1777

The Year of the Hangman

George Washington
C. W. Peale
COURTESY OF THE PENNSYLVANIA ACADEMY OF FINE ARTS

1777

The Year of The Hangman

JOHN S. PANCAKE

The University of Alabama Press
University, Alabama

This book is for
John and Connie

Library of Congress Cataloging in Publication Data

Pancake, John S
    1777, the year of the hangman.

    Bibliography: p.
    Includes index.
    1. United States—History—Revolution, 1775–1783
—Campaigns and battles. I. Title.
E233.P27   973.3'33   76-30797
ISBN O-8173-5112-4

Contents

Preface

ANYONE WHO HAS READ THE HISTORY OF THE WAR OF INDEPENDENCE CANNOT fail to be fascinated by the campaign of Gentleman Johnny Burgoyne. The story evokes pictures in the mind's eye: scarlet-coated Englishmen; the green and blue uniforms of the German mercenaries; the flash of brass and silver and steel accoutrements; the swarms of Indians in their war paint; the whole moving through the green forests or sailing the blue waters of lakes and rivers. Even the names have a lyrical tone: Richelieu, Champlain, Oriskany, Ticonderoga, and La Chine. Not the least part of the fascination is the fact that the fate of the expedition marked a turning point in the history of the war.

It is not surprising that there has been a host of chroniclers, scholars, and novelists, and those who fall in a category somewhere between because their artistry bridges the gaps that footnoted facts cannot, and so allows some scope for imagination (and may teach more history than the rest).

It is this fascination that has been partly responsible for the present writer's exploration of this particular part of the history of the war. There was also the fact that no scholar since Hoffman Nickerson in his *Turning Point of the Revolution* (1926) has attempted a detailed study of the British invasion from Canada, although there has been a vast amount of literature on specific aspects of the campaign.

Nor has any study to date attempted to link the Canadian expedition to the concurrent operation of General Sir William Howe in Pennsylvania in such a way as to present a complete story of the campaign of 1777 from the point of its inception and launching by the American Secretary, Lord George Germain, to the point where it was reduced to a shambles at the end of the year.

There is another gap which needs to be filled. As T. Harry Williams has reminded us, wars are won and lost by men who fight each other on the battlefield. But war also intrudes itself into the lives of the whole people of a nation, and the present study attempts to show this, if only in a limited way. It would be highly instructive, for instance, to present more about the state of mind of the English people, the social and economic factors that resulted in less than a full commitment of Britain to the suppression of the American rebellion.

On the American side it would be of great interest to find out to what extent this was truly a people's war.

So at the end of an investigation of this sort one is left with more questions than at the beginning—and a devout wish that some day he or others may answer them.

As I have noted elsewhere, anyone who says "I wrote a book" states considerably less than the truth. *We* wrote this book, and this includes: my wife, Frances, who had the frustrating experience of typing much of the manuscript in such odd sequences that she professes to know nothing about the campaign of 1777; Boyd Childress and Bruce Ellis, students *par excellence*, who were splendid research assistants, and who just may know more about the source materials than I do; Hugh Rankin of Tulane University, who generously read the manuscript (in record time) and who corrected many errors; Howard Miller of the Psychology Department of The University of Alabama, who enthusiastically took on Sir William Howe as an outpatient; John Ramsey of the History Department of the University of Alabama, who was kind enough to advise me on the French alliance; Richard Brough of the Art Department of the University of Alabama, who reproduced the map of the northern theatre of operations; Douglas Jones, Dean of the College of Arts and Sciences, who wangled a special leave of absence.

I am also indebted to the long-suffering staffs of the libraries of The University of Alabama, the University of Virginia, Washington and Lee University, Virginia Military Institute, The Chicago Historical Society, the city of New York, the New York Historical Society, and the William L. Clements Library at the University of Michigan.

The New York Historical Society, the New York Public Library, and the William L. Clements Library have generously allowed me to use quotations from manuscripts in their collections.

This work would not have been possible without the generosity of the Research Grants Committee of the University of Alabama, enabling me to take time off from my teaching duties.

For any errors of fact or aberrant conclusions I take full responsibility.

University, Alabama   JOHN S. PANCAKE

1777

The Year of the Hangman

"I left Congress on the 11th of November, 1777, that year which the Tories said, had three gallows in it, meaning the three sevens."
—John Adams

Prologue

IF GEORGE WASHINGTON AND HIS CONTEMPORARIES HAD BEEN TOLD THE American history books would have contained sections entitled: "The American Revolution: 1763 to 1789" they would have been amazed. Washington remarked on his return to his farm at the end of the Seven Years' War that "we are much rejoiced at the prospect of peace which 'tis hoped will be of long continuance." For the frame of the colonial mind had as yet conceived of no serious quarrels with the mother country, much less the notion of American independence.

Yet what Professor Lawrence Gipson has called the Great War for Empire had given England a preponderance of power which ultimately proved her undoing. France and her allies were dismayed at the drastic shift in the balance of power and anxious for an opportunity to redress it. As Benjamin Franklin noted, "Every nation in Europe wishes to see Britain humbled, having all in turn been offended by her insolence." When her American colonies revolted England's enemies welcomed the opportunity, and their aid was crucial to the success of the War of Independence.

For the Americans in 1763, there was relief that the threat of New France which had hovered over the Northern horizon for more than a century was finally gone, although they did not perhaps perceive that they thereby became less dependent on the mother country. Loyalty is rooted in mutual needs and common hopes and fears. At the beginning of the eighteenth century 200,000 colonists were strung along the Atlantic littoral from Massachusetts to the Carolinas, a thin rim of Britain's empire. Their existence was vitally dependent on support from England. By 1763 the population had exploded to two million and the colonies were not only prosperous but remarkably self-reliant.

It might be noted in passing that their self-confidence generated a myth: that they, not the redcoats, had won this war, and veterans' tales of Louisbourg and the Plains of Abraham lost nothing in the telling in the years after 1763. For such men of valor British regulars posed no serious problem when it came time to assert American rights by force of arms.

In fact, at the beginning of the French war, Americans had been extremely reluctant to aid the British army. Not a single colony came near meeting the quotas of men and supplies which the home government requested. Pleas and threats alike fell on deaf ears, for colonial assemblies controlled taxes and appropriations, including the salaries of the governors. Many a faithful servant of the crown, faced with royal displeasure 3,000 miles away or the wrath of the colonial assembly just across the street, was bludgeoned into submission by the power of the legislative purse. General Edward Braddock, on the eve of his fateful march to the forks of the Ohio, complained that Pennsylvania and Virginia "promised great matters and have done nothing, whereby instead of forwarding they have obstructed services." Only when the war government of William Pitt, driven to desperate measures, agreed to reimburse the colonies for wartime expenses, did colonial patriotism become as swollen as colonial purses. Royal officials had the uneasy feeling that one of the badly wounded casualties of the war was British authority in America.

England emerged from the war staggering under an enormous national debt, and a program of imperial retrenchment was inaugurated. George Grenville, a capable administrator but sadly lacking in imperial statesmanship, was the first of a series of ministers who attempted to set Britain's economic house in order. He began by instructing customs officers to begin enforcing the trade laws, a proposal which was not only startling but financially disastrous to crown officials who had been thriving off the bribes of colonial merchants. Under Grenville's whip they had no choice but to turn on their erstwhile benefactors and recover their former affluence by zealous— and often fraudulent—enforcement of intricate and complicated customs laws. Customs officials were entitled to a percentage of confiscated goods and cargoes, and their legal racketeering outraged colonial merchants.

Lord Grenville also began to cast up the accounts on the colonial books. He discovered that the administrative cost of the American colonies was several times as great as the revenue which they contributed. To Grenville's orderly mind this was an untidy situation and he set about to remedy it through taxation. To his credit, he asked for advice, even consulting that foremost expert in American affairs, Benjamin Franklin. The solution which Grenville hit upon was the Stamp Act of 1765 which levied a tax on all kinds of legal and commercial paper—newspapers, contracts, invoices, wills, and the like.

The reaction in America was as violent as it was unexpected. In Virginia, Patrick Henry declared that "taxation of the people by themselves . . . is the only security against burthensome taxation, the distinguishing characteristic of British freedom, . . ." and lit the fuse which exploded into colonial defiance. Protest groups called the Sons of Liberty held torchlight parades and hanged Grenville in effigy. Colonial boycotts were declared against British goods, and nine colonies sent representatives to a Stamp Act Congress in New York to address a petition to the Crown. Colonial newspapers rallied public opinion: "Taxation without representation is tyranny!"

Two things are worth noting about the Stamp Act crisis. Although there were virtually no precedents to guide them, Americans displayed a remarkable talent for revolutionary techniques of protest. Whig editors showed an immediate appreciation of newspapers as weapons of propaganda. The Sons of Liberty not only organized popular support but injected an atmosphere of enthusiasm—and, not incidentally, thoroughly terrorized the opposition. The boycotts added the reality of economic pressure to constitutional arguments of principle. Considering the slowness of communications and the diversity of colonial interests it was an amazing performance. From the passage of the Stamp Act by Parliament in March, 1765, only seven months elapsed before the Stamp Act Congress published its protest.

The second point was less apparent in both America and England. In protesting the constitutionality of the Stamp Act, the colonists were raising serious questions about the nature of the British Empire. They seemed to be assuming the existence of a sort of federal structure in which a considerable degree of self-government belonged by right to their own colonial assemblies. If Parliament lacked the most fundamental of all powers, the power to tax, what authority did it have? Perhaps it was fortunate that the colonies did not press the point in 1765. Parliament vehemently denied any limitations on its powers in the Declaratory Act of 1766, but since it was accompanied by the repeal of the Stamp Act, few Americans bothered to dispute the issue. In England the Stamp Act and its repeal were minor issues, which were quickly dismissed by members of Parliament who knew little and cared less about the American colonies. But as the controversy with the mother country grew in the years that followed, it became increasingly clear that what the colonies insisted were English rights and English liberties had acquired a distinctive brand which read "Made in America."

For example, when the Stamp Act Congress spoke of being taxed only "with their own consent, given personally or by their representatives," Englishmen were not only irritated but puzzled. A member of Parliament felt that he represented the whole empire—he certainly did not consider that he was the spokesman for the populace of the "rotten borough" from which he was elected. But Americans had developed a republican system; that is, a representative conceived of himself as the voice of the people who had elected him, and as being responsible to them.

As with the political system, so it was with other American institutions. Jefferson attacked the established church in Virginia, not because of religious intolerance, but because established religion was an anachronism which violated the rule of reason. With thousands of Baptists, Presbyterians, and Methodists peopling the Virginia back country it seemed ridiculous to maintain in law what did not exist in fact. Americans deplored the English "rotten boroughs," not because people in the colonies could not vote, but because, even with property qualifications, a substantial number of adult males could and did vote. The Stamp Act and the Townshend Acts which followed two years later they considered to be a corruption of English constitutional principles, and they insisted in all sincerity that their cause was the cause of English liberty. Theirs was an Enlightenment philosophy overlaid with the imprint of New World experience. In short, Americans were preaching what they were already practicing.

So it was that as late as 1773 few colonists were thinking in terms of American independence. Indeed, the explosive clash between soldiers and citizens in 1770 known as the Boston Massacre was followed by a period of calm which dismayed radical agitators like Sam Adams. But Lord North, the latest of a succession of ministers through whom George III attempted to rule, managed to revive the dispute. At his request Parliament passed the East India Company Act, better known as the Tea Act, which attempted to aid the great corporation by granting to it a monopoly on the sale of tea in America.

The Act itself was not onerous, but by this time the colonists were convinced that it presaged an attempt to revive Parliamentary authority. Committees of Correspondence were soon busy organizing colonial resistance. The confrontation came in Boston a few days after Christmas, 1773. The Boston Sons of Liberty boarded one of the East India Company ships and dumped its cargo of tea into the Boston harbor. The reaction of Parliament was swift and severe for George III, through Lord North, now commanded a majority in Parliament for the first time since 1763. There was no question of Parliament's belief in its authority. The port of Boston was closed until the tea was paid for; the Massachusetts assembly was prorogued and courts were authorized to issue changes of venue so that persons charged with serious crimes could be tried outside the colony; and army commanders were authorized to quarter their troops on private property (although not in private residences, as Sam Adams alleged). The authority of government was concentrated in the hands of the royal governor, General Thomas Gage, who was also commander-in-chief of the British Army in America.

Action and reaction followed in rapid succession. By the fall of 1774 half a hundred delegates from the colonies had organized the First Continental Congress in Philadelphia. They professed their loyalty to the Crown, but on terms which were hardly compatible with England's concept of the empire. John Adams framed the proposition:

> . . . The foundation of English liberty, and of all free government, is a right in the people to participate in their legislative council: and as the English colonies . . . cannot be properly represented in the British Parliament, they are entitled to a free and exclusive power of legislation in their several provincial legislatures, where their right of representation can alone be preserved, in all

cases of taxation and internal polity, subject alone to the negative of their sovereign. . . . We cheerfully consent to the operation of such Acts of the British Parliament as are . . . restrained to the regulation of our external commerce, for the purpose of securing the commercial advantages of the whole empire. . . .

Adams' proposal was essentially the principle of dominion status by which Britain later held together her far-flung empire. But such proposals were lost on the government at Whitehall. Among other things, it seemed to suggest that Americans considered themselves the equal of Britons, a notion as dangerous as it was outrageous.

Though they denied the authority of Parliament the colonists insisted that they were loyal subjects of the King. Their relationship was defined by their colonial charters, granted by authority of the Crown and consisting of a contractual relationship between the colonists and the King. This idea had its roots in the philosophy of John Locke, who had justified the Glorious Revolution on the basis of a "social contract" that existed between the rulers and the ruled. Such a contract could only exist between equals, and the logical corollary was that the people could call the ruler to account if he violated the terms of the contract. The dispute between the colonies and the mother country was thus founded in the tradition of English Enlightenment philosophy, but by no means accepted in English practice: that government is in its nature an agreement between equal contracting parties and that the rulers are accountable to the ruled.

The First Continental Congress did not stop with a petition of protest. The members adopted resolutions of nonimportation, nonexportation, and nonconsumption. They also created a Continental Association which provided for committees throughout the colonies to see that the resolutions were enforced. The Congress then adjourned, but not before its members agreed to meet again within a year to deliberate on further action which might be necessary.

The meeting of the First Continental Congress was a momentous step along the road to independence. In adopting its restrictive resolutions the Congress had enacted what amounted to legislation, and it had provided the machinery to enforce it. These were functions normally exercised by governments; and, like a government body, Congress provided for its own continuity by agreeing to meet again.

Probably Americans did not themselves appreciate the full significance of what they had done. Certainly it did not penetrate the limited vision of Parliament, the ministry, or the King. Lord North's reaction was to frame a reply to Congress' petition which was designed to hoodwink the colonists and at the same time assuage the sensibilities of Parliament. Its blatant trickery outraged some members of Parliament and deceived the Americans not at all. The ministry's bad faith is revealed in the instructions to General Gage in January, 1775, which urged him to take "a more active and determined part" in dealing with troublemakers in Massachusetts.

When the Second Continental Congress met in May it found that further steps had indeed been taken. New England militia had fought British troops at Lexington and Concord, and so began a civil war which was to last eight years.

Congress made a last appeal to the King in the summer of 1775, mostly to satisfy Whig-Loyalists, Americans who fervently supported the cause of liberty, but hoped against hope that a solution could be found which would not force them to renounce their country. The King's Proclamation confirmed their worst fears. It declared the colonists to be rebels and soon afterward Parliament ordered the interdiction of American trade. Thus the King, who had been appealed to as "the party of the first part" in the social contract, had betrayed his trust. For many Americans the problem had been reduced to its simplest terms. Either they must submit and abandon their fight for liberty, or take the only other avenue left open to them—independence. And the clarity with which they perceived the choices made many colonists aware of what they had already intuitively sensed: that somewhere along the way they had become more American than English.

ONE

The War Begins: 1775

IN 1842 CAPTAIN LEVI PRESTON, A NINETY-ONE YEAR OLD VETERAN OF THE War of Independence, was interviewed by the historian, Mellen Chamberlain. Captain Preston, it turned out, had never read Sydney or Locke, never drunk tea, nor did he recall ever having seen a stamp. But he was very explicit about why he had fought. "Young man, what we meant in going for those red-coats was this: We always had governed ourselves and we always meant to. They didn't mean we should."

THE APPEAL TO ARMS

General Thomas Gage is a familiar name to anyone who has read about the War of Independence. After all, Gage started it by sending his redcoats to Lexington and Concord on April 19, 1775. Yet Thomas Gage is a faceless shadow-man who only gave the orders which sent the soldiers on their desperate mission. He was not at the head of those men when they faced Captain John Parker's militia on the Lexington Common nor when the battered, bloody ranks staggered back to Boston, ripped apart by swarms of minute men. In the American tradition Gage is a villain, but he conjures up no remembered personality. The tall, swarthy Howes, "Sir Billy" and "Black Dick," fat-faced George III, swaggering "Gentleman Johnny" Burgoyne, savage Cornwallis who could turn cannon on his own men to win a battle — these men make pictures in the mind's eye. Gage gave his fateful orders and a few months later left America forever.

Yet Gage ought to be remembered if for no other reason than that he had a thoroughly sound appreciation of the situation of the colonies in the spring of 1775. He had served in North America for twenty years, twelve of them as commander in chief of the British army in America. He had survived frequent clashes with civilians and had displayed a resolute composure in the face of petitions, protests and as bad language as Whig editors could muster, which was bad indeed. In 1773 he had gone to England on leave and had returned in the spring of 1774 not only as commander in chief but as governor of Massachusetts. His first duty was to put into effect the Boston Port Bill, closing the city to all trade until its citizens paid for their very expensive tea party of the previous December.[1]

As tension increased in Boston and the surrounding countryside Gage reiterated to the ministry warnings which he had been sounding ever since his return. He was never hostile toward nor contemptuous of Americans (his wife was a native of Brunswick, New Jersey); but he was positive that the authority of the Crown must be firmly asserted. "If you yield to [colonial] menaces there is an End of your Sovereignty; and I shall expect they will very soon make laws for you, and take the same method to enforce them," he wrote in June, 1774. He was also convinced that an overwhelming demonstration of authority "should be effectual at the beginning. If you think ten thousand Men sufficient, send Twenty, if one Million [pounds] is thought to be enough, give two, and you will save both Blood and Treasure in the end." And finally, in December, 1774, mindful that his regulars numbered only about 4,000 men, he urged the ministry to "send me a sufficient Force to command the Country, by marching into it and sending off large detachments to secure obedience through every part of it." Instructions from the Earl of Dartmouth, Secretary of State for the Colonies, arrived in Boston on the 16th of April, 1775. They left no doubt that the ministry expected action and that Gage was free to pursue his own inclination to take a hard line. But there was no mention of twenty thousand men, or even ten.[2]

In dispatching troops to Lexington and Concord on the 18th of April Gage's ostensible purpose was to arrest some of the most notorious Whig leaders and to seize stores of arms which the militia were said to have collected. But his real purpose was undoubtedly to scotch the rebellion by a display of force, "to command the country by marching into it." Before the bloody day was over Gage had to commit one third of his entire force of which seventeen percent were casualties. The Patriots not only turned out by the thousands but pursued the troops to the very outskirts of Boston.

The story of New England farmers springing to arms and besieging the British in Boston is a well-known one.[3] (It also gave birth to the myth that the nation would always turn out enough volunteer citizen-soldiers to fight its wars. American leaders from George Washington to George Marshall knew differently.) To Gage mobs of angry New Englanders were a familiar story. But this time there was a shocking difference. Instead of venting its spleen and dispersing, this mob stayed and its members steadily increased. By early June there were between 12,000 and 15,000 men surrounding Boston and they were loosely organized into an army. It might not have been much of an army by Gage's precise British standards, but every night for six weeks sentry fires winked relentlessly from Roxbury to Chelsea. General Hugh Earl Percy, who had fought the militiamen on April 19, commented, "Whoever looks on them as an irregular mob will find himself very much mistaken."[4]

By early June the first reinforcements had arrived from England. These included parts of six regiments and brought Gage's total effective force to about 6,500 rank and file. The reinforcements also included three major generals, William Howe, Henry Clinton, and John Burgoyne whom the ministry had sent as "advisers" to Gage. Of these the senior was General Howe. He had seen previous service in the Seven Years' War and it was rumored that he might succeed Gage. This created a situation which was both frustrating and embarrassing to Gage, since he had as his junior officer the man who might be promoted in rank and possibly was his successor.

In response to instructions from the ministry and in a last attempt to avoid the cataclysmic course of events, Gage issued a proclamation declaring martial law but offering amnesty to all rebels except the ringleaders, the Adamses, John Hancock, and Joseph Warren. Whatever hopes Gage had for a reconciliation may well have been extinguished when General Burgoyne, sometime London playwright, offered his literary talents in composing the proclamation. The resulting combination of bombast and insult was a literary and diplomatic disaster, "replete with consummate impudence, the most abominable lies, and stuffed with daring expressions of tyranny," according to the *Pennsylvania Journal*.[5]

It was Burgoyne who had reacted to the idea that the British were besieged by saying, "Well, let *us* get in, and we'll soon find elbow room." After Bunker Hill he seemed to resent the fact that soldiers on both sides dubbed him "General Elbow-Room," but then Burgoyne was a slow learner on the subject of America and Americans. Henry Clinton, a man of more sober and meticulous mind than Burgoyne, also urged more elbow-room and Howe seems to have concurred. By the second week of June the coterie of generals agreed that their force was too small to break out of the encirclement, especially since there seemed to be no feasible objective beyond the American lines. But the situation did seem to call for the occupation of the two peninsulas, Charlestown and Dorchester, which jutted out into the harbor to the north and south of Boston.

At the American headquarters at Cambridge General Artemus Ward heard rumors from Boston of the British plans. A veteran of the Seven Years' War, Ward had risen from sickbed to take command of the militia after Lexington and Concord. If he appeared cautious and indecisive to some it was because he stubbornly refused to risk his fragile "army" of untrained, undisciplined troops in any madcap offensive. The line he had established from Winter Hill around to Dorchester was formidable, and his bluff, no-nonsense attitude earned him the respect, if not the adulation, of the conglomeration of officers and men who came to (and often left) the crowded camps.

On June 16 Ward finally yielded to the urgings of his subordinates and sent Colonel William Prescott to occupy Bunker Hill on the Charlestown Peninsula. When Prescott reached the ground he decided to fortify Breed's Hill, and by daylight on the 17th his men had entrenched themselves on its crest. Later in the morning the line was extended on the left to the Mystic river where Connecticut militia under Captain Thomas Knowlton hastily threw up a "breastwork" consisting of fence rails, rocks, and hay. About noon Knowlton was joined by Colonel John Stark's New Hampshire militia, bringing the total of Prescott's command to about 1,500 men.[6]

General William Howe took charge of 2,500 redcoats and by early afternoon he had crossed to the peninsula. Howe intended to make short work of this rabble of upstart farmers who were finally offering to make a stand-up fight. He sent half his force under General Hugh Pigot against the redoubt on Breed's Hill, while he himself led an attack on the rail fence defended by Knowlton and Stark.

It was still the age of picture book wars and this battle had thousands of spectators watching from the hills and housetops in Boston. Through the eddying smoke of the British bombardment the double line of redcoats could be seen moving forward, sunlight flickering on bayonets and accoutrements, "one of the greatest scenes of war that can be conceived." As Pigot's line reached the crest of Breed's Hill Prescott's men "rose up and poured in so heavy a fire upon us that the oldest officers say they never saw a sharper action." The British line staggered to a halt and then retreated.

Out of view of the spectators in Boston, beyond the curve of the hill, Howe's right wing was advancing against the rail fence. In a surprising display of discipline most of the militiamen held their fire until the British were within easy musket range. Then "an incessant stream of fire poured from the rebel lines. It seemed a continued sheet of fire. . . . Our light Infantry were served up in companies against the grass fence and without being able to penetrate. . . . Most of the Grenadiers and Light Infantry at the moment of presenting themselves lost three-fourths, and many nine-tenths, of their men. Some had only eight and nine men a company left, some only three, four and five." The red line recoiled, "fell into disorder" and retreated.

It was a mind blowing experience for William Howe—"*a moment that I never felt before.*" But he did not waver from his purpose. He pulled his battered lines together and launched a second attack. Again the troops met a shattering fire which "put the regulars to flight who once more retreated in precipitation."

But Prescott, Knowlton, Stark and the militiamen were done. The third assault, reinforced by 400 men under Clinton, found many of the Americans out of ammunition, although a handful met the British bayonet charge with clubbed muskets. Even in retreat the militia "continued a running fight from one fence, or wall, to another," noted Lord Rawdon of the Grenadiers.[7]

General Burgoyne watched the battle from Boston, and said "the day ended with glory," and Rawdon reported that "we have . . . given the rebels a signal defeat." But to William Howe it was "what I call this unhappy day. . . . The success was too dearly bought." Howe was an eighteenth century general whose doctrine was to fight his regulars "under circumstances the least hazardous to the royal army; for even a victory attended by a heavy loss of men on our part, would have given a fateful check to the progress of the war. . . ." The price Howe paid at Bunker Hill was devastating. Of something more than 2,500 men engaged 1,050 had been killed and wounded including 92 officers. This was forty-two percent of his force, a prohibitive loss in any era of warfare. Howe confessed that "when I look to the consequences of it . . . I do it with horror." A week after Bunker Hill the British army could muster only 3,400 rank and file, present and fit for duty.

For Thomas Gage it was the final blow to his American career. Lord George Germain, soon to be appointed Secretary of State for the Colonies, had already expressed the opinion that "General Gage . . . finds himself in a situation of too great importance for his talents." After the news of Bunker Hill orders were issued for his recall and he returned to England in October, although he was not formally relieved of his command until the spring of 1776. Yet his report to Lord North contained the clearest perception of the significance of this first full-dress battle of the war. Gage's grammar was bad and his blunt language probably either offended or amused his superiors. But Gage knew Americans and he understood the enormity of the crisis. "These people show a spirit and a conduct against us they never showed against the French, and every body has judged of them from their former appearance and behavior when joyned with the King's forces in the last war; which has led into great mistakes.

"They are now spirited up by a rage and enthousiasm as great as ever people were possessed of, and you must proceed in earnest or give the business up. . . . I have before wrote your Lordship of my opinion that a very large army must at length be employed to reduce these people. . . . or else to avoid a land war and make use of your fleet. I don't find one province in appearance better disposed than another. . . ."[8]

THE BIRTH OF THE AMERICAN ARMY

The Second Continental Congress convened on May 10, 1775, three weeks after Lexington and Concord and a little less than six weeks before the battle of Bunker Hill. Its members were preoccupied with many problems and complexities, not the least of which was that they were in a state of armed rebellion against the Crown while some of its most influential members were convinced that reconciliation could still be achieved. Whig-Loyalists like John Dickinson, James Duane, and Robert Morris could not easily bring themselves to renounce their loyalty to Britain.[9] The radicals, that is, those who were beginning to think of independence, were inclined to move slowly lest they alienate these conservative supporters. It must be remembered that the Congress was an illegal body and the Whig movement which sanctioned it represented a minority of the American people. To propose such a portentous issue as independence its advocates had to be sure, not just of a majority vote, but of virtual unanimity in Congress. It was not until a year had passed that

Jefferson, the Adamses and other radicals were to feel confident enough to propose separation from England.

Meantime, there was the war. Congress, which had originally assembled for the purpose of confronting the home government with an organized protest, found itself willy-nilly forced to govern. It is a commentary on the rising spirit of American nationalism that the members never considered leaving the conduct of the war to the individual colonies. John Jay went so far as to advocate that the "Union depends much upon the breaking down of the provincial Conventions."[10]

From the beginning the Massachusetts assembly and the Committee of Safety assumed that Congress would take over the responsibility for the army, and on May 16 a petition was dispatched to Philadelphia urging "to your consideration the propriety of your taking the regulation and general direction of it, that the operations of it may more effectually answer the purpose designed for it." There is no record of formal action by Congress, but on June 17 James Duane noted that "Congress have agreed to raise, at the Continental expense, a body of fifteen thousand men," and the next day John Hancock referred to a Congressional appropriation for "a Continental Army."[11]

Having adopted an army Congress next set about selecting its commander. In later years John Adams remarked somewhat petulantly, that when the history of the American Revolution was written, "The essence of the whole will be that *Dr. Franklins electrical rod smote the Earth and out sprang General Washington.*" If Adams was then perturbed that his own career would be lost in the giant shadow of the father of his country he might reflect that he had only himself to blame, for it was he who proposed that Washington command the new army. In 1775 Adams was not so much concerned about creating America's first authentic hero as he was with finding a commander in chief who was both capable and politically acceptable. No one was more aware than Adams that colonial unity was a fragile thing, and the new general and his army would be the principal instrument through which this unity would be forged and strengthened. He, more than any one else, would personify the American cause.

So Adams' keen political eye singled out Washington. It would be a Southerner and a Virginian who would command an army of New Englanders. Washington's patriotism was unquestioned, but he was no radical. He was a planter and an aristocrat, but his massive frame and rugged features suggested a man of great physical power and endurance. He was a superb horseman and he had "an easy, soldier like air and gesture." It may well be that the big Virginian's most important asset was that he *looked* like a commander in chief.

Washington's military experience was limited. He had served four years in the French and Indian War, much of it with the British commanders, Braddock, Forbes, and Bouquet. He was therefore well acquainted with army routine and administration. He had also served for two years as commander of the Virginia militia guarding a frontier which stretched three hundred and fifty miles from Fort Cumberland in Maryland to Fort Bedford in southwest Virginia. Undoubtedly Washington regarded this as the most thankless and unrewarding duty of his early career, but it must have taught him invaluable lessons. Here he learned that while legislatures might vote troops for duty, any resemblance between the number authorized and the number that appeared in the field was usually coincidental. He experienced the frustration of relying on untrained militia who might flee in panic at the mere rumor of the approach of the enemy. He learned that neither militia nor legislators could be ordered about, but must be handled, each in their own fashion, with delicate care. Considering the choices which confronted Congress it had chosen a man who was somewhat limited in military qualifications, but who was especially attractive politically and personally. Whether he could measure up to the enormous task remained to be seen. Washington himself declared "with the utmost sincerity, I do not think myself equal to the Command I am honored with."[12]

Having chosen the commander in chief Congress then selected five major generals and eight brigadiers. Of these Nathanael Greene was to prove indispensable. Four more could be said to have rendered valuable services and two died before their fine promise could be realized. Israel Putnam never achieved the success expected of this most famous veteran of the French and Indian War, and four others were clearly incompetent. If one recalls the dubious quality of the generals at the outset of most of the wars of the United States, the conclusion is that the men at Philadelphia did very well. If nothing else, they used unerring judgement in selecting the commander who would lead the army to victory.

Washington left the capital on June 23, 1775, and nine days later he arrived at army headquarters in Cambridge. There he found "a mixed multitude of people . . . under very little order or government." He was informed that there were 20,000 men on the rolls, but when he asked for a return of those present and fit for duty (a process which took eight days) the number had shrunk to 13,743.

For the next six months Washington struggled to create an army out of the chaos around Cambridge. "I dare say the men would fight very well (if properly officered) although they are an exceeding dirty and nasty people," he noted soon after his arrival. The general himself soon earned the respect, if not the affection, of the army. It discovered that the commander in chief was a severe disciplinarian and a hard task master. "The strictest government is taking place and great distinction is made between officers and soldiers. Everyone is made to know his place and keep it. . . ."[13]

Autumn brought the first crisis, but not from the threat of the British in Boston. Most of the American soldiers had agreed to serve for eight months, or until approximately the end of the year. Washington feared that a "Dissolution . . . of the present Army will take place unless some early Provision is made against such an Event." The enlistments of the Connecticut regiments were due to expire on December 10 and most of the troops prepared to go home. The officers made strenuous efforts to reenlist the men for an additional year but by the end of November Washington was so discouraged that "I should not be at all surprised at any disaster that might happen." In desperation he appealed to Massachusetts and New Hampshire for temporary replacements. The response was enormously gratifying. Into the lines on December 11 marched the first regiments of 5,000 militia—boiling mad at being called from their firesides in the dead of winter. As the Connecticut troops marched off "through the lines they were so horribly hissed, groaned at, and pelted that I believe they wished their aunts, grandmothers, and even sweethearts, to whom . . . they were so much attached, at the devil's own place." The pace of reenlistments quickened and Washington marvelled at having had "one army disbanded and another to raise within the same distance of a reenforced enemy." By January, 1776, the army numbered about 15,000 men of whom one third were militia.[14]

General Howe replaced Gage in October but made no move to leave the security of Boston. Some reinforcements had arrived from England but his army still counted less than 10,000 men present and fit for duty. As winter advanced life in the besieged city deteriorated. Supplies ran short and "Death has so long stalked among us that he is become less terrible . . . than he once was." Soldiers plundered to such an extent that Howe ordered "the provost to go his rounds attended by the executioner with orders to hang upon the spot the first man he shall detect. . . ."

By the New Year Washington was becoming impatient. He admitted that "to have the eyes of the whole continent fixed, with anxious expectation of hearing some great event, and to be restrained . . . is not very pleasing." His hopes for an offensive were emboldened by the arrival of a train of artillery.[15]

The genius behind this achievement was a twenty-five year old artillery colonel named Henry Knox, who had been ordered to bring in the guns from Ticonderoga, which had fallen to the Americans in May. Possessed of a booming voice, a huge girth, and a vast amount of energy, Knox contrived to transport the guns across winter ice and snow on forty-two sleds drawn by eighty yoke of oxen. Although a mild winter provided less freezing weather than he would have liked, by early January Knox had bulldozed his way across Lake Champlain and down the Hudson to Albany. The distance from Albany to Boston is today traversed by 165 miles of the Massachusetts Turnpike. In 1776 Knox delivered fifty-two cannon and fourteen mortars to the artillery park in Cambridge in eighteen days.[16]

Washington now decided to fortify Dorchester Heights and threaten Howe's position in Boston. The American movement was made under cover of darkness on March 4. If the little redoubt on Breed's Hill a year earlier had surprised the British, the sight of the elaborate works on Dorchester Heights on the morning of March 5 left them dumfounded. Howe is said to have exclaimed, "Good God! Those fellows have done more work than I could have made my army do in three months."

On March 7 Howe announced that he intended to evacuate the city, and ten days later, accompanied by over 1,000 Loyalists, he embarked his troops for Halifax. The British made no move to destroy the city and the American guns were silent. As Washington's troops approached cautiously toward the town they saw that the lines were apparently manned by British sentries. Closer inspection revealed that they were dummies, and on one of them was a placard which read, "Welcome, Brother Jonathan."[17]

So a year after the war began the British army had been driven from American soil. It was true that the ministry had agreed with Howe that Boston should be abandoned. But Washington had forced the enemy to leave at a time of his choosing, not theirs, and his threatening guns had forestalled any inclination on the part of the redcoats to sack the town. The evacuation of Boston was a tremendous boost to American morale.

In the process the new commander in chief had showed himself fully capable of his responsibilities. If his actions had not been brilliant, the fact that he had methodically carried out his task, overcome serious obstacles and made no mistakes, constituted a kind of brilliance. Most of all he had convinced both Congress and the army that he was to be trusted.

TWO

The American Secretary

ENGLAND'S MILITARY SYSTEM WAS ENTIRELY CONSISTENT WITH EIGHTEENTH century rationalism. Because weapons systems were not very destructive and because economic considerations limited the size of armies, the eighteenth century accepted war as a necessary element in the international order of things. Eighteenth century statesmen tacitly admitted that behind the moral poses of diplomacy and the elaborate language of treaties there lay the threat of brute force as the ultimate sanction of international law. The revolution which began in America in 1775 caught the British government off guard, not only in the inadequacies of its military establishment but in the narrowness of its imperial vision.

GERMAIN AND THE STRATEGY OF RECONQUEST

He was the son of a peer of the realm and at the age of four he was entitled to be called Lord George Sackville. His father was briefly lord lieutenant of Ireland and the son was a lieutenant colonel of cavalry by the time he was thirty-four. A year later in 1741 he was elected member of Parliament and so became one of those soldier-politicians who were familiar figures in late eighteenth century England. His military career in the War of Austrian Succession was outstanding and on the eve of the Seven Years' War he was promoted to major general.

In 1758 Sackville was assigned as second in command under the Duke of Marlborough in the British expedition sent to the continent in support of the Prussian army, and on Marlborough's death he became the British commander. At the battle of Minden in 1759 he was accused by the Prussian commander in chief, Prince Ferdinand, of being dilatory in obeying an order to attack. Sackville's pride was stung and he returned to England demanding a court martial which would justify his conduct. It is probable that if he had been less insistent the government would have been happy to drop the whole matter, since at one point Sackville was asked to specify the grounds on which he wished to be charged. But he conceived that his honor had been impugned and he was finally accused of disobedience of orders. A more astute politician would have foreseen that the scales of justice were too heavily weighted by politics, for now the affair became a political football between contending factions headed by the King and William Pitt on the one side and the young prince who was to become George III on the other. But Sackville's stubborn— even arrogant—belief in the justice of his cause led him to persist. He was convicted and the vindictive old monarch, George II, ordered the verdict posted in every regiment of the army, and had Sackville's name struck from the list of Privy Councillors.

Eighteenth century British politics was constituted not only of a vast amount of corruption but of bitter feuds in which elegant language furnished only a thin veneer for slashing insults and outrageous personal attacks both in and out of Parliament. Although Sackville had been convicted only of dis-obedience to orders in a trial which was admittedly shot through with polit-ical prejudice, he found himself the target of slurs and insults which ques-tioned both his courage and his honor. This must have been insufferable for a man whose overbearing manner gave evidence of deep-rooted pride. In the five years of political banishment which followed the court martial his self-control and composure were severely tested.

George II died in 1760 and young George III succeeded to the throne. In the confusion of factions, cliques and blocs which had shattered England's traditional two-party system the young King made slow headway. He recog-nized that Sackville had been a casualty of political warfare, but even the King had to move warily in rehabilitating the man who was already plagued by the "Ghost of Minden." In 1765 during the debates surrounding the Stamp Act Sackville took a strong stand in Commons in support of the Declaratory Act which asserted Parliamentary supremacy over the colonies. At about this time he received a minor appointment as vice-treasurer of Ireland and had his name restored to the Privy Councillors' list. These were insignificant marks of recognition, to be sure, but they brought an end to his political exile.[1]

It was not until 1770 that George III was able to stabilize his executive control. The head of his ministry was Lord North, an amiable, conservative man who handled the political and financial affairs of the Crown. He was likeable and level-headed, though he often appeared indolent and inattentive during Parliamentary debates. But from this somnolent air of studied indif-ference his lordship could deliver a sudden thrust which was as acute as it was unexpected; or the opposition might find its argument punctured by a barb of sarcasm and wit which left the House roaring with laughter. By 1775 the North ministry had achieved a degree of durability and permanence. Yet despite his shrewdness, and his skill at picking his way through the political swamps and jungles, North was deficient in both originality of thought and resolution of purpose.

When the colonial calm in America was broken by the dispute over the Tea Act Lord North welcomed the support of Sackville (who had taken his aunt's family name of Germain as a condition of inheriting her fortune in 1770). The passage of the Intolerable Acts found him supporting North along the same lines that he had taken in 1766. When the question of the repeal of the Intolerable Acts was brought before the House early in 1775 Germain made it clear that conciliation must be on the ministry's terms. He would listen to American petitions, he said, but not to American demands for rights which they did not possess. By the time the news of Lexington and Concord reached London in the summer of 1775 Germain had established himself as one of the ablest spokesmen for the ministry on the American question. He was frequently consulted by the members of the cabinet, especially by William Eden, under-secretary for the Southern Department. Germain's advice was detailed and emphatic. Gage must be recalled and military and naval forces must be concentrated immediately. "As there is not common sense in protracting a war of this sort, I should be for exerting the utmost force of this Kingdom to finish this rebellion in one campaign." He also recommended that Howe replace Gage and that New York be occupied as the center for British naval and military operations.[2]

The sentiments expressed by Germain fully accorded with the policy which had been developing for more than a year. When the meeting of the First Continental Congress in September, 1774, gave clear evidence that the colonies intended to resist the Intolerable Acts, George III wrote Lord North that since "the New England governments are in a state of rebellion, blows must decide whether they are to be subjects of this country or independent." With the King striking the key note the subsequent line of ministerial policy was to subdue the rebellion in the colonies by military force, and only then to consider what changes in colonial policy might be advisable.

An important factor in the development of this policy was a serious misunderstanding of the strength of the Loyalists. The government acted on the assumption that the trouble in America was the work of a small number of dissident radicals who had no considerable popular support, and who were confined largely to New England. This was an understandable miscalculation and was not a serious misreading of intelligence from America. What was much more serious was the assumption that the overwhelming majority of Americans would actively respond in the crisis and vigorously support the home government in its suppression of the rebels. The King and his ministers failed to recognize that in the beginning many Americans were apathetic to both sides, and that the Whigs had been unusually effective in scotching the organization of Loyalist support.

Lord Dartmouth, soon to be supplanted by Germain as the American Secretary, was probably not aware of the perceptiveness of his admonition to William Howe when the latter was informed of plans for a military expedition to South Carolina in the fall of 1775:

> In truth the whole success of the measure His Majesty had adopted depends so much upon a considerable number of the inhabitants taking up arms in support

of government, that nothing that can have a tendency to promote it ought to be omitted: I hope we are not deceived in the assurances that have been given, for if we are, and there should be no appearance of a disposition in the inhabitants of the southern colonies to join the King's Army, I fear little more will be effected. . . .[3]

Dartmouth had already expressed his desire to be relieved as Secretary for the American Colonies and it is probable that North had decided to elevate Germain to the post by the end of the summer of 1775. As usual this involved complicated arrangements at which Lord North excelled. Dartmouth must be placated by suitable rewards, both pecuniary and honorary. Germain must be given enough authority to execute policy without offending the Secretaries of the Northern and Southern Departments who showed signs of resenting an upstart commoner who headed a newly created (1769) department. But Germain was finally installed less than a month after Parliament convened in the fall of 1775.

At the time of his appointment Lord George was fifty-nine years old. He was a tall, imposing figure of a man with a strong face dominated by keen blue eyes. He had a rather haughty manner which many found formidable and even forbidding. His subordinates knew him as a driving, insistent task-master who could still be considerate and courteous. He took little part in the social life of London, partly because he put in long hours in the American Department and partly because he had few friends. In fact, it was this lack of influential intimates or strong family connection that made his position a difficult one. His views on American colonial policy were popular, but Lord George was not. He had no difficulty finding support both in the ministry and in Commons, but there was no very wide margin for error. He must succeed or convey the appearance of success if he were to remain in power.

On October 26, 1775, less than a month before Germain took office, Parliament assembled to hear the King's decision to seek a military solution to the American rebellion. It is doubtful if George III or his ministers were aware of its full implications. The decision was the culmination of a series of actions, or perhaps reactions, that had occurred over the past year. Gage had sent his troops to Lexington and Concord in response to instructions from the ministry urging "a more active and determined part." By the summer of 1775 George III had issued a proclamation of rebellion in which he directed "all our officers, as well civil as military . . . to use their utmost endeavors to with stand and suppress such rebellions."

Now, in October, the King asserted that the colonies had begun the war "for the purpose of establishing an independent empire," and announced his intention to "put a speedy end to these disorders by the most decisive exertions." Alexander Wedderburn, a member of the cabinet, led the support of the King's policy in the House of Commons. "Sir, we have been too long deaf; . . . faction must be curbed, must be subdued and crushed; Our thunders must go forth; America must be conquered." The Opposition protested the use of force to no avail. Young Charles James Fox thought that Lord North was "the blundering pilot . . . [who] had brought the nation into its present condition." And the rabble rouser, John Wilkes, now Lord Mayor of London viewed the war as "fatal and ruinous to our country. . . . An human mind must contemplate with agony the dreadful calamities and convulsions which are the consequence of every civil war, and especially a civil war of this magnitude and extent." With prophetic insight Sergeant Adair insisted that the policies advocated by the ministry, whether "they are followed by defeat or success, . . . will, almost with equal certainty destroy the power, the glory, the happiness of this once great and flourishing empire. It is my opinion that we cannot conquer America; I have no doubt that we cannot acquire or maintain a beneficial sovereignty over her by violence and force." But the majority was unimpressed and regarded the idea of serious American resistance as ridiculous. When the debate was over the House voted 176 to 72 to support the ministry's war policy.[4]

King, Lords, Commons, generals and ministers all concurred in the decision to subdue the rebellion by force and only then to work out a policy of conciliation. It would be unjust to say that the decision was heedless, that George III and his ministers blundered mindlessly into disaster. It is true that there was little understanding of the depth of American resistance and of the quickening spirit of colonial unity. It is perhaps ironic that part of the failure to appreciate the rise of American nationalism was the fact that England's own national pride was outraged by the audacity of colonial resistance. The idea that an illegal Congress would deny the supremacy of Parliament was as obnoxious as the notion that an American "rag, tag and bobtail" should defy British regulars.

Moreover, Britain and its king were not prepared for what Professor Robert Palmer has called The Age of Democratic Revolution. This was the first colonial war of independence in modern history and the first rebellion which had a popular base. The political and military minds of the late eighteenth century were conditioned by the Age of Limited Warfare in which armies were finely tooled instruments of national policy. Marlborough and Frederick the Great did not allow the glories of military victory to obscure diplomatic objectives. Wars were concluded, not with the conquest and ruin of nations, but at the point where one nation had had its military and economic strength strained to the extent that it would agree to concessions. A treaty might demand from the vanquished a piece of territory, a trade concession, or even a change of dynasties, but nations were rarely required to give up their national existence. The Treaty of Paris of 1763 which ended what Professor Lawrence Gipson called the Great War for Empire was the result of a delicate negotiation in which demands on France were pushed to the farthest tolerable limit—but no farther. Britain's own resources had been stretched to the point where the national debt was almost insupportable. To provoke France into a renewal of the conflict was unthinkable.

Yet George III and his ministers saw no correlation between the diplomacy of limited warfare and the American rebellion. In demanding that the Americans submit to Parliamentary authority and, after July, 1776, to renounce independence, England was committing herself to the kind of war to which eighteenth century statesmen were not accustomed, a war of conquest which could be ended only by destruction of the enemy. As the king had earlier noted, "The dye is now cast, the colonies must either submit or triumph."

THE GREAT TROOP LIFT

"There was at once an end to all circumlocutory reports and inefficient forms, that had only impeded business, and substituted ambiguity for precision; there was. . . . no trash in his mind." So a minor official described Lord Germain's assumption of the office of American Secretary. The task that faced him was formidable. If the ministry was to realize its hope for a swift and decisive suppression of the rebellion the first step was the transportation of an expeditionary force to America. This of itself posed monumental logistical and administrative problems. The governmental system through which the war effort must be executed was shot through with antiquated bureaucratic procedures, and conflicts which were rooted not only in politics but in petty personal jealousies, family rivalries, and the greedy quest for sinecures and patronage.

To act with efficiency and dispatch in such circumstances would tax the energies and even the courage of the stoutest leader. Policy was shaped in the Cabinet whose members were constitutionally spokesmen for the King. In reality the King took the initiative only in matters of broadest policy and then only if he could be sure that his policies would be supported in Parliament. As the direction and execution of policy evolved from the Cabinet the King's role became one of advice and suggestion, although such suggestions were rarely ignored. For example, the plan for Burgoyne's expedition of 1777 was given in initial form by Germain in consultation with, and approval of the Cabinet. It was then laid before the King who suggested certain alterations or attached certain conditions. These were incorporated into the final plan and the American Secretary then became responsible for its execution.

In carrying out war plans Germain had to deal with several executive departments. The most important—and the most amorphous—was the army. The King, as Captain-General, was the head of the army and George III, like all Hanoverians, took great pride in his knowledge of military matters. He was familiar with every regiment in the army, its reputation and that of its commander, and he preferred to control the army directly. He was assisted by a secretary at war but this minor official was responsible only for administrative details and finance. Not until 1778 was a military man, Lord Jeffery Amherst, named commander in chief. For all practical purposes the operational control of the army was exercised by the American Secretary, and he was also responsible for its manpower requirements and the deployment of forces. Since the largest military unit was the regiment, training was left almost entirely to the regimental commanders.

The navy was a far different matter. The First Lord of the Admiralty, the Earl of Sandwich, was a powerful and independent figure and the Lords Commissioners of the Admiralty Board were professional officers who also had a great deal of political influence. The Admiralty exercised control over a fleet of several hundred vessels and a vast administrative and logistical machinery that included shipyards, storehouses, naval bases scattered all over the world, a vast purchasing system, and a recruiting service. Its control of operations was such that no military strategy could be carried out without the First Lord's advice and consent.

Supply and transport were even more complex. The navy had its own Victualling Board through which it secured supplies and hired ships to carry them. Army supplies were procured by the Treasury which also hired ships for their transportation. Troop transports were hired by the Navy Board. Artillery and ordnance for both services as well as army engineers were furnished and transported by the Board of Ordnance which was completely independent of both the army and the navy. Germain had also to keep in mind the military and naval requirements of the Northern and Southern Departments. The government was aware from the beginning of the American rebellion that there was the threat of French intervention. The Secretary of the Northern Department, whose responsibility included Europe and the North Atlantic, had to be constantly concerned about the security of the Channel and the threat of a sudden descent by the French upon the coast of England.[5]

In such a situation the need for energetic and unifying leadership was essential. Lord North could handle the complexities of patronage and soothe the frictions of political rivalries, even manage the defense of the ministry in Parliament, but he could not provide resolution and cohesive administration. The King could bring the considerable weight of his prestige to bear, could lend his stubborn determination to the support of his ministers, but he could not exercise the kind of sweeping powers that absolute monarchs had wielded in the past. The very fact that he was king made it necessary for him to proceed with caution lest he arouse the ancient Whig animosities against arbitrary royal power. If the administrative maze was to be penetrated, if the ponderous machinery of government were to generate energy, the American Secretary must provide the driving force.

The first task confronting Germain was manpower. It was obvious that requirements were far in excess of what the King and his ministers had imagined when the crisis in America first developed. General Gage may have been thought facetious when he suggested before Bunker Hill, "If you think ten thousand men sufficient, send Twenty . . ." but by the fall of 1775 Howe was requesting 11,000 reinforcements to supplement the 9,000 men he already had in Boston. Germain planned not only to meet this request but to send an additional 10,000 men to Canada. By the beginning of 1776 it was known that American forces had successfully invaded Canada and were besieging Quebec. Germain proposed not only to lift the siege but to send Governor-General Carleton enough troops to enable him to take the offensive.

At first glance such numbers seemed out of the question. The total strength of the British army in 1775 was less than 50,000 men. Lord Barrington, the Secretary at War, held out a gloomy prospect for recruiting and his pessimism was confirmed by reports of recruiting officers. "Never did the recruiting parties meet with such ill success in every part of this Kingdom as at present, so invincible is the dislike of all ranks of people to the American service. . . ." The government had hoped to hire large numbers of troops from Russia but Catherine II rebuffed the British in the summer of 1775. Germain then turned to the German states of central Europe for help. By March, 1776, he had concluded agreements for 4,636 men from Brunswick, 12,000 from Hesse-Cassel, and 668 from Hesse-Hanau, a total of 17,304. Of these 5,000, mostly Brunswick troops, were sent to Canada and the remainder to General Howe in New York. From England Germain allocated nine British regiments and McLean's Highland Corps, about 5,000 men, to Carleton. Howe was to have a detachment of the Guards and a Highland corps, which, together with the Germans and the force which he had at Halifax, would bring his total strength to more than 25,000 men.

The assembling of troops was only the beginning of the task; transports and escorting warships must be organized to make the voyage across 3,000 miles of ocean. In the early part of 1776 Germain discovered that not only was the campaigning of armies seasonal but so was the Atlantic crossing. The governors of North and South Carolina had reported that large numbers of southern Loyalists were prepared to rise against the Whigs and needed only to be supported by regulars to put down the rebellion in the South. Germain had an expedition of 2,500 men ready on December 1, 1775—except for the Ordnance Department which did not have its store ships ready until the middle of the month. Then a northeast wind locked the ships in the Thames estuary for two weeks. Not until the first of the year was Sir Peter Parker able to collect his ships at Spithead. He then sailed for Cork to pick up the Irish regiments where another five weeks were lost. The convoy finally put to sea in the middle of February, only to be scattered by a North Atlantic gale. The ships were painstakingly reassembled and again set out for their rendezvous off the coast of North Carolina. During the crossing the fleet was again scattered and it was not until May that the expedition reached Cape Fear, too late to support the Loyalists who had been defeated at Moore's Creek Bridge. General Clinton, commanding the expedition, was persuaded by the naval commander, Sir Peter Parker, to lead an abortive attempt against Charleston, and it was not until the middle of July that the expedition finally reached New York, with nothing to show as to results.

One of the most disillusioning of Germain's discoveries was the fact that almost all of the supplies for the army must come from England. These included not only arms, uniforms, tents (with pegs and poles), axes, kettles, and all the myriad items of housekeeping equipment, but also food and forage. The fact that the army was largely confined to coastal bases meant that only a limited amount of food could be foraged from the countryside or purchased from Americans. In 1776 alone one hundred and five ships carried to New York 912 tons of beef, 3,500 tons of pork, 4,900 tons of bread, 800 tons of oatmeal and rice, and 390 tons of butter. At least that was the amount the government contracted for. Not only was there enormous wastage but contractors were notoriously careless about packaging and storage of supplies. A combination of venal government inspectors, profiteering contractors, and the long sea voyage made serious inroads on the quantity and quality of foodstuffs. ". . . I have had the mortification to see Butter taken out of Firkins and Stones etc., put in lieu to compleat the weight," wrote a commissary general in Canada. A soldier noted, "The pork seemed to be about four or five years old. It was streaked with black toward the outside and was yellow farther in, with a little white in the middle. The salt beef was in the same condition. The ship biscuit was so hard they sometimes broke it up with a cannonball, and the story ran that it had been taken from the French in the Seven Years' War. . . ."

To organize and implement the complex elements of this troop lift required an enormous amount of administrative skill and sheer energy from Lord George Germain. Ordnance, Admiralty, and Treasury had to be simultaneously coaxed and bullied to furnish ships for ammunition and guns, troops and supplies. The Highlanders must be embarked on the Clyde, the Germans at North Sea ports on the Continent, the Guards at Spithead, the Irish regiments at Cork. Howe had requested landing craft, Carleton needed prefabricated ships for Lake Champlain, wagons must be built for hauling ordnance. Embarkation orders to regimental commanders had to be coordinated with orders to naval escort commanders; sailing instructions issued to transport captains; camp equipment for twenty-nine battalions must arrive at its destination at the same time as the regiments. Admiral Palliser, who bore the burden of the work of the Admiralty, began to sense the enormity of the task.

> It seems the demands from the small army now in America are so great as to be thought impossible to furnish. The waggons and draft cattle [horses] is prodigious. If this is the case, what will it be when we have another army there above 20,000 men, if they can't make good their quarters, and command carriages and cattle, and subsist and defend themselves without the aid and defence of the fleet, who, whilst so employed can perform no other service? I think some people begin to be astonished and staggered at the unexpected difficulties we are in.[6]

It was shortly after this that poor Palliser discovered that another 10,000 troops were destined for Canada. Yet it should be noted that despite the unprecedented task required of it the Admiralty met the prodigious demands of the American Secretary.

Germain's tireless efforts, his air of certainty and optimism, infused the ministry and its bureaus and boards with an energy and vitality that had not been known since the days of William Pitt. Confident that one bold stroke would bring an end to the revolt in America and finally establish his own reputation, Germain prepared to send overseas the greatest trooplift in modern history until the twentieth century.

News from Canada revealed that American forces had driven all the way to Quebec where they were besieging the slender forces under Governor-General Carleton. Relief for the northern provinces was therefore given top priority and early in March eight British regiments and 2,000 Brunswickers sailed for the St. Lawrence. In just two months, an amazingly short time for a westward crossing, the vanguard of this force crashed through the melting ice of the spring thaw and delivered reinforcements to Quebec. Accompanying the force was General John Burgoyne who was to direct the field operations of the troops under Carleton's command.

Early in May the first contingents of troops for General Howe left England: 3,500 Highlanders, 1,000 of the Guards, and 8,200 Hessians. The shortage of transports delayed the departure of 4,000 more Hessians until July. Thus it would be well into the summer before Howe's force would be assembled and organized for the campaign. But the General was nevertheless greatly impressed "at the decisive and masterly strokes for carrying such extensive plans into immediate execution as has been effected since your Lordship has assumed the conduct of the war."[7]

THE HOWE BROTHERS

By the time Germain came into office in the fall of 1775 William Howe had already been picked for the American command. In 1775 he was forty-six years old and he had spent twenty-eight of those years in the army. He was just under six feet tall with heavy, swarthy features; not a handsome man, but genial and pleasant, well liked by his officers and respected by his men. He had had an outstanding career, most notably as colonel of the 58th Regiment under Wolfe during the Seven Years' War. He had fought with distinction at Louisbourg in 1759, and had led the "forlorn hope" up the heights to the Plains of Abraham outside Quebec, enabling Wolfe to achieve his great victory.

He became a member of Parliament after the war while continuing on active service with the army. His political career was not notable and it was said that the first speech that he ever made in Parliament was in 1778 when he defended the conduct of his campaign in America. He was promoted to major general in 1772 and shortly afterward he was placed in charge of training light infantry. These were lightly equipped, highly mobile troops who could act as regimental scouts and skirmishers, and maneuver in open or extended formation. Howe had just completed this assignment when the fighting began in America.

He was obviously not a man of strong political convictions. He told his Nottingham constituents that he opposed the ministerial policy of coercion, saying he would resign his commission if asked to serve in America. But when he realized that the army was to be employed on a large scale he privately notified Lord North that he was available for assignment. This was welcome news because many senior officers, including Lord Jeffery Amherst, had declined service in the colonies. The fact that much of Howe's service had been in America and that he was an expert in light infantry tactics made him the logical choice for the command. Germain had indicated his approval even before he took office, noting that "Nobody understands that discipline [light infantry] so well as General Howe who had the command of light troops, and who will . . . teach the present army to be as formidable as that he formerly acted with." Germain was aware of Howe's record on conciliation but probably did not consider the general as having a great deal of political weight. Or perhaps he recognized that Howe's announced views had behind them very little conviction.[8]

Lord Richard Howe, William's older brother, posed an altogether different problem. The Howes had powerful family connections and the oldest brother George Augustus Viscount Howe had died a hero's death at Ticonderoga in 1758. George Howe was one of the few British officers who did not despise colonial militia and at his death he became an American hero. The Massachusetts assembly voted two hundred and fifty pounds for a statue to his memory which stands in Westminster Abbey. Whether the younger brothers' sympathy dated from these events or not, Richard, now Viscount Howe, had on several occasions spoken in Parliament in favor of conciliation.

He was three years older than William and his swarthy, craggy features gave him a rough-hewn appearance that befitted a man who had spent thirty-five years in the Navy. He had had an excellent record in the Seven Years' War, establishing a reputation of unquestioned personal courage and as a commander who took care of his men. "Give us Black Dick and we fear nothing," was said to be the toast of the sailors, a recognition of their respect for his skill as a fighter and their regard for him as a captain. By 1775 he had been promoted to admiral, held the sinecure of treasurer of the navy, and had served on the Board of Admiralty.

Richard Howe carried considerably more political weight than his brother. He was an active member of Parliament, especially where naval affairs were concerned, and he was accorded the deference due the head of a family with powerful connections. He regarded the rebellion in America as a tragedy; he believed that a solution could be found and that he himself might be the instrument through which reconciliation could be achieved.

Here he found a sympathetic supporter in Lord North, who was determined to create a peace commission if for no other reason than to placate the opposition. Yet North also shrank from the idea of a long and bloody conflict which would leave Englishmen and Americans angry and embittered. The hard-line policy advocated by Germain and the King, and Parliament's insistence that the colonies acknowledge its supremacy as a precondition for settling the imperial relationship did not bode well for colonies contented and useful to the empire.

If Lord Howe was to achieve his purpose he must first secure a position of power. And to do this he must mask his conciliatory attitude from Germain and George III. His ambition was aided by the fact that the King had as much difficulty in finding candidates for the naval command as he had had in supplanting Gage.

George III had an almost unlimited constitutional power to wage war, but the workaday world of English administration and politics was a maze of complexities. There is an aprocryphal story that early in his reign the King's mother had admonished him, "George, *be king.*" The son took the admonition seriously, but he was wise enough to realize that, in the political realities of eighteenth century England, he must contrive to rule by building a combination of political forces that could execute his will. From a politician's point of view the decade of the 1760's was a bedlam through which there moved an array of cliques and factions—the "Bedford Gang," the Grenvillites, the "Hero of the Mob," John Wilkes, and a host of others. It was not until 1770 that the King found in Lord North a minister and a coalition that would do his bidding.

Intricately interwoven into the political fabric were the personal ambitions of individuals whose loyalties and family connections the King dared not ignore. To these complications must be added the fact that many high ranking military and naval officers were Members of Parliament. (In addition to the Howes, Lord Cornwallis and Lord Rawdon, Clinton and Burgoyne were M.P.'s.) In order to command support for his American policy George III and his principal ministers, North and Germain, had always to control the myriad threads of this political and military tapestry so that the pattern would produce the desired results. The fact that the King was able to do so and adhere steadily to his American policy for seven years is a commentary on his skills as a political leader. George III may have been stubborn, but he was not the bumbling oaf so often depicted in American histories. Like his brother William, Lord Howe began to make himself more acceptable to the ministry by appearing to concur in the military policy advocated by Germain. At the same time he maneuvered through his friends in and out of Parliament to secure the command of naval forces in North America.

At this point chance intervened to give Howe unexpected leverage with Lord North and the ministry. The death of Sir Charles Saunders created a vacant lieutenant-generalcy of marines, a sinecure awarded to naval officers which carried a salary of £1,200 a year. North awarded the post to Admiral Hugh Palliser—and was immediately confronted by Lord Howe, who reminded North that the post had been promised to him. Howe threatened to resign unless the injury to his pride and his pocketbook were not repaired. There now began an intricate and time-consuming game as Lord North tried to extricate himself. He simply could not afford to lose the support of Lord Howe, a man with powerful family influence who was also a distinguished naval officer and a responsible member of Parliament, qualities which were in short supply in 1775. It was not long before Admiral Howe was openly demanding not only a fleet command but the position of American peace commissioner. North's task was complicated by the fact that the Earl of Sandwich, First Lord of the Admiralty, disliked Howe, and Germain still suspected that Howe favored conciliation. In the weeks that followed, North's twistings and turnings included an effort to get Palliser to resign, a quarrel with Admiral Keppel, and a strenuous effort to placate Germain and Sandwich. More than two months later, early in February, 1776, Lord Howe was appointed commander in chief of the North American fleet and named peace commissioner. As a sop to Germain's suspicions, William Howe was also appointed a commissioner, presumably to prevent the admiral from indulging any leniency toward the colonies.[9]

The episode is interesting from several viewpoints. Certainly the ministers were influenced by political and family pressures into appointing to a position of great sensitivity a man that none of them thought particularly well-qualified. Certainly Lord Howe had indulged in a kind of blackmail to further his own ambitions. But it was precisely his rare reputation as an outstanding seaman and able member of Parliament that forced the ministry to succumb. And if Howe was driven by a desire for position and fame, there is no reason to doubt that he was equally moved by the belief that in his dual role he would be in a unique position to save England her American empire.

It was in these circumstances that Howe and Germain, after a bitter wrangle, finally reached an agreement on the instructions of the peace commission. Still suspecting that Howe was too inclined to conciliate, the American Secretary determined to place such strictures on the mission as to leave no room for appeasement. Lord Howe was given no powers to negotiate a permanent peace nor was he to acknowledge Congress as representative of the colonies. He was directed to declare each colony, county, or town "at peace" only after all revolutionary assemblies were dissolved, all armed bodies disbanded, and royal officials once more established in office. He was not to discuss terms or conditions of settlement of any sort until an area had been declared "at peace." In short, the colonists were to lay down their arms and submit; only then would they learn the bases for settling their differences with the mother country.

These stipulations vexed Lord Howe. He especially objected to the requirement that the colonies acknowledge the supremacy of Parliament "in all cases whatsoever," the language of the Declaratory Act. He recognized that this was the essence of the quarrel with the mother country and that to flaunt this in the face of colonial opposition would stifle any spirit of compromise. He insisted that the odious requirement be dropped and finally succeeded, but the concession was meaningless. Germain was careful to keep a firm hand on the peace commission, and to insure that it was stipulated that when the commissioners declared a colony at peace their action would have to be ratified in London before further terms of settlement could be negotiated.

Admiral Howe's success as fleet commander was deemed much more important in ending the trouble in America. In addition to lending support to the army Howe was expected to enforce the Restraining Acts by interdicting colonial trade and destroying colonial shipping; to carry the war to the ports and harbors of the American coast; to seize all military supplies and even impress seamen into the navy. In a word, the ministry expected his lordship to rely on the vigorous application of force to bring peace in America.

The strangulation of colonial commerce was designed to complement the objectives of the British armies. As previously noted General William Howe had been ordered to move from Boston to New York in the autumn of 1775, but he had thought it best to spend the winter in Massachusetts. The first move for 1776, then, would be to occupy New York City and establish it as a base of operations. From this point several prospects appeared feasible. It was expected that the sizeable force sent to Canada would allow Carleton and Burgoyne to go over to the offensive. This suggested the possibility of coordinating an invasion from the north with a movement by Howe up the Hudson. Massachusetts and the rest of New England would then be open to attack from the west. The seizure of Rhode Island would also offer possibilities both as an important naval base and as an entering wedge to New England. But Germain had no intention of dictating details to his American commanders. "These operations must be left to your judgement and discretion," he wrote in identical letters to Howe and Carleton, "as it would be highly improper, at such a distance, to give any positive orders, especially as so much confidence is placed in your knowledge and military experience."[10]

The plans for 1776 were not very specific because the parts of the machinery were not in place. At the end of April Quebec was still besieged by the Americans, Howe was still in Halifax, and the first elements of his reinforcements had barely cleared English waters. Germain had perforce to depend on his commanders in America to seize opportunities as they were presented and shape their strategy to the occasion. And in addition to the geographic objectives there was, as General Howe pointed out, the need to deal a blow which would shatter American morale, "to check the spirit which the evacuation of Boston will naturally raise among the rebels." He thought that "it is probable that the leaders, urged on by the people and flushed with the idea of superiority, may be the readier brought to a decisive action, than which nothing is more to be desired . . . as the most effectual means to terminate this expensive war. . . ."[11]

Lord George Germain had come a long way from the court martial which had convicted him of disobedience—the gossips still whispered "cowardice"—at Minden. He had assumed direction of the first great imperial crisis that England had faced since 1763. He at once grasped the dimensions of the problem posed by the decision to suppress the rebellion by force of arms. If the decision itself ultimately proved to be fatal, Germain staked his reputation on it, and he brought to the war effort a single-minded determination and a display of driving energy not seen since the days of the great Pitt. In drawing the comparison some discrepancies are obvious. Haunted by the "Ghost of Minden" Germain could never assume the heroic stature that inspired such patriotic fervor in the followers of Pitt. Perhaps this was impossible in a war in which Englishmen were fighting Englishmen. And Germain did not have at hand an Amherst or a Forbes or a Wolfe to execute his will.

THREE

Dress Rehearsal: 1776

From his base at Halifax Sir William Howe wrote to Lord Germain on April 26, 1776:

> There is not the least prospect of conciliating this continent until its armies have been roughly dealt with; and I confess my apprehensions that such an event will not be readily brought about, the rebels get on apace, and knowing their advantages in having the whole country, as it were, at their disposal, they will not be readily brought into a situation where the King's troops can meet them on equal terms. Their armies retiring a few miles beyond the navigable rivers, ours cannot follow them from the difficulties I expect to meet in securing land carriage. It cannot be denied that there are many inhabitants in every province well affected to the Government, from which no doubt we will receive assistance, but not until His Majesty's arms have a clear superiority by a decisive victory.[1]

William Howe does not get high marks for brilliance in the history of the War of Independence, but this is as clear and concise a statement of the military problem as was ever expressed by an English or ministerial leader.

The day before Howe wrote his dispatch the American Secretary had issued instructions to his brother, Admiral Lord Richard Howe. As noted, the admiral was not only given command of naval forces for the campaign in America but had been named, along with his brother, as peace commissioner to receive the colonies' submission. Yet this last title was misleading, for what Germain envisioned was a decisive victory which would smash American armed resistance and be followed by a dictated peace. On May 11 Lord Howe's flagship HMS *Eagle* set sail for America.[2]

THE CANADIAN OFFENSIVES

While the American army had been forcing the British out of Boston Congress had taken under consideration another military objective. It was not surprising that both Massachusetts and Connecticut should focus their attention on Ticonderoga, located at the upper end of Lake Champlain.

Ever since Samuel de Champlain had accompanied the Hurons south against the Iroquois in 1609 the Richelieu river-Lake Champlain-Hudson river depression had been a pathway for Indian and white warriors alike. As England and France struggled for supremacy in North America during the Seven Years' War this natural highway took on an immense strategic importance. At its upper end (that is, southern end) the lake narrows to a width of less than half a mile where it is joined by the swift unnavigable waters from Lake George. Fort Ticonderoga was situated at this strategic point and was considered the key to the invasion route.

The idea of seizing Ticonderoga occurred almost simultaneously to Benedict Arnold and Ethan Allen. Captain Arnold had marched to Cambridge with his company of Connecticut militia when the New England troops gathered after Lexington and Concord. At his request the Massachusetts Committee of Safety early in May authorized Arnold to recruit 400 men to take the fort and its artillery, which numbered over a hundred guns.

In the meantime a motley force of Connecticut and New Hampshire troops had assembled at Castleton in the "Hampshire Grants" (Vermont) and had elected Ethan Allen as their colonel. Allen was a lean, tough frontiersman who had become notorious as the leader of the Green Mountain Boys during the hotly contested boundary dispute between New York and New Hampshire. There had been several armed clashes with the New Yorkers and Governor Tryon had put a price of £100 on Allen's head.

When Arnold heard of the gathering of Allen's men he hurried to Castleton, presented his commission and claimed the command. The Boys declared that they would march with no one but Allen. After a furious exchange of words the two commanders finally reached an agreement to share authority, probably because each recognized in the other a stubbornness that matched his own. The joint expedition of about 200 men reached the lake opposite Ticonderoga on May 10, 1775. Early the next morning about half of them crossed under cover of darkness and burst upon the handful of British soldiers manning the works. Allen brandished his cutlass over the head of Captain Delaplace, the fort's commander, and demanded his surrender "in the name of the great Jehovah and the Continental Congress." At least, so Allen later wrote in his version of the adventure; it was strange language from a man who had no authority from Congress and who had written a pamphlet on deism.[3]

The Americans pressed northward in the days that followed. Arnold and Allen each led raiding parties all the way to the Richelieu, but by early June the troops were back at Ticonderoga. The fortress was stripped of its guns and it was at first decided to abandon the Lake Champlain position. But the public outcry, especially from New York and New England, caused Congress to reconsider. It was reported that the British were urging the Indians of the Iroquois Confederacy to attack American forts and settlements and Congress was reluctant to relinquish its hold on Lake Champlain. It therefore appointed Major General Philip Schuyler to organize and command a Northern Army.

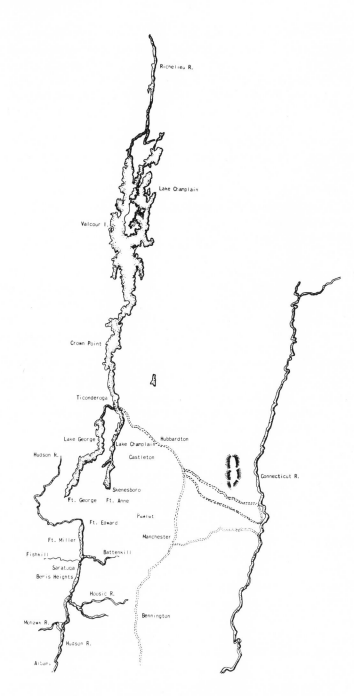

THE CANADIAN INVASION ROUTE

At about the same time Congress received a dispatch from Benedict Arnold, who had been replaced as commander at Ticonderoga and was on his way back to Massachusetts. Arnold reported that Sir Guy Carleton, the governor-general of Canada, had only a corporal's guard with which to defend the whole province. A force of two thousand men, said Arnold, could not only clear the enemy from Lake Champlain but should be able to capture Montreal and threaten Quebec. This opened a glittering prospect to Congress, and at the same time confronted it with the paradox of its position. The delegates would, a few weeks later, vote a petition to the King professing their loyalty and asking for reconciliation with the mother country. Although this would be done primarily to placate the Whig-Loyalists, could the colonies, while professing to be fighting in defense of their liberties, undertake what amounted to a campaign of conquest? Moreover, it was by no means certain that the Canadians were prepared to receive the blessings of liberty, American Whig style, since the latter had only recently inveighed against the Quebec Act which confirmed Catholicism as the approved religion of the French *habitants*. Yet the prospect was alluring and if the Canadians were not persuaded it would at least deprive the British of a base for military operations against the northern colonies. Accordingly, Schuyler was ordered to take the offensive against "St. Johns, Montreal and any other parts of the country." The general and his staff went to Ticonderoga on July 18.[4]

Philip Schuyler was the scion of one of the Dutch patroon families of the Hudson Valley and he had married Catherine Van Rennselaer, whose family was even more prominent and wealthy. His mother was a Van Cortlandt, and so Schuyler was typical of the landed gentry of the Hudson River Valley whose family connections and vast land holdings enabled them to rule New York. He had been a member of the New York Assembly since 1768 and was a man of considerable influence in the clannish, factional politics of the colony. The revolutionary New York Provincial Congress had nominated him to Congress for the rank of major general in 1775, probably as much in deference to his political influence as to his military experience.

Arnold had urged the necessity for prompt action against Canada but this was more easily said than done. At Ticonderoga Schuyler found a garrison of about 600 men, many of them ill, most of them undisciplined. These and other troops in the area were badly supplied and the enlistments of many were about to expire. New York had voted additional troops, but the assembly had noted that "they have no arms, clothes, blankets or ammunition, the officers no commissions, our treasury no money, ourselves in debt. It is vain to complain. . . ." It was the sort of situation with which American commanders would soon become painfully familiar. In addition, Schuyler, a New Yorker, did not have the capacity to inspire confidence in the New Englanders. He was an aristocrat and a patroon whose large land holdings and dignified manner made him an object of considerable skepticism among the democratic militiamen and their officers. Schuyler was honest and brave, an able administrator, and unselfishly devoted to the Patriot cause. But his health was chronically poor and all during the campaign he was plagued with a "bilious fever and violent rheumatick pains."

It was not until the middle of August that a northern army was finally assembled, but even then Schuyler delayed to attend a conference of Indians at Albany. In his absence General Richard Montgomery, his second in command, decided to wait no longer. The antithesis of Schuyler when it came to action, the young brigadier was convinced of "the necessity of a vigorous and speedy effort to crush [the British] naval armament before it got abroad." On August 28 he embarked 1,200 men and eight days later, on September 5, he reached St. Johns on the Richelieu, where Schuyler rejoined the command. After some confusion and a brief retreat the Americans besieged St. Johns and finally forced its surrender. But the ill-conducted operation had taken fifty-five days and not until the first week in November was the way to Montreal open. By the 13th Montgomery had forced the capitulation of Montreal, although Governor-General Carleton managed to escape down the St. Lawrence to Quebec.[5]

In the meantime a second striking force against Canada had been organized under the command of Benedict Arnold, who had been promoted to brigadier general. With 1,100 men Arnold had started from the mouth of the Kennebec river in Maine on September 19, 1775, intending to penetrate the wilderness by way of Lake Megantic and the Chaudiere river and descend on Quebec. Among the units of Arnold's force was a company of riflemen under the command of Daniel Morgan, Indian fighter and veteran of the French and Indian War.

Arnold's march to Quebec was an epic of hardship and bravery. Beset by bad weather, bad maps and hunger, Arnold's force was reduced to making porridge out of barber's powder and moccasin leather. When they reached the headwaters of the Chaudiere the men collapsed, but the tireless Arnold drove ahead to the nearest Canadian village and brought food back to his men. The command emerged on the St. Lawrence opposite Quebec on November 8. The march had taken forty-five days instead of the anticipated three weeks and they had come 350 miles instead of 180.

But the worst of bad luck foiled the expedition. A message sent to Montgomery fell into the hands of the British and the defenders of Quebec were warned. Montgomery finally arrived on December 3 bringing the total force of the invaders to about 2,000 men. Despite the cold of Canadian winter, sickness, lack of supplies and expiring enlistments, the Americans kept the city in a state of siege. On December 30 they launched a desperate assault under cover of a driving snowstorm. In the bitter struggle Montgomery was killed, Arnold was wounded, and the giant Morgan was captured. The attackers were finally beaten off, but they did not lift the siege. Held to their task by the iron determination of the wounded Arnold they stayed before the city until spring. Despite the pleas of Schuyler to Congress and Washington the first reinforcements did not reach Arnold until April 1, 1776. By that time it was too late. Soon afterward Carleton began to receive the first of the reinforcements from England and, early in May, he drove off the Americans in such confusion that many of their supplies and the wounded had to be abandoned. Altogether the Americans had lost about 100 killed and wounded and 400 captured. It was a dismal ending to the hopes for the conquest of Canada.[6]

By the time the American retreat had reached St. Johns, Washington and Congress had at last begun to send significant numbers of men and supplies. On the first of June General John Sullivan was sent to the Northern Army in command of about 8,000 men. With characteristic optimism Sullivan decided that the course of the campaign could be reversed and he launched a reconnaissance in force of 2,000 men against Trois Rivieres on the St. Lawrence. But General Carleton had now received the full complement of his reinforcements from England which consisted of 10,000 men and General John Burgoyne. The American attack on Trois Rivieres ran squarely into the main body of Carleton's force advancing up the St. Lawrence and was smashed and scattered. What had begun as an American offensive suddenly became a scrambling retreat. The Americans barely escaped to Isle-aux-Noix at the northern end of Lake Champlain. Temporarily out of reach of the British, the army was now attacked by an even more deadly enemy, smallpox. By the end of June Sullivan's force had been reduced by more than half, and what was left was ill-fed and ill-equipped. Malaria and dysentery now struck down many who had escaped the pox and Isle-aux-Noix became a filthy pest hole. Early in July the sick, dispirited army finally returned to Crown Point, their point of departure ten months before.

When Carleton arrived at the Richelieu he considered that naval control of Lake Champlain was a necessary condition to a further advance southward. Since no vessels had been sent from England he began to build a fleet. He was also preoccupied with his duties as governor of Canada and as the summer dragged on he was frequently absent at Quebec reorganizing the provincial government. He seems to have felt no urgency in pressing his advance, for he turned down a proposal by Burgoyne to make a diversionary attack from the west by way of Lake Ontario and the Mohawk Valley. It was not until the first week in October that Carleton finally launched his fleet on Lake Champlain to seek out a hastily assembled little force commanded by Benedict Arnold. Arnold fought his usual stubborn and skillful battle off Valcour Island but his guns could not match the weight of the British metal. He brought his badly mauled boats out of action under the cover of darkness and fog, but two days later Carleton caught up, completely destroyed the remnant, and occupied Crown Point. By October 27 the British advance parties were probing the defenses of Ticonderoga.[7]

The campaigning season was now well advanced and Carleton was forced to make a decision. Should he seize Ticonderoga and press on southward? Should he hold Crown Point as an advance base, or should he withdraw to the St. Lawrence? To the dismay of Burgoyne Carleton decided to abandon Crown Point and pull back to Canada. "I think this step puts us in danger . . . of losing the fruits of our summer's labor & autumn victory," said Gentleman Johnny.[8]

From Carleton's point of view there were good reasons for his decision. He was, after all, governor of Canada and the political affairs of the province were still in a tangle. A winter campaign over a long supply line was out of the question, since Howe, in New York, had given no indication that he intended to move up the Hudson. Even a decision to hold Crown Point would necessitate a lengthy line of communication and supply if it were not to suffer the same exposure that led to the fall of Ticonderoga.

A more important question is why Carleton delayed the entire summer in preparing for his advance southward. The ease with which he brushed Arnold aside suggests that the naval problem was not very serious, and the confusion and discouragement of the American forces would have made them vulnerable to a determined attack or even a reconnaisance in force. Yet Carleton showed no sense of urgency and indeed seemed to be pointedly ignoring Germain's instructions to support Howe.

Without reaching any firm conclusions, some tentative explanations may be put forward. Despite his autocratic manner and haughty bearing Carleton was a genuinely humane man. He treated American prisoners captured at Quebec with every consideration "to convince all His Majesty's unhappy subjects that the King's mercy and Benevolence are still open to them."[9] He saw to it that the wounded were treated and paroled home when they recovered. He paroled several captured American officers including Daniel Morgan—and may well have regretted it a year later when the "Old Waggoner" led his riflemen against Burgoyne at Saratoga. All this suggests that Carleton considered reconciliation to be the solution to the American rebellion as opposed to the hard line military policy of Lord Germain.

As previously noted, he was concerned about political and administrative problems created by the Quebec Act and he made frequent trips back to the capital during the summer of 1776. If the ministry considered that the rebellion was the major concern of the governor-general, Carleton obviously did not. His commission as major general was senior to Howe's, and he despised Lord George Germain. Under the circumstances Carleton felt free to judge for himself where his duty lay, and he was, on the whole, well satisfied with what he had accomplished. In desperate circumstances he had saved Canada from conquest and had driven the enemy from its borders, for which the King awarded him the red ribbon of a Knight of the Bath. From the point of view of continental strategy Carleton may have missed a golden opportunity. But from the citadel of Quebec the governor-general had a different view.

THE MISSION OF THE HOWES

On June 29, 1776, Daniel McCurtin, an American soldier on Staten Island, "was upstairs in an outhouse and I spied as I peeped out the Bay something resembling a wood of pine trees trimmed. I declare, at my noticing this, I could not believe my eyes, but keeping my eyes fixed on the very spot . . . in about ten minutes the whole Bay was full of shipping as ever it could be. I declare I thought all London was afloat." The sight which distracted him was the arrival of General Howe and his army from Halifax. (Unfortunately, "Just about five minutes before I see this sight I got my discharge," and the journal ends; future generations were thus deprived of the subsequent views of Rifleman McCurtin on the backside of American history.) With the arrival of substantial reinforcements, Howe had decided to make New York his base for the campaign of 1776. On July 12 HMS *Eagle*, flying the pennant of Admiral Richard Lord Howe, arrived off New York after nine weeks at sea.[10]

The dates are important. Lord Howe's peace commission had been the subject of discussion in the colonies for months. Whig-Loyalists in and out of Congress still hoped for a reasonable offer of settlement by the Crown. By alternately holding out expectations of reconciliation and the spectre of military conquest they had hoped to stem the radical movement for independence. Robert Morris, wealthy financier who abstained in the final vote for independence, had succinctly stated the dilemma of Loyalists in April: "Where the plague are these Commissioners, if they are to come what is it that detains them; it is time we should be on a certainty and know positively whether the liberties of America can be established and secured by reconciliation or whether we must totally renounce connection with Great Britain and fight our way to total independence."

Yet winter ended and spring came in with General Howe's army still at Halifax, so there was not a single regiment of the British army on American soil when Richard Henry Lee introduced his resolution on June 7, "that these United Colonies are, and of right out to be, free and independent States. . . ." The great debate began, although it was less a debate than a period when the delegates awaited instructions from their provincial governments. Members of Congress were thorough republicans and they did not intend to vote on such a momentous question until they were directed to do so.[11]

If General Howe saw any relationship between his arrival at New York and the decision which was being reached in Philadelphia, he gave no sign. He prudently put his troops ashore on Staten Island on July 3 and awaited the reinforcements which Germain had promised him. Even so, the appearance of the British brought radical activity in New York to a halt, and its delegates in Philadelphia abstained from voting for independence on July 2. When the *Eagle* dropped anchor on July 12 the United States was ten days old.

This is not to say that spirited action by General Howe or an earlier arrival by his Lordship would have forestalled completely the vote on July 2. Admiral

Howe and Lord Germain were thinking in terms of submission followed by reconciliation at a time when the colonies were debating independence. Yet a fuller appreciation of the intentions of the radicals and a better understanding of the issues involved might have enabled the Howes to employ both military and diplomatic means to weaken support for the radicals. It was not until the last week in June, for example, that New Jersey denounced Governor William Franklin and instructed its delegates to join the other colonies in declaring independence. Considering how quickly the Whigs of New Jersey collapsed five months later, it is interesting to speculate on what their reaction would have been had Howe lodged his army in New York instead of Halifax during the winter, or if he had put a few regiments ashore at Sandy Hook when he finally arrived on the 25th of June.[12]

As it was Lord Howe proceeded as if the Declaration of Independence had never occurred. Officially, of course, he refused to acknowledge the existence of the United States and, in seeking an interview with Washington, insisted on addressing him as "George Washington, Esq., etc., etc." The commander in chief's reply was simply to convey "my particular compliments" to the Admiral and the General. Within a few days a packet of dispatches from Lord Howe was intercepted by American soldiers and sent to Congress. From these documents, which included instructions to royal governors and letters to private individuals, it was clear that, however eager the peace commissioners might be to open negotiations, there was simply nothing to negotiate. Aside from issuing pardons to individuals and receiving submission of the "colonies," the Howes had no authority. These revelations, which were published in the Whig press, snuffed out the last hope of the waverers.[13]

Lord George Germain, believing from the beginning that a military solution was necessary, did not stint in his support of the plans for 1776. He had urged General Howe to move his base from Boston to New York not only to rid himself of the hornet's nest of New Englanders, but also because New York had the best port facilities in America and because its geographic position made it an ideal center from which Howe's operations could be conducted. Centrally located on the Atlantic coast, it lay at the southern end of the Richelieu-Lake Champlain-Hudson trench which would provide a communications route to Canada. In addition New York City was thought to be a center of Loyalism and it was believed that neighboring New Jersey and Pennsylvania might be easily won over if Loyalists in those areas were given military support.

General Howe told Germain that, once he had established himself in New York, his principal objectives would be to win a decisive victory over the American army and isolate New England. The latter might be accomplished either by the occupation of Rhode Island or a move up the Hudson to link with Carleton, or both. By early spring, then, Germain, Carleton, and Howe had all agreed on the general plan, and had announced their intentions to make it operational at the earliest possible moment. The American Secretary had conceded to his commanders that, as noted above, they must exercise their own "judgement and discretion" in the execution of their respective phases of the plan.

For the campaign of 1776 Howe estimated that a total of 20,000 men would be needed for his operations in New York and New England, plus 2,000 men to garrison Halifax. This meant that Germain would have to more than double Howe's force of something less than 9,000 men which the latter had brought to New York. If Carleton was expected not only to beat back the American invasion but go over to the offensive he would need a force of 10,000 men. Considering the fact that the total strength of the entire British army in 1775 was less than 50,000 men this constituted an enormous demand on the American Secretary as well as on the Admiralty which would have the job of lifting these troops overseas.

As noted above, Germain authorized a force which not only equalled Howe's estimates but exceeded them. The sudden demand for manpower was met by hiring mercenaries from the German states, principally Hesse-Cassel and Brunswick. Twelve thousand Hessians were sent to Howe along with 3,500 Highlanders and 1,000 volunteers from the Guards, bringing his total force at New York to nearly 26,000 men. Of the 10,000 man force sent to Carlton, half were Germans.[14]

But the hopes for an early beginning to the campaign, for that "decisive Action . . . to terminate this expensive War" soon vanished. Howe's Halifax force did not arrive until the end of June. An expedition of 3,500 men under General Henry Clinton had been diverted southward in the vain hope of supporting Loyalist risings in the Carolinas. The British attack was repulsed at Charleston and Clinton finally rejoined Howe at New York at the end of July. The main body of reinforcements, the Guards and the Hessians, did not arrive until August 12. William Howe was an orderly man. Not until he had assembled his entire force with all its supplies and equipage, did he begin his offensive. Even then he avoided a direct attack on Manhattan.[15] On August 22 he began landing 15,000 men on Long Island.

This ended a long period of watchful waiting for George Washington. After the evacuation of Boston he had correctly guessed that the next move of the enemy would be against New York, and he shortly sent General Charles Lee to Manhattan to supervise the erection of fortifications. The island was surrounded by navigable waters on three sides; Lee's pessimistic conclusion that the city could not be defended was hardly surprising. But he did believe that the Americans could punish the British severely by a vigorous resistance. Subsequently, when Washington arrived in New York in mid-April, he directed the construction of two forts, Washington and Lee, on either side of the Hudson at the northern end of Manhattan to guard the approaches to the upper Hudson valley. Remembering the British experience in Boston, Washington also fortified Brooklyn Heights on Long Island which overlooked the southern tip of Manhattan across the East River. To him this may have appeared to be another Dorchester Heights, from which the British guns could make the lower end of Manhattan untenable and open the East River to the British fleet. Finally he stationed some militia across the river at Amboy in New Jersey to guard against a landing there. Washington had thus attempted to provide for all contingencies, but in reality none of them could be adequately met considering the meager and undisciplined force at his disposal.

When the British landed on Long Island Washington hurried to the scene. He already knew that General Greene, who commanded on Long Island, was ailing and he had delegated John Sullivan to take charge. During the next four days there was fitful movement on both sides, a cautious sparring, as Howe planned his attack. Washington was still fearful that the British might storm Manhattan directly, but he filtered more regiments across to Brooklyn until about half his force, 10,000 men, was committed. On the 24th came still another change of command. General Israel Putnam, veteran of the French war and senior to Sullivan, pleaded with Washington to be given charge on Long Island and Washington acceded to his request. "Old Put" was still regarded as the most seasoned of the generals and it seems not to have occurred to the commander in chief that Putnam was not familiar with the fortifications or the terrain. The most prominent feature was an escarpment of wooded hills which formed a natural defensive position about a mile and a half east of the fortifications in Brooklyn. Sullivan was placed in command of an advance force of 3,500 men manning this height. The right wing was anchored on the south shore at Gowanus Bay and was commanded by William Alexander, a self-styled Irish peer who claimed the title of Lord Stirling. The center was commanded by Sullivan himself while the left or northern end of the American line simply petered out—in military terminology, it was "in the air." Washington inspected these dispositions on the 26th and made no suggestions. Putnam took his post in the fortifications in Brooklyn.

On the morning of August 27 General Howe launched his attack. About 5,000 men, mostly Germans, advanced directly against the American position and began to skirmish along Stirling's front while 10,000 men under Clinton and Cornwallis swung to the north and circled the unprotected American left flank. The envelopment was a complete surprise and the British fell on the rear of the American line like a clap of doom. Complete disaster was avoided when Stirling swung his Delaware and Maryland troops ninety degrees to the north, and rammed them straight into the van led by General Cornwallis. It was a measure of Stirling's determination and the courage of these raw troops that the British vanguard was halted and temporarily thrown back, allowing many of Sullivan's command to escape. The Maryland and Delaware regiments lost 250 men and both Stirling and Sullivan were captured. The British pursued the fleeing Americans into the outer works of the fortifications at Brooklyn, at which point Howe called off the attack.

Did he miss a golden opportunity to destroy the American army and capture its commander in chief? Clinton thought so and so did innumerable critics of Howe after he was recalled in 1778. Howe later admitted that he could have carried the fortifications at Brooklyn, but "the loss of 1,000 or perhaps 1,500 British troops, in carrying those lines of the enemy, would have been but ill-repaid by double that number of the enemy." It has often been said that Howe's memory of the slaughter on Breed's Hill had instilled in him a fatal caution which he carried with him for the rest of the war. But there are reasonable explanations for his decision. There was no evidence that Howe knew of Washington's presence on Long Island and, more important, no reason at this point for Howe to recognize the enormous value of Washington's indomitable leadership to the American cause. Nor did Howe's decision allow the Americans to escape. They were still tightly pinned between the British and the East River from which Howe believed there was no escape, especially since the fleet would shortly be able to move up the river and seal off the way to Manhattan. "The most essential duty I had to perform was not wantonly to commit his majesty's troops where the object was inadequate." Howe had, after all, struck his decisive blow and he may well have expected the rebellion was about to collapse.

For two days, August 28 and 29, the Americans held their position, but it became increasingly clear to Washington that he had not only been defeated but that the Long Island detachment, more than half his force, was in dire peril. Only a northeast wind, which had blown steadily down the East River for the past several days had prevented Admiral Howe from interposing his vessels across the line of retreat. In the darkness and fog of the night of August 29–30 Washington ferried his entire force to the safety of Manhattan. It was a magnificent maneuver and it showed the commander in chief at his best. Planning and discipline—and luck—had made possible the evacuation of over 9,000 frightened, wet, dispirited men with so much dispatch and so little noise that the British did not react until the last elements of sentries and the small covering force had pushed out into the stream. Even the artillery, except for the heaviest guns, was brought off.[16]

The Retreat from New York

The defense of New York presented Washington with formidable problems. He was faced with an enemy that had overwhelming superiority in numbers and experience of its soldiers. British naval support enabled the Howes to land troops and give fire support to any spot of their choosing. Yet the American commander had not done well in his first test of battle in the field. He had divided his force for understandable reasons, but he expected too much of both his troops and his generals. Sullivan might be blamed for the stunning success of Howe's envelopment but Washington had himself inspected the lines and had made no move to protect the exposed flank. He had been present during the battle but had issued none but routine orders during the course of the action. Of the principal subordinates (Greene excepted) Putnam had shown no capacity at all; Sullivan and Stirling had proved themselves to be hard fighters, but incapable of controlling a battle field or even a considerable part of it. There was one small bright spot in the otherwise dark picture of the engagement. In the morning hours of the 27th there was sharp skirmishing along the center and right while the British waited for Clinton to reach his flanking position. During these sporadic fire fights the Americans stood up well and displayed considerable poise in the presence of the enemy. In addition when Stirling counterattacked, William Smallwood's Marylanders and John Haslet's Delaware Continentals behaved like veterans; and "General Lord Stirling fought like a wolf."

But this did nothing to dispel the pall of gloom which descended over Washington's headquarters and over the entire army. Once more militia began to leave for home. Enlistments fell off sharply, and despite some replacements, Washington's strength fell below 20,000 by the end of the first week in September. The commander's soldierly sense of propriety was outraged by breaches of discipline especially among militiamen, whose officers were obviously incapable of controlling the men in the presence of the temptations of the "big city." Colonel Laommi Baldwin wrote his wife that in his duties as officer of the day, "going the grand round with my guard of escort, [I] have broke up the knots of men and women fighting, pulling caps, swearing, crying 'Murder' etc., hurried them off to the Provost dungeon by the half dozens, there let them lay mixed till next day. Some are punished, some get off clear— Hell's work. . . ."[17]

Fortunately for the dispirited and disorganized army, the Howes chose this moment to resume their role as peace commissioners. The two prisoners of war, John Sullivan and Lord Stirling, found themselves guests of Admiral Lord Howe aboard the *Eagle*. His Lordship avowed his friendship for America, declared that the war was most unwise, and gave his guests to understand that Parliament would ratify whatever terms he could arrange with the "colonies." He urged Sullivan to convey these sentiments to Congress so that a conference could be arranged. Sullivan agreed and on September 2 he came to Philadelphia, insisting that Howe was willing to negotiate with Congress and make concessions. Hopes rose among the moderates and the radicals were afraid to refuse the invitation. They gambled that the Admiral was overstating his authority, since to negotiate with Congress would be, in effect, to recognize its legitimacy and that of the new independent nation. Benjamin Franklin, John Adams and Edward Rutledge, the latter a moderate, met with Lord Howe on Staten Island on September 11. Franklin and Richard Howe "had been in long habits of friendship and intimacy," so the discussion was amiable, but the Americans soon discovered that Howe had nothing to offer. As John Adams put it, "The whole affair . . . appears to me, as it ever did, to be a bubble, an ambuscade." It was the end of the peace commission. Patriots, Loyalists, moderates and the Howes themselves finally and fully understood

George III's self-fulfilling prophecy, now more than two years old, "The colonies must either submit or triumph."[18]

While Congress played out the game with Lord Howe, Washington gained a two-week respite. It finally became evident that New York was untenable and he began to make plans for a slow withdrawal. His inclination was to put the town to the torch and thus reduce its usefulness to the British, but Congress instructed that "no damage be done to said city by his troops, on their leaving it." On September 13, the withdrawal began.

The decision was made barely in time to avert disaster. On September 15, Howe landed 9,000 redcoats and Hessians at Kip's Bay on the eastern side of Manhattan. It is doubtful if the thinly held American defenses could have seriously impeded the operation, but the militia abandoned their trenches without firing a shot and their panic quickly spread. Washington arrived at the scene and he and his subordinates tried desperately to rally the fugitives. As the soldiers continued to flee in blind panic, the frustrations and disappointments of the past weeks which were bottled up beneath Washington's monumental calm and composure at last exploded in a towering rage. "The General was so exasperated that he struck several officers in their flight, three times dashed his hat on the ground, and at last exclaimed, 'Good God! Have I got such troops as those?' It was with difficulty his friends could get him to quit the field, so great was his emotions."

Two circumstances saved Washington from disaster. The first was the fact that, pursuant to the decision of the Council of War three days earlier, the army had already begun to move to a defensive position at Harlem on the northern end of Manhattan. The second factor was another inexplicable pause by General Howe. The last of the Americans, about 5,000 men under Putnam's command, were hurrying north along the west side of the island, but Howe made no attempt to cut them off; instead he turned north along the East River. At one point his leisurely march paralleled Putnam's sweating militia, separated only by what is now Central Park.

By the evening of the 15th the two armies faced each other at Harlem Heights, the last of Putnam's fugitives safe within the American lines, although there had been a heavy loss of supplies and artillery. Washington's position was a strong one and he seems to have been confident of his ability to bloody Howe "if the generality of our troops would behave with tolerable resolution." When the British conducted a reconnaissance in force on the morning of the 16th the Americans checked them; then, as each side fed more troops into the fight, the Americans drove the British, including eight companies of the famous Black Watch regiment. Washington broke off the engagement after each side had lost about 200 men, killed and wounded. Among the dead was Thomas Knowlton who had defended the rail fence at Bunker Hill. It was no more than an oversize skirmish but coming as it did on the heels of the disgraceful scene at Kip's Bay, "you can hardly conceive the change it made in our army. The men have recovered their spirits and feel a confidence which before they had quite lost." And, most gratifying of all Howe left Washington alone for almost a month.[19]

It was a month of disappointments and frustrations. Malingering, lack of discipline, desertions, and thievery testified to the most critical weakness of the army, lack of capable officers. Colonel Stephen Moylan confessed that he was not qualified as quartermaster general and was replaced by General Thomas Mifflin. Any kind of training was impossible because militia units came and went so often that by the time they learned the rudiments of duties and drills their enlistments expired. Even the Continental troops had only three more months to serve. ". . . Such is my situation" wrote Washington, "that if I were to wish the bitterest curse to an enemy this side of the grave, I should put him in my stead with my feelings."

In the middle of October Howe moved again, this time with another amphibious flanking maneuver, but again conducted with such indecision and at such a leisurely pace that Washington had ample time to withdraw to White Plains. This time Howe risked an attack on October 26 and in the engagement which followed Washington was outmaneuvered and thoroughly beaten. But again Howe did not press his advantage. (It should be remembered that on October 27 Carleton was before Ticonderoga, and was making his decision to withdraw to Canada. Did Howe consider pushing Washington aside and penetrating up the Hudson? Despite the fact that the operational plan discussed by Howe and Germain had referred to isolating New England by "an operation on the Hudson" and the instructions to Carleton indicated cooperation with Howe, there is no evidence that Howe considered a move northward after the battle of Long Island, nor that he and Carleton ever communicated on the subject.) Instead, Howe turned his attention southward to the two American fortresses, Lee and Washington on opposite sides of the Hudson. The American commander decided that the forts should be abandoned, since he was now in no position to support them, but he allowed himself to be dissuaded by his generals. Putnam and Greene were convinced that Fort Washington, east of the Hudson, could withstand a British attack. On November 14 the British stormed it and Colonel Robert Magaw, who had sworn he could hold "till the end of December" surrendered the fort and its garrison of nearly 3,000 men before nightfall. Six days later an alert American patrol's timely warning allowed Greene to escape from Fort Lee, with 1,000 men of its garrison.[20]

Even before the loss of the Hudson forts Washington had once more divided his army. To General Lee he designated a force of 7,000 men to operate in the neighborhood of White Plains. General Heath was allotted 2,500 and left at Peekskill to guard the Hudson Highlands. Washington himself with less than two thousand men moved down the west side of the Hudson to Newark, New Jersey. He counted on the garrisons of the fallen forts and the New Jersey and Pennsylvania militia to augment this slender force but, as noted, only about 1,000 men from Fort Lee had escaped, and the militia response was negligible.

By the 28th of November he was forced out of Newark by the approach of a British force under Lord Cornwallis. At Brunswick he was joined by Lord Stirling with his division of 1,000 men. The hard drinking, hard fighting Irishman was a welcome sight but his men were "broken down and fatigued—some without shoes, some had no shirts." The soldiers, as always where the opportunity offered, were addicted to "Barrel Fever" which had its own peculiar symptoms, and "which differs in its effects from any other fever—its concomitants are black eyes and bloody noses."[21]

Now came the first signs of lack of confidence in the commander in chief. Repeated and urgent requests to Charles Lee to bring his 7,000 men to join Washington were answered by a variety of excuses and justifications which only thinly concealed Lee's conviction that "a certain great man is most damnably deficient." Even Washington's long-suffering adjutant, Joseph Reed, was writing to Lee, "You have decision, a quality often wanting in minds otherwise valuable. . . ." There was no difficulty in making a decision now. Tired, hungry and cold though they might be, the little army of 3,400 men was driven out of Brunswick on December 1, passed through Princeton and arrived at Trenton on the Delaware on the 3rd. Again Washington was granted a respite as Howe came down from New York to snap the leash on Cornwallis. It was four days before the British again took up the pursuit. By this time the Americans had stripped the left bank of the Delaware of every boat and scow they could find, and had crossed over into Pennsylvania.[22]

In self-governing states where responsibility is divided it is not very difficult for war leaders to report failure as success, and in so doing they are frequently led into self-deception. Germain had been chosen, in the face of considerable opposition, to preside over the reestablishment of British authority in the colonies. He had, in turn, chosen Sir William Howe to succeed Gage in the confident expectation that he would destroy the rebel army. Since Parliamentary support was necessary if the American Secretary and his commander were to retain their positions and reputations, it would have been surprising if either had admitted failure. On the contrary, the enemy, said Sir William was "much depressed at the success of His Majesty's arms," and Germain noted that Howe "finishes his campaign most honorably for himself and most advantageously for the country." The King indicated his approval by awarding the American commander the Red Ribbon of the Bath.[23]

During 1776 Lord Germain's enormous energies had produced a troop lift overseas the magnitude of which was unparalleled in military history until the twentieth century. Yet neither Germain nor Howe was very explicit as to objectives and priorities. Scattered through the welter of their correspondence from the autumn of 1775 through the summer of 1776 were four ob-

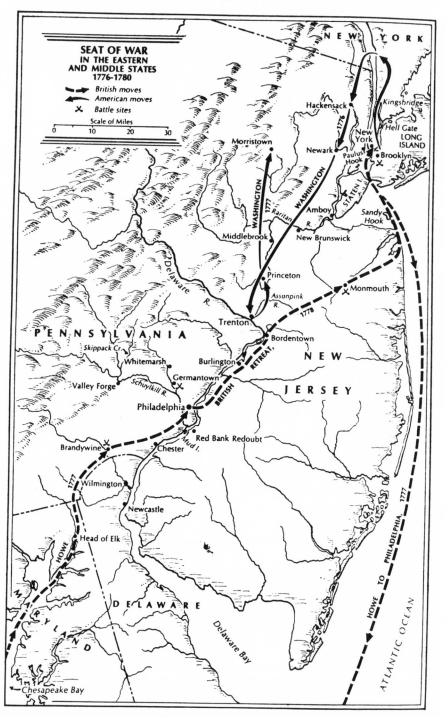

jectives to which both had agreed: the occupation of New York; striking decisively at the American army; a juncture with Carleton's northern force; and the occupation of Rhode Island. A fifth objective had been undertaken by Germain, the expedition to South Carolina, which had been driven off. Finally, in the autumn of 1776, Germain had suggested that Howe "pay a visit to Philadelphia," and Howe indicated that he intended, "in the disposition of the winter cantonments," to occupy New Jersey.

Howe had certainly accomplished the occupation of New York and he had brought Washington "to a decisive action" at Long Island. But whether his subsequent maneuvers had been designed "as the most effectual means to terminate this expensive war" is a question that has been debated by critics then and now. Howe himself reported on September 25, ten days after his landing at Kip's Bay, that there was "not the slightest prospect of finishing the contest this campaign. . . ."

As for the other objectives, Howe had made not the slightest effort to support Carleton nor did he show any interest in a "visit to Philadelphia." And not until late December was Clinton dispatched to Rhode Island, where the British succeeded only in occupying Newport.

In his dispatch of August 10 Howe had mentioned, almost as an afterthought, the occupation of New Jersey. Now, in November, having driven the Americans beyond the Delaware, he decided to leave a chain of garrisons to secure the state. There is no indication that Howe gave any thought to an occupation policy except for the promulgation of an amnesty to all who would declare their loyalty to the Crown. The choice of Hessians to comprise most of the occupation force seems to have been dictated by nothing more than the usual British tendency to give the dirty chores to their mercenary allies. Yet the success or failure of this objective may have been the most fateful of all.[24]

FOUR

Crisis in New Jersey

It was perhaps the darkest hour of the war. Even if the remnant of the forces under Lee and Heath joined him Washington's army could count less than 10,000 men. Already, on December 1, some militia enlistments had expired and many more were simply walking out of camp and going home. The Continental troops would end their term of service on the last day of the year. Congress had fled from Philadelphia to Baltimore without offering any prospect of reinforcements. Confidentially, Washington wrote to John Augustine Washington: "*If every nerve is not strain'd* to recruit the New Army with all possible expidition, *I think the game is pretty near up. . . .*" But his discouragement did not break the iron will. Dr. James Thacher reports a remark which may be apocryphal but not out of character. "My neck does not feel as though it was made for a halter," said the commander in chief. " . . . We must retire to Augusta County in Virginia, and if overpowered, we must cross the Allegheny Mountains." But Washington was not yet ready to take to the back country. He still had an army, even if only for a few more weeks.[1]

Meanwhile, Howe retired to New York for the winter. But he reiterated his intention to "quarter a large body of troops in that [New Jersey] district." He therefore left a chain of cantonments stretching across the state from Perth Amboy to the Delaware. It was the first attempt by the British to establish and maintain control of an area from which they had driven the enemy. In many respects it was a crucial test of England's ability to carry out its program of reconquest, and if it was successful it would constitute a long stride toward ending the war.[2]

The Revolution in New Jersey

The struggle between Whigs and Tories in New Jersey followed much the same course as the revolutionary movement in the other colonies. Its people developed the same American identity and the same stubborn resistance to Parliamentary authority. Most of the Anglican clergy defended the Crown while Presbyterians and most other dissenters made cause with the Whigs. In the southern part of the state the Society of Friends, impelled by conscientious objection to violence, stolidly refused to take sides in the war. Gen-

scientious objection to violence, stolidly refused to take sides in the war. Generally speaking, debtor groups tended to join the Whigs since they were waging a constant battle against the conservative propertied classes.

The situation was complicated by the legacy of the original New Jersey charter, the Council of Proprietors. The proprietors had long since ceased to function as recruiters and promoters of colonization and confined their activities to selling property, recording and notarizing land titles, and collecting quit rents. Yet the proprietary holdings were still considerable and in 1775 a twenty-fourth share of a proprietary right was worth £1,200 a year. Not only did the farmers protest the payment of quit rents but they frequently challenged the proprietary titles. They brought suits attempting to show that the only valid titles were those granted under royal patents or those derived from Indian purchases. There were riots in 1770 in the course of which the demonstrators raised the cry of "Liberty and Property" directed, not against the Crown, but against the proprietors and their detestable henchmen, the lawyers.[3]

The Council of Proprietors formed the nucleus of a coterie of powerful land holders and colonial officials who were known as the "Perth Amboy Group." Prominent among them were Courtland Skinner, a proprietor and the attorney general of the colony, and Frederick Smythe, chief justice of the colony. Peter Kemble, father-in-law of General Gage, was president of the Governor's Council and his son, Stephen, was an officer on General Howe's staff. Altogether there were some twenty or thirty families who represented the economic, social, and political elite of the colony.[4]

Any attempt to make hard and fast distinctions of economic or class interests inevitably produces important exceptions. William Paterson, an outstanding lawyer, became attorney general of the revolutionary state government. William Livingston, whose family was prominent in New York, became New Jersey's first revolutionary governor. John Witherspoon, the brilliant Scot who was president of Princeton, was one of the most vocal supporters of the Whig cause. His students made a point of attending graduation exercises in American made clothes and, after Lexington and Concord, they formed a military company (in which, appropriately, all were officers). Francis Hopkinson, a former member of the Governor's Council, was elected to both Continental Congresses and Lord Stirling, another Council member, was one of Washington's commanders.[5]

The guns of Lexington and Concord precipitated a revolutionary upheaval in New Jersey. In the summer of 1775 the Whigs seized the initiative by electing a Provincial Congress which adopted an "Association" of the people which "forms a social compact." The Congress ordered the establishment of local Committees of Inspection (also called Committees of Observation) in every county and town. These committees circulated the "Association" for signatures by the inhabitants and sometimes rather rudely brought recalcitrant individuals and districts into line.

British authority in the colony was represented in the person of Governor William Franklin, illegitimate son of Benjamin Franklin. This handsome, affable gentleman was also a skilful politician and he courageously attempted to maintain Royal authority. But as the revolutionary movement grew, as committees and congresses were organized, Franklin found himself helpless to oppose them. One reason was that he had no police force. Regular troops had been withdrawn from the area some years before, and the Whigs in New Jersey had followed the example of other colonies in getting control of the militia.[6]

A more important reason was the failure of the Loyalists to take a firm stand alongside the governor. While Franklin remained at his residence in Perth Amboy, refusing to acknowledge the authority of the Provincial Congress, prominent members of the colonial establishment made every effort to avoid committing themselves. Courtland Skinner, who later raised a Loyalist regiment, gave evasive answers to a Committee of Inspection and it was not until December, 1775, that the Whigs intercepted one of his letters which revealed his Loyalist sympathies and forced him to flee. Chief Justice Smythe, a cautious man, avoided antagonizing the Whigs until 1777 when he finally went into the British lines. Stephen Skinner's views were so misunderstood that he was elected to the Provincial Congress in the spring of 1775 and was not arrested as a Loyalist until more than a year later. Peter Kemble, sometime Council president whose son was serving with the British army, managed to trim his sails to the political winds enough to avoid Whig reprisals, and he was a gracious host to American officers when the army wintered near his estate in 1775–1776.

The Provincial Congress was soon requiring loyalty oaths, even of its own members, and it passed a treason law which provided for barbaric penalties for offenders. Estates of Tories who had "deserted" to the enemy were confiscated and those of dubious loyalty were required to give paroles. Families of Loyalists in the vicinity of New York were moved to the interior of the state and Patriot militia did short terms of "Tory hunt service." On July 2, 1776, the Provincial Congress adopted a constitution for the independent state of New Jersey. Governor Franklin was arrested and imprisoned.

But the summer began with the arrival of Howe's fleet and army in New York. Staten Island, the initial British base of operations, was only a cannon shot across the water from the farms of Middlesex and Essex counties. Resentful Tories who had endured the high-handed Committees of Inspection became bolder in the proximity of this military might. Armed clashes broke out in Hunterdon and Monmouth counties and Tory raiders began to collect in the Great Cedar Swamp in the south. Although local Patriot militia prevented a concerted uprising militiamen were reluctant to leave their homes for service in the army, and Washington released some of his New Jersey regiments to defend Powle's Hook (modern Paulus Hook) and Newark.

The British victory on Long Island and Washington's retreat had a devastating effect on the Patriot cause. The wealthier Tories sought refuge inside the British lines and the boldness of the Tory partisans increased. As Washington abandoned New York and retired into New Jersey he brought in his wake the British advance commanded by Lord Cornwallis, creating "a great to Do of Moveing of Goods and talk of hideing Earthly treasure."[7]

Washington was deeply disappointed at the failure of the militia to rally to his support, but he understood their frame of mind. "When danger is a little removed from them, they will not turn out at all. When it comes home to them, the well-affected, instead of flying to Arms to defend themselves, are busily employed in removing their Family's and effects, while the disaffected are concerting measures to make their submission [to the British], and spread terror and dismay all around."[8]

The "disaffected" lost no time in turning on their tormenters. Northern New Jersey quickly fell to the Loyalists who hunted down their enemies as savagely as had the "Tory hunters." John Hart, speaker of the Assembly, fled to the Sourland Hills after the Tories murdered his wife and ransacked his home. The state legislature decamped from Trenton, met briefly at Burlington, and then disbanded until spring. "The State," wrote General Alexander McDougall on December 22, "is totally deranged, without government, or officers, civil or military, in it, that will act with any spirit. Many of them are gone to the enemy for protection. . . ."

On November 30 General Howe proclaimed a pardon for all who would take an oath of allegiance within sixty days, and it was now the turn of the Tories to "persuade" their fellow-citizens to declare their loyalty. Samuel Tucker, former president of the Provincial Congress, was taken prisoner, but obtained his release by accepting Howe's pardon. Two other members, John Covenhoven and Henry Garritse, also accepted British protection along with thousands of less prominent inhabitants who found it expedient to side with the winner.

Courtland Skinner, powerful leader of the Amboy Group, was commissioned a brigadier general with authority to raise five regiments, a total of 2,500 men. But Tories proved to be no more eager for long-term enlistments than their Whig counterparts. They preferred to enlist in the Loyalist militia "Associations" which enabled them to draw muskets and ammunition to harass their Whig enemies.[9]

By the middle of December it appeared that the British conquest of New Jersey was complete. As Howe prepared to go into winter quarters he decided to secure the state by a line of garrisons extending from Perth Amboy, opposite Staten Island, through Brunswick and Princeton to the Delaware river towns of Trenton and Bordentown. "My principal object," said Howe, "in so great an extension of the cantonments was to afford protection to the inhabitants, that they might experience the difference between his majesty's government, and that to which they were subject by the rebel leaders."

There was indeed a difference, but not of the kind Sir William meant. Red-coats and Hessians were much more thorough and efficient in their looting than the Americans, and they made no distinction between Tory and Patriot. They "carried off their furniture . . . and piled up looking glasses with frying pans in the same heap, by the roadside. The soldier would place a female camp follower as a guard upon the spoil, while he returned to add to the treasure." Young Stephen Kemble, a native of New Jersey and a member of General Howe's staff, attested to the fact that the British incursion was "marked by the Licentiousness of the Troops, who committed every species of Rapine and plunder."

Both Howe and Cornwallis issued stern orders against looting but both were back in winter quarters in New York. It was not long before more serious breaches were being committed. A committee of Congress reported *"inhuman treatment of those who were so unfortunate as to become prisoners,"* and *"the lust and brutality of the soldiers in abusing women."* Such reports were no doubt exaggerated but the indignation of the Loyalists confirmed the fact that there was considerable substance to the charges.

The severity of the Tory reprisals and the indiscriminate looting by the soldiers was fatal to Howe's hopes for a peaceful conquest. The British invasion laid the ground for a bitter internecine struggle that lasted until the end of the war. By the middle of December, 1776, the Whig partisans had unleashed a fierce guerilla counter-attack that kept British and Tory nerve ends raw. On December 11 a member of Howe's staff reported the theft of 700 oxen, 1,000 sheep and hogs, 400 cattle, and 8 baggage wagons. During the next week parties of militia on their way from the north to join Washington's army captured 75 Tories. A Hessian officer reported that it was "very hard to travel in New Jersey." Rebels hid their weapons "in some nearby bushes, ditches or the like; when they . . . see one person or only a few, they shoot at their heads, then thrown their muskets away . . . and act as if they know nothing about it." Colonel Johann Rall, commanding the Hessians at Trenton, lost so many dispatch riders that he decided to bring the problem to the attention of General James Grant, commanding at Brunswick, by sending his dispatches under an escort of 100 men and two guns. General Grant does not seem to have been either amused or impressed.[10]

Yet these were sporadic and uncoordinated harassments. If they drove the Hessians to distraction and irritated the British command, they did not threaten British control of the state. Moreover, the ebbing of American fortunes was not confined to New Jersey. Washington was painfully aware that the entire American cause was in grave peril. He must have wholeheartedly agreed with Joseph Reed when the latter wrote: "We are all of the opinion, my dear General, that something must be done to revive our expiring credit, [and] give our cause some reputation. . . . Even a failure cannot be more fatal than to remain in our present situation. In short, some enterprise must be undertaken . . . or we must give up the cause."[11]

The Guns of Trenton

On the western bank of the Delaware above Trenton, Washington began to collect the remnants of what had been, less than four months before, an army of 20,000 men. He ordered General Gates to bring in the regiments of Continental troops which had been sent to the northern army, and only reluctantly decided to leave Heath's little command at the Hudson Highlands. For more than two weeks he had been urging Charles Lee to join him in accordance with the plans made when the army left New York, but Lee had other ideas. Dispatch after dispatch went out from headquarters and the answers from Lee were equivocal and argumentative. Lee had been given 7,000 men comprising the best regiments in the army, but Washington's urgent request "to hasten your march as much as possible" drew from Lee a vague suggestion that "it will be difficult I am afraid to join you; but cannot I do you more service by attacking their rear? I shall look about me tomorrow and inform you further."

On December 12 Lee carelessly rode out of his lines near Basking Ridge to White's Tavern "for the sake of a little better lodging." The next morning a British patrol captured him as he finished a leisurely breakfast, and he remained in enemy hands until the summer of 1778. The loss of this most experienced of Washington's subordinates added to the gloom that was descending on headquarters. John Sullivan, Lee's successor, brought in the vagrant command on the 20th, but only 2,000 men paraded for the commander in chief's inspection, and Gates' seven "regiments" had shrunk to 600 rank and file. Again it was the militia that brought Washington's army up to something resembling respectability. Nearly 2,000 Maryland and Pennsylvania troops came in commanded by General John Cadwalader and Colonel James Ewing, so that as of December 20 the force west of the Delaware numbered about 7,500 men. But the enlistments of the Continental troops would expire at the end of the year. Unless there were reenlistments or replacements the Continentals would be reduced to less than 1,400 effectives. "This handful, and such militia as may choose to join me, will then compose our army."[12]

In addition to collecting his troops Washington needed to collect his wits. The man who had always advocated concentration of forces had divided his army, and had allowed himself to be talked into decisions that had lost the two forts on the Hudson with their invaluable men and supplies. Even when he reached Trenton, on December 3, he had made as though to attack the pursuing British although he was outnumbered almost two to one. Once across the Delaware he had attempted to spread his regiments over a twenty-five mile front which left him weak at all points. By carefully destroying or bringing off all the boats on the east bank of the Delaware, he had temporarily thwarted the enemy's pursuit, but Washington dreaded a hard freeze which would allow the British to cross the river into Pennsylvania and threaten Philadelphia.[13]

The most feasible way to regain the initiative seemed to be to strike a blow against Howe's tenuous line of cantonments. The idea probably occurred to others besides the commander in chief. The keys to the success of such a movement would be surprise and concentration of forces which would give the Americans a decided advantage in numbers. Intelligence reports placed the enemy force in Trenton at about 2,000 men, all Hessians, commanded by Colonel Johann Rall. About six miles further down the river at Bordentown was another contingent of some 1,500 men commanded by Colonel Von Donop. Three more regiments were reported quartered at Princeton. This information was fairly accurate although the estimate of Hessian strength at Trenton was exaggerated by about twenty-five percent.

Above all, there must be secrecy. Washington did not call a council of war, as he usually did before a major operation. He did not even issue the orders for the attack until the morning of the 25th, the day when the troop movement was to begin. These orders called for a main force of 2,400 men to attack the garrison at Trenton. General Cadwalader was to cross at Bordentown to distract Von Donop. Colonel Ewing was to take 700 men across the river below Trenton to seal off the enemy's escape downriver.[14]

On a bitter cold Christmas night Washington's main force began its embarkation. Colonel Henry Knox, the stout artillery chief whose voice was as big as his girth, acted as "beachmaster," his stentorian commands reaching above the blustery northeast wind as he directed men and equipment into the boats. Eighteen guns were manhandled aboard, more than three times as many as were usually employed with such a force of infantry. Knox's artillerymen were an elite corps, well trained and confident. Washington was undoubtedly well aware of their quality and of the special value of artillery in bad weather.

John Glover's regiment, composed largely of seamen from Marblehead, Massachusetts, manned the forty-foot "Durham boats." These were flat-bottomed craft drawing less than two feet of water, used to haul iron ore and grain on the Delaware, and they could hold 100 men. They were pointed at both ends and propelled by four pole-men who sank their long poles in the river bottom and then "walked" the boats forward. For three hours the Marblehead men battled the wind and floating ice as the boats passed back and forth, and it was not until 3 a.m. that the last of the men and guns were across to New Jersey. Only four hours of darkness remained and their objective was still nine miles away. It was obvious that the army would not be in a position for a dawn attack, as Washington had planned. The troops set off down the road to Trenton, measuring their pace to the progress of the guns.

About halfway to Trenton Washington divided the command, sending Sullivan along the river to attack the lower town while he rode with Greene's division toward the upper end. Each division was accompanied by nine guns,

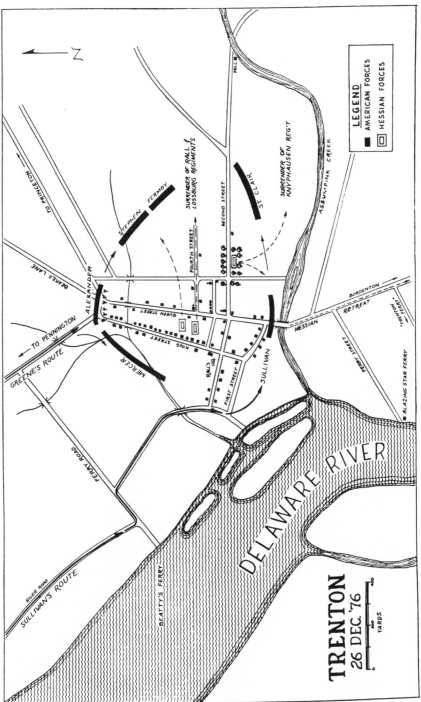

four at the head of each column. Daylight came and both wings were still short of Trenton. The wind now carried rain and sleet which glazed the road and numbed the thinly clad soldiers. It was almost eight o'clock when Greene's van approached the first Hessian pickets posted along the Pennington Road.

This road came into Trenton from the northwest, ran across the northern edge of the town and continued northeast toward Maidenhead and Princeton. The two principal streets, King and Queen, ran south from this road and perpendicular to it. The head of these two parallel streets was Greene's objective. At the far end of Trenton, King and Queen Streets merged to cross a bridge over Assunpink Creek, this being the only easy exit to the south. The Assunpink bridge was Sullivan's objective.[15]

Much has been said about the slothfulness of the Hessian commander, Colonel Rall, and the fact that his soldiers were suffering from massive hangovers as the result of their Christmas celebration. There is no question but that much of this is true. But all the Hessians were not asleep. Lieutenant Andreas Wiederhold was in charge of the outposts on the night of December 25–26 and he attended to his duties. At daybreak he sent patrols up both the Pennington Road and the River Road. With the coming of full light the patrols returned and reported that all was quiet. If Washington had been able to keep his schedule both his columns would probably have been discovered. As it was, about eight o'clock Wiederhold stepped out of the building housing the pickets to get a breath of fresh air and saw Greene's vanguard about one hundred and fifty yards away.

Driving in the Hessian outpost the Americans broke into a stumbling, sliding, sprawling run. Urged on by Washington they poured into the upper end of King Street, then slipped between the buildings and into alleyways, pressing the enemy toward the center of the town. Shots from the other end of King Street signalled the simultaneous arrival of Sullivan. But the driving snow and sleet rendered many of the muskets useless. Quickly the way was cleared for the guns, vents kept dry by leather plugs and powder charges encased in starched cloth smeared with tallow. Young Captain Alexander Hamilton swung two six-pounders into action at the head of King Street. As the Hessians attempted to form the American guns boomed into their ranks and broke their formation. Captain Thomas Forrest posted six guns at the head of Queen Street and fired salvos into the flank of an attack that was forming against Sullivan, who was seizing the Assunpink bridge.

Meantime, Hugh Mercer's Virginians pressed into the town from the western side of King Street and linked up with Sullivan's left. Lord Stirling's brigade advanced down King and Queen Streets in the wake of the artillery fire. As Stirling, Mercer, and Sullivan squeezed the Hessians they retreated to the eastern outskirts of Trenton. Greene, however, had not committed his whole command and he now sideslipped the regiments of Adam Stephen and Roche de Fermoy out along the Princeton road to the northeast. Rall's men were now surrounded but the Hessian commander bravely attempted to rally his men. He placed himself at the head of one of his regiments and ordered a charge but his troops were driven back and Rall himself was shot from his horse, mortally wounded. Major von Dechow, the second in command was also killed. A little before nine o'clock the last of the Hessians grounded arms, the officers raising their hats on the tips of their swords to indicate surrender.

Twenty-two of Rall's men were dead and 948 were captives. About 500 escaped to Bordentown or Princeton. Two Americans had been killed, possibly frozen to death, and only a handful were wounded, among them Lieutenant James Monroe and the commanding general's cousin, Captain William Washington.[16]

Included in the spoils were forty horses, six field guns, 1,000 muskets and bayonets, and enough trumpets, clarinets, and hautboys for two bands. There were also forty hogsheads of rum which the commander in chief ordered staved in. But one must suppose that these veterans had learned all the arts of war and there must have been a few cases of "barrel fever." At least one group managed to salvage not only a cask of rum but also a hogshead of sugar. The whole was dumped into a rain barrel, stirred with a fence rail, and punch was served using shoes for cups. What gastric and cerebral effects this had on poorly fed soldiers who had marched and fought in the bitter cold for twelve hours is not recorded, but the imagination boggles.

There had been no news from either Cadwalader or Ewing, so Washington decided to cross back into Pennsylvania. In fact, Cadwalader had gotten part of his men across but could not land his guns, and so abandoned the attempt. Ewing made no effort to brave the storm and the river. But the threat to the Hessians at Bordentown was nonetheless achieved by a stroke of good fortune. On December 22 a detachment of militia had moved up from Philadelphia and skirmished with Hessian outposts not far from Bordentown. On the 23rd Von Donop reacted by pursuing them to Mount Holly, some ten or twelve miles southeast of Bordentown, and was thus too far away to help Rall. By early morning of the 27th Washington's men were back in Pennsylvania, worn to exhaustion and anxiously awaiting supplies which would restore their strength.

The battle had been a marvel of tactical neatness, considering the lack of training of both officers and men in offensive battlefield maneuvers. When the two columns divided on the way to Trenton Washington had had the officers set their watches with his. Whether he really believed that the attack would be so closely coordinated, the fact was that Greene and Sullivan had struck within minutes of each other. Greene had displayed fine judgement in keeping Stephen and Fermoy clear of the melee and then moving them out to snap the trap shut on the enemy retreat. But the outstanding performance of the day was surely that of young Henry Knox. Each attempt by the Hessians to rally their forces had met a blast from the guns, especially effective on a day when many of the soldiers' muskets failed to fire. Knox was promoted to brigadier on December 27.

There was indeed ample honor for all and when Washington reported to Congress he said simply that "were I to give preference to any particular Corps, I should do great injustice to the others." The men were enormously pleased with themselves. Pennsylvania soldiers said in lofty disdain that "engaging the English is a very trifling affair—nothing [being] so easy as to drive them over the North River." Somewhere on the long road from Brooklyn Heights to Trenton this little army had become part of that rare breed called "veterans."[17]

PRINCETON

The effect of the victory at Trenton was electric. Washington had "pounced upon the Hessians like an eagle upon a hen. . . . If he does nothing more he will live in history as a great military commander." In Baltimore, "This affair has given such amazing spirit to our people that you might do anything or go anywhere with them." From the President of the Pennsylvania Council of Safety came encouragement of a more tangible sort. "We are sending off reenforcements of militia, in hopes this very important blow may be followed up. . . . Our militia are turning out by degrees, but this will give them new stimulus. . . ."

Washington was greatly encouraged and hoped to continue his offensive. He remained west of the Delaware only because supplies had not arrived to feed his tired men. He was further encouraged by news from Cadwalader, who was no ordinary militia general. He reported his failure but added that he still intended to take his force into New Jersey which "would cause a diversion that would favor any attempt you may design in future. . . ." Cadwalader added that the militia "are in good spirits and enlist very fast."[18]

But militia could not replace Continentals. Washington must retain a substantial number of his hard-bitten veterans as the nucleus of his army. There was no way for him to launch an offensive before the first of the year and by that time the enlistments would expire. Much as he hated speech-making Washington resolved to make a personal appeal to these troops who "were absolutely necessary to lead on the more raw and undisciplined."

The Continental regiments were paraded and, after offering a ten dollar bonus for six weeks additional service, he told them plainly that they had done all that he had asked them to do, "but we do not know how to spare you." The drums rolled and, after an agonizing interval, "one said to another, 'I will remain if you will,' . . . A few stepped forth, and their example was immediately followed by nearly half who were fit for duty. . . ." When an officer asked if the men should be enrolled Washington's answer was, "No! Men who will volunteer in such a case as this need no enrollment to keep them to their duty."

He was ready to challenge the enemy again. Cadwalader and the other militia commanders were summoned and for the third time in five days the army crossed the Delaware. He was in Trenton on New Year's Eve when dispatches arrived from Congress at Baltimore informing Washington that he had been made virtual dictator for six months. He was authorized to raise troops "in the most speedy and effectual manner from any or all of these United States . . . to displace and appoint all officers under the rank of brigadier general . . . to take, wherever he may be, whatever he may want for the use of the army, if the inhabitants will not sell it, allowing a reasonable price for the same. . . ." This grant of "powers . . . of the highest nature and almost unlimited extent" could be viewed as a vote of confidence, but it also meant that Washington would receive all the blame if he failed. He answered by saying, "Instead of thinking myself freed of all *civil* obligations by this mark of confidence, I shall constantly bear in mind that as the sword was the last resort for the preservation of our liberties, so it ought to be the first to be laid aside when those liberties are firmly established. . . . I shall instantly set about making the most necessary reforms in the Army."[19]

By New Year's Day Cadwalader had come in with 2,100 men and 1,600 more Pennsylvania militia raised by General Thomas Mifflin had arrived. This brought his forced to somewhat more than 5,000 men along with the whole of Knox's artillery train, forty guns.

He now learned that Lord Cornwallis himself had come out from New York to deliver a counterattack. With a swiftness that was uncharacteristic of the British his lordship routed the New Jersey garrisons from their winter quarters and, five days after the news of Trenton reached New York, Cornwallis was in Princeton. Leaving 1,500 men in the college town and another 1,500 at Maidenhead the British pressed toward Trenton.

The movement caught Washington napping. Instead of scattered garrisons spread across the state he was faced with 5,000 regulars under a commander who obviously did not intend to waste time in getting to the business at hand. Hastily the American commander pushed out a reconnaissance in force along the Princeton road commanded by Colonel Edward Hand who made contact with Cornwallis about noon on the 2nd. Hand fought his men tenaciously and harassed the enemy to such an extent that he forced them to abandon their marching formation and advance the last few miles in line of battle. It was not until about four o'clock that Hand finally pulled his men into the American lines on the south side of Assunpink Creek across from Trenton. As the British approached, Knox's forty guns greeted them, and Daniel Hitchcock's Rhode Island Continentals defended the bridge with a steady rifle fire. Cornwallis withdrew to Trenton for the night and Knox's howitzers continued to lob an occasional shell into the town.

Washington now found himself squeezed into much the same kind of cul-de-sac as he had himself fashioned for Rall. One soldier remembered that "our army was in the most desperate situation I had ever known it; we had no boats to carry us across the Delaware . . . to cross the enemy's line of march between this and Princeton seemed impractical . . . [in] the south part of Jersey there was no support for an army. . . ."

In fact, there was a way "between this and Princeton." Cornwallis had not taken care to close the back roads which led off to the right of the American lines, roads which Colonel Reed and General Cadwalader knew well. Having decided that the odds were too great to risk a battle, Washington sought advice from a council of war. Probably he had already made up his mind to slip off by the right flank since patrols reported that the way was clear. However, unseasonable weather had thawed the ground and muddy roads would make slow going for the soldiers and monumental work for the gunners. The council readily agreed that a retreat to Princeton was the solution and the troops began to move at midnight.

Five hundred men were left behind to keep the campfires burning and make appropriate noises with pick and shovel. Three guns continued to send an occasional shell across toward the enemy camp. The rest of the men moved out silently, careful not to rattle their arms, the wheels of the guns muffled with rags. Washington's incredible luck was still with him, for the wind shifted to the northeast and the temperature dropped sharply. By two o'clock on the morning of January 3rd the muddy roads had frozen solid. It was another cold, slow night march but the weather was clear. As always, the soldiers had to adapt their pace to the guns, "frequently coming to a halt, or stand still, and when ordered forward again, one, two, three men in each platoon would stand, with their arms supported, fast asleep." Daylight came "bright, serene, and extremely cold, with a hoar frost which spangled every object." About eight o'clock the vanguard arrived at a Quaker meeting house about a mile and a half from Princeton. Here a back road led off to the right toward the town, along which Washington intended to make his attack by flanking the British defenses. Parallel to this road and about three-quarters of a mile ahead to the north lay the main Post Road from Trenton to Princeton. Hugh Mercer with about 350 men was to push ahead and destroy a bridge at Worth's Mill to prevent reinforcements to the enemy from Trenton.[20]

A few minutes after Mercer had started on his errand and Sullivan's division was filing off on the back road, firing was heard to the north in the direction of Worth's Mill. Colonel Robert Mawhood, commanding the British garrison at Princeton, had taken the Post Road for Trenton shortly before eight o'clock at the head of the 17th and 55th regiments. As he passed Worth's Mill Mawhood spotted Mercer's force coming up to his left and turned on it, driving the Americans back toward the main body. Mercer rallied his men and checked the British advance momentarily, but as the superior enemy force increased its pressure Mercer and Colonel John Haslet of the Delaware Continentals were both shot down. The men broke and were pushed back

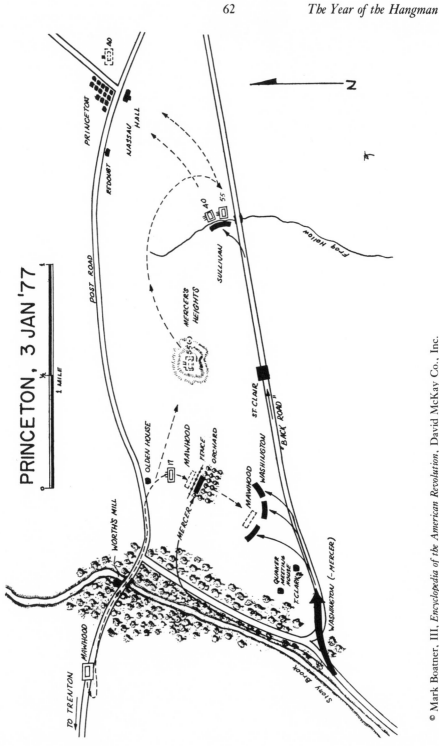

PRINCETON, 3 JAN '77

1 MILE

TO TRENTON

MAWHOOD

WORTH'S MILL

POST ROAD

OLDEN HOUSE

MAWHOOD

FENCE
ORCHARD

MERCER

MERCER'S
HEIGHTS

MAWHOOD

WASHINGTON

ST. CLAIR

BACK ROAD

QUAKER
MEETING
HOUSE

T. CLARK

WASHINGTON (–MERCER)

Stony Brook

SULLIVAN

Frog Hollow

40

55

PRINCETON

REDOUBT

NASSAU
HALL

40

into the advance elements of Cadwalader's Pennsylvanians. The raw militia panicked and for a brief time it looked as if another Kip's Bay was developing.

But the panic was not universal. In the midst of the melee the gunners of Captain John Moulder's battery cooly swung their "long" four-pounders into action and slammed charge after charge of grape and canister into the advancing British. Washington's towering figure loomed through the smoke a scant thirty yards from the enemy line as he rallied the Pennsylvanians and directed Hitchcock's veterans into line. He built up the formation with Hand's tough riflemen. The line advanced with Washington at its head and he himself gave the order to halt and fire. The British broke and the big Virginian could not restrain himself. "It's a fine fox chase, my boys!" he roared and spurred his horse in pursuit of the flying redcoats.

The remainder of the Princeton garrison was surrounded and captured. Washington estimated the British losses at 400 men of whom 100 were killed. His own losses were 40 killed and wounded. But among the dead were General Mercer, an officer of proven ability, and John Haslet, whose Delaware Continentals had performed so brilliantly at Brooklyn Heights, and had been in virtually every action since then. It was a tribute to the young colonel that long after his death the regiment continued to be called Haslet's Continentals.

After helping itself to the scanty stores of food and blankets the army moved out. Cornwallis could be expected to be close on their heels, so Washington abandoned an attack on Brunswick. There were simply no more swift marches left in these exhausted, hungry men. From Princeton the commanding general led them northwest out of the path of the pursuers. A veteran sergeant made a rather clinical report on what had obviously been his own extensive study of the psychology of facing the enemy: "In this battle and that of Trenton there were no ardent spirits in the army, and the excitement of rum had nothing to do in obtaining the victories. As I had tried [gun] powder and rum on Long Island to promote courage, and engaged here without it, I can say that I was none the less courageous here than there."

On January 6, twelve days after the Christmas embarkation on the Delaware, the little army went into winter quarters in Morristown.[21]

"The unlucky affair of Rall's Brigade has given me a winter campaign," General Howe wrote to Germain on January 8, ". . . our quarters were too much exposed, and it is necessary to assemble our troops; that is now done and all is safe." What Sir William was saying, as delicately as possible, was that New Jersey had been abandoned by the British except for a garrison at Perth Amboy, across from Staten Island, and another at Brunswick, ten miles further inland. Even these two posts were harassed by the Americans in the months that followed. A British officer at Brunswick noted almost casually that "our Foraging Parties meet with the Rebels as usual, and a Man or two Killed now and then;" and a Hessian at Elizabethtown complained, "One can no longer lie down to sleep without thinking: this is your last night of living."[22]

More important than the failure in New Jersey was the fact that the Howes had missed their chance to bring the war to an end. From Long Island to the Delaware there had been one opportunity after another to bring Washington "to a decisive action" and most of these had been lost, not so much by Washington's skill as by Sir William's indolence or stupidity. Even the victories at Trenton and Princeton were impressive only against the background of dark despair that had fallen on the American cause. Granted that Washington had displayed magnificent courage and determination, and had managed the little campaign with great skill, he would have been a poor general indeed if he had failed to rout Rall's 1,500 men with his own force of 2,500. At Princeton, with more than four times the strength of his opponent, he had barely escaped disaster before he finally drove the enemy.

But the stunning success of the campaign could not be denied. On January 20 Howe was somewhat more frank with Lord Germain: "I do not now see a prospect of terminating the war but by a general action, and I am aware of the difficulties. . . ." But, as always, he found an excuse, albeit a rather lame one. ". . . The Enemy moves with so much more celerity than we possibly can with our foreign troops who are too much attached to their baggage. . . ."

Germain was not at all pleased with the news of Trenton and Princeton, although he perforce defended Howe's conduct publicly. He informed Howe that he disapproved of the leniency which had provoked the proclamation of November 30 and reminded the general that "it [is] necessary to adopt such modes of carrying on the war, that the Rebels may be effectually distressed, so that through a lively experience of Losses and sufferings they may be brought as soon as possible to a proper sense of their Duty." In short, Sir William was to wage war, not peace.[23]

The gloom in the British camp was shared by the Loyalists. "The minds of the people are much altered," wrote young Nicholas Creswell. "A few Days ago they had given up the cause for lost. Their late successes have turned the scale and now they are all liberty mad again. Their Recruiting parties could not get a man . . . no longer since than last week, and now the men are coming in by the companies. Confound the turncoat scoundrels and cowardly Hessians together. . . . Volunteer Companies are collecting in every County on the Continent, and in a few months the rascals will be stronger than ever. Even the parsons . . . have turned out as Volunteers and Pulpit Drums or Thunder or whatever you may please to call it, summoning all to arms in this cursed babble. D——— them all."

From one end of the country to the other Patriot despair changed to jubilant hope. "Washington retreats like a General and acts like a hero," trumpeted the *Pennsylvania Journal*. "If there are spots on his character, they are like spots on the sun. . . ." The *Freeman's Journal* urged that "whilst we are united in our sentiment, vigilant in our duty, and active in our operations, we need not dread the thunder of cannon, nor tremble at the names of heroes arrayed in all the splendor of a corrupt court, or crowned with faded laurels which have been plucked by the hands of tyranny."[24]

So the dark crisis of 1776 passed. The Americans had not yet won this war. But Britain had lost an irretrievable opportunity to win it.

FIVE

Arms and Men

THE CREATION OF THE AMERICAN ARMY MARKED A MILESTONE IN THE HISTORY
of modern warfare. Until 1775 eighteenth century wars were fought by relatively small armies composed of highly trained soldiers. The American army,
of necessity, was made up of citizen soldiers who were mustered into the
ranks, given the barest minimum of training, and often sent almost immediately into battle.

In 1790 the War Department reported that there had been 396,000 enlistments of all kinds in the national and state armed forces between 1775 and
1783. This included, of course, a large number who had enlisted more than
once. Considering the fact that there were probably no more than 250,000
men of military age available for duty a fair estimate would seem to be that
about 100,000 men bore arms at one time or another during the War of Independence. Less than one third of this number, about 30,000, were under
arms at one time. The largest return of the regular, or Continental army under
Washington's command was in October, 1778, when the commander in chief
reported 18,742 men present and fit for duty.[1]

The myth persists to this day that the soldiers who defeated the British
regulars were veteran Indian fighters, crack shots who harried the redcoats
from ambush with their deadly long rifles. In fact, probably ninety percent
of the American soldiers were recruited from areas east of the Appalachians
and were a generation or more removed from the frontier. Most of them had
never seen a wild Indian in their lives and few had ever fired a shot in anger.
Most of them were familiar with fire arms, for most were farmers and hunters, so their fire was somewhat more accurate than their British counterparts.
But their weapon was a smoothbore musket which had a maximum effective
range of seventy-five yards and took from twenty to thirty seconds to reload.
On the battlefield a fire delivered at pointblank range (twenty-five to thirty
yards) rarely inflicted more than ten percent casualties.[2]

The close-ordered ranks of British regulars were the subject of much derision by Americans then and since, but eighteenth century generals knew
what they were about. Only when soldiers were organized into disciplined
ranks so that their limited fire power could be concentrated and controlled
could an army be effective. American derision changed to terror at Brooklyn
Heights when the serried ranks of redcoats advanced against the Americans,

halted to deliver a fire at thirty paces, and then charged with levelled bayonets. General Washington insisted that his army be trained according to the practice of European military science, and the first occasion on which his Continentals met the British on something like equal terms (i.e., without benefit of fortifications or superior numbers) was at Monmouth Courthouse in 1778. It was an army which had been trained the previous winter by the Prussian drill master, Baron Von Steuben.

THE REDCOATS

"The success was too dearly bought," said General Howe after the battle of Bunker Hill. His dismay reflected not only his awareness of the limited number of soldiers in Boston, but the fact that the entire British army in 1775 numbered only about 45,000 men. Of this number 20,000 were committed to Ireland, Gibraltar, and other outposts of Britain's vast empire.

The basic unit of the British army was the regiment. Regiments were sometimes combined into brigades, divisions, wings or corps, but these were usually temporary organizations for special purposes or limited time periods. Lord Cornwallis' force that came out of New York to attack Washington at Trenton was referred to as both a corps and a division. A brigade of the Guards that served in America consisted of fifteen men from each of sixty-four companies of the King's household troops.[3]

The infantry regiment consisted of ten companies, eight of regular infantry and two flank companies. One of these consisted of grenadiers, so called because when they were incorporated into the regiments in the seventeenth century the men were selected for the size and strength necessary to throw grenades into the enemy ranks. By 1775 the grenades had long since disappeared but the tall, rugged grenadiers were still regarded as elite troops. The other flank company was composed of light infantry. These men were lightly built, active and quick-moving, and were usually picked for their marksmanship.

If several regiments were combined into a corps or there was an especially difficult assault to be made the flank companies were sometimes detached from their regiments and formed into a special regiment. At Bunker Hill Howe formed a regiment from eleven light infantry companies to attack the rail fence on the left of the American line.

Each company consisted of a captain, two lieutenants, two sergeants, three corporals, and thirty-eight privates. The total, including a drummer, was forty-seven officers and men. The regimental staff included a lieutenant-colonel, chaplain, two surgeons and, of course, the colonel commanding. It should be noted that reports of troop strength (or casualties) were made in terms of "rank and file," which meant the total of privates and corporals. A colonel who reported his regiment at full strength would therefore be accounting for 410 men.[4]

The standard weapon for the infantry of both armies was a smoothbore musket approximately four and a half to five feet in length with a calibre range from .69 to .80. A recruit was trained in the complicated loading procedure until he could fire every twenty seconds. If this were done on command twelve separate orders were necessary to complete the evolution.

Powder and shot were made up into paper cartridges. These were carried in a cartridge box made of wood and leather which afforded some protection from dampness, but were not proof against heavy rain. In loading his weapon the soldier extracted a cartridge, bit off the end of the paper spill, and poured a few grains of powder into the priming pan. He then closed the pan and poured the remaining powder and the ball into the muzzle of the musket, using the paper as a wad, and ramming the whole firmly into place. He then pointed his weapon in the general direction of the enemy and fired, bracing himself against the vicious recoil. When he pulled the trigger the hammer or cock, which held a bit of flint, fell upon the lid of the pan (called the frizzen) creating a shower of sparks and flipping up the frizzen to expose the powder. The resultant flash ignited the propellant charge through a touch hole bored through the barrel.

It is not surprising that these crude weapons often failed to fire. A worn flint, damp powder, a clogged touch hole—all these could cause a failure. There was also human failure. An enemy fire delivered at thirty yards while a soldier was reloading was not conducive to steady hands and cool nerves, especially when the enemy might at any moment burst through the dense cloud of smoke with his deadly bayonet levelled. If the soldier were under fire for the first time his performance usually left a great deal to be desired. It was not remarkable to see a number of ramrods sailing through the air when a volley of counterfire was delivered. And in the crash of musketry it was hard to tell if one's own weapon had fired. So it was commonplace after a fight to find on the battlefield muskets loaded to the muzzle with unexpended charges.[5]

The field artillery of the British army was organized into four battalions (or regiments) of eight companies each. Although their total company strength was only 116 there were, for this specialized army, six officers and eight non-commissioned officers. Nine bombardiers, eighteen gunners, and seventy-three matrosses (privates) completed the complement. Field guns ranged in size from enormous 24-pounders to tiny 3-pounders. A 12-pounder required ten to twelve horses to haul its 3,200 pounds of dead weight so that 6- and 9-pounders were increasingly used by both armies as a concession to the bad roads and rough terrain of the American countryside. Gun teams were handled by civilian drivers who were hired by the army.

All field guns, regardless of size, had approximately the same range of about 2,000 yards, but were generally not effective beyond 1,000 to 1,200 yards. The standard piece fired a fairly flat trajectory and used solid shot, grape, or canister. Grape consisted of clusters of iron balls about two inches in diameter. Canister was, as the term implies, simply an iron container filled with musket balls. A 6-pounder had a bore of about 3.6 inches and the gun tube was about five feet long. The gun was trained by a long pole called a tiller or handspike which was inserted through a ring in the gun trail, so that the entire gun and carriage was slewed to left or right. The range was set by an elevating screw or wedge.

In addition to the regular field guns there were also mortars and howitzers. Mortars were stubby, massive pieces mounted on flat, immobile beds at a fixed angle of 45° to 70°. They fired high-trajectory explosive shells, the range determined by the size of the powder charge. Howitzers were the compromise between regular field guns and mortars. They were mounted on wheeled carriages, but the short trail and stubby barrel enabled them to fire high-trajectory explosive shells as well as the standard solid shot, grape, and canister. Although their effective range was decreased by the short barrel length they were very versatile guns.

It was the usual practice to allot two guns to each regiment, although by the time of the War of Independence commanders on both sides were beginning to use much higher ratios and to employ massed artillery operating independently of the infantry regiments. The rate of fire achieved in both armies was remarkable considering that the loading was similar to, though less complicated than loading a musket (a gun could be primed and loaded at the same time). Captain George Pausch, an artillery officer of the Hesse-Hanau regiment, gave a demonstration for General Burgoyne and his officers during which his gunners fired twelve rounds per minute.[6]

Mounted troops were traditionally divided into two categories: cavalry, that is, troops trained to fight from horseback; and dragoons, who were technically mounted infantry who rode to the battlefield and then dismounted and fought on foot. In practice, the dragoons performed as cavalry and the two terms were often used synonymously. There were only four regiments of cavalry in the British army and none served in America until the end of the war. Dragoons were used for outpost duty, scouting and reconnaissance, and especially to harry a retreating enemy whose formations had been broken. Since horses were in short supply there was almost never a sufficient force of dragoons available to appear in battle formations. There were Hessian dragoons with Burgoyne's army but they had no horses and were therefore relegated to infantry duty.

Despite their public assurances to the contrary the ministry and the King did not make the mistake of planning for a short war. As already noted, when General Howe asked for 20,000 men for the campaign of 1776 Germain not only exceeded his request but sent an additional 10,000 troops to Canada. Before the war was over 56,000 men had been sent to North America and the West Indies.[7]

Peacetime enlistment in the British army was for life, and it was obvious that the expansion of the army, as well as the navy, would never be accomplished under the normal peacetime conditions. "Sad work everywhere in recruiting," wrote the British adjutant-general, Edward Harvey, late in 1775. "In these damn times we must exert zeal."

The most usual way to enlarge the army was for the King to grant a commission to a regimental commander, who in turn recruited his men, for which he received a bounty, and pay and subsistence for his men. George III was reluctant to incur the additional expense of raising new regiments until the existing ones had been brought up to strength. But enlistments were encouraged by an order of December, 1775, which provided that volunteers would receive a guinea and a half bounty and could be discharged at the end of three years or the conclusion of the war, "at the option of His Majesty." In addition, vagrants, smugglers, and those convicted of minor crimes might enlist as a means of escaping imprisonment. It is not surprising that jails and prisons became a favorite haunt of recruiting officers. By 1779 additional inducements had been added, among them doubling the bounty and allowing the conscription of convicted criminals.[8]

The obvious conclusion is that those who were enlisted were for the most part riffraff and vagrants, and those whose earning power was so low that a guinea and a half bounty was irresistible. From such "disorderly persons" and "incorrigible rogues" the ranks of the army were filled, scarcely "such Recruits as a Battn. might choose to take in times of profound Peace." But under hard-eyed sergeants these recruits became soldiers, and whatever identity they might have had as civilians was lost as they merged into and became a part of the regiment. This new identity led to the development of a fierce pride and loyalty that was so intense that it could become explosive. Soldiers of Fraser's famous 71st Highlanders were threatened with transfer to another regiment, which would have forced them to stop wearing their kilts. They mutinied and thirty of them were killed before they could be subdued.

A private's pay was eight pence a day but so much of this was deducted for various "off-reckonings" that the soldier rarely received any hard cash. As one contemporary observed, ". . . when all deductions are made, for clothing, for necessaries, for washing, for the paymaster, for the surgeon, for the multiplied articles of useless and unmilitary fopperies (introduced by many colonels to the oppression of the soldier for what they call the credit and appearance of the regiment) there is not sufficient surplus for a healthful subsistence; and as to the little enjoyment and recreation, which even the meanest rank of men can call their own in any country, the brave, the honorable veteran soldier, must not aspire to."[9]

So the army existence was desperately hard. But then in the eighteenth century all life among the lower classes was harsh, and punishments, even for petty crimes, were cruel and brutal. Similar brutalities existed in the disciplinary code of the army. Petty offenses such as malingering or failing to pass inspection might bring confinement to barracks on bread and water for a week. Serious breeches of discipline brought drastic penalties. Striking an officer was a court martial offense punishable by a sentence of 800 lashes. Delivered full force with a cat-o'-nine-tails such punishment might kill a man, and would certainly cripple him for weeks.

The poverty of the average soldier made him a chronic thief. Thomas MacMahan and his "wife" were convicted of theft, he being sentenced to 1,000 lashes, she to "100 lashes on her bare back, at the Cart's Tail, in different portions and most conspicuous Parts of the Town, and to be imprisoned for three months." Two soldiers convicted of robbing a storekeeper were shot.

Drinking, gambling, and women provided most of the diversions for the British redcoat. That estimable chronicler of army life, Sergeant Roger Lamb, relates that privates would often gamble away their uniforms, and be forced to borrow clothes from their comrades in order to muster for inspection. Women were commonplace with the army. It was said that Burgoyne's army was accompanied by 2,000 women when he invaded New York, and Sir William Howe issued a general order authorizing six women per company in the campaign of 1776, a total of 2,776 women and 1,904 children. Some few of these were undoubtedly wives, and there is convincing evidence that many of the women, wives or not, were remarkably loyal to their men, some even accompanying the troops to the battlefield.[10]

All in all the British regular soldier, despite his miserable existence, proved to be a formidable opponent. Trained as he was in monotonous drill and rigid formations, he moved when he was supposed to move with predictable precision and speed. Because he performed as he was expected to perform he was, man for man, the superior of his American counterpart on the battlefield. Burgoyne paid tribute to the courage of his infantry: "Men of half [your] bodily strength and even Cowards may be [your] match in firing; but the onset of Bayonets in the hands of the Valiant is irresistible. . . ." English officers lost a good many battles in the War of Independence but almost never because of the failure of the redocat.[11]

Officers owed their positions to two factors, social rank and money. It was not very difficult to become an officer if one came from an upper or middle class family. Younger sons of the nobility who sought army careers were placed in a regiment at an early age, ordinarily sixteen. A subaltern's commission could be purchased in most infantry regiments for £1,200. From that point the officer advanced by finding a vacancy created by death or retirement and purchasing it. If he rose from ensign to lieutenant-colonel in his regiment, the total cost was £3,500. Usually the senior subaltern was given preference for vacancies up to the rank of major. Above that rank the officer encountered stiffer competition, since the rank of lieutenant-colonel might carry with it a regimental command. It became necessary for the aspirant to find a sponsor from the higher military ranks or from a patron in the government. He might find himself favored because of his excellent record, but he was more apt to be promoted for family or political reasons.[12]

At first glance the system appears impossible as a means of producing capable and competent commanders. In the peace-time establishment senior officers only occasionally saw duty with the troops, preferring instead to enter politics or to indulge in the games society played. A regimental colonel might be in his seventies, for there was only half-pay retirement for officers too infirm for active duty. But the coming of war usually eliminated the physically and mentally disabled. Sponsors rarely backed a candidate who was a proven incompetent, for if the officer failed his disgrace discredited the man who recommended him. It is doubtful if William and Richard Howe would have received their American commands if they had not had excellent records, since their failure could (and, in the event, did) adversely affect those who had backed their appointments.

In the absence of any professional schooling it is difficult to see how officers could be better trained than simply by serving with a regiment. A lad of sixteen, if he were not a complete dullard, would likely be a capable lieutenant by the time he was twenty-one. The truism that senior sergeants are the backbone of the army was no less applicable in the eighteenth century, and an erring young subaltern could usually be guided through the first years by the tactful wisdom of non-commissioned officers.

Unless he had an independent income the junior officer was rarely able to live much above the level of a middle class tradesman or mechanic. If the purchase system blocked his way to advancement he found an outlet for his energies in perfecting the efficiency of his platoon or company. He was often widely read in the military literature of the day and occasionally gained a reputation as a military scholar. An officer was a gentleman and was accepted as a peer by his fellows, even those who might have titles of nobility; "off parade . . . It ought to be the characteristic of every gentleman neither to impose, nor submit to, any distinction but such as propriety of conduct, or superiority of talent, naturally create." In short, the major must not assume an overbearing attitude toward a lieutenant—especially as the lieutenant might turn out to be properly addressed as "M'lord."

The highest ranking generals and admirals were often from families of the nobility. Francis Lord Rawdon, Hugh Earl Percy and Lord Cornwallis, for all their patrician background, were hard and skilful fighters. Not a few officers earned titles in the performance of their duties. Guy Carleton, as noted, was knighted for his defense of Canada in 1776 and ten years later he became Lord Dorchester. The large number of officers of the nobility was not surprising, for eighteenth century Britons had not forgotten the Civil War which had brought Cromwell to power, and other unsuccessful rebellions against the Crown. What better way to preserve order and secure property than to entrust control of the military to the landed gentry?

It should also be noted that at the beginning of the war there were twenty-three members of Parliament who held commissions in the armed forces, and that among their number were both Howes, Clinton, Burgoyne, and Cornwallis. This may seem strange to Americans who have traditionally kept the military carefully separated from politics. But Britain during the period of her great empire undoubtedly benefitted from the mutual understanding of the military and political problems of imperial control. The United States in the twentieth century has come to understand that politicians and generals have difficulty solving global problems if each operates in isolation from the other.[13]

If in hindsight the British officer corps seemed shot through with inefficient fops who held their positions through a capricious system of selection, it should be remembered that every system before and since has had its share of bumblers and nincompoops. If William Howe appears inordinately lazy and dull, if "Gentleman Johnny" Burgoyne comes on as a braggart and a blunderer, their counterparts have appeared in other times and circumstances. It is too much to expect that every war will produce a Wolfe or a Wellington.

THE CONTINENTALS

Two days after Lexington and Concord the Massachusetts Committee of Safety began enlisting men into a provisional army. The soldiers took a rather simple oath to obey their officers and to submit to orders and regulations. They agreed to remain in the army until the end of the war, and so were known as the "Eight Months Army." Congress adopted it in the middle of May, 1775, and General Washington took command of it a year and a day before the Declaration of Independence.

In the weeks that followed Washington labored to organize the inchoate assemblage into an effective fighting force. Uniforms were scarce although Congress promised "a suit of clothes" for those who reenlisted. The shortage of arms constituted another problem but almost any of the muskets which these first volunteers often brought with them were as effective as the British "Brown Bess." Artillery was much more difficult to acquire, but some was obtained from colonial arsenals and more from forts abandoned by the British. Soon significant supplies of arms of all sorts came in from abroad, especially from France.[14]

By the spring of 1776 Washington had come to believe that a standing army of regular soldiers was a necessary requirement for winning the war. Congressional leaders thought that the war would be a short one, and they shared the traditional Whig aversion to standing armies. "We already see the growing thirst for power in some departments of the army," Elbridge Gerry remarked darkly in the fall of 1775, "which ought to be regulated so as to keep the military subservient to the civil in every part of the United Colonies." The subsequent history of the United States has provided so little ground for such fears that there is a tendency to smile at the Founding Fathers for their paranoia. But politicians in 1775 were students of history and they cited examples from Caesar to Cromwell to demonstrate their point. Indeed, the dreary history of Congressional procrastination and political malingering in the states suggests that a commander in chief with only a little less patience and patriotism than George Washington might have changed the course of revolutionary history as profoundly as did Napoleon.[15]

It was these considerations which led Congress to limit the enlistments of the "Eight Months Army" and the policy was continued for 1776. Not until Washington was driven from New York and the army was at the edge of disaster did the leaders awake to the fact that their theoretical fears were wasted in the reality of the imminent collapse of the revolution. Belatedly Congress authorized an army of eighty-eight regiments to be enlisted for three years or the duration of the war. But by this time the first flush of patriotic ardor had cooled and those who felt the call to duty found it more convenient to enlist in their state militia for terms of from two to six months. The army that was recruited in the winter of 1776–1777 was the real beginning of the "regulars."

When recruiting first began in 1775 the adjutant general directed that officers were prohibited from enrolling "any deserter from the ministerial army, nor any stroller, negro or vagabond." By 1777 a more realistic attitude dictated the acceptance, not only of such undesirables, but slaves and convicts. This was often the result of state laws which permitted men called to duty to furnish substitutes, and if the price was right recruiters accepted almost anyone, even "miserable sharp looking Caitiffs, [and] hungry lean fac'd Villians." It was true that some substantial citizens joined the ranks in the early days of the war, shopkeepers, farmers, and artisans who were moved by a sense of duty and patriotism. But by the beginning of 1777 the Continentals were reduced to less than a thousand men consisting of what must have been the toughest bodies and spirits in the country.[16]

By the spring of 1777 Congress had turned the problem of recruiting over to the states by assigning to each a quota and providing for the payment of a fee for each enlistment in the Continental army. Both Congress and the states had long since resorted to bounties to persuade men to serve in the ranks. In fact, during the early years offers of bounties to serve in the state militia often exceeded those offered by Congress. By the Act of 1776 privates who agreed to enlist in the national army received twenty dollars and one hundred acres of land. Local townships and counties offered additional bounties of their own in order to meet their quotas.

Such inducements make it clear that while some few of the troops may have joined the army because they felt an obligation to do their duty such high-minded motivation did not suffice for most. It must be remembered that patriotism is an outgrowth of history and tradition, of which the new nation had almost none. Loyalty was much more strongly rooted in the states and even in regions of the states. Soldiers often adamantly refused to serve in regiments from other states and they even objected to "foreign" officers as their commanders. Some may have responded to the romantic appeal of the recruiting broadsides "to see this beautiful country" but the thought of leaving home was probably a stronger deterrent. A lad from the Hampshire Grants who travelled to Boston found himself in surroundings as strange as if he were on the other side of the world. Homesickness was the most widespread of the diseases of the camps. It was sometimes only a few weeks after enlistment that the soldiers felt "such an unconquerable desire of returning to . . . their homes, that it not only produces shameful, scandalous Desertions among themselves, but infuses a like spirit in others."[17]

By 1777 Washington was writing that "we may fairly infer that the country has been pretty well drained of that class of Men whose tempers, attachments and circumstances disposed them to enter permanently . . . into the army. . . ." Whatever mixture of motives there may have been to enlist and remain in the service, it is fair to assume that an essential ingredient was material reward of money and land. And it must be supposed that a large proportion of the men were those very vagabonds and strollers against whom recruiters had earlier been warned.[18]

But is there any reason to suppose that they were bad soldiers? As human raw material they were certainly no worse than the recruits of the British army. Is it not fair to assume that the Continental soldier also came to regard his regiment as "home," that to him the army, with all its hardships and privations, afforded the kind of security and companionship that he had not found on the outside?

In the case of one group of soldiers motives are somewhat easier to define. With the organization of the army the new nation faced the oldest of American dilemmas, the black man. Both Congress and General Washington opposed the enlistment of Negroes in 1775, and both were forced to swallow their prejudices in the face of the realities of war. Although neither gave any formal sanction, at the end of 1775 the commander in chief issued a general order which read: "As the General is informed, that numbers of Free Negroes are desirous of inlisting, he gives leave to recruiting officers to entertain them, and promises to lay the matter before Congress, who he doubts not will approve it." Rhode Island, New York, and Maryland had, by 1777, authorized the recruitment of regiments of Negro slaves.[19]

But the reality of the enlistment of black soldiers had little to do with the law. The combination of whites who wanted to avoid service by furnishing black substitutes and recruiting officers who were under pressure to fill their quotas resulted in the appearance of considerable numbers of black Americans in the Continental ranks. Officers might rail at "the strangest mixture of Negroes, Indians, and whites, with old men and children, . . . [whose] nasty lousy appearance make the most shocking spectacle," but the regiments had to be filled. It has been estimated that about 5,000 identifiable black men served in various branches of the armed forces during the War of Independence. In August, 1778, Washington's adjutant general reported 755 black troops serving in fourteen regiments of the New York Continental Line; if these were typical regiments Negroes constituted about ten percent of their strength.[20]

The assumption that all black soldiers were freemen (slaves being disbarred from enlistment unless by the consent of their masters) must have been a powerful incentive for fugitive slaves seeking refuge. Once accepted into the ranks it became very difficult for masters to recover them. Dr. Israel Ashley of Westfield, Massachusetts, was drafted into the service. He intended to provide his slave, Gilliam, as a substitute but to his dismay he found that Gilliam had already enlisted for three years. The doctor's appeal to General Gates for the return of his property fell on deaf ears. Attempts by masters in Virginia to reclaim their slaves after the war led Governor Benjamin Harrison to appeal to the General Assembly, "not doubting that they will pass an act giving these unhappy creatures that liberty which they have been in some way instrumental in securing to us." The governor had his way.[21]

For the free Negro the security of the army—food, clothing, and shelter— offered considerable attraction. He was still subjected to the degradation accorded a Negro at any level of society. He was usually given the most undesirable duties, orderly, cook, teamster, and every other dirty work which is the lot of men in the army. But he nonetheless enjoyed the status of being a soldier. The bounty of money and especially of land were rewards which he found difficult to obtain elsewhere. There was little inducement for him to desert and he usually served out his full enlistment. For the slave the reward for honorable service was freedom. It might be several years away but he had long since learned that to endure was to survive.

Serious as were the problems of recruiting, they must sometimes have seemed insignificant beside the problems of training and discipline. These were especially difficult at the outset of the war because there was no cadre of veterans to teach the men the most fundamental facts of camp life. So the general orders of the commander in chief himself were taken up with such elementary details as reminding officers "to keep their men neat and clean," and "to see that they have straw to lay on." Time and again it was necessary to repeat "Orders that have been given against the firing of small arms, it is hourly practised." Similarly, "There is a bad custom prevailing of the Non-Commissioned Officers and Soldiers absenting themselves from Guard, under the Pretense of going for Provisions." The men had not only to be instructed in personal cleanliness but in the necessity for keeping the camps clean. "One Man a Company to be appointed Camp Colour man, from every Company in every Regiment in the Army, whose particular duty it must be . . . to sweep the Streets of their respective encampments, to fill up old Necessary houses and dig new ones, to bury all Offal, Filth, and Nastiness, that may poison or infect the health of the Troops . . . and by persevering in the constant and unremitting Execution thereof, remove the odious reputation, which (with too much reason) has stigmitized the Character of American troops." Washington was trying to make the army *respectable*.[22]

The most serious disciplinary problem was desertion, and Washington never solved it to his satisfaction. Some soldiers left because of hunger or homesickness, others because they were impatient with the boredom and drudgery of camp life. Should these men be severely dealt with? Would a few exemplary executions or long prison terms have a salutary effect? Or would such stringent measures discourage enlistments and keep the repentent from returning?

In the first months of his command Washington was inclined to be lenient. Where simple desertion was the charge thirty-nine lashes became the standard penalty. As the army began to take shape, as he attempted the "new modelling of it," to make it "in every point of view entirely Continental," discipline became more severe. Deserters were executed, or sentenced to serve "on an American frigate" for the duration, or tarred and feathered and forced to run the gauntlet of their companies. By the time the army went into winter quarters at Morristown in 1777 he had again come around to a more lenient point of view. Severe punishment for one deserter was accompanied by pardons for ten, and in April, 1777, he issued a blanket pardon for all deserters who would come in within a month.[23]

Breakdown of discipline could usually be traced to two sources. One was lack of the basic rewards which every soldier had a right to expect, food, prompt pay, and clothing. The army seldom had enough of any of these. The other serious flaw lay in the failure of the officer corps. Men accused of drunkenness or malingering and disorderly behavior could scarcely be expected to respond when officers were guilty of the same offenses. One may well imagine the circumstances which produced the charge against Private James McDaniel, accused of "foregoing an order of General Putnam's to obtain a quart of rum, and for abusive language." Of 900 officers who served at one time or another with seven New York regiments during the war 135, or over fifteen percent, deserted. All too frequently officers were drunkards or cowards, cheated the men of their pay, and in general fell far short of the standards set by the commander in chief:

> . . . At a time when everything is at stake, It behooves every Man to exert himself. It will not do for the Commanding Officer of a Regiment to content himself, with barely giving Orders, he should see (at least know) that they are executed. He should call his men out frequently and endeavor to impress them with a just sense of their Duty, and how much depends on subordination and discipline. Let me therefore not only Command, but exhort you and your Officers . . . to Manly and Vigorous exertion at this time, each striving to excell the other in the respective duties of his department.

Washington made it clear that he preferred officers who were gentlemen. He was appalled at the New England custom of electing their commanders and he insisted that an officer must set himself apart from his men; otherwise they would "treat him as an equal; and . . . regard him as no more than a broom-stick, being mixed together as one common herd; no order, nor no discipline can prevail; nor will the Officer ever meet with that respect which is essential to due subordination."[24]

The quality of the officers was probably neither better nor worse than the citizenry of the nation has always furnished in time of war. The trouble was that, like the men in the ranks, they seldom stayed for very long. For those who did not desert, resignation provided an honorable way of quitting the service. Officers who were gentlemen were also those who had the most to lose by an extended tour of duty. By April, 1778, Washington was complain-ing that officers' resignations were being submitted at the rate of two or three a day.

A case in point is the career of Samuel Smith, a young officer of the famous First Maryland regiment. Son of a wealthy merchant and engaged to a Balti-more belle, Smith served faithfully through the campaigns from 1776 through 1778. He commanded the defenses of the Delaware forts in 1777 for which Congress voted him a sword, an honor not lightly given. By 1778 he was a lieutenant colonel, but the rather considerable fortune of his father had been wrecked by the war. In the fall of 1778 he resigned his commission and went home to run the family business. He served in the Maryland militia and rose to the rank of brigadier general. He also restored the family fortunes, mostly through contracts with the state and with Congress to supply the army. Far from being considered a slacker he was called "General" Smith for the rest of his life and was a charter member of the Society of the Cincinnati.[25]

By the end of January, 1777, Washington's force at Morristown had been reduced to 3,000 men of which less than a third were Continentals. It was at least some consolation that there were not so many mouths to feed, and the army did not suffer as it did the next winter at Valley Forge, or when it re-turned to Morristown in 1779. Even so, much of the army's food was forcibly seized in the surrounding countryside by foraging parties, who frequently clashed with British detachments on similar errands. Washington justified this on the basis of the grant of extraordinary powers from Congress in Decem-ber and because it denied supplies to the enemy. But he tried to proceed with caution. He was well aware that the heavy hand of the military would arouse deep resentment among some civilians, and he recognized that the popular support of the revolutionary cause must not be jeopardized. A year later, under similar circumstances he pointed out, "To acts of legislation or civil authority [the people] have ever been taught to yield a willing obedience, without reasoning about their propriety; on those of military power, whether immediate or derived originally from another source, they have ever looked with a jealous and suspicious eye."[26]

As spring came in so did the recruits, but enlistments still fell short of expec-tations. In addition to the eighty-eight battalions which Congress hoped to raise in the states Washington himself was authorized to recruit sixteen regiments. plus three of artillery, 3,000 dragoons, and a corps of engineers. Had the entire authorized force been raised, the total would have been 75,000 men. As it was, by the middle of May forty-three regiments of about 200 men each had been assembled at Morristown. Almost as important, as the ranks began to fill, supplies came from France: 20,000 muskets, 1,000 barrels of powder, 11,000 flints, and an assortment of other supplies, notably clothing and blankets. Although it was to be another year before France became a formal ally, the French foreign minister, the Comte de Vergennes, had seized the opportunity to weaken an ancient foe, and for more than a year unofficial aid had been making its way across the Atlantic.

The army that began to prepare for the summer campaign was far short of the 20,000 men with which Washington had begun the campaign of 1776, but his efforts to create a "fixed and settled force" had made him less dependent upon "the practice of trusting the Militia." Counting dragoons, artillery, and engineers, the Continentals numbered over 9,000 men. Never again would the commander in chief be reduced to the shadow force which had brought him to the edge of extinction in the winter of 1777.[27]

THE MILITIA

Early in 1776 Francis Lord Rawdon, despite his baptism of fire at Bunker Hill, was still convinced that "we shall soon have done with these scoundrels, for one only dirties one's fingers by meddling with them." It was a continuing source of amazement to the British that American citizen-soldiers could constitute a serious threat to the British army.

This was in part due to the low opinion of colonial militia that English officers had acquired during the Seven Years' War. Wolfe thought Americans were "the most contemptible cowardly dogs you can conceive. There is no depending on them in action." In his more pessimistic moments Washington would have been inclined to agree, but he noted that "a people unused to restraint must be led, they must not be drove, even those who are ingaged for the War must be disciplined by degrees."

English officers tended to regard all soldiers as the lowest level of English society. They expected, and got, servile respect from the ranks, and they assumed that Americans were simply "a set of upstart vagabonds, the dregs and scorn of human society." Colonel (later General) James Grant, who had served in Florida and therefore qualified as an expert, stated categorically in Parliament, "They would never dare face an English army and did not possess any of the qualifications of a good soldier."[28]

Political leaders accepted the army's verdict. Alexander Wedderburn told the Commons in 1774, ". . . Our thunders must go forth; America must be conquered." And Richard Rigby, M.P., assured the members that tales of colonial resistance "was an idea thrown out to frighten women and children."

There were other observers who were more discerning. Hugh Earl Percy, who had met the Massachusetts militia one April morning in 1775, remarked, "They have men amongst them who know very well what they are about." Thomas Gage, who had observed Americans in two wars, reported to the ministry that "in all their wars against the French they never shewed so much conduct attention and perseverance as they do now."[29]

When American revolutionary leaders found themselves faced with "the Necessity for Taking up Arms" they were not especially perturbed by the lack of an army. Some were deluded by the myth of the American victory over the French and Indians, but their more tangible expectations were based on the existence of the militia organizations. The militia tradition had its origins in the early years of English colonization to take care of the exigencies of the expanding frontier. First the Indians and then the French and the Dutch had threatened the tiny settlements, and the mother country had never sent troops to defend her outposts overseas until the latter part of the Second Hundred Years War.

Left to fend for themselves the colonial assemblies enacted laws which created militia organizations. In 1631 Massachusetts Bay required that all men between the ages of sixteen and sixty be supplied with arms, and local officers were made responsible for compliance. Two years later the Plymouth colony decreed that every man must have a musket, sword, cartridge box, powder, and ball. In the same period Virginians were required to take their muskets to church on Sunday so that they would be ready for drill after the service.

By the 1760's the militia had pretty much deteriorated into a semisocial organization which met a few times a year, and gave the men folks an excuse for fun and games. The ranks on parade were liable to be ragged as much from an excess of rum as a lack of discipline. But there was a tradition that every man should own a weapon and that every man had an obligation for military service. What may have passed unnoticed in England was a phenomenon remarked on by Governor Berkeley of Virginia at the time of Bacon's Rebellion: "Unhappy is the man who governs a people who are poor, indebted, discontented, and *armed*."[30]

As the crisis with England grew more serious in the 1770's there was a revival of militia activity. Muster days became more frequent and a serious air pervaded the farmers who assembled for drill. The threat against which they were obviously preparing was not from a foreign foe but from the authority of the Crown. Although colonial governors were nominally in control of the militia by virtue of their office of commanding general, in colony after colony the Whigs began to gain control of the militia organization, especially in New England where officers were elected.

The most famous of the militia units—and the most short-lived—was the "minute men." Each regiment in Massachusetts designated one third of its number to be prepared to "come in at a moment's warning," and it was these troops that harassed Gage's redcoats on their expedition to Lexington and Concord. Many of the "minute men" stayed on and fought in the battle of Bunker Hill. Many joined regiments and enlisted in the "Eight Months Army." Others simply went home when they felt that the emergency was over. They left a name and a legend in American military history, but by summer's end they had disappeared.[31]

Following the colonial pattern the states organized their militia primarily for defense against an invading enemy, and to "keep the peace" locally. This meant providing enforcing authority for the local committees of safety who were charged with suppressing "enemies," that is, Loyalists. The militia were also expected to march to the aid of Washington's army when Congress or the commander in chief thought it necessary.

In colonial times a sort of conscription system existed in the sense that local officers were responsible for seeing that able-bodied men were armed and ready to deal with emergencies. The new state governments made custom and practice more explicit. In Connecticut all males between the ages of sixteen and sixty were required to enroll, with exceptions which are surprisingly similar to those of today. Exempted were state and national officials, ministers, students and teachers at Yale, Negroes, Indians and mulattoes. Officers were elected and it was possible to purchase a substitute, or, if none could be found, to pay a fine of £[32]

North Carolina passed a similar law in the summer of 1776. To the usual list of exemptions was added the Quakers, but they were required to pay a fee of £10, presumably for the expense of hiring a substitute. The state was divided into five military districts, each under the command of a brigadier general. The men were divided into five classes: the first, consisting of men over fifty years of age, who were not required to serve on active duty; the other four to be called in rotation for a term of service of not more than sixty days.

In Pennsylvania the first Militia Act was passed as a result of pressure from the Pennsylvania Association, a volunteer group that was political as well as military. The Associators insisted that those who did not contribute to the cause by volunteering for service be required to pay a fee, and a sum of £3/10 was levied. All adult males between the ages of eighteen and fifty (not excepting Negroes and Indians) were eligible. Sons between the ages of sixteen and eighteen might serve in place of their fathers. There were the usual occupational exemptions and provisions for hiring substitutes.

Each county was to enlist a regiment of from 440 to 680 men under the supervision of county lieutenants and sub-lieutenants. Officers were elected, but all colonels and majors had to be property owners and all officers had to be qualified voters. Each regiment was divided into eight classes to be called to service in rotation for no more than sixty days. County lieutenants were authorized to hire substitutes the expense for which the state would presumably collect a fee from delinquents who failed to turn out. Despite the sweeping nature of the system recruitment was not very effective. In 1777 Captain

Thomas Askey's Cumberland County company turned out only forty-four men, of whom ten were substitutes and thirteen were hired by the county lieutenants.[33]

The service of the militia as reinforcements for the army left more than a little to be desired. Washington delivered his low opinion of these troops frequently and at length, of which one in the fall of 1776 was typical:

> To place any dependence upon Militia, is, assuredly, resting upon a broken staff. Men just dragged from the tender Scenes of domestick life; unaccustomed to the din of Arms; totally unacquainted with every kind of Military skill, when opposed by Troops regularly train'd, disciplined and appointed, makes them timid and ready to fly at their own shadows. Besides, the sudden change in their manner of living, (particularly lodging) brings on sickness in many. . . . Men accustomed to unbounded freedom, cannot brook Restraint which is absolutely necessary to the good order and Government of the Army; without which licentiousness, and every kind of disorder triumphantly reign. To bring Men to a proper degree of Subordination, is not the work of a day, a Month or even a year; and unhappily for us and the cause we are Englaged in, the little discipline I have been laboring to establish in the Army . . . is in a manner done away with by such a mixture of Troops as have been called together within these few months.[34]

Yet in spite of their presumed worthlessness Washington could not have kept an army together without the militia. The 5,000 men who turned out in December, 1775, got him past the critical termination of the "Eight Months Army" and two-thirds of the skeleton force at Morristown in the early part of 1777 was composed of militia. If they had failed at Trenton they had responded magnificently at Princeton where Cadwalader's Pennsylvanians had held the line at the crisis of the battle. On many other occasions they were to display a splendid elan, especially when they were led by capable officers and supported by veteran Continentals.

A word should be said about the riflemen, since they achieved a fame in some degree unwarranted in the history of the army. These men were Indian fighters from the frontier whose accurate fire astonished all who witnessed it. But the frontiersmen posed problems. Products of the back country settlements and conscious of their elite status, they did not take to army discipline. In the fall of 1775 Pennsylvania riflemen precipitated a riot at Prospect Hill near Boston and thirty of them were arrested for "disobedient and mutinous behaviour."

On the battlefield another weakness of the riflemen was exposed, one inherent in the weapon which made them famous. The accuracy of the rifle stemmed from the fact that the ball was tightly fitted into the barrel which was rifled; that is, there were spiral grooves cut on the inner surface which gripped the tightly seated ball and gave it a spin, giving it greater accuracy and a range three times that of the musket. The tight seal of the ball was achieved by fitting a greased patch over the muzzle when the ball was rammed, and this increased the reloading time. Furthermore, the rifle barrel could not be fitted with a bayonet. The result was described by Colonel George Hanger, a British officer who was captured at Saratoga:

> When Morgan's riflemen came down to Pennsylvania from Canada, flushed with success gained over Burgoyne's army, they marched to attack our light troops under Colonel Abercrombie. The moment they appeared before him he ordered his troops to charge them with the bayonet; not one man in four had time to fire, and those who did were given no time to load again; the light infantry not only dispersed them but drove them for miles over the country.[35]

The riflemen were to be found in both the militia and the Continental line, but at the peak of their strength they never constituted more than ten percent of the armies to which they were attached. They constituted a valuable weapon—Hitchcock's Rhode Islanders at Trenton and Morgan's brigade at Freeman's farm—but the rifle was scarcely "the gun that won the Revolution."

The militia in general proved to be a source of disappointment as adjuncts to the regular army. The system of rotation used in most states meant that even the few months of discipline and drill with the army were largely wasted. By the time the raw troops had learned the rudiments of march and maneuver their time was up and their replacements had to be trained anew. More important, most of them had never seen action in battle and if they did participate in a campaign this experience, too, was lost when the regiments were rotated home. So it was not surprising that, as Washington concluded, "Men who have been free and subject to no controul cannot be reduced to order in an Instant . . . and the aid derived from them is nearly counterbalanced by the disorder, irregularity and confusion they occasion."[36]

A far more important effect of the militia may well have been in areas outside the main theatres of the war. Much has been made of guerrilla warfare and its effects on enemy supply and communication lines, and certainly this had its impact. But the real prize of the American Revolution was the allegiance of a majority of the people who, in the early stages of the war, did not commit themselves. The winning of independence was, in the final analysis, a numbers game. The objectives were not so much New York or Charleston or the Hudson River Valley but control of the civilian population. When Germain and the King talked, at first confidently and then wistfully, of the rising tide of Loyalism which would eventually take over the task of reconquest, they dimly perceived the real issue over which the war was being fought. But the Patriots understood far better that "loyalty" was in most cases to be read as "interest" and that while "life, liberty and pursuit of happiness" made a fine catch phrase, it had to be understood in concrete terms.

The percentage of the population devoted to either the Patriot or Loyalist cause at the beginning of the war thus becomes relatively unimportant. Standing between them was a large majority of Americans, probably as great as Patriots and Loyalists combined, who were undecided and neutral, who did not want to risk their lives and fortunes on any cause. They may or may not have understood the issues involved but they rather naively believed that they could continue to pursue the even tenor of their lives. Yet these people found their opinions altered, and indeed their whole lives changed when the war came to their doorstep. "The war" did not necessarily mean the marching ranks of Continentals and redcoats. John Hart, whose wife was murdered by Tory renegades, found the war suddenly very real. When Patriot committees of safety, backed by militia, offered a choice between military service and possible imprisonment as suspected Torys, "liberty" took on a special meaning. When Hessians plundered barns and corncribs the "pursuit of happiness" became difficult, to say the least. A thousand local clashes, betwen militia and Tories, acts of mob violence, even petty annoyances, all of which might be peripheral to campaigns and battles, had a decisive effect in destroying the illusions of that segment of the population who had begun by thinking that they could stand aloof from the conflict. The political education of many Americans may have begun with the exhortations of Whig editors and pamphlets like *Common Sense*, but the lessons were driven home when the county lieutenant appeared to make up the militia muster list. The very act of enrollment and participation in drills forced most adult males to declare themselves. This may have been the reason why the law in many states required a man to turn out for muster in person, even though he intended to provide a substitute when he was called to active duty.

This does not mean that military operations were not important. New Jersey was firmly in Patriot hands until Howe's invasion of 1776, but upon his approach the Patriot militia disintegrated and local leaders went into hiding. Loyalists, emboldened by the appearance of the redcoats, organized their own militia and were soon harrying the countryside. They in turn collapsed after the American victories at Trenton and Princeton caused Howe to withdraw his garrisons. Even after the military theatre of operations moved elsewhere, the bitter struggle in New Jersey continued until the end of the war. The history of New Jersey was repeated in one form or another until the end of the war.

As Professor John Shy puts it: "In this sense, the war was a political education conducted by military means, and no one learned more than the apathetic majority as they scurried to restore some measure of order to their lives."[37]

In a way, the warfare of the eighteenth century represented the ideal employment of what Clausewitz called "the ultimate weapon of diplomacy." Though it was cluttered with rules and conventions that amuse the modern military scientist, wars were narrow in scope, seldom touching the civilian population with mass destruction or atrocities. Even the casualties were small. The diplomatic objectives were reasonable and limited. Warfare was thus the epitome of that enlightened rationalism on which the eighteenth century prided itself. Campaigns were conducted in warm weather and battles were avoided in place of chess-like maneuvers. The perfectly conducted campaign would place the enemy in such a hopeless tactical position that he would refuse to risk a battle, withdrawing from the field and leaving his objective to the superior general.

Washington revealed early in the war that he was not only a student of eighteenth century warfare but a disciple as well, thereby revealing his own failure to appreciate the special nature of a war of revolution: ". . . It is impossible to forget," he wrote in the fall of 1776, "that History, our own experience, the advice of our ablest friends in Europe, the Fears of the Enemy, and even the Declarations of Congress demonstrate, that on our side the war should be defensive. It has even been called a War of Posts. That we should on all Occasions avoid a general action, or put anything to the Risque, unless compelled by a necessity into which we ought never to be drawn."[38]

Eighteenth century wars should be understood in their social and economic setting. A considerable cleavage existed between the British army and the society which it served. The gap was less distinct in the officer corps because the purchase of commissions led inevitably to an increasing number of officers from the middle class. But the rank and file were filled with large numbers of the unproductive elements of the lowest level, the English classes, and it was here that the distinction was most marked.

The industrial revolution was just beginning in England but there was already an enormous demand for productive workers, especially skilled artisans. If Great Britain did not support the American war with her full resources—meaning especially man power—it was because her politicians did not think it necessary or proper to sacrifice her economy to inflated notions of national pride. Why conscript productive workers into a national army and so drain the very labor force which was in short supply? Citizen-soldiers were of considerably less value than citizen-workers. This was the rationale which limited conscription to vagrants, "strollers," criminals and "public idlers," rather than those who were gainfully employed. Volunteers were tempted by bounties, but these were not high enough to appeal even to an apprentice who had regular employment. Rather than tap this useful class the government considered hiring German mercenaries as a superior investment.

For Americans the war posed a different problem. While England could and did lose the war without catastrophic consequences to her position as a world power, the outcome would determine the very existence and survival of the United States. The full resources of lives and fortunes were to be called forth to win independence—that is, to avoid the alternative of unconditional surrender. Yet despite the exhortations of the leaders in Congress and in the states, the American army which emerged was cast in much the same mold as other eighteenth century armies. Not because of government policy, but in spite of it. The Continental ranks were filled from the lowest levels of American society. Even the words which describe the recruits, "lean fac'd caitiffs," "worthless dogs," the "meanest, idlest, most intemperate and worthless," are the same as those used by British recruiters. This was because those who could afford it sent substitutes and those who could not enrolled in the militia so that they would not have to absent themselves from farms or businesses for long. A soldier of some means and substance who did enlist for a long term could rarely resist an appeal for help from home occasioned by family distress or hardship. If he was not granted leave he simply went home.[39]

There is, of course, no way of knowing how many soldiers of the Continental army served from a sense of duty and how many were society's "losers," for whom the army, miserable as it was, provided a security that was better than none. But, taking into account the number of substitutes, the honorable alternatives (an officer's commission or militia service), and the fact that bounties became more and more generous in order to induce enlistments, it seems fair to infer that a relatively small number of Continentals were what could be called "solid citizens." But, as in the case of the redcoats, there is also reason to agree with General Washington that "in a little time we shall work these raw materials into good stuff."[40]

The militia constituted an unknown quantity in the eighteenth century military equation. European theory was based on waging war between two or more armies of known strength. The quality of arms, the presence or absence of fortifications, the quality of generalship, and other factors could be calculated with some precision. But how was one to calculate an unknown number of soldiers of unknown quality who might reinforce Washington's army, or suddenly appear to harass outlying posts, or whose presence created a countryside of hostile civilians?

British leaders who were used to wars waged between governments only dimly perceived that in dealing with a popular revolution they were waging war on the American people.

SIX

Germain and
the Generals

THE BRITISH PLAN OF CAMPAIGN FOR 1777 WAS QUITE SIMPLY AN EXTENSION and elaboration of the campaign of 1776. It did not originate with any particular person nor did it contain any startling new ideas. From the point of view of Lord George Germain, at least, it commended itself because it would be coordinated so as to lend maximum effectiveness to British military power in North America, and because troops and commanders were already in place on the western side of the Atlantic. The stupendous overseas lift of men and supplies which had preoccupied so much of his and the ministry's effort in 1776 would not have to be repeated. The invading Americans had been cleared from Canada, and the possession of New York gave the Howe brothers a central base from which they could achieve maximum flexibility of naval and military operations.

The focus of the plan was the axis of the Richelieu river, Lake Champlain, and the Hudson. A force from Canada would fully exploit the objectives that Carleton had failed to achieve in 1776 because of the lateness of the season (or, as Germain thought, Carleton's slothfulness). It would penetrate to Albany and there be joined by an offensive force from New York. Control of the Hudson-Lake Champlain line would prevent the American movement of large bodies of troops and supplies between New England and the rest of the colonies. Control of the Hudson Highlands, Albany, and Ticonderoga would give the British bases in the interior of the country from which they might penetrate especially into New Hampshire and Connecticut. As a memorandum in the Germain papers puts it:

> By our having the entire command of the communications between Canada and New York, which is both convenient and easy, being almost altogether by water, the troops from both these provinces will have it in their power to act in conjunction, as occasion or necessity may require. In consequence whereof, the provinces of New England will be surrounded on all sides, whether by His Majesty's troops or navy, and liable to be attacked from every quarter, which will divide their force for the protection of their frontier settlements,

while at the same time all intercourse between them and the colonies to the southward of the Hudson's River will be entirely cut off.[1]

THE PLAN GERMINATES

On November 30, 1776, as the British pursued Washington's retreating army across New Jersey, Howe wrote to Germain recounting what he intended to do during the remainder of 1776: send Clinton to occupy Rhode Island; and occupy New Jersey by establishing a chain of posts from Perth Amboy to the Delaware.

He then launched into a detailed proposal for the campaign of 1777. Clinton's conquest of Rhode Island would pave the way for a force of 10,000 men which would advance "into the country towards Boston and, if possible, reduce that town." Another force of 10,000 men was to advance up the Hudson to Albany to join with an army moving south from Canada. Five thousand men were designated for the defense of New York city, and a third "defensive army" of 8,000 men, commanded by Lord Cornwallis, was to cover New Jersey "to keep the southern [Washington's] army in check, by giving a jealousy to Philadelphia, which I propose to attack in the autumn, as well as Virginia, provided the success of other operations will admit an adequate force." For this grandiose plan Howe requested 15,000 additional reinforcements to bring his army to a total of 35,000 "effective men."

As Clinton was designated for Rhode Island and Cornwallis for New Jersey it must be assumed that Howe himself would lead the expedition "up the North [Hudson] River to Albany." Since he believed the northern invasion force would not reach Albany "earlier than the month of September" it is difficult to understand how he then expected to attack Philadelphia "as well as Virginia."[2]

But the November 30 letter is worth careful notice because in it Howe's attention was directed in general to the north and New England, and the focus of his own movement was up the Hudson to Albany and a junction with the army from Canada.

On the same day that he wrote to Germain Howe issued his proclamation of pardon. As noted previously considerable numbers of people in New Jersey accepted it in the hope that they would be protected from the pillaging and looting of British and Hessian soldiers as they pursued Washington to the Delaware. Howe was still hoping to fulfill his role as peace commissioner and he was greatly encouraged by the response to his offer of amnesty. There were also reports of "the opinions of the people being much changed in Pennsylvania," which may account for the subsequent changes in his own thinking about the campaign of 1777.

On December 20, six days before the disaster at Trenton Howe sent a supplemental dispatch to Germain. He reported the increasing strength of Loyalist opinion "in which sentiment they would be confirmed by our getting possession of Philadeliphia [.] I am from this consideration fully persuaded the principal army should act offensively on that side where the enemy's chief strength will be collected." He went on to propose that the New England expedition be deferred until reinforcements arrived from England. And the joint expedition against Albany was now reduced to "a corps to act defensively upon the lower part of Hudson's River to cover New Jersey on that side, as well as to facilitate in some degree the approach of the Army from Canada." These objectives could be attained with his present force of about 20,000 men, although he urged Germain to send "every augmentation of troops . . . to this port [New York]. . . ."

The most significant aspect of this last dispatch was the shift in priorities. In the original plan of November 20 Philadelphia was almost an after-thought and a main striking force of 10,000 men was designated for Albany. By December 20 Howe had become afflicted with that most chimerical of all British delusions, the rising of the Loyalists. It had lured Clinton's expedition to South Carolina in the summer of 1776 and it was to become the most fatal of all the British miscalculations about the war for America. But in the euphoria surrounding the flight of Washington from New York across New Jersey, and the wholesale applications for pardons, Howe's optimism was understandable. He became convinced that Loyalism was rampant in Pennsylvania and that possession of the American capital was the key to British success.

Before Germain could fully digest the varied diet which his American commander was serving up there arrived still another dispatch from Howe, dated January 20, 1777. This was written, of course, after Trenton and Princeton had forced the British to abandon most of New Jersey, wiping out the gains of the December campaign. There was a tone of deep pessimism in this addendum to the plan for 1777. It was clear that Howe was keenly conscious of his failure in New Jersey although he made a half-hearted attempt to blame the Hessians and their dead commander. He now said that 20,000 reinforcements would be necessary if his campaign were to have any chance of success and expressed the fear that the capture of Philadelphia might not be as decisive as he had hoped. (Howe surely could not have really expected a reinforcement greater than the one he had received in 1776; an impression is conveyed of a commander preparing to defend a future failure by having his request a matter of record.)[3]

Germain's reaction to his American commander's proposals was curious. Replying to Howe's November 20 dispatch Lord George spoke of "your well digested plan," a phrase he may have regretted when he received the proposal of December 20 and the gloomy forebodings of mid-January. He was, he said, "really alarmed" by the size of the request for reinforcements. The most that Howe might expect would be about 8,000 men, a figure that was subsequently reduced to slightly less than 6,000.

After considering Howe's latest proposals Germain replied on March 3. The King, he said, had approved "your proposed deviation from the plan which you formerly suggested, being of opinion that the reasons which have induced you to recommend this change . . . are solid and decisive." Lord George said nothing in this letter about the expedition from Canada, although he had spent several weeks planning the campaign in detail with Burgoyne and had received the King's approval of it only three days before.[4]

The omission is striking. Although Howe knew that a northern invasion was planned he had deliberately downgraded his own part in support of it to the point that it barely received mention in the December 20 projection of his movements for the coming campaign. It is possible that at this point Howe was not aware of the elaborate nature of the Canadian expedition or of Germain's high hopes for it. But the astonishing fact is that Lord George's letter, in which he gave Howe official notice of the King's approval of his plans, contained not the slightest mention of the British invasion from Canada.

GENTLEMAN JOHNNY

Six days before he sent George III's assent to Sir William the American Secretary received a long memorandum from General John Burgoyne entitled "Thoughts for conducting the war from the side of Canada." If Germain had not read it when he wrote to Howe, he knew that it contained a detailed summary of the plan for a British offensive from Canada, and that Burgoyne would be its commander.

John Burgoyne had reached the climax of a colorful and tempestuous career. It was rumored that he was the illegitimate son of Lord Bingley because he had made Burgoyne's mother a major beneficiary of his estate. Burgoyne himself eloped with Lady Charlotte Stanley, daughter of the Earl of Derby, which forced the young couple to live for a time in genteel "exile" on the continent. But the marriage ultimately provided him with the powerful family connection so necessary to either military or political preferment. At the age of twenty-one Burgoyne purchased a commission in the Royal Dragoons and by the beginning of the Seven Years' War he was a captain.

He distinguished himself in the campaigns in Portugal where he served under General Wilhelm von der Lippe who was regarded as one of the finest artillerymen in Europe. It may have been in Portugal that Burgoyne acquired his belief in the importance of artillery. He seems to have been a better than average student of military science and he produced several treatises, especially on the psychology of discipline. He came to believe that English soldiers were more intelligent than those of most European armies and that officers should appeal to the reason and sensibilities of their troops as well as to their pride and patriotism. Burgoyne practiced what he preached, and it was because he earned the respect and affection of his men that he was dubbed "Gentleman Johnny."[5]

He was fairly typical of his time and class. He became a member of Parliament, he gained a reputation as a gambler and *bon vivant*, and he developed some talent as a playwright. But beneath the surface of the urbane, convivial gentleman was a streak of hard ruthlessness. London gossip had it that he was not above "taking his stand at gaming table, and watching with soberest attention for a fair opportunity of engaging a drunken young Nobleman at Piquet." Gentleman Johnny had a driving ambition for fame and place.

When the war began in America he was fifty-three years old and a major general. He was sent to Boston with Howe and Clinton to "assist" Gage, but the fact that he was the junior of the generals convinced him that this was a dead end. By the end of 1775 he had returned to England, voicing his opinions of the war in America, subtly disparaging Gage, and pushing his claims for recognition and promotion. He published a treatise early in 1776 suggesting the idea for an invasion from Canada, and this may have been responsible for his assignment as Carleton's second in command when troop reinforcements were sent to Canada in the spring. His wife was desperately ill at the time and Burgoyne had protested that only his duty to King and country had forced him to leave her side (she died while he was in America).

Burgoyne was home once more in December, 1776, unhappy with his role and pushing for a high command. His timing was fortuitous. A smouldering quarrel between the American Secretary and Sir Guy Carleton had exploded when Germain was sharply critical of Carleton's mismanagement of the expedition on Lake Champlain in 1776. He even went so far as to suggest that the defeats at Trenton and Princeton were indirectly attributable to Carleton's bungling. The Governor-General replied in a tone of aspersion and resentment that even shocked the King.

Aware of the friction between Carleton and Germain Burgoyne again suggested an offensive from Canada and he did not hesitate to urge "a more enterprising Commander." In February his plans were nearly ruined by a dispatch from Sir William Howe. Sir William assumed that Clinton would be given the Canadian expedition and asked that Burgoyne be assigned to New York, presumably as Howe's second in command. The King approved the suggestion.

Burgoyne did not intend to be shouldered aside. It was primarily to promote his own fortunes that he had composed the "Thoughts" and its comprehensive detail was designed to demonstrate his familiarity with the problem. Lord Germain was sympathetic. Even so, Clinton's senior rank would probably have won him the Canadian command. He was back in England in February and there were hints from several of the ministers that he had only to ask and the assignment was his. But Clinton was of that odd sort who refuses to grasp at opportunity—and afterward complains resentfully about how they were victims of slights and discriminations. He did not ask and Burgoyne and Germain were vastly relieved.

Henry Clinton was a study of conflicting qualities and emotions. He had perhaps the best military mind of all the British generals. Time after time his analyses of military problems sorted out the central kernel from the chaff. Yet he possessed a diffidence, a lack of confidence which all too often prevented him from acting with decision. He counted Burgoyne his friend and the numerous letters which passed between the two indicate that the friendship was mutual. But Burgoyne would scarcely have allowed friendship to stand in the way of his ambitions. Clinton, on the other hand, had "a delicacy upon those matters that would not permit me to do anything of that kind [push his claims]." Besides, he pointed out, Burgoyne was familiar with the country, "knew better what to do and how to do it."

So in the end Clinton went back to the very job from which he had hoped to escape. His relations with Howe had become abrasive and bitter, and the commander in chief seldom accepted his suggestions. Clinton had come home determined either to secure another command or resign. It was typical of him that he did neither. He was assuaged by the Red Ribbon of the Bath and returned to New York for his last and bitterest quarrel with his commander.

The plan that Burgoyne submitted to Germain was, as noted, not original with him. During the French and Indian War British and French forces had attacked and counterattacked in both the valley of the Mohawk and the route of Lake Champlain and the Hudson. Fort Stanwix, Ticonderoga, and Crown Point had stood for years as monuments to the importance that both nations had attached to these routes. What Burgoyne proposed was a two-pronged attack utilizing both lines of advance. The principal thrust was to be by way of Lake Champlain and the Hudson, with an army of no less than 8,000 men. The expedition down the Mohawk would be a token force of Canadian rangers and Indians designed to protect the western flank of the main body, suppress any local threats from Patriot militia, and enlist the support of the Tories who were reported to be numerous in the Mohawk Valley. The objective of both forces was Albany, some ten miles below the confluence of the Mohawk and the Hudson.

"These ideas," said Burgoyne, "are formed on the supposition, that it be the sole purpose of the Canadian army to effect a junction with General Howe, or after cooperating so far as to get possession of Albany and open communication with New York, to remain upon the Hudson's River, and thereby enable that general to act with his whole force to the southward."[6]

No doubt Burgoyne knew of the ambiguous nature of Howe's plans which encompassed both the taking of Philadelphia and supporting in some way the northern army. The statement above may have been an implied question. Was he to expect a junction with Howe or was he merely to "open communication?"

When the plan was submitted to the King, George III made a number of comments. He took pride in the fact that he was well informed on military affairs and his notes justify the claim. One of his comments gave the answer to the question implicit in Burgoyne's statement of objectives: "As Sir William Howe does not think of acting from Rhode Island into Massachusetts, the force from Canada must join him at Albany." When Germain drew up the order to put the plan into execution he directed Sir Guy Carleton (nominally the command link between Germain and Burgoyne) "to give him [Burgoyne] orders to pass Lake Champlain, and from thence, by the most vigorous exertion of the force under his command, to proceed with all expedition, to Albany, and put himself under the command of Sir William Howe."

By the widest latitude of interpretation, this could mean either that Germain expected Howe himself to arrive at Albany to take command of the joint force, or that Howe would be back in New York in time to assume jurisdiction over Burgoyne when he "opened communications."

Yet Germain's method of notifying Howe of what was expected of him in the coming campaign was merely to send him an information copy of his instructions to Carleton. Howe later claimed that, prior to his departure for Philadelphia, he did not receive any order from Germain positively directing him to support Burgoyne, and technically he was correct.[7]

But what was happening was a gradual and subtle shift of authority without either Howe or Germain being fully aware of it. A change had come over Sir William since he had first begun formulating his plans in November, 1776. At that time Washington's army seemed on the point of either destruction or disintegration. Another year's campaigning, a concerted strategy that would strike devastating and coordinated blows at the rebels and the war would be over. Howe's tone was as hopeful and enthusiastic as he had ever allowed himself to be. But at the turn of the year came the disasters at Trenton and Princeton and the rebellion revived. The reverse had bitten deep, the characteristic pessimism had reasserted itself. And with the pessimism came a great stubbornness. Convinced of the revival of Loyalism to the southward, lured by the prospect of the capture of the American capital, Howe fixed his eyes steadfastly on Pennsylvania. He would erase the Trenton blunder; ". . . by the end of the campaign we shall be in possession of New York, the Jersies, and Pennsylvania." By March, 1777, Sir William had become oblivious to Germain's attempts to control or restrain him. It was not insubordination in the sense that he defied Germain's orders. He simply ignored them.

In England Howe's demands for reinforcements dismayed Germain and he flinched at the idea of going to Parliament for additional money and men. His enormous efforts of 1776 had made deep inroads on the ministry's political capital. Beset by increasingly sharp attacks from the opposition in Parliament, grumblings from his colleagues in the cabinet, and the fragile sensibilities of Burgoyne, Clinton, and Carleton, Germain shrank from any gesture or reproof which might alienate his American commanders.

In fact, one of those unfortunate episodes involving family sensibilities and court favors may have complicated matters for the American Secretary. The treasurer of the navy Sir Gilbert Elliot had died in January leaving vacant a position which carried a salary of four thousand pounds a year. Lord Richard Howe had previously held this sinecure and was considered likely to receive it again—so thought Lady Caroline Howe. She was the widow of George Howe, oldest of the brothers, who had been killed in America during the

Seven Years' War. Lady Howe was the jealous guardian of the family interests at court and she made it clear that, though Lord Howe would not solicit the post, he would certainly accept it if offered. Lord North, immersed as usual in the impenetrable maze of obligations owed and favors due, awarded the office to Welborn Ellis. Caroline Howe and other powerful family friends were soon at pains to inform all and sundry of exactly how an ungrateful ministry had slighted those who were its most faithful servants.[8]

The Howe brothers had been brought forward for the American command at considerable political cost on the confident assertion by Lord Germain that their abilities would insure a victorious conclusion to the rebellion. He had backed his favorites to the hilt and he had no recourse now but to defend their conduct and give them his confident support. To have dismissed Howe would have been to sink himself. But in dealing so gently with Sir William the American Secretary had unwittingly become Howe's prisoner. Viewed as a whole, the correspondence between Germain and Howe conveys the impression that the general was giving the orders—with a bewildering array of modifications—and the minister was almost supinely acquiescing.

If this was true, Germain gave no overt sign. The great plan was now complete. With the posting of orders to Governor-General Carleton (copy to Sir William Howe) Lord George confidently expected that Britain's great engine of war would roll forward inexorably and crush the American rebellion. To provide additional assurance that the operation would not falter Germain sent Major Nisbet Balfour to New York as his special emissary to prod the British high command to action.

Spring Comes To America

After the withdrawal from the New Jersey interior in January the British army was divided for the remainder of the winter, about half quartered in New York city and the other half encamped along the Raritan at New Brunswick and Perth Amboy. Despite the pall cast over headquarters by the failure in New Jersey (and a dispatch from Germain calling it "extremely mortifying") Howe did his best to provide entertainment for his officers and important citizens of the town. Although he was gloomy about the prospects for the coming campaign Sir William did not allow this to suppress his naturally gregarious nature and his expansive social tastes. There were balls and fireworks, dinners for prominent Loyalists, receptions for generals and admirals, and "play at Vingt et Un." Howe had discovered the charms of Mrs. Joshua Loring, wife of the commissary of prisoners, and their dalliance led one young Loyalist to decide that the campaign against the rebels would begin "whenever he shall think proper to leave Mrs. Lorain and face them."

For the rank and file it was not so easy. Confinement to winter quarters was always a dispiriting experience. With no fresh food available the soldiers subsisted on weevily biscuit, worm-eaten peas, and maggoty beef. The troops in New Jersey were even more miserable. Crowded into makeshift quarters they were subjected to the added indignity of constant harassment by coveys of Continentals and militia that roamed the countryside. Parties of redcoats who attempted to forage outside their lines rarely did so with impunity. One contingent of nearly 500 British soldiers returning from a raid was set upon by Pennsylvania militiamen who scattered the raiders and recovered forty wagons of plunder and 200 horses and cattle. The Hessians were especially guilty of indiscriminately looting Tories and Whigs alike. Thus were many converts made to the American cause.

Washington took great pains to defer to civilian sensibilities. After Trenton he had distributed the Hessian baggage to those who were victims of enemy pillaging; he himself issued orders for severe punishment for looting by American soldiers. And he saw to it that accounts of British depredations received full coverage in the Pennsylvania and New Jersey press. When Howe's deadline for accepting pardons expired on January 30, 1777, Washington promptly countered with his own proclamation. Those who had accepted British protection had thirty days in which to renounce their allegiance to the Crown or go into the enemy lines. Those who did neither would be considered enemies of the country. It certainly did not improve Howe's spirits when, soon after the expiration of Washington's order, a dispatch arrived from Germain criticizing his amnesty policy and reproving him for acting so leniently toward the rebels.

The British commander, nonetheless, decided to try again. On March 15 he issued another proclamation which again offered a pardon, but on much more stringent terms. This time those who accepted were not allowed to return to their homes but must either enlist in one of the Loyalist regiments or be returned to England. This new order proved to be more successful and there were numerous desertions from Washington's army into the British lines.

But as spring came and the weather grew milder Howe made no move to bestir himself. The only spark of energy came from the Earl of Cornwallis. American outposts had pushed to within seven miles of Brunswick where a force of about 500 men under General Benjamin Lincoln was posted at Bound Brook. On April 18 his lordship suddenly debouched from his cantonment with 2,000 men, crossed the Raritan, and drove for Lincoln's outpost. Militiamen supposed to be watching the river crossing failed to warn the Americans and they barely escaped encirclement. There was a brisk skirmish in which Lincoln lost his guns and suffered about seventy-five casualties before Nathanael Greene brought up his division and forced Cornwallis to retire.

All this was somewhat confusing to the American commander in chief. A few weeks earlier an enemy raiding party had attacked an American supply depot at Peekskill in the Hudson Highlands. This had lead Washington to believe that Howe might be starting northward, and he had ordered John Sullivan to reinforce the river forts with eight newly recruited regiments. Now Cornwallis' demonstration in New Jersey seemed to warn of a movement toward Pennsylvania.

Later in April Howe sent Governor William Tryon with 2,000 men to raid Connecticut. The objective was a large American supply depot in Danbury. The British landed at Fairfield and marched unopposed to Danbury where they burned not only a large quantity of supplies but a good part of the town.

As the raiders retreated an American force hastily gathered by Benedict Arnold attempted to cut them off. Although his 600 men were only about one third the size of the British, Arnold boldly threw them in against the redcoats, stubbornly contesting their retreat. But his force was too small and the raiders escaped.

Arnold was in Connecticut because, despite his proven reputation as perhaps the hardest fighter in the army, five junior brigadiers had been promoted over his head to major general. Arnold had left the army in disgust, and only a tactful appeal from General Washington had prevented his resignation. The coincidence that placed him in the vicinity of Danbury was a fortunate one, for Congress finally acknowledged his abilities by promoting him to major general. Arnold was mollified sufficiently to return to General Philip Schuyler's northern command.[9]

Washington puzzled to fit all these events into some kind of pattern that might indicate Howe's intentions. But the British commander's strategy was as obscure to some of his own subordinates as it was to the Americans and what Howe had in mind was outside the range of Washington's speculations. It certainly must have come as a shock to Lord George Germain.

Under the date of April 2 Howe informed Germain that he had abandoned his plan for an overland march from New York to Philadelphia because of "the difficulties and delay that would attend the passage of the Delaware . . . I propose to invade Pennsylvania by sea, and from this arrangement we must probably abandon the Jerseys. . . ."

By sea! However ambiguous Howe may have been about his cooperation with the Canadian expedition the fact that his army would be between Washington and Burgoyne afforded willy-nilly some assurance of support. If Washington followed Howe's march toward Philadelphia or moved to block him this would remove the American southern force from any position from which it could threaten Burgoyne. If the American commander ignored Howe and moved toward the Hudson Sir William would know it instantly and take the necessary precautions.

But to go to Philadelphia by sea was to leave Burgoyne entirely on his own. Not only would Howe be out of position to support the northern army, he would even be out of communication with it, especially while he was at sea.

If any doubt remained in Germain's mind of Howe's aberration it was dispelled by a dispatch that Howe had written to Carleton, a copy of which accompanied his letter to Germain. To the Governor-General Sir William wrote: "Having but little expectation that I will be able, from the want of sufficient strength in this army, to detach a corps in the beginning of the campaign to act up Hudson's River consistent with the operations already determined upon, the force your Excellency may deem expedient to advance beyond your frontiers after taking Ticonderoga will, I fear, have little assistance from hence to facilitate their approach, and as I shall probably be in Pennsylvania when that corps is ready to advance into this province, it will not be in my power to communicate with the officer commanding it, as soon as I would wish; he must therefore pursue such measures as may from circumstances be judged most conducive to the advancement of his Majesty's service consistently with your Excellency's orders for his conduct."

The most that Howe could offer in the way of assistance was to "endeavor to have a corps upon the lower part of Hudson's river sufficient to open communication for shipping thro' the Highlands." What may have been most significant about this latest communication was the aura of pessimism which pervaded it. "Restricted as I am from entering upon more extensive operations by the want of force, my hopes of terminating the war this year are vanished."[10]

And what of Major Balfour, who was aware of the ministry's expectations and whose mission it had been to represent those wishes to the commanders in New York? Balfour's influence on Howe's decision may be deduced from the latter's letter to Germain on May 22, two weeks after Balfour's arrival in New York. Howe merely reported Tryon's raid on Danbury and the news that Burgoyne was expected to be on Lake Champlain in June. His own army, he said, was encamped on the Raritan and he gave no hint of when he expected to move on Philadelphia.

The only reference to any of the suggestions conveyed by Balfour was in a dispatch of June 3. To the ministry's suggestion that a raiding expedition into New England might discourage recruiting for Washington's army, Howe again referred to his lack of reinforcements and noted that such an expedition would interfere with the major operations "that have received royal approbation and which are already too curtailed by the want of land force. . . ."

In the meantime Germain had gone to the King with the news of Howe's April 2 dispatch containing the latest deviation from the plan of campaign. The result of their conference was an instruction to Howe (May 18) which, once more, can be understood only on the assumption that Germain and the King were, in effect, at the mercy of the whims of their commander in chief in America. The King, wrote Germain, "does not hesitate to approve the alteration which you propose, . . ." But he added the important condition that "it will be executed in time for you to cooperate with the army ordered to proceed from Canada and put itself under your command." There was every indication, both in Howe's April 2 letter to Germain and in his letter to Carleton which he enclosed, that Howe did not intend to do more than "endeavor" to open the lower Hudson to "communicate" with Burgoyne. Nevertheless, Germain's dispatch on May 18 closed with the notation that "his Majesty entirely approves of your letter to Sir Guy Carleton."[11]

Perhaps Germain was resigned to the fact that there was nothing he could do at this late date to alter Howe's course of action. If his dispatch took the usual eight weeks to make the westward crossing of the Atlantic Howe would not receive it until mid-July when he would presumably be fully launched on his sea voyage (in fact, Howe did not receive it until August 12). If Howe and Burgoyne were successful Germain would have given no offense. If the great campaign fell apart because of lack of cooperation, he, like Howe, had his justification on the record.

There was still a faint hope. Sir Henry Clinton had left late in April to resume his duties as Howe's second in command. He was thoroughly conversant with Burgoyne's plans and with the ministry's views. He was himself convinced that victory depended on the coordination of British forces. Moreover, Sir Henry never hesitated to speak his mind to his chief, although seldom with any success.

Cat And Mouse In New Jersey

With the coming of warm weather the army in New York became restless yet the British commander seemed in no hurry to begin the campaign. To the ministry he pointed out "the delays which may attend the evacuation of the Jersies" but he issued no orders to the army on the Raritan. April passed into May and now Sir William complained that he had not received sufficient tents to take the field. Finally, having talked of delays in getting the army out of New Jersey, he began a series of maneuvers *into* New Jersey, presumably either to disguise his intentions or to force Washington out of his position behind the mountains at Morristown. Howe evidently hoped to maneuver him into open country and bring the Americans to battle.

Washington had already concluded the obvious, that Howe would either take his army up the Hudson or strike overland for Philadeliphia. At the end of May he moved his army south to Middlebrook, about ten miles northwest of New Brunswick where he could keep an eye on the road to Philadelphia and still be in a position to fall back into a defensive position in the Watchung Mountains.

In the second week in June Howe made his first feint. Marching west from New Brunswick he seemed to be offering Washington a chance to get between the British and New York. But reports came into headquarters at Middlebrook that Howe had left his heavy baggage in Brunswick and that he had no boats for crossing the Delaware. The further Howe advanced, the further he was separated from his base but Washington simply waited. New Jersey militia and Morgan's deadly riflemen now began to harass the redcoats, picking off stragglers and snapping at outposts and detachments.

After about a week Howe suddenly withdrew his army toward New Brunswick, simulating a hasty retreat. The Americans followed with the divisions of Nathanael Greene and "Mad Anthony" Wayne closing on the rear of the British column. The pursuit continued to New Brunswick but the American units had trouble coordinating their movements and Washington cautioned his commanders not to press too hard. As the British continued their withdrawal toward Amboy the Americans broke off the pursuit, but the move had succeeded in drawing the American commander out of his defensive positions at Middlebrook.

On June 26 Howe tried to close the trap. Marching swiftly out of Amboy in two columns he attempted to cut the Americans off from Middlebrook and the sanctuary of the New Jersey hills. But the effort was too great for his men. The heavily clad troops suffered from the intense June heat, and small parties of sniping militiamen stung the lumbering column. Lord Stirling, commanding the advance American division, briefly found himself in serious trouble. The belligerent Irishman further imperilled his position by standing and fighting. The British column under Cornwallis smashed him and almost cut him off but the long march and the hot, humid weather halted the pursuit. Washington was amply forewarned and withdrew to Middlebrook, leaving the two armies in the same positions they had occupied three weeks before. Howe refused to risk an attack and the American commander in chief would not be drawn from his prepared defenses.[12]

Having already decided to take his army to Pennsylvania by sea Howe pulled back through New Brunswick to Amboy and on June 30 ferried the entire force across to Staten Island. It was, of course, a logical move, one that was in fact long overdue if the British were to make the most of the remainder of the summer. But it had an unfortunate effect on the army. After the frustrations and confinement of winter quarters officers and men had had high hopes for the spring. Their spirits had lifted as they began what many thought would be the final campaign of the war. Now, in the first week of July, a month's campaign had not only been fruitless but aimless. New Jersey was abandoned, the army was back in New York, and the commander in chief had fallen into another of his strange lapses of torpid inactivity.

It was a dispirited and idle army that Sir Henry Clinton found when he arrived in New York on July 5. He was alarmed that the summer was so far advanced for he knew that Lord Germain and the King expected two results from the coming campaign: that Philadelphia would be captured, and that Howe would have made a junction with Burgoyne. He now learned for the first time that Howe planned to go to Philadelphia by sea. Sir Henry was dismayed. He had earlier expressed to Germain his doubts that there would be time for a campaign to Pennsylvania and a return to the Hudson to assist Burgoyne. Now he was certain of it.

Clinton and Howe had never gotten along well, although it was part of Clinton's paradoxical personality that he could sincerely admire his superior. All

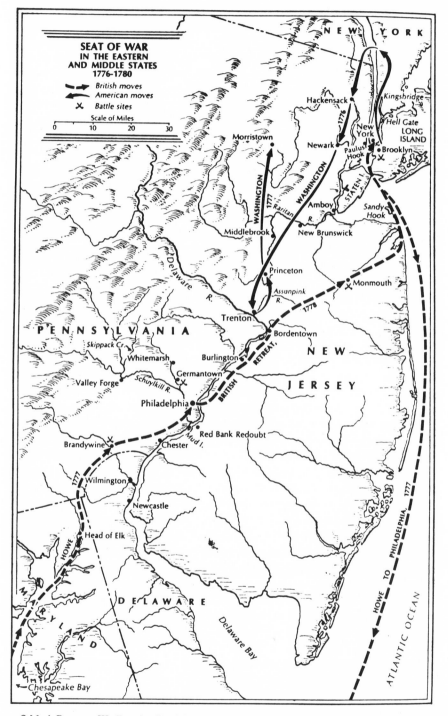

SEAT OF WAR
IN THE EASTERN
AND MIDDLE STATES
1776-1780
➤ British moves
← American moves
✕ Battle sites
Scale of Miles
0   10   20   30

© Mark Boatner, III, *Encyclopedia of the American Revolution*, David McKay Co., Inc.

through the campaign of 1776 they had disagreed, Clinton expressing his opinions with a forcefulness and frankness that was surprising in view of the diffidence he had lately displayed at court. During 1776 he had insisted that it was Washington's army, not the occupation of territory that was the real objective (Did he now remind Howe that he had spent a month pursuing that same army in New Jersey when he should have been on his way to Pennsylvania?). He had proposed a flanking movement to cut off Washington's army during the American retreat of December, 1776. He steadfastly refused to believe that much reliance could be placed on the Loyalists.

Now, in the summer of 1777, Clinton vehemently denounced the strategy proposed by his commander. In going to Philadelphia by sea, he argued, Howe could not possibly bring the Americans to a decisive engagement unless Washington wished it. Holding Pennsylvania and New Jersey at the end of the campaign would require an army of occupation as well as extensive support from the Loyalists in whom Clinton had no more faith than he had had a year ago. In such circumstances support for the army on the Hudson became impossible.

Howe professed (not withstanding Germain's dispatch to Carleton) that he did not understand the purpose of Burgoyne's expedition and that he had no specific instructions to support it. Clinton removed his doubts. "I told him [the] government did not seem to hold that language, but freely declared—too freely—I thought this [movement by sea] must finish it. He stared." Was it possible that Howe never really grasped the ministry's intention, that he had not realized the importance Germain attached to Burgoyne's invasion? Clinton seemed to think so. Having relegated the Canadian army to a minor role in his own thinking it never crossed Howe's opinionated mind that Germain and the King might disagree.

But if Clinton's emphatic assertion of the ministry's view came as a surprise to Howe it did not alter his fixed intention. He finally silenced Clinton with what, to his involuted logic, must have been an unanswerable argument: ". . . he had sent home his plan, it was approved, and he would abide by it." But Germain and the King had not approved a sea voyage to Philadelphia.

To Clinton, Howe's decision was simply unbelievable. By mid-July Burgoyne was reported at Ticonderoga, and Sir Henry, at the moment of Howe's sailing, flatly told his chief that "*he intended to deceive us all, and, though he was pleased to say he was going to sea . . . I should expect to see him return with the first southerly blast and run up the North River.*"[13]

On July 23, with his troops finally embarked, Howe and the fleet disappeared beyond the southern horizon.

SEVEN

The Suppression of
the Loyalists

In April, 1776, the Baltimore Council of Safety ordered a detachment of militia to Annapolis to arrest Governor Robert Eden on the charge of giving aid to the enemy. Major Mordecai Gist, the detachment commander, reported to the State Council of Safety before proceeding with his mission. That august body sent the detachment back to Baltimore and shortly afterward issued a reprimand to the Baltimore council chairman, Samuel Purviance, for exceeding his authority. Two months later Governor Eden was allowed to take his departure peacefully. The fact that the Baltimore Council of Safety had acted on the recommendation of the Continental Congress carried no weight with the state council of Maryland.

The episode is illustrative of the dilemmas presented by the problem of Tory or Loyalist subversion. Eden was one of the few colonial governors who made a genuine effort to reconcile the conflicting views of the colonists and the home government in the crisis of 1775. His moderation had earned him the respect of the colonists, especially those in the more conservative eastern counties, and he was personally popular in Maryland. His friends, some of whom were members of the state council, were shocked at the idea of humiliating him by placing him under arrest.[1]

When the war came in 1775 enthusiastic Whigs throughout the colonies began a campaign to "overawe the disaffected." Mobs harassed notorious Tories, breaking into their homes, terrifying their families, and often subjecting the victims themselves to tar and feathers or other physical abuse. Yet on the whole there was surprisingly little bloodshed. Alexander Graydon recalled that a Tory who had shouted out his allegiance to George the Third was given mild treatment compared to the bloody vengeance of the French Reign of Terror twenty years later; ". . . his bravado would unquestionably have brought the offender to the lamppost and set his head on a pike."[2]

The irony of rebels suppressing disloyalty by attacks on people who proudly called themselves Loyalists was lost on most of the Whigs. But they realized that the success of the Revolution depended not merely on winning adherents but in stifling the opposition. Who, then, were the opponents of the Revolution? Among Americans who had voiced their opinions since 1763 almost all

had expressed disapproval of one or another of the measures of the home government that became known collectively as the "new colonial policy." When
the Whigs shifted the focus of their struggle from the defense of their liberties
as Englishmen to independence, they lost a sizeable number of supporters.
Joseph Galloway, a prominent member of the First Continental Congress,
became one of the leading supporters of the Crown after 1776. John Jay, Robert and Gouverneur Morris, and James Duane were also opposed to independence, hoping for reconciliation even after July, 1776. Yet in the end they
remained faithful to the Whig cause. John Dickinson, author of the famous
Letters from a Pennsylvania Farmer, was so torn by his deep-rooted loyalty to
England that he could not bring himself to sign the Declaration of Independence. Yet he served in the Delaware militia and was sent back to Congress
by his Delaware constituents in 1779.

Thus distinctions were blurred and this greatly complicated the Whig
problem of what today we would call internal security. Moreover Americans
prided themselves on the fact that they were men of reason who could conduct
an orderly revolution.

THE MOBS

It is important to remember that those who eventually came to be judged as
enemies of the Revolution were themselves American and an integral part of
the community in which they lived. As the Whig movement progressed from
protest to resistance to independence the differing loyalties put a serious strain
on the social fabric of these communities. When these men—and their families—many of whom had been respected leaders of their county or town,
found their homes surrounded by mobs threatening them with violence, the
shock was sometimes overwhelming, and the trauma deep and lasting.

The period of greatest confusion and perplexity over the division of loyalties came in the initial stage of the war. Although Americans were in a state
of rebellion against Great Britain it was more than a year after Lexington and
Concord before they had governments, either state or national, that possessed
some kind of legitimacy. The first act of the Maryland revolutionary convention which met in April, 1775, was to swear allegiance to King George.
The members then proceeded to elect delegates to the Second Continental
Congress.[3]

Most of the interim governments were hastily formed and were primarily
concerned with raising and fitting out troops and meeting other problems
created by the emergency of war. The regular processes of government were
left largely to local governments, along with the problem of the suppression of
the Tory opposition.

The most obvious potential enemies were royal officials. Some had used
their positions to bully and tyrannize, but these were probably the exception
rather than the rule. After all, even royal officials were mostly Americans

and had lived peaceably with their neighbors all their lives. As the revolutionary movement gained momentum their positions became increasingly difficult. As holders of royal office they were committed to uphold Crown authority. When, as most believed, the rebellion was suppressed, and they had compromised their loyalty they would be called to account. In the meantime there was the question of survival.

Lieutenant Governor Thomas Oliver of Massachusetts was confronted by a crowd of 4,000 angry citizens of Cambridge on September 2, 1774. Oliver was a respected land owner and leading citizen but he had accepted his appointment under the Massachusetts Government Act, which had dissolved the assembly and virtually ended self-government in the colony. This made him the focus of attention for the aroused Whigs. The crowd did not appear to be in a dangerous mood so Oliver addressed them, answered some of their questions, and persuaded them to disperse. Shortly afterward a rumor spread that troops were being sent to Cambridge from Boston and the crowd reappeared, some of its members armed. Five spokesmen "of decent appearance" were admitted and presented a demand that Oliver resign his office. Fearful for his family, Oliver agreed to sign a resignation, although he entered a notation that he had done so in the face of threats. Some of the crowd objected to this but moderates among them persuaded the rest to go home. The next day Oliver and his family fled to Boston where he resumed the duties of his office. Even though he had acted under duress, the lieutenant governor was disturbed by the fact that he was breaking an oath. He finally concluded, ". . . I still had it in my power to die or to make the promise. I chose to live."[4]

Other marked men were members of the Anglican clergy. Many of these churchmen were politically naive and extremely conservative in their views. Most regarded defiance of authority as a mortal sin and it would not have been unusual to hear sermons from their pulpits defending the divine right of kings.

Jonathan Boucher, an Anglican clergyman from Annapolis, announced that he would preach a sermon in which he would instruct his parishioners that "they could not be sure they were right and doing good; and so their truest wisdom as well as duty . . . was, as the Prophet advised, to *sit still*." When Boucher arrived he found his church filled with 200 armed men. He grimly determined to deliver his message and started to mount to his pulpit, "my sermon in one hand and a loaded pistol in the other." He was suddenly seized by "one of my good friends," who urged him to desist, saying that men had been ordered to fire on him if he entered the pulpit. After some scuffling and arguing, Boucher concluded "that there was but one way to save my life. This was by seizing Sprigg [the leader of the armed men] . . . by the collar and with my cocked pistol in the other hand, assuring him that if any violence was offered me I would immediately blow his brains out. . . ." The two marched to Boucher's horse—Sprigg "had the meanness" to order his drummers to play the "Rogue's March"—and the sturdy minister escaped.[5]

American revolutionaries were the first to recognize that the press could be a powerful weapon in promoting their cause. The obvious corollary was that the Tory press must be silenced. Here the Whigs ran into an ideological conflict that obviously disturbed them, for the tradition of a free press was strong in the colonies, and it was not easy to reconcile attacks on Tory editors with the struggle for liberty. James Rivington, editor of the *New York Gazetteer*, at first made a sincere effort to steer a middle course, inviting expression of opinion from both sides. But by 1775 his obviously Tory sympathies led to his condemnation by a Whig meeting and his press and offices were destroyed by the New York Sons of Liberty. Young Alexander Hamilton, although he had already attracted attention as a radical pamphleteer and orator, remarked, ". . . I cannot help condemning this step." The New York Provincial Congress investigated the charges against Rivington and exonerated him upon his pledge to sin no more. Nevertheless he sailed for England early in 1776 and did not return until the British occupied New York.[6]

The local work of suppressing the Loyalists fell to the old Committees of Correspondence or the more recent committees created by the Continental Association (to enforce the nonintercourse resolutions of the First Continental Congress). These constituted themselves as committees of safety at both the county and state levels. Since there were no statutory codes to guide them the committees had to decide cases on the basis of their own notions of justice. In small rural communities the suspect's local reputation and character might count as much in his defense as the evidence. Committeemen were usually aware that in such a heated atmosphere old personal scores might be paid by bringing charges based on false testimony, and that a witch hunt might result. They were also conscious of the fact that their verdicts were as often based on a sense of the feeling of the neighborhood as their own sense of justice.

Difficult problems arose in that gray area where an accused might have spoken out against the Whig cause without having advocated support of the Crown or the measures enacted by Parliament. In late 1774 and early 1775 there were many who believed that radical Whigs were leading the colonies down the road to war and that bloodshed must be avoided at all costs. In June, 1775, Elisha Adams, Timothy Hammant, and Jonathan Cutler were accused in Medway, Massachusetts, of being "unfriendly and inimical to the just rights and liberties of America and measures for recovering the preservation of the rights, liberties and constitution thereof." The evidence consisted of one's protest against bloodshed, another's prediction of a race riot in Boston, and the sinister fact that the third had sold his horse two days before the battle of Lexington and Concord.

The three were asked to unite with the community in opposing British tyranny. When one replied that he could not "see any reason nor justice in riotous actions in the later times" the committee allowed that such an opinion did not conflict with his pledge to "exert myself in a just and constitutional way. . . ." The charges against the accused were dismissed.[7]

Such leniency was the rule rather than the exception in most of the proceedings of the committees from 1774 to 1776. The exceptions could usually be found in those areas where tensions were high and where overt hostilities by one side or the other outraged the people of the community. In Virginia the Nansemond Committee of Safety decreed that the Reverend John Agnew be ostracized for persisting in preaching obedience to the Crown. The stubborn Anglican refused until a mob forced him to stop preaching entirely, but except for the original judgement of the committee he was not punished further. However, when the royal governor, Lord Dunmore, decided to raise an armed force to oppose the Whigs, and especially after he offered freedom to any slaves who joined him, the temper of the area changed sharply. The aroused Virginians defeated Dunmore outside Norfolk in December, 1775, and then burned the town, forcing its inhabitants, Whig and Tory alike, to flee. Once the threat of Dunmore was removed, Virginians relaxed their vigilance to an extent that alarmed some Patriot leaders. James Madison complained that although Benjamin Haley's words and actions "gave abundant proof of his being an adherent to the king" he was only fined twelve shillings and sentenced to one hour in jail.[8]

From first to last the most troublesome problem for the Pennsylvania Whigs was the Society of Friends. Their militant pacifism forbade them from participating directly or indirectly in the war. Although many of them were wealthy and politically powerful they aroused a good deal of resentment, especially among the westerners who accused the self-righteous Quaker merchants of putting guns in the hands of the Indians, and now were enriching themselves by trading with the British. Yet religious diversification in American society, and the strong hold that religion of whatever faith had on community life in the colonies precluded any systematic attack on the sect. North Carolinians and Rhode Islanders seem to have adopted much the same view toward the Friends in those colonies.

Most of the Quakers attempted to follow a policy of reconciliation. The Philadelphia Meeting of the Suffering early in 1775 urged its members to "demean themselves as peaceable subjects and to discountenance and avoid every measure tending to excite disaffection to the King as the supreme magistrate or to the legal authorities of government."

Moses Brown, a wealthy merchant of Rhode Island, became a member of the Society of Friends in 1773. He urged Rhode Islanders to seek reconciliation, but his ostentatious pacifism became somewhat tainted after the British seized one of his ships and arrested his brother. Brown went to Boston and secured the release of both in return for which he agreed to use his efforts to curb hostilities in Rhode Island. For the moment the tensions were relaxed between the Patriots and the Friends, and Brown and his fellows earned a grudging respect for the extensive program that they carried on for the relief of refugees and other destitute people during 1775 and 1776.[9]

THE LAW

In August, 1776, Asa Porter of Haverhill, New Hampshire, was jailed for plotting to induce the British to send troops from Canada to invade New Hampshire. Porter, it was alleged, was organizing a band of armed Tories to cooperative with the invaders. The Haverhill Committee of Safety passed the case to the New Hampshire assembly. The evidence against Porter was not very substantial, but the accused defended himself on quite a different ground.

He challenged the constitutionality of the whole proceeding against him. He pointed out that in American legal practice "it doth not consist with the liberties of the people that the same body which hath the power of making laws should also have the power of executing the laws or determining causes of individuals." Moreover the legislature, even if it had judicial power, was determining treason without having passed a law that defined it. Finally it was examining evidence without a formal charge having been brought and was denying Porter's right to trial by jury. Porter was paroled and rearrested several times, but he continually bombarded the assembly with appeals and petitions, and their refusal to hold him in custody may have indicated that the members were sufficiently troubled by his arguments to bury them in procedural red tape.[10]

In the absence of constitutional or legal sanctions the colonies tended to follow English common and statutory law and to operate through their colonial court systems. In most of the New England and middle colonies revolutionary provincial congresses were elected, but constitutions were somewhat slow to take shape. In Virginia a constitutional convention was in session in the summer of 1776, but it was some months before the frame of government was complete. Massachusetts did not ratify a constitution until 1781. The Second Continental Congress in Philadelphia, though it assumed responsibility for the army and other functions of a national nature could only make suggestions to the states. Lacking constitutional authority to tax, to conscript troops, or, indeed, to take any measures without the consent of the states, it is not surprising that Congress avoided the perplexing problem of Loyalist subversion.

The American rebels were obviously having a difficult time defining treason. It was not until a few days before independence that Congress finally faced the problem. On June 24 it passed a resolution suggesting criteria for disloyalty. Those who levied war against the "united colonies," were adherents to George III, or gave aid and comfort to the enemy should be adjudged guilty of treason. It was six months to a year before most of the states responded. Maryland passed an act providing for the death penalty for "adherents to Great Britain" on July 4, 1776, but New York did not legislate against treason until 1781, relying instead on English common law. It passed a test law—a law providing for the administration of an oath as a test of loyalty—in December, 1776.

Most states also specified lesser crimes of subversion. Those who encouraged recognition of the sovereignty of George III, who discouraged enlistments in the army or advised against resistance to Britain, who disseminated false information, or maintained communications with the enemy were liable to less severe punishments. Two of the most widespread crimes were counterfeiting and trading with the enemy (the former was considered subversive as well as criminal).

Edward Perry, a Maine lumberman, supplied masts under contract to the royal navy in Nova Scotia. Perry was required by the local committee to post a bond of £2,000, but there was little the committee could do about "seizing" the huge mast timbers. After some hesitation it released Perry (who had displayed no other signs of disaffection) but ordered him to move to an inland town.

By 1777 most of the states came to the conclusion that there had to be some means of identifying the "disaffected." In short, the Patriots were driven to the axiom that those who were not for them must be against them. The means employed to effect this was the test oath.

The wording varied from state to state but in general the person taking the oath swore that he renounced his allegiance to the Crown, would do nothing that would compromise the freedom and independence of the United States, and would report to the authorities any conspiracies or treasonable acts of which he had knowledge. It should be noted that rarely did test oaths require any positive action, although in some states the test oath was administered by those who made up the militia rolls, so that swearing to or signing the test oath made one liable for militia conscription.[12]

In the early stages of the war committees of safety were often loath to convict suspects when there was only the flimsiest kind of evidence. The test oath bound the suspect to future good conduct and in effect put him on notice that he was being carefully watched by the authorities. The committees now had recourse to deterrence rather than punishment as a means of checking disaffection.

By 1777 many states, on Congress' recommendation, were calling on all inhabitants to take the oaths, thereby inaugurating a sweeping campaign of intimidation (New Hampshire, New York, North Carolina, and Georgia required test oaths only of civil and military office holders). In the twentieth century many Americans are outraged and insulted at the idea of loyalty oaths, but it must be remembered that large segments of the population in America in 1776 were in the process of switching allegiances. Many of the stoutest supporters of the Whig cause had held civil or military office under the Crown and thus welcomed the opportunity to proclaim their loyalty to the new nation. As Professor Don Higginbotham has suggested, an analogy might be drawn between the Patriots and the twentieth century immigrant who is proud of his new citizenship when he becomes naturalized. Those who refused to take the oath were disarmed and deprived of some of their rights, such as the right to vote, to run for office, or to bring civil suits in court. In some cases they were exiled, either to the British lines or to some destination outside the United States. In two states, Delaware and New Jersey, property of nonjurors was seized, and in New York, Maryland, and Delaware their taxes were doubled or trebled.[14]

Those who refused to take the oath were kept under surveillance especially during military crises. In the fall of 1777 after Howe occupied Philadelphia those who refused to take the oath were jailed without bond. When the British shifted their major military effort to the South in the latter years of the war and invaded the Carolinas penalties became increasingly severe. South Carolina nonjurors were banished and threatened with death if they returned. Georgia had no test oath until 1781, but those who refused to take it were automatically adjudged guilty of "high crimes and misdemeanors."

By the end of 1777 all the states except New York had enacted laws for the suppression of loyalism, although time and experience made necessary additions and modifications. In all states except Delaware and Georgia test oaths were established to separate friend from foe. It had taken almost two years for the Patriots to translate their concern over subversion into law. Yet on the whole the record was not bad, especially if one compares the American Revolution with other revolutions of the eighteenth and early nineteenth centuries which were often characterized by witch hunts and mass executions.[14]

THE ENFORCERS

The administration of both laws and test oaths was carried out by the committees of safety in cooperation with local justices of the peace. These officials usually had at their command the local militia who hunted down and arrested suspects, and who were occasionally called on to deal with armed bands of Tories who were so bold as to try to raise the standard of counterrevolution. The militia, then, performed as a sort of local constabulary in addition to preparing themselves for service with the army. As noted above, administering test oaths and drawing up militia rolls was often done at the same time, usually by the county lieutenant. In many states conscript laws specified that all who were subject to military duty were required to appear in person for drills and other militia training. Thus every man publicly identified himself as a supporter of the Revolution, even though he might have a substitute ready to serve in his place when the regiment went to active duty.

Suspects were brought before the local justice of the peace and the charge, with supporting evidence, was presented. The justice might himself dispose of the case if the charge was not serious. Mrs. John Davis of Woodbury, Connecticut, came under suspicion after her husband left home and joined the British army. Several people of the town presented affidavits attesting to Mrs. Davis' unquestioned adherence to the Patriot cause and the local justice dismissed the charges. A year later Davis deserted from the British and returned home. He was believed when he said that he was a convert to the American cause and the local justice of the peace instituted a petition to the General Assembly to grant him a pardon.

In more serious cases the justices of the peace held what amounted to preliminary hearings. In Fairfield, Connecticut, the local constable delivered John Cannon to Justice Thaddeus Betts, charging Cannon with coming from the British lines with a pass signed by the former governor of New Jersey, William Franklin. Since Cannon might be a British spy, Betts ordered him jailed to await trial in Superior Court. In Massachusetts courts of special session, composed of three to five justices of the peace, tried persons accused of treason, spying, and other serious crimes of subversion. In most states defendants who were convicted were allowed to appeal to the state assembly or the highest state court.

Punishments ranged from fines and the posting of bonds for good behavior in cases of minor offenses to banishment and imprisonment for serious crimes. Prison sentences were limited because there were simply not nearly enough jails. In New England, especially, the courts seem to have been more concerned about future behavior of the accused and neutralizing subversion than in reprisals against the Tories themselves. There was only one execution in Connecticut during the entire war.[15]

The middle states differed somewhat from New England because the problem of disaffection was much more widespread and the percentage of Loyalists was much higher. New York city became a haven for Loyalists from all parts of America, and sizeable numbers were enlisted in provincial corps of the British army. It was here that Major Robert Rogers, the famous ranger of the French and Indian War, organized raiding parties that terrorized Patriots on Long Island and the Connecticut coast. Here also Burgoyne's invasion in 1777 raised the hopes of enthusiastic Loyalists on the lower Hudson and in the Mohawk Valley, and frightened many others into fearful neutrality.

Under these circumstances local committees of safety often proved unequal to the task of checking subversion and aid to the enemy. Early in 1777 the New York Convention authorized the trial of traitors by military courts martial. The previous year a state Committee and Commission for Detecting and Defeating Conspiracies had been set up; now, assisted by a militia corps, the commission began to sweep the state, using the militiamen to round up suspects, and organizing courts-martial. In April and May, 1777, eighteen accused were convicted and sentenced to death. The Convention approved fourteen of these. During the three years of its existence the commission heard over a thousand cases of disloyalty. In 1778 New York passed a test oath law and failure to take it was punished by banishment or imprisonment. By this time local committees of safety had become merely administrative arms of the state committee, rarely deciding any cases on their own or exerting much influence.[16]

A similar pattern developed in New Jersey. Here the state's executive body, the state Council of Safety was given virtually complete control of detecting and punishing disloyalty. Its energetic attorney general, William Paterson, soon had the council travelling throughout the state, conducting its own prosecutions and rendering judgements. Such action was highly suspect so far as constitutional theory was concerned, but constant incursions of British troops during 1776 and 1777 disrupted the regular court system and the Whigs had to exert the full force of their authority to check the rather sizeable number of Tories and waverers.[17]

The effect of troop movements and military campaigns on the fortunes or misfortunes of the Loyalists was nowhere better illustrated than in Delaware. This smallest of the states had perhaps the highest percentage of Loyalists, and Patriots frequently had to call on their neighbors in Maryland and Pennsylvania for militia to help contain Tory uprisings.

Howe's invasion of Pennsylvania in 1777 brought hopeful Loyalists into the open, and when the British fleet appeared in the Delaware Loyalist pilots were on hand to guide the ships upriver and armed bands were ready to join forces with the redcoats. When Howe announced his decision to go to the Chesapeake, Loyalists were bitterly disappointed. One of them, Thomas Robinson, went aboard the flagship and begged Howe to put 500 regulars ashore in Delaware. This gesture, he said, would bring out 5,000 Loyalists who were ready to fight. Although Howe had been attracted southward by word of widespread Loyalist support, Sir William headed for the Chesapeake and what he believed to be prospects for greater support in southern Pennsylvania. With his departure went the best opportunity for a counterrevolution in Delaware.[18]

Pennsylvania, like New York, relied principally on state authority vested in a touring committee of safety. The problem of the Society of Friends proved just as nettlesome after systematic procedures had been established as before. The Whig majority—if indeed it was a majority—dared not completely antagonize this considerable body of militant neutrals, who steadfastly refused to aid either the American or British war effort. There were enough unscrupulous merchants masquerading under Quaker guise to antagonize the Patriots and in the summer of 1777 the Continental Congress urged the state to disarm and arrest the "disaffected," a measure obviously aimed at the Friends. Eleven prominent Quakers were arrested by the militia and, after interminable legal proceedings, they were exiled to Winchester, Virginia, where they lived under surveillance until the end of the war.

Enactment of a test oath met with equally stubborn resistance, not only from the Society of Friends, but from lesser sects like the Dunkards and Mennonites. The latter especially became victims of vigilante groups, notably where their numbers were small. Pennsylvania was one of the first states to use confiscation laws to suppress disaffection, and gangs of outlaws masquerading as militia descended on isolated communities and literally stripped the inhabitants bare. Eventually the Friends were forced to accommodate themselves to reality. They ceased condemning the American cause and, in effect, claimed only such consideration as might be given any religious group. They intensified their program for the relief of refugees and the destitute, and thus an uneasy truce was established between Friends and Patriots.

The fate of the Loyalists in Philadelphia during and after the British occupation of 1777 and early 1778 points up the frustration and impotence that they so frequently experienced with the British army. During the winter of 1777–1778 Joseph Galloway secured an appointment as Superintendent of Police. Using his powers broadly Galloway restored order to the city, suppressed trade with the enemy, and restored civil government. In a remarkably short time the city was flourishing, foreign trade had resumed, the Loyalist exiles had returned.

Then, in the spring of 1778, Sir Henry Clinton, the new commander in chief, announced that the British were evacuating the city. In vain, Galloway urged the British to retain the city, if for no other reason than as a model for what could be accomplished by the restoration of English rule. But Clinton was adamant and Philadelphia instead became an example of the fate of Loyalists who put their trust in the British army.[19]

In all the states the militia were an essential ingredient in the enforcement of state authority. Governor Clinton of New York thought that suppression of disaffection was the militia's most important duty and General Schuyler frequently called on them for such purposes. As we shall see, he used them to hold the Indians of the Six Nations in check, and he smashed an incipient rising of Highland Scots in Tryon county in early 1776. In Fairfield county, Connecticut, Whig militia nipped a Loyalist rising in the bud in the fall of 1776, and it was roving bands of militia between the lower Hudson and Saratoga that were to play havoc with communications between Burgoyne and New York during the campaign of 1777. We have already noted how militia harassed outposts in the vicinity of British bases, ambushing foraging parties and killing or capturing stragglers. In such situations it was difficult for the redcoats to extend their influence to Loyalist sympathizers in the surrounding countryside.[20]

The failure of the Loyalists to make a more significant contribution to the cause of England's reconquest of America can be attributed to several factors. The most obvious is the thoroughness and swiftness with which the Whigs in the states set up measures for controlling and neutralizing Tories and would-be Tory sympathizers. The dispersal of power among the states undoubtedly hamstrung the American war effort in general, but it was a blessing in disguise for counteracting subversion. Congress passed this problem to the states by default and it would appear that the states, with their local court systems, committees, and militia already in place, were much better equipped to meet the problem.

Whig leaders early realized that it was important to get control of the militia, the only organized "police force" in the colonies, and they were successful in getting Whig officers elected or appointed, and in using the militia organization as a means of promoting the revolutionary cause. Equally important was the fact that committees of safety were, in general, careful to avoid witch hunts and campaigns of terror. Certainly there were many unjust convictions, innocent people who were victimized, and property illegally and arbitrarily confiscated. All too often militia units were covers for outlaw gangs who pillaged and looted friend and foe alike. But by and large the committees exercised admirable restraint, giving those who were accused every opportunity to recant their loyalty to the Crown. By 1777 even those against whom the evidence of treason was overwhelming were tried under proper legal procedures and their rights were safeguarded. The Tory argument that Whig rule was mob rule was effectively answered, and waverers were encouraged to believe that the newly independent state governments were capable of creating an orderly society.

The failure of the British authorities to support and encourage the Loyalists more successfully may be attributed to both circumstance and negligence. It was soon apparent that Howe's strategy of extending British authority over large areas by the use of occupation troops was beyond the capacity of the forces under his command. The British abandonment of Philadelphia in 1778 was dictated not by lack of concern for the Loyalist, but by strategic considerations growing out of the entrance of France into the war.

Yet those Loyalists who actively and enthusiastically supported the Crown were usually met with indifference or downright contempt. Loyalist regiments were often badly equipped. Their officers were given provisional rank and they were never fully accepted by the British officer corps. Burgoyne, Howe, and Clinton all shared the basic disdain of Englishmen for Americans and they consistently expressed their lack of faith in the Loyalists as effective soldiers.

Germain and his generals continually overestimated the strength of the Loyalists, especially in terms of the numbers available for military duty. Expressions of loyalty to England did not necessarily mean active participation, and there were probably as many summer soldiers and sunshine Loyalists as there were Patriots.[21]

In the final analysis, then, the Loyalists never had a base from which to launch a counterrevolution. Almost everywhere those who might have been emboldened to raise the King's standard found themselves surrounded by neighbors who were either hostile or apathetic. Given the rapidity and thoroughness with which the states implemented the machinery of suppression, by 1777 any hope that Germain and the ministry may have had for Americanizing the war was at an end.

EIGHT

The Northern Invasion

FOR THE THIRD TIME IN TWO YEARS JOHN BURGOYNE CAME TO NORTH AMERICA. He had achieved the hope of every general, an independent command, and orders for a campaign that would make him a national hero. England was tired of the Howes and Clinton, commanders whose campaigns were unlucky and inconclusive. Burgoyne was the new star in Britain's firmament and the colorful, flamboyant Gentleman Johnny was fully prepared to take the center of the stage in the war for America.

"THIS ARMY MUST NOT RETREAT"

The army that assembled at Montreal was, at first glance, a polyglot of nationalities and even of races. Yet its elements had been carefully specified by Burgoyne and Germain. The regular troops consisted of an almost equal number of redcoats and German mercenaries, most of whom had been sent to Canada in the great troop lift of 1776. They had had a year to become accustomed to the climate and other vicissitudes of America. Of the allotments of reinforcements which Germain made for 1777 only 1600 were consigned to Canada.

The British force consisted of seven regiments: the Ninth, the Twentieth, the Twenty-First, the Twenty-Fourth, the Forty-Seventh, the Fifty-Third, and the Sixty-Second. Three other regiments were left as a garrison for Carleton, less their flank companies which were detached to the invading force. On his July 1 return of troops Burgoyne listed "total rank and file (sick included)" of these regiments as from 542 (9th) to 524 (47th). If these figures are correct their strength was from twenty-five to thirty percent greater than the normal British regiments. As was customary when a large number of regiments was serving together, the flank companies were combined into two regiments of grenadiers and light infantry. These, together with the 24th Regiment, formed the "advance corps" commanded by Brigadier General Simon Fraser.

Fraser was a hard-bitten Scot who had served under Wolfe at Louisbourg and Quebec in the 62nd Royal Americans. He had subsequently been named colonel of the 24th and had come to Canada with it in 1776 where he had been given the "local rank" of brigadier general. The grenadiers were commanded by Major John Acland whom the Baroness Riedesel described as "a plain, rough man, and was almost daily intoxicated; with this exception, however, he was an excellent officer." The light infantry was commanded by Major the Earl Balcarres who was often the commanding general's late night companion at cards and drink, but this did not seem to impair his ability to get into the thick of every fight.

The remaining British force was divided into two brigades. The 9th, 47th, and 53rd regiments comprised the first brigade commanded by Brigadier General Henry Powell; Brigadier General Hamilton commanded the second brigade made up of the 20th, the 21st, and the 62nd. The British troops were designated as the right wing of the army and were commanded by Major General William Phillips. Phillips was a violent-tempered artilleryman of thirty years' service who had distinguished himself in the Seven Years' War. As an artilleryman he would normally have never gotten an infantry command, but Burgoyne was so impressed with his aggressiveness that he had named him second in command as an "emergency measure."

Burgoyne's artillery park contained 138 guns ranging from huge 24-pounders to 4.4-inch mortars. Knowing that his first major objective was Ticonderoga he assembled a train of two 24-pounders, four 12-pounders, eighteen 6-pounders, six howitzers, and twelve smaller pieces, altogether forty-two guns. The British right wing totalled about 3,600 infantrymen and 400 artillerymen.

The left wing consisted of the Germans, mostly from Brunswick, commanded by Major General Friedrich von Riedesel. The Baron was thirty-nine years old and had spent twenty years in the armies of Hesse-Hanau and Brunswick. His good looks and hearty, jovial manner were infectious, and he was an intelligent, quick-witted commander. His force consisted of the Regiments Rhetz, Riedesel, Specht, Barner, Hesse-Hanau, a regiment of grenadiers, and a regiment of dragoons (who had no horses). There was also a company of Hesse-Hanau artillery commanded by the redoubtable Captain Pausch.[1]

The German mercenaries were the ministry's answer to England's troop shortage. For almost a century the rulers of the central European states had used their armies as a lucrative source of income. Although American propagandists and the Opposition in Parliament professed to be shocked that "the German slave had been hired to subdue the sons of Englishmen and freedom," Great Britain had often employed such troops during the Second Hundred Years' War. In fact the availability of these troops was one of the reasons why England and other nations were able to maintain such small standing armies.

The treaty that was concluded with the Duke of Brunswick in January, 1776, was fairly typical. The soldiers were hired at the rate of £7.4s:4½d. per man plus an annual subsidy of £11,500 and a payment of £46,000 when the troops had completed their service. The Duke was also to be compensated "at the rate of the levy money" for every soldier who was killed or wounded. Altogether the 5,700 troops furnished from Brunswick cost the royal treasury about £150,000. During the entire course of the war nearly 30,000 German troops served in America.

The soldiers from the German states were recruited and trained much like those of the British army, although the pressure of the despotic dukes and princes on recruiting officers made them more indiscriminate and heavy-handed. The regiments contained not only the usual number of unemployed vagrants and drifters but "foreigners," that is, those not native to the dukedom or principality. A student travelling from Leipzig to Paris found himself impressed into a regiment of Hesse-Cassel along with "a bankrupt tradesman from Vienna, a fringemaker from Hanover, a discarded secretary of the post-office from Gotha, a monk from Wurzburg . . . a Prussian sergeant of hussars, [and] a cashiered Hessian major. . . ." Yet, like the British regular, the German recruit became a disciplined, tough, efficient soldier.

The Brunswickers in Burgoyne's army included a company of jägers who were armed with short, heavy rifles; there was also a considerable number of musicians. The latter were considered very important for the morale of the troops and the soldiers often marched into battle not only with bands playing but with the soldiers themselves singing lustily.

It was natural that there should be some friction between the British and the Germans. Captain Pausch thought it was because "the Devil of Jealousy has been aroused because the English see that my men drill quicker and more promptly, and because, also, the spectators do us the justice publicly to acknowledge this to be the case." There were occasional fights between the two nationalities, and at one point an order was issued forbidding the Germans from carrying side arms. Captain Pausch entered a strenuous protest "since were they to depend on boxing for protection, some would return to Germany cross-eyed and some blind." General Riedesel and Burgoyne seem to have gotten along well enough although the German complained that Burgoyne did not consult him or keep him informed of plans and operations.[2]

The total of Burgoyne's regular rank and file, then, numbered about 6,600 men. To cover the two wings of the army and to provide scouts, artificers and other auxiliaries Burgoyne hoped to recruit 2,000 Canadians and Loyalists and 1,000 Indians. British expectations were, as usual, far beyond reality. The French *habitants* were impassively apathetic, "awkward, ignorant, disinclined to the service, spiritless." Only 150 could be enlisted and to these were added about 100 Loyalists. This force was to act as a screen for Phillips' right wing.

Riedesel's screen was made up of Indians. Burgoyne expected to recruit a large force of warriors and on the surface this appeared to be a reasonable expectation. Western New York was the homeland of the powerful Iroquois Confederacy whose allegiance to the British dated back to the first European settlements in North America. Samuel de Champlain had accompanied a war party of Algonquins against the Iroquois in 1609 and thus the struggle between England and France for control of North America paralleled the hereditary hostility between the Iroquois and the Algonquins.

In more recent years Sir William Johnson, the Indian superintendent for the Northern Department, had cemented the alliance by marrying Molly Brant, sister of the Mohawk chief, Joseph Brant. Sir William had spent a lifetime in close association with the Indians. He knew their ways, was sympathetic to their interests, and had taken care to see that they received continuous government subsidies. He had built a fortress-like "castle" on the upper Mohawk which became known as Johnstown, and at his death in 1774 his son, Sir John, assumed his father's duties. He was assisted by Guy Johnson, a distant relative, Daniel Claus, Sir William's son-in-law, and John and Walter Butler. All were Loyalists and all held commissions in the militia of Tryon County, which included the whole Mohawk Valley west of Schenectady.

Yet this seemingly powerful hold on the Six Nations was seriously weakened soon after the outbreak of the war by the genius and determination of General Philip Schuyler. The Butlers and Guy Johnson went to Canada at the outbreak of hostilities, but Sir John remained at Johnstown surrounded by a guard of 150 Mohawk braves. In January, 1776, Schuyler marched on Johnstown with 3,000 militiamen at his back and arrested the Indian superintendent. He convinced the Indians that their territory would be respected if they would stay out of the white man's fight. Overawed by the militia, the Indians agreed. When Johnson was released on parole he fled to Canada. All this damaged British prestige severely and the Indians were in a dubious frame of mind when Burgoyne called them to a council at St. Johns on the middle of June, 1777. Here he issued a proclamation calling on them to "go forth in the might of your valour and your cause;—strike at the common enemies of Great Britain and America;—and disturbers of the public order, peace and happiness; destroyers of Commerce; parracides of the state."

It may have been the idea of Indians restoring law and order in America that reduced Lord North to tears of laughter when the proclamation was read in Parliament. Or it may have been when Burgoyne insisted that the Indians give "most serious attention to the rules" which forbade the killing of women, children, prisoners, and the aged. "You will receive compensation for the prisoners you take," continued Gentleman Johnny, "but you shall be called to account for scalps."[3]

The proclamation elicited a sonorous response from Indian orators at the Council and enthusiastic whoops from the assembled warriors, but only 400 of the expected 1,000 responded. Only after the word had spread to the far western tribes did another 400 drift in, lured by the prospect of loot. The Indians, in fact, became a chronic source of irritation to Burgoyne who was constantly pestered by demands for money, supplies, and ammunition, and their irregular comings and goings made them difficult to control. Their leader was

St. Luc de la Corne, a sixty-five year old French Canadian, veteran of the
frontier wars who had just served fourteen months in a Yankee prison.

Taken together Burgoyne's total effective force of Indians, provincials,
and regulars was about 7,500 rank and file. But there was another way of
looking at the invasion force which might well have given its commander a
pause. Adding officers, non-commissioned officers, civilian employees, and
camp followers, Burgoyne had over 10,000 mouths to feed. As was usual with
British armies there were a number of women, and not only camp followers.
Several officers' wives and their women servants accompanied the army.
Among these were the Baroness Riedesel, with her three children aged one
to six, and Lady Harriet Acland who was pregnant.

Artillery, supplies, and equipage necessitated a tremendous amount of transport. Burgoyne's commissary general estimated that it would take 1,125 carts
to haul rations for the entire force for 30 days. Carleton had neglected this
phase of the expedition's preparation and Burgoyne waited a month after his
arrival at Quebec before he requested 400 horses for his artillery train and
another 1,000 animals to draw 500 carts carrying his provisions. The carts
were hastily built of green wood and the quartermaster procured less than
half the number of horses which had been requisitioned. This was not thought
to be serious at the time since the principal objective of the army was Ticonderoga at the upper edge of Lake Champlain and could be approached by
water. Burgoyne expected that once this American strong point was reduced
the way to the Hudson and Albany would be open. Transportation between
the lake and the river was a problem which would be met in due time. The distance, after all, was only twenty miles.

By the middle of June the army was assembled at St. John's on the Riche-
lieu, and Carleton came up from Montreal to take formal leave of Burgoyne.
On June 14 a review was held under the royal standard, a banner rarely dis-
played except in the presence of the monarch. It bore the three golden lions of
England, the red lion of Scotland, the harp of Ireland, and the *fleur-de-lis*, that
quaint symbol of the ancient claims of English sovereigns to the throne of
France. After appropriate rounds of wining and dining and the firing of salutes
Carleton returned to Quebec and Burgoyne embarked his army.

By June 21 the various contingents of soldiers, Indians, sailors and camp
followers had made their way up the Richelieu and debouched into the lower
end of Lake Champlain. There they formed into a spectacular column, the
Indians leading in their big war canoes. Then came two ship-rigged schoon-
ers, *Royal George* and *Inflexible*, followed by a long line of bateaux crowded
with colors: red-coated British infantry; the green of the jägers; the blue coats
of the Brunswickers, with their glittering cap plates; "in such perfect regular-
ity as to form the most complete and splendid regatta you can possibly conceive." A closer scrutiny would have revealed that the red coats had been
trimmed down to jackets by cutting off the skirts, that many of the Brunswickers were ill shod, and that the whole army was somewhat threadbare after a

year in Canada. But the soldiers were in good spirits from the generals down to the German privates who strained at the oars of the bateaux. "At first they made bad work with it; but after a while they rowed nicely," observed Captain Pausch.

By June 30 the invaders had reached Crown Point, fifteen miles north of Ticonderoga. Here Burgoyne issued the last of his exhortations, an order to the army. For once he was brief and to the point:

> The army embarks tomorrow, to approach the enemy. We are to contend for the King, the Constitution of Great Britain, to vindicate the Law, and to relieve the oppressed—a cause in which His Majesty's Troops and those of the Princes his Allies, feel equal excitement. The services required of this particular expedition, are critical and conspicuous. During our progress occasions may occur, in which, nor difficulty, nor labor, nor life are to be regarded. This Army must not Retreat.[4]

TICONDEROGA

Ticonderoga was built on a high bluff overlooking the narrow neck of water at the upper end of Lake Champlain. Stretching to the south and east an arm of the lake continued for almost twenty miles to Skenesboro. Lake George formed a parallel arm to the west connected to Lake Champlain by an unnavigable creek.

The fort was commanded by Major General Arthur St. Clair. As a twenty-two year old ensign in the 60th Regiment he had fought with Wolfe at Quebec. After the Seven Years' War he had settled in America and become a wealthy Pennsylvania land owner. He served in Canada in 1776 and had commanded a militia regiment at Trenton. Promoted to major general he was sent to the Northern Department in June to replace Gates as commander at Ticonderoga. Although the fort had undergone considerable repairs since its capture by the Americans in 1775, its defense still posed a number of problems.

In order to understand the geography of Ticonderoga it should be remembered that Lake Champlain makes a turn to the west so that a vessel sailing through the narrows to the upper arm of the lake is heading only one or two points south of due west. The headland on which the fort was located lay less than half a mile from the opposite shore which was dominated by a hill called Mount Independence. Since it was within cannon shot of Ticonderoga it had to be fortified. The American garrison had connected Mount Independence with the fort by a boat bridge and had constructed a log and chain boom across the narrows. They believed that this would effectively block the passage of vessels into the upper arm of Lake Champlain. They had also cleared a rough track through the forest from Mount Independence eastward to Hubbardton to link with the main road to the Hampshire Grants in Vermont. To the southwest of Fort Ticonderoga another hill called Sugar Loaf rose 800 feet above the lake. Although it was only 1800 yards from the fort its slopes were considered too steep and rugged to allow guns to be mounted. The land approaches from the west were protected by a crescent-shaped series of trenches and redoubts called "the old French lines." Finally, to the northwest was Mount Hope which guarded the road and the stream from Lake George. Altogether Ticonderoga and its supporting positions constituted 2,000 yards of lines, fortifications and outworks.

The fort had been built originally by the French in 1755 and subsequent occupants had added to and refined it along lines dictated by European military engineers. Because it had figured so prominently in the military history of North America Ticonderoga had acquired an impressive mystique as the "Gibraltar of North America." Its complex of lines and ramparts epitomized the kind of strong point which figured so prominently in the European doctrine of strategic posts guarding important geographic areas. The British were sure that Ticonderoga was the key to the conquest of New York, if not the entire continent, and Americans, including General Washington, thought so too. Their political ideology might be revolutionary but American military strategy was orthodox European.[5]

The very complexity of the fortress was its greatest point of weakness. The French, the English, and now the Americans found that establishing and maintaining a garrison large enough to man the entire works presented formidable problems in logistics. This was why the fort had fallen so easily to the Americans in 1775, and it may well have been the consideration that led Carleton to abandon the upper end of Lake Champlain in 1776.

A garrison post imposes an especial strain on discipline. Although General St. Clair put the American soldiers to work repairing and strengthening the trenches and block houses, they complained that this was not proper duty for soldiers. Long weeks and months in this distant outpost were tedious and the troops became bored and quarrelsome—and sick. "Our men are harassed to extreme weakness by fatigue. . . . what can be expected from a naked, undisciplined, badly armed, unaccoutred body of men? . . ." The New York legislature, despite the nagging insistence of General Schuyler, was no more willing to furnish supplies in 1777 than they had been in 1776. Schuyler in desperation dispensed $10,000 of his own money, and his reward was to be charged with mishandling of government funds. During the winter of 1776–1777 Congress had yielded to blandishments of the friends of General Horatio Gates by making him commander of Ticonderoga, semi-independent of the command of the Northern Department. Schuyler blew up and went to Philadelphia to demand an investigation. By late spring the issue was apparently resolved to Schuyler's satisfaction. Gates refused to serve under Schuyler and St. Clair succeeded him, arriving at Ticonderoga on June 12, 1777.

There he found what was left of ten Continental and two militia regiments, some of only forty-five men, the largest 265. Major Benjamin Whitcomb had nineteen scouts, Thomas Lee about the same number of rangers and there were perhaps 375 artificers. Altogether the garrison numbered about 2,500 men present and fit for duty. Had they manned the entire position from Mount Independence to the old French lines there would have been about one man per yard. St. Clair had three brigadier generals as subordinates, the Frenchman Roche de Fermoy, John Paterson of Massachusetts, and Enoch Poor of New Hampshire.

General Schuyler arrived on June 19 to confer with St. Clair. Although Burgoyne had complained that "the whole design of the campaign" had been published in Canada "almost as accurately as if it had been copied from the Secretary of State's letter," the news had not reached St. Clair. Congress had heard that the Canadian army would move by sea, presumably either to Boston or New York. Schuyler himself was dubious about the feasibility of defending Ticonderoga but "without orders from Congress, he dare not undertake on himself the responsibility of a measure [retreat] which would create a great outcry." So reported young Colonel James Wilkinson who had been appointed deputy adjutant by Gates and continued to serve under Schuyler. On June 20 a council of war was held. It concluded that both sides of the lake should be defended but that if they were attacked by a major force of the enemy, "the number of troops now at this post, which are under 2,500 effectives, rank and file, are greatly inadequate to the defense; . . ." and that "we think it would be imprudent to expose the army to be made prisoners by the enemy; and that, therefore, it is prudent to provide for a retreat." The council recommended that the retreat follow two lines, by the road east to Hubbardton and Castleton, and by boat southward up Lake Champlain.[6]

Although Schuyler was present at the council his views are not recorded. He left Ticonderoga and shortly afterward appealed to Washington for help. Washington, threatened by Howe's army in New Jersey, could only agree to "hold in readiness" four regiments in the Hudson Highlands. In the midst of all this uncertainty only General Gates, whose many faults did not include bad military instincts, predicted that Burgoyne would move south in force to link up with Howe and control the Hudson.

By the last week in June St. Clair knew that a British force was on the lake. Although Major Whitcomb was a seasoned veteran of frontier warfare he and his scouts could not penetrate the screen of Indians under the skillful leadership of St. Luc de la Corne. The American commander finally concluded that the slowness of the enemy's advance was caused by his hesitancy in attacking the fort; he therefore must have a small force. It seems not to have occurred to St. Clair that a very large force, with its artillery and baggage, would also move slowly.

Burgoyne reached Crown Point in the last week in June and set up a temporary base. From there he moved his troops to a point about three miles from Ticonderoga and began to disembark. Fraser's advance corps and the British right wing were assigned to the western side of the lake with Riedesel and the Germans on the east. On July 2 Burgoyne ordered the advance. Riedesel's command was to move against Mount Independence and seal off the road to Hubbardton. Fraser was ordered to circle to the west and attack the old French lines. He also expected to cut off the garrison at Mount Hope, but St. Clair forestalled him. Early on the morning of the 2nd the garrison set fire to their works and hurried into the American lines.

Fraser's attack was a comedy of errors on both sides. The British advance was screened by Indians directed by Captain Fraser, the general's nephew. The Indians were drunk, and, their courage thus emboldened, they dashed helter-skelter toward the American positions, sweeping Captain Fraser and some of the regulars along with them.

General St. Clair took personal charge of the American defenses. He ordered his inexperienced men to sit down on the firing step and wait for his order, hoping that their inability to see the advancing enemy would keep them from firing (or running) prematurely. But it was his own adjutant, the ubiquitous Colonel Wilkinson, who spoiled the game. As a few British skirmishers moved within musket range the eager young colonel took it upon himself to order a sergeant to fire at one of the exposed redcoats. At the sound of the shot the defenders, officers and men alike, sprang to their feet and discharged a thunderous fusillade. Most of the muskets were pointed "at an elevation of twenty degrees, and the artillery without any direction." When the heavy cloud of smoke finally eddied away the attackers were running like mad, but only two Indians and one soldier had fallen before the awesome volley. The light infantryman whose reckless exposure had provoked Colonel Wilkinson was one of the fallen, but he was found to have succumbed to liquor rather than lead.[7]

It was this prisoner, in fact, who gave St. Clair his first real knowledge of what he was up against. Placed in confinement, the soldier was deceived by a fellow "prisoner" who posed as a Tory and St. Clair was apprized of the fact that he faced an overwhelming force of regulars. If he needed further convincing a new development soon made his situation critical.

The evacuation of Mount Hope gave the British access to the Sugar Loaf. One of Burgoyne's engineers, Lieutenant Twiss, reported to General Phillips that he thought a battery could be gotten to the summit. The old artilleryman was quick to seize the opportunity. "Where a goat can go a man can go and where a man can go he can drag a gun," he said and turned his furious energy to the task. By the morning of July 5 the British had a battery mounted which commanded both the interior of the fort and the narrows of the lake.

St. Clair did not hesitate. He paused only long enough for a hasty council of war to confirm his decision and then ordered a retreat. The baggage, the sick, and a guard of 600 soldiers were loaded into boats and evacuated up Lake Champlain towards Skenesboro. The rest of the army crossed the bridge under cover of darkness to Mount Independence. Scouts reported that the road to Hubbardton was still open so the army began its withdrawal. So silently did the Americans move that not until almost daylight did General Fraser realize they were gone.

Without waiting for orders the commander of the advance corps hastily assembled 750 men and took the road in pursuit. Burgoyne ordered Riedesel to follow with a supporting force. But St. Clair was moving too fast. By late afternoon of July 6th he had reached Hubbardton where he left a rear guard under Colonel Seth Warner to delay the pursuit. St. Clair and the rest of his force pushed on to Castleton. Altogether it was a highly creditable performance. St. Clair had marched almost thirty miles in a day losing only about fifteen percent of his force as stragglers, many of whom caught up with Warner. The July heat brought Fraser to a halt three miles short of Hubbardton.

Warner's force camped for the night, a violation of St. Clair's orders to follow the main force to Castleton. Moreover the inexperienced colonel failed to post pickets, although he must have known that the British were close on his heels. His rear guard consisted of three undermanned Continental regiments which, together with the stragglers, amounted to about 800 men.

At dawn on July 7 Fraser surprised the Americans at breakfast and drove Nathan Hale's New Hampshire regiment right out of the fight. But Warner recovered quickly and established a line that checked the British advance with a galling fire. The British took more than twenty casualties including Major Grant of the 24th killed and the Earl of Balcarres who was wounded. Fraser sent his grenadiers clawing and scrambling up the steep hill overlooking the American left flank, but was soon threatened on his own left by Colonel Turbott Francis' Massachusetts regiment. As the fight raged back and forth Riedesel's German advance guard arrived, a company of jägers and eighty grenadiers and light infantry. Fraser was on the point of launching a bayonet attack in a desperate effort to stop the threat to his right flank. Riedesel drove the jägers straight in to his support and swung the rest of his small force up the hill against the opposite flank. Warner's men wavered and then broke as Colonel Francis was shot dead. Warner ordered his troops to disperse and rendezvous at Manchester.

The little battle, the first real encounter between Burgoyne's invasion force and the troops of the Northern Department, was notable for several reasons. It was a bloody business, for the combined British and German losses were 198 killed and wounded, including fifteen officers. This was more than twenty percent of their force. The American losses were 325 killed, wounded, and captured. After the initial panic of Hale's troops Warner's men had done well, firing from cover and severely punishing Fraser's command. This was the kind of fighting they understood best, but it could not cope with Fraser's aggressiveness. In the end, discipline and bayonets drove the Continentals from the field. Finally, although the British chronically complained about the ponderous slowness of the Germans, Riedesel's troops had kept pace with Fraser's advance corps, and the little German had shown unerring judgement in directing his 120 men to the key points to break the American line.

The noise of the battle reached St. Clair at Castleton. He sent his aides to direct two militia regiments who were within supporting distance to go to Warner's assistance. The militia declined and St. Clair's own troops displayed a mutinous reluctance to join the fight. Wearily, the general turned eastward toward Schuyler's headquarters on the Hudson.

Meantime, the remaining Americans with the baggage and sick were making their way up the southern arm of Lake Champlain. Believing the log boom would deter pursuit by water, they arrived at Skenesboro and began leisurely unloading their boats. But the British were only a few hours behind. A few well-aimed cannon shots had broken the boom and the enemy followed hard on the heels of the fugitives. Their attack sent the small American force flying to the southeast where they took refuge at Fort Anne, a tumble-down stockade halfway to the Hudson. Here they stood off a small force of British pursuers and then made their way to Fort Edward on the Hudson where they found General Schuyler with a corporal's guard of 700 men.

The pursuit of the Americans had left Burgoyne's army scattered all over the landscape between Ticonderoga, Hubbardton, and Skenesboro. Troops were separated from their baggage and commands were dispersed. Riedesel brought his advance corps in on July 8 and the next day Fraser's chewed up brigade came up with over 200 American prisoners. The wounded on both sides had been left on the field at Hubbardton. By July 11 Burgoyne had reassembled his scattered forces at Skenesboro. The great American fortress at Ticonderoga had fallen and the way to Albany was open.[8] There was, however, one small fly in Burgoyne's ointment. He had expected that Carleton would garrison Ticonderoga, but the governor-general pointed out that he had positive orders from Germain that he was to have no authority over the expedition once it left Canada. Burgoyne was forced to leave more than 900 redcoats and Brunswickers to man the defenses of the fortress.

THE SPIDER AND THE FLY

The fall of Ticonderoga generated shock waves in England and America. Its exaggerated importance as the key to the continent produced unwonted despair in Philadelphia, and jubilation in Whitehall. When the news reached London George III is said to have rushed into the Queen's chambers (surprising her in her chemise) exclaiming, "I have beat them! I have beat all the Americans!"

Across the channel in Paris the news reached Benjamin Franklin early in September. The French foreign minister, the Comte de Vergennes, had been under increasing pressure from the British to call a halt to the aid being furnished to the United States. Whitehall was particularly incensed that Vergennes permitted American privateers entry to French ports. The French and their Spanish allies were beginning to bristle as much at English arrogance as at English demands. Franklin hoped that Louis XVI was reaching the point where he could be persuaded to redress the European balance of power by depriving England of thirteen of her American colonies. The news of Ticonderoga brought such expectations to an abrupt halt.

In Philadelphia there was dismay on all sides and savage denunciations of Schuyler, especially from the New Englanders. They now felt vindicated in their support of Gates for command of the Northern Department. "I think we shall never be able to defend a post until we shoot a general," exclaimed John Adams. For General Washington the news was "an event of chagrin and surprise, not apprehended nor within the compass of my reasoning. . . ." This stroke is severe indeed, and has distressed us much."

Schuyler protested that "not the most distant Hint of such an Intention [to withdraw from Ticonderoga] can be drawn from any of my Letters to General St. Clair," but he was silent about the council of war on June 20. Nor could he show any positive order for St. Clair to defend the fort in the face of a superior enemy. St. Clair himself did not quibble. "It was done," he said, "in consequence of a consultation with the other general officers . . . and had their opinion been contrary to what it was, it would have nevertheless taken place, because I knew it would be impossible to defend the post with our numbers. . . . I may have the satisfaction to experience that although I have lost a post I have eventually saved a state."[9]

As the clamor over his behavior swelled Schuyler went to Fort Edward to do what he could to restore the situation. Twenty-three miles separated him from Burgoyne's base at Skenesboro. Although the region divided the basin of Lake Champlain from the valley of the Hudson there were no mountains or even high hills to mark the watersheds. In 1777 the land was heavily wooded and crisscrossed by streams which meandered sluggishly through swampland which covered much of the country. A single rough track led from Skenesboro along Wood Creek to Fort Anne, the tumble-down relic of the Seven Years' War. Here the fugitives from the retreat had checked the British pursuit on July 7 before withdrawing the remaining ten miles to the Hudson.

Schuyler reached Fort Edward that same day, and for almost a week he boldly held his position with less than a thousand men. Finally St. Clair came in from Castleton and Colonel John Nixon arrived from Peekskill with 600 Continentals. This brought Schuyler's command to just under 4,500 men, a mixed body of 2,800 Continentals and about 1,600 militia.

Schuyler did not intend to make a stand at Fort Edward, but he did want to make life as miserable as possible for the British. Emboldened by the fact that Burgoyne sent no advance parties to secure the route to the Hudson the American commander sent a thousand axmen back into the woods and swamps. They systematically destroyed every bridge and causeway. They dug ditches to divert streams and turned stretches of the road into muddy bogs. For days their axes rang through the virgin timber, felling huge trees so that the branches interlaced to create a nightmare tangle along the road.

Schuyler urged the few settlers to drive off their livestock and burn their crops so that there would be no forage or food for the invaders. The axmen pressed as far north as Fort Anne but except for occasional harassment by Burgoyne's Indians the British made no attempt to halt their work.

Having created a veritable jungle to delay the enemy Schuyler abandoned the ramshackle works at Fort Edward and withdrew his force down the Hudson to Saratoga. There he halted and sent out urgent pleas for reinforcements, but he was losing men by desertion almost as fast as he gained recruits. On July 24 Wilkinson reported that "in the short space of five days, our continental force was reduced to less than 3,000, and our militia to about 1,300 men . . . the greatest part badly armed, and both men and officers half-naked, sickly and destitute. . . . Our troops . . . instead of recovering confidence, lost spirit; and the panic became more general than ever."

By August 3 Schuyler had retreated again, this time to Stillwater, twenty-five miles south of Fort Edward. The constant withdrawal in the face of the enemy was calculated to make Burgoyne's line of communication at Ticonderoga more tenuous, but it nevertheless fueled the criticism of Schuyler which had been mounting ever since the abandonment of Ticonderoga. His appeals to Washington for help placed the commander in chief in a dilemma. General Howe had embarked his army on transports on July 23 and disappeared over the Atlantic horizon; with his destination unknown Washington hesitated to send more reinforcements northward. In an effort to stimulate militia response in New England he dispatched Benedict Arnold and Benjamin Lincoln to report to Schuyler.[10]

Arnold was the most experienced combat officer in the army. His knack for inspiring loyalty in the men under his command suggested that he might instill some of his own fighting spirit into the troops on the Hudson. Arnold's quarrelsome, abrasive personality kept him in constant hot water with Congress and his military superiors, and was probably responsible for the delay in his promotion. But he respected and admired George Washington, and his service under Schuyler in 1776 had resulted in mutual confidence and a curious affinity between this tough, hard fighter and the aristocratic patroon.

Washington had at first probably judged Benjamin Lincoln too much by appearances, but finally recognized that he "was an abler man than his great bulk and loose jowel would indicate." Lincoln had caught the commander in chief's eye while serving as a general in the Massachusetts militia. Washington had paid him the compliment of mistakenly recommending him for promotion to major general of the Continental Line and Congress had complied. Lincoln reported to Schuyler who promptly dispatched him to New England to recruit militia.

Schuyler's delaying tactics began to bear fruit, unpopular though they were. Burgoyne was now at the point where he had to make some critical decisions. He must now abandon the easy water communication with Ticonderoga and Canada. He might have retraced his steps to the foot of Lake

George and moved south by this western arm to a point only nine miles from the Hudson. But this would have involved hauling his bateaux and artillery across the portage below Ticonderoga. According to Captain John Money, Burgoyne's quartermaster, "it would have taken a fortnight to transport 400 bateaux from Lake Champlain to Lake George. . . ." The British commander accordingly decided to move his troops directly from Skenesboro to Fort Edward and use the Lake George route for his provisions and supplies.

Burgoyne also decided to take most of his artillery, for which he was later severely criticized. But he reasoned that "artillery was extremely formidable against raw troops." Also the Americans might be expected to adopt defenses "at which they were beyond all other nations expert . . . that of entrenchment covered with strong abbatis, against which the cannon, of the nature of the heaviest described [24-pounders], and howitzers, might often be effectual, when to dislodge them by any other means might be attended with continued and important losses." And artillery would be necessary for "the intention of fortifying a camp at Albany."

It took the British several days to collect their scattered forces and their baggage after their headlong pursuit of the Americans. By July 10 they had begun the laborious task of clearing away the ruin left by Schuyler's axmen. It was heavy work and the engineering parties were harassed by the sultry summer heat, and clouds of gnats and mosquitoes. At the outset a causeway two miles long had to be constructed across the worst of the swamp. Heavy rains made the streams run full and British working parties were obliged to build over forty bridges. Axmen, most of them Canadians, struggled to clear the tangle of trees, their branches so densely matted that they could not be hauled aside, but had to be cut through. Nearly a week was consumed in opening the road to Fort Anne and it was not until July 24 that the road to Fort Edward was finally clear. Burgoyne took four days to move fourteen miles to Fort Anne. On the 28th, Fraser's advance corps was sent forward and two days later the British right wing occupied Fort Edward. Bringing up the rear Riedesel's Germans came in and by August 9 Burgoyne's entire force was finally assembled on the Hudson.[11]

There now ensued another delay. Ammunition and stores for thirty days had to be assembled and bateaux dragged across from Fort George, for Burgoyne intended to use the river to transport his supplies. It was to be almost a month before the British were prepared to cut their communication with Canada and make the final dash to Albany.

Meantime the general and his officers were enjoying what ease they could find in the North American wilderness. ". . . Burgoyne liked having a jolly time of it and spending half the night singing and drinking and amusing himself in the company of the wife of the commissary, who was his mistress and, like him, loved champaign." There seems to have been plenty of food and drink although Burgoyne had ordered that "officers are depended on not to encumber the service with more baggage than shall be absolutely necessary."

But headquarters did not stint and Baron Riedesel found himself the recipient of occasional cases of Madeira. The Baroness Riedesel and Lady Acland joined the army in the middle of August. "The surrounding country was magnificent" related the little baroness, ". . . when it was beautiful weather we took our meals under the trees. . . . It was at this place I eat bear's flesh for the first time, and found it of capital flavor."[12]

On August 3 Burgoyne received a dispatch from Sir William Howe, dated July 17: "My intention is for Philadelphia, where I expect to meet Washington; but if he goes to the northward, contrary to my expectations, and you can keep him at bay, be assured I shall soon be after him to relieve you. . . . Sir Henry Clinton remains in command here [New York], and will act as occurrences may direct." Burgoyne does not seem to have been perturbed by this news. Nor did he show any alarm over the delays which daily consumed his supplies and cost him wear and tear on his transport. Having spent more than a month on the road from Skenesboro to Fort Edward, he appeared unconcerned at the prospect of abandoning his supply line with thirty days provisions to reach an objective more than fifty miles away.

Whether the idea of drawing the British farther and farther from Ticonderoga and Canada before engaging them was a preconceived strategy of the American high command is an open question. But by midsummer its merit was obvious. General Washington gave it expression in mid-August when he advised:

Independent of the Inconveniences that attend a Situation, where the Rear and Flank are constantly exposed to the insults of light parties which may be at every moment harassing them; the necessity of never losing sight of the means of a Secure Retreat, which ought to be the first object of an Officer's Care, must be exceedingly embarrassing where there is a Force in such a position as to endanger it. If a respectable Body of Men were to be Stationed on the Grants, it would undoubtedly have the effect intimated above, would render it not a little difficult for Mr. Bourgoigne to keep the necessary Communication open, and they would frequently afford opportunities of intercepting his Convoys.[13]

LORD GEORGE GERMAIN
Joshua Reynolds
COURTESY OF THE CLEMENTS LIBRARY,
UNIVERSITY OF MICHIGAN

GEORGE THE THIRD
Allan Ramsey
COURTESY OF COLONIAL WILLIAMSBURG

JOHN BURGOYNE
Joshua Reynolds
COURTESY OF THE FRICK COLLECTION

SIR WILLIAM HOWE
C. Corbutt
COURTESY OF THE CLEMENTS LIBRARY,
UNIVERSITY OF MICHIGAN

GEN. SIR WILLIAM HOWE
BRITISH COMMANDER IN CHIEF M.P.
From an English print 1777

DANIEL MORGAN
C. W. Peale
COURTESY OF THE INDEPENDENCE
NATIONAL HISTORICAL PARK

HORATIO GATES
C. W. Peale
COURTESY OF THE INDEPENDENCE
NATIONAL HISTORICAL PARK

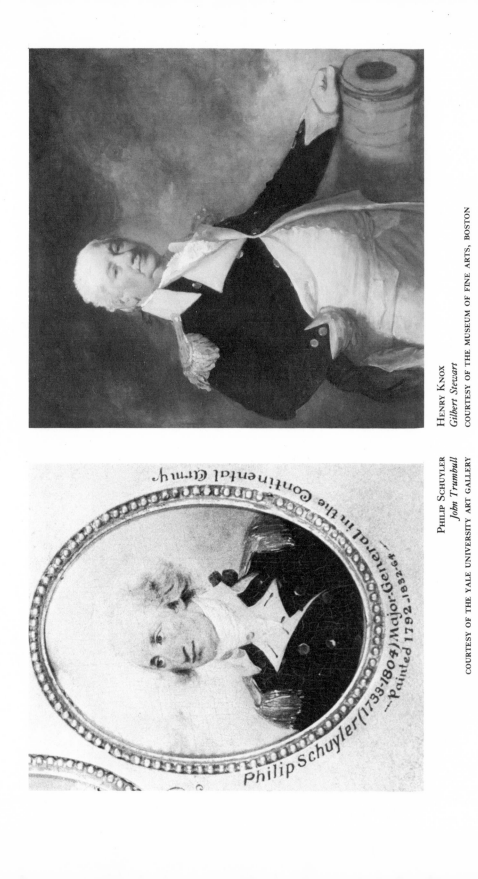

PHILIP SCHUYLER
John Trumbull
COURTESY OF THE YALE UNIVERSITY ART GALLERY

HENRY KNOX
Gilbert Stewart
COURTESY OF THE MUSEUM OF FINE ARTS, BOSTON

NATHANAEL GREENE
C. W. Peale
COURTESY OF THE INDEPENDENCE
NATIONAL HISTORICAL PARK

SIR HENRY CLINTON
A. H. Ritchie
COURTESY OF THE CLEMENTS LIBRARY,
UNIVERSITY OF MICHIGAN

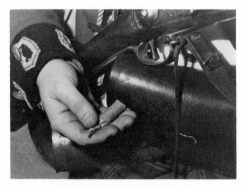

1. " . . . handle cartridge"

2. " . . . tear cartridge"

Firing a Musket

3. " . . . prime"

4. " . . . close frizzen"

5. " . . . load"

6. " . . . ram"

7. " . . . full cock"

8. " . . . fire!"

9. A "soldier" of the 42nd
Highlanders

" . . . those dear, ragged Continentals."
Trego
COURTESY OF THE VALLEY FORGE HISTORICAL SOCIETY

NINE

The Gathering Storm

As HE PAUSED ON THE HUDSON, PREPARING HIS ARMY FOR THE FINAL DRIVE on Albany, Burgoyne was confident. Ticonderoga had fallen and the enemy was scattered into the hills of Vermont. Only Schuyler's little army, not much more than half his own numbers, stood in his way, and it appeared doubtful if they intended to stand and fight. There were rumors that the Loyalists were increasing in strength and boldness, "and I have certain intelligence that the country around Fort Stanwix is in alarm." Burgoyne shared with Germain the assumption that the populace of northern New York awaited only the appearance of his triumphant army to display their loyalty to the Crown.[1]

THE CRISIS IN NEW YORK

New York was a prime example of the geo-politics of the American Revolution. The entire length of the Appalachian ridge from New England to the southern coastal plain is broken in only two places and both are in New York. One is the Champlain basin. The other is the Mohawk Valley, not as well travelled by the armies of the eighteenth century, but destined to become vastly more important as the transportation link between the Hudson and the Great Lakes. The state itself lies like a wedge between New England and the states to the south. This geography gave New York a political and imperial importance beyond that of any other region in the United States. On the upper Mohawk river in Tryon County Sir William Johnson and his son, Sir Guy, presided over the affairs of the Six Nations of the Iroquois Confederacy and of all the tribes of the Northern Department. At the confluence of the Mohawk and the Hudson Albany was the *entrepôt* for the fur trade. At the mouth of the Hudson New York city was already gaining recognition as potentially the greatest port in North America. Here were not only the headquarters for the British army and navy but the center of supply contractors and merchant factors for British trading firms which gave the city closer ties with England and Europe. Its population of 25,000 was twelve percent of the population of the entire state, and it dominated the Lower Counties.

The first test of strength in the revolutionary crisis came in the wake of the meeting of the First Continental Congress. That body's passage of resolutions for nonimportation, nonexportation, and nonconsumption of British goods was accompanied by a recommendation that each colony create "associations" to urge the enforcement of the resolutions. Collectively these were known as the Continental Association.

This recommendation was duly considered by the Committee of Fifty-One of New York city originally set up in the spring of 1774 as a committee of correspondence. Although the group was committed to opposing ministerial and Parliamentary policy, especially the Intolerable Acts, it contained a considerable number of conservatives who eventually could be called Whig-Loyalists. The committee passed Congress' recommendation along to the towns and counties for action, but the response of local leaders was apathetic. The more conservative group was centered around the DeLancey family while the moderates looked to the Livingstons for guidance. These two factions may well have been contending as much for power as for principle, and it is confusing to label them as radicals or conservatives. The Tory party (DeLanceys) included many who accepted the idea of the Association but who were reluctant to sacrifice their financial interests or to entertain any idea of disloyalty to the Crown. The true radicals, mostly in New York city, denounced the Committee of the Fifty-One for foot-dragging and accused DeLanceys and Livingstons alike of being obstructionist and delaying the implementation of the boycott. The moderates gave in to the pressure by inducing the colonial assembly to send petitions of remonstrance to the King.

The critical point was reached in the spring of 1775 when the Whigs called on the legislative assembly to vote approval of the actions of the First Continental Congress and to choose delegates for the Second Continental Congress which was about to convene. The assembly refused, and the Whigs thereupon abandoned the legal machinery of the colony and elected their own Provincial Congress. The DeLancey group lost considerable prestige, but continued to lend at least token support to the struggle for American rights. Whig-Loyalists such as John Jay, William Duane, and Isaac Low continued to carry considerable weight with the moderates, while the radicals led by Isaac Sears and Alexander McDougall attempted to force the revolutionary movement into more militant opposition to the home government.[2]

Yet the radicals were unable to seize the initiative, to overwhelm the conservatives as the Adamses had done in Massachusetts, or Patrick Henry and Thomas Jefferson in Virginia. There were several reasons for their failure. Perhaps most important was the fact that the DeLancey faction did not take an adamant stand of unqualified support for the Crown. They retained their influence on the new Committee of Sixty and their presence probably accounted for the lack of a viable network of county committees of safety. Moreover, the Committee of Sixty, the dominant revolutionary organization in the colony, was beset by internecine frictions and quarrels which constantly threatened its facade of unity.

Another factor was the intelligent leadership of Governor William Tryon and his deputy, Cadwallader Colden. Tryon had already served as governor of North Carolina when he came to New York in 1771. He was a capable administrator and a good politician, and in the beginning he announced that he "would not be dealt with or crossed for Party Purposes." He judiciously courted the Livingston group through appointments and other political favors and maintained a nice balance between amiability and tolerance on the one hand, and firm assertion of authority on the other. By coincidence he returned from a leave of absence in England on the same day that General Washington passed through New York on his way to command the troops at Boston. The citizenry greeted the general enthusiastically on the morning of his arrival and "huzzaed for Tryon in the evening." A few days later, in July, 1775, the radicals moved to arrest Tryon. Philip Schuyler, recently appointed a major general by Congress, intervened and produced an order from Washington forbidding Tryon's arrest.

One of the most effective weapons in the governor's hand was his influence in granting land patents. The colonial secretary, Lord Dartmouth, wrote Lieutenant Governor Colden in 1774: "Their [land speculators'] Pretensions will meet with every Countenance and Support that can be shewn consistent with Justice; for I can with truth say that the conduct of that Province in general . . . has been such as justly intitles its well disposed and peaceable Inhabitants to His Majesty's particular Favor and Indulgence." Tryon and Colden secured approval for grants totalling 433,000 acres from April, 1775, to July, 1776, of which 275,000 went to prominent Tories.

Over 300,000 acres of this land lay in the area east of Lake Champlain. In fact, one of the largest grants went to Colonel Peter Skene, the Loyalist who attached himself to Burgoyne's staff. The Colonel received a patent for 120,000 acres and was commissioned governor of Crown Point and Ticonderoga. These grants, of course, exacerbated the quarrel between the great land barons of the Upper Hudson (of whom Schuyler was one) and the settlers in the Hampshire Grants. It is not too much to say that this dispute had a powerful influence in promoting radicalism in the Vermont area and a countervailing propensity toward loyalism among the inhabitants of the Upper Hudson.[3]

Another powerful source of royal influence, especially in the vast region of the upper Mohawk Valley embraced by Tryon County was Sir Guy Johnson. His influence with the Six Nations has already been noted. Johnson was also a large landholder whose numerous tenants might be expected to rally to his leadership. Although the Tryon County Committee was industrious in attempting to organize the Whig forces, their efforts were not notably successful. In the elections to the Second Provincial (New York) Congress in the fall of 1775 the county elected two delegates. One resigned to become chairman of the County Committee. The other departed for the meeting of the Congress in New York City but two months later he had not arrived. Although the committee promptly chose new delegates the incident was perhaps illustrative of the problems of organization in the widely scattered rural areas.

The First Provincial Congress which met in the fall of 1775 was still lukewarm in its support of the Whig cause. It professed support of the Association but it was laggard in providing for the raising of troops and in carrying out its own resolution for the suppression of Tories. By November so many members were absent that the Provincial Congress dissolved. October elections for a new Congress, with voting limited to freeholders, brought confused results. Apathy and factionalism took their toll and in three of the fourteen counties elections were delayed for several weeks. Two counties did not elect any delegates and when the Second Provincial Congress finally met early in December, 1775, only half the countries were represented.

Meantime, royal authority had suffered two set-backs. Guy Johnson, the Butlers, and Daniel Claus had retired to Canada, leaving only Sir John at Johnson Hall with his corporal's guard of Mohawks. In New York City Governor Tryon found it expedient to move his quarters to a British warship in the harbor. Even so, the new Provincial Congress moved slowly. The reasons for its hesitancy were not hard to find. Anchored in New York harbor were HMS *Asia*, a ship of the line, and her consorts whose menacing guns threatened Manhattan. Her captain had orders from Admiral Samuel Graves to bombard the town if the ships were molested and there were rumors that Lord Dartmouth would order reprisals against any town that raised troops for the rebel army.

By the end of the year the New York Whigs found themselves like a nut in the jaws of a nut-cracker. The King's Proclamation of 1775 declared the colonies to be in a state of rebellion and ordered a naval blockade of the Atlantic ports. This was ample demonstration of the radical contention that the government did not intend to relax its restrictions against the American colonies. But it was also common knowledge that General Howe was to be reinforced and that he planned to seize New York City as his base of operations for 1776. When General Charles Lee was sent to New York in January, 1776, to fortify the town against attack the Committee of Safety was in a panic. Many Tories fled the city and "you would scarce see any person or but few in the streets carts and waggons all employed in carrying out goods and furniture. . . ."[4]

Although the committee protested that heavy-handed tactics would convert many people to Toryism Lee refused to be cowed. He began removing cannon and stores from the city forts and threatened retaliation against the Tories if the fleet interfered. By April his belligerence had so alarmed the city fathers that they protested to General Washington. Lee was transferred shortly afterwards, but the commander in chief delivered a stinging rebuke to the New

York authorities for allowing communications between the British naval vessels in the harbor and people in the city.

While the Whigs thus vacillated the Tories failed to take advantage of the situation. They too were caught between threats, the Sons of Liberty on one side and royal authority on the other. Both sides undoubtedly recognized that the King's Proclamation reduced the choices to independence or unconditional surrender to whatever settlement the home government decided to make with the colonies, but neither wanted to make an overt commitment. In the last elections of the colonial assembly the Whigs won a heavy majority, and Governor Tryon predictably prorogued it almost as soon as it convened.

During the first four months of 1776 most of the Whig Loyalists moved into the ranks of the revolutionaries. After a year of war, as John Jay observed, ". . . it is natural to suppose that the Sword must decide the Controversy—and with a View to that object our Measures should in great Degree be taken."

The elections of the Fourth Provincial Congress in April chose 101 delegates from all fourteen colonies. County committees of safety were now becoming more effective at turning out voters. The state committee cut off supplies to British naval vessels and warned the people to prepare for sterner measures. But, as Washington began to move his troops into the city, the lame duck Third Provincial Congress failed to raise the quota of troops fixed by Congress. It was accused of leniency towards Tories, a charge underlined by General Washington's discovery of a Tory rebellion plot on Long Island.

The introduction of Richard Henry Lee's resolution for independence in the Continental Congress on June 7 drove New York Whig-Loyalists to their last desperate strategem. Jay proposed that discussion of independence be postponed until the new Provincial Congress could convene. This was unanimously approved in the dying days of the Third Congress. The New York delegation in Philadelphia was therefore without instructions on independence and so abstained from voting on July 2.[5]

In New York Lord Richard Howe's vast fleet came over the horizon and the Provincial Congress hastily adjourned to White Plains. It was there that its successor, the Fourth Congress, convened on July 9. Gouverneur Morris may have given the most honest explanation for New York's tardy acceptance of independence: *"We are hellishly frightened but don't say a word of that* for we shall get our spirits again. . . ." Once committed the Whigs did indeed begin to recover their spirits. As Robert Livingston put it after the disastrous battle of Long Island, "I am amazed at the composure I feel tho' I have everything at stake, & the enemy are already in possession of one third of my income."

The British occupation of the city and the lower Hudson valley was greatly encouraging to the Loyalists. As in neighboring New Jersey the Whig movement collapsed and Tory militia turned on their erstwhile tormenters. Governor Tryon and royal authorities had their hands full administering loyalty oaths. Many who had been prominent on Whig committees in the lower counties hastily departed. Others professed that they had been coerced into cooperating with the rebels, and now took the oath of allegiance to the Crown. By October, 1776, Loyalist refugees who had fled to escape the American army streamed back into the city. The Provincial Congress, now rid of its anxieties about New York, was emboldened to take energetic measures for the suppression of the Tories on the Upper Hudson. In the fall of 1776 the state committee of safety sent a special investigating committee to Albany to cooperate with General Schuyler. County and local committees were urged to disarm potential enemies and directed to use the militia to suppress any Tory uprisings.

Burgoyne's invasion had a disastrous effect on the revolutionary cause in the early summer of 1777. There was never any serious danger of a real Tory uprising, but the fall of Ticonderoga and Schuyler's retreat down the Hudson in July had a serious effect on his enlistments. The country was not prepared to welcome Burgoyne with open arms, but neither was it prepared to risk its collective lives and fortunes. "I am exceedingly chagrined at the pusillanimous spirit which prevails, . . ." said the commander of the Northern Department in mid-July.

As July came to a close a crisis had been reached that was not only military but political. The success of Burgoyne's invasion would not only mark a triumph of British strategy. There was also every reason to think that the Whigs would collapse before a successful military conquest just as they had in New Jersey in 1776. The revolutionary movement in New York was about to be decided by the outcome of the clash between rebels and redcoats.[6]

BENNINGTON

Although he did not realize it, Burgoyne's passage from the Lake Champlain watershed to the Hudson marked more than the crossing of a geographical divide. From the time of his arrival on the Hudson Gentleman Johnny's luck began to run out.

He had foreseen that his supply problem would be a serious one since he was now 185 miles from Montreal. Moreover, Sir Guy Carleton, obedient to the letter of his orders from Germain, refused to furnish a garrison force for Ticonderoga. This meant that in order to guard his supply line—possibly a line of retreat—Burgoyne felt obliged to garrison the fort with the 53rd Regiment and the Brunswickers of the Regiment Prince Frederick, about 900 men in all. Having decided to assemble thirty days' supplies at Fort Edward for his final drive to Albany, it might be supposed that Burgoyne would cut himself loose from his tenuous link with Canada. But eighteenth century doctrine, with its emphasis on fortified posts and lines of communications, would not permit it.

Burgoyne's situation was complicated by lack of horses. He had expected to be furnished 1,500 animals in Canada but had received only 500. The poorly built carts with which he had been equipped had broken down badly in the rough country between Lake Champlain and the Hudson. Finally, there was the sad state of Riedesel's dragoons. Clad in their heavy leather britches and huge cocked hats they were still horseless, clumping along in their jack boots and spurs. Riedesel had been urging Burgoyne to find mounts for them and now, at Fort Edward, Burgoyne decided to send an expedition into the Hampshire Grants where he was told livestock was fat and numerous. Since horsemen would be needed to round up and drive the 1,300 or so animals that were needed Burgoyne chose Lieutenant Colonel Friederich Baum's Brunswick dragoons for the raid. Fifty German jägers (riflemen), 100 grenadiers, fifty British regulars, and 300 Canadians, Loyalists and Indians brought the force to about 700 men. One of the Loyalists was Colonel Philip Skene, who was to recruit Tories in the region and act as a sort of aide and emissary for Baum, who spoke no English.

The German commander's instructions were detailed and covered a whole range of objectives. In addition to collecting draught animals and wagons Baum was to "try the affections of the country, to disconcert the councils of the enemy," to gather intelligence, and even "to tax the several districts." The specific objective was Bennington, about thirty-five miles to the southeast. British headquarters received a report just before Baum's departure that the rebels had established a supply depot there, and Burgoyne changed Baum's orders at the last moment in order to avail himself of this windfall. The only obstacle to Baum's advance was thought to be the remnant of Seth Warner's command which had been scattered at Hubbardton.[7]

It is obvious that Burgoyne's intelligence, which was gathered by Indians and Tories, was beginning to falter, for it failed to report the existence of a force of 1,500 men assembled by a veteran commander, John Stark. In the middle of July the settlers in Vermont had appealed to New Hampshire for help against the enemy invasion. The New Hampshire assembly had generously responded by an appropriation of funds and an authorization for Stark to raise a corps of militia. Stark was another of the Continental officers who had been offended by the Congressional promotions of January, 1777. Although he had fought with distinction at Bunker Hill, in Canada, and at Trenton, he had been passed over for brigadier general and had resigned his Continental commission in disgust. Understandably stiff-necked about his treatment and typically New England in his distrust of "them"—meaning Schuyler, New Yorkers, Congress or anything else south and west of the Green Mountains—Stark insisted that he be accountable only to the legislature and that he be authorized "to act separately for the protection of the people or the annoyance of the enemy."

By the last week in July Stark had raised 1,500 men and marched them to Manchester, about twenty-five miles north of Bennington where he was joined by Seth Warner. A few days later General Benjamin Lincoln arrived with orders from Schuyler to move part of this force to the Hudson. Stark displayed his orders from the sovereign state of New Hampshire and declared that he, not Schuyler or Lincoln, was giving the orders. The politic Lincoln agreed to try to work out a plan which would allow the New Englanders to remain between the invaders and their homes and at the same time cooperate with Schuyler. Lincoln went back to report to headquarters on the Hudson and Stark moved to Bennington, leaving Warner at Manchester. So it was that the late intelligence that directed Baum to Bennington failed to report that it was occupied by a force over twice his numbers.

The German commander left the Hudson on August 11. Two days later he reached the little village of Cambridge and the next day, August 14, began to move south to the Walloomsac river where he made his first contact with the Americans. Stark, equally ignorant of the presence of an enemy, had sent out a force of 200 men in response to a report of "a party of Indians." The Americans delayed Baum by destroying a bridge and for the first time the German commander became aware of the size of Stark's force. He sent a report to Burgoyne on the morning of August 14, and later in the day a second dispatch requested reinforcements, although Baum was confident and apparently unconcerned about the safety of his force. At about the same time Stark learned that he had more than an Indian raid on his hands, and sent orders to Warner to bring in his corps from Manchester. That afternoon Baum made his approach to Bennington and Stark formed a defensive line, but since it was late afternoon the German commander went into camp on high ground overlooking the western approach to the village. Stark withdrew about two miles to the east.

Now the weather intervened. Rain came in a steady downpour. All day on the 15th the two forces huddled in their camps, soaked to the skin, their weapons useless. At Burgoyne's headquarters at Fort Miller Lieutenant Colonel Heinrich von Breymann with a body of 550 men moved out on the road to Bennington although there was no urgency to his mission; he was simply supporting an operation that was apparently going well but might encounter unforeseen trouble. From Manchester Warner's men were also on the march, but making slow progress over bad roads and rough country. The rain continued throughout the night and into the morning of the sixteenth.[8]

About noon the weather began to clear and Stark decided to launch an attack. Baum's position represented a tactical compromise. His main force occupied a commanding hill where he constructed a redoubt. But he also wanted to defend the bridge across the Walloomsac about a half a mile away. Here he posted a force of grenadiers and Canadian rangers. The two positions were loosely linked by three detachments between the hill and the river. Still another detachment guarded the rear.

These scattered elements would probably have had difficulty supporting each other against a simple frontal assault, especially by a force as large as Stark's. But the American commander, with Warner's force about to come up, decided to attack Baum's detachments in detail by flanking parties. He was aided by the fact that the Brunswicker made several bad guesses. In igno-

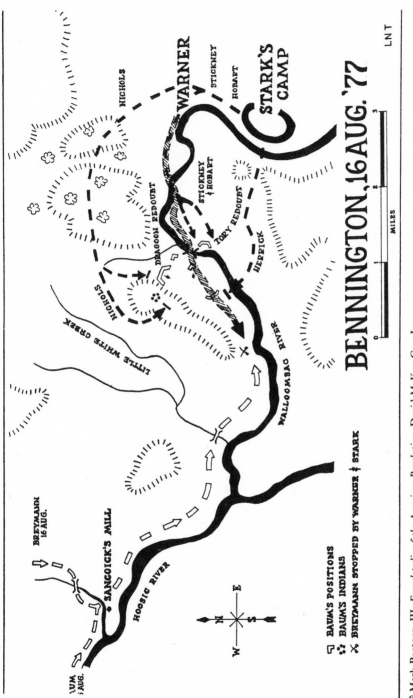

BENNINGTON, 16 AUG. '77

⌐ BAUM'S POSITIONS

∴ BAUM'S INDIANS

✕ BREYMANN STOPPED BY WARNER ⚬ STARK

© Mark Boatner, III, *Encyclopedia of the American Revolution*, David McKay Co., Inc.

rance of the fact that he was opposed by an experienced commander Baum noticed but failed to realize the threat of Stark's flanking parties. He concluded that they were leaderless fragments who were probably retiring.

Colonel Skene persisted in his assurances that the countryside contained many Loyalists. Skene had circulated the word that when they came in to join the British they were to wear pieces of white paper in their hats as identification. The Americans picked up this bit of information and several parties of them displaying scraps of paper, infiltrated among Baum's scattered positions before they were recognized.

About three o'clock the Americans opened fire and the British suddenly found themselves assailed from all sides. Considering that over 1,000 untrained militia had been widely deployed the coordination of the attack was remarkable. The separated parts of Baum's command collapsed under the fierce attack and the detachments were soon surrendering or trying to escape into the surrounding forest. As the Americans began to close on the German strong point at the redoubt, a sheet of fire and a thunderous roar marked the destruction of Baum's ammunition wagon. This was the signal for the final assault which drove the dragoons from the hill. Baum and a few followers almost hacked their way clear with their cavalry sabres, but the German commander was finally cut down by musket fire and the fight ended.

The militiamen began to scatter, some pursuing the escaping enemy, most of them looting the baggage and equipment. It was into this confusion that Seth Warner finally brought his command. Simultaneously Breymann appeared from the west, unaware that Baum was even engaged since the jumble of mountains and valleys had deadened the sound of firing. As the German light infantry collided with the first elements of Stark's men they drove the Americans back on the main body. Stark seems to have favored retreating in the face of this new threat but the timely arrival of Warner's men halted Breymann's advance. Suddenly alive to his danger Breymann drew up into a defensive position and beat off a sharp attack by the Americans. Both sides were exhausted by the sultry heat and the day's marching. Soon the Germans began to run short of ammunition and Stark and Warner got more men into action. Breymann began a fighting withdrawal and darkness finally ended the engagement. Breymann pulled his battered column back toward the Hudson. Twenty-five percent of his force had been killed or wounded and he had lost his guns.

Bennington was a disastrous combination of bad luck and bad judgement for the British. Chance had placed Stark at Bennington, and chance had allowed the weather to clear before Breymann could join Baum. With the two forces combined Baum's position would have been a tough nut for the Americans to crack even with the addition of Warner's brigade. (It should be noted in passing that the Germans, ridiculed by their British allies and by historians for their lumbering, heavy-footed marching, covered the twenty-five miles to Bennington in the same time that it took Warner's men to march the same distance from Manchester.) Burgoyne's force was now reduced by nearly 1,000 men of all ranks. The British left 207 men dead on the field at Bennington and 700 officers and men prisoners of the Americans. Counting Breymann's wounded, the missing, and deserters the loss was fourteen percent of Burgoyne's force, of which half were regulars.[9]

The defeat seems not to have seriously dampened the morale of Burgoyne's men. "We shall soon be in a position to move on toward Albany," wrote a Brunswick soldier on August 18. "The unhappy occurrence . . . has not dispirited us." But it did dispirit the Indians. Shortly after Bennington they held a council and most of them decided to go home. Only eighty of the 500 or so who had accompanied Burgoyne as far as the Hudson now remained. Of the Loyalists "I have about 400 (but not half of them armed), who may be depended upon. The rest are trimmers merely actuated by interest." These departures seriously handicapped the British reconnaissance. Before Ticonderoga the Americans had great difficulty penetrating the screen of Indians and Loyalists to secure information about enemy numbers and movements. After mid-August it was the British who lacked intelligence of the enemy.

If the spirits of the troops were unimpaired a shadow of doubt began to nag Burgoyne. "Had I latitude in my orders, I should think it my duty to wait in this position, or perhaps as far back as Fort Edward"—was he already preparing the record for failure?—"where my communications with Lake George would be perfectly secure; . . . but my orders being positive 'to force a junction with Sir William Howe' I apprehend I am not at liberty to remain inactive longer. . . ."

Still, said Gentleman Johnny, "I do not yet despond." But before the week was out he was again overwhelmed by bad news, this time from the west.[10]

Drums Along the Mohawk

The key to the American defense of the Mohawk Valley was Fort Stanwix, guarding the portage between the Mohawk River and Wood Creek leading to Lake Oneida and thence to Lake Ontario. Built by the French during the Seven Years' War, the geometric precision and elaborate outworks of its eighteenth century military engineering presented an odd contrast to the primitive forest surroundings. The fort was located on the only dry ground between the two waterways; except in its immediate vicinity the area was heavily wooded and marshy. A road down the Mohawk forded the river a short distance below and followed the left bank eastwards to Fort Dayton and Albany. By the spring of 1777 the fort had fallen into a bad state of repair and reflected the apathy of the local militia. A handful of troops garrisoned the tumbleddown works and the Tryon County Committee of Safety reported, "More than half of our inhabitants are resolved not to lift up arms in defense of their country."

In April General Schuyler ordered Colonel Peter Gansevoort and his 3rd

New York Continentals to occupy Fort Stanwix and that energetic young officer immediately set about repairing the fortifications. In May he was joined by his second in command, Lieutenant Colonel Marinus Willett, who had been a radical firebrand in the early days of the Revolution and had fought with Montgomery in Canada. The two young officers fell to work repairing the works and drilling the garrison. They cajoled and wheedled supplies from Albany and urged that more reinforcements be sent. Warnings from the Oneida Indians, one of the Six Nations that took sides with the Americans, convinced the commanders that the fort was in danger. By mid-July they had definite news of St. Leger's expedition and they redoubled their efforts to get the fort in a condition of readiness.[11]

Colonel Barry St. Leger was the commanding officer of the 34th Regiment which had been left on garrison duty in Canada. His selection as commander of this flanking foray was no accident for Burgoyne had designated him in the initial planning of the campaign. He had spent half of his forty years in the army and had won a reputation as a frontier fighter under Abercrombie and Wolfe in the Seven Years' War.

St. Leger's command left La Chine, just above Montreal, on June 23. Indian scouts reported from the upper Mohawk that Fort Stanwix was in ruins and manned by less than 100 men. The expedition included 100 men each from St. Leger's 34th Regiment and the 8th Regiment, eighty jägers of the Hesse-Hanau Regiment, and thirty artillerymen who served two 6-pounders, two 3-pounders, and four 4.4. inch mortars. There were also 350 Tories of the King's Royal Americans commanded by Sir John Johnson, dubbed the "Royal Greens," and a company of John Butler's rangers. About 100 Canadian bateaumen and axmen were hired as workmen. The total rank and file of St. Leger's white troops was about 750 men.

The first leg of his journey was up the St. Lawrence, 140 miles to Lake Ontario. This strenuous stretch was made in bateaux, thirty to forty feet long, which could be propelled by poles, sails, or oars and were sufficiently seaworthy to withstand turbulent rapids or windy weather on the lakes. As the main body toiled up the river Daniel Claus and Sir John Johnson went ahead to rally the Indians of the Six Nations. By July 14 they were at Oswego on Lake Ontario where they were joined by Joseph Brant. Now began the task of persuading the warriors assembled at Oswego to join St. Leger.

The Indians were suspicious of all white men, American or British. Only nine years before, the Treaty of Fort Stanwix had established an Indian boundary at Unadilla Creek (near Utica), and already the whites were pushing beyond it. The Iroquois understandably did not want to get involved in a white man's fight unless there was something in it for them. Probably Joseph Brant persuaded them that if Fort Stanwix fell they could drive the white settlers back beyond the Treaty line.

The Indians needed other assurances. They wanted it understood that the whites would fight with them, that there would be no heavy casualties, and that there would be plenty of loot. Claus pointed out how easily the great fortress at Ticonderoga had fallen; ". . . when I come before that fort [Stanwix]," he said, "and the commanding officer shall see me, he . . . will not fire a shot, but will surrender the fort to me." Whether impressed by the oratory or by the promises, about 800 Iroquois, most of them Mohawks, agreed to accompany the British.

By the time St. Leger reached Oswego at the end of July a scouting party had come in with prisoners taken near Fort Stanwix. From them St. Leger learned that the fort was "garrisoned by upward of 600 men; the repairs far advanced, and the rebels expecting us, and were acquainted with our strength and route." Another party reported that a convoy of supplies was on its way up the Mohawk toward Stanwix. Speed was now essential and St. Leger detached a force of thirty regulars and 200 Indians under Brant to invest the fort and intercept the supplies. They reached Stanwix late on August 2 only moments after the supplies had been landed and hauled inside the walls.

St. Leger brought the main force in two days later, between 1,500 and 2,000 troops and warriors. He established two camps, one on Wood Creek for the white troops and an Indian encampment at what was called the Lower Landing on the Mohawk. In between he set up a loose picket line of Indians. Warriors and German sharpshooters kept up a desultory fire on the fort.[12]

St. Leger was confronted with a situation not at all to his liking. Fort Stanwix was not only adequately defended but the timely arrival of supplies had furnished "provisions sufficient to support the garrison [for] six weeks." He must therefore settle down to a siege which would delay his advance and would without doubt try the patience of Brant and his warriors. Despite his experience in frontier warfare St. Leger was too thoroughly conditioned by eighteenth century military dogma to consider bypassing the American fort. He sent out axmen "for opening Wood Creek (which the enemy with the indefatigable labor of one hundred and fifty men . . . had most effectively closed up) . . . for a present supply of provisions and transport of artillery."

Meanwhile Tryon County was at last bestirring itself. The committee of safety had been warned by a half-breed Oneida named Thomas Spencer on July 30 that "there is but four days remaining of the time set for the king's troops to come to Fort Schuyler [Stanwix]. . . . one resolute blow would secure the friendship of the Six Nations, and almost free this part of the country from incursions of the enemy." The chairman of the committee of safety, Nicholas Herkimer, was also commander of the militia. He was a stolid, soft-spoken German who several months before had held a conference with Joseph Brant in an effort to persuade the Indians to remain neutral. It was rumored that Herkimer had allowed himself to be faced down by the Mohawk chieftain. Nor did it help matters that the general's brother was a ranger captain with St. Leger.

Nevertheless 800 militia answered General Herkimer's muster order and assembled at Fort Dayton on August 4. Perhaps it was the threat of Brant's

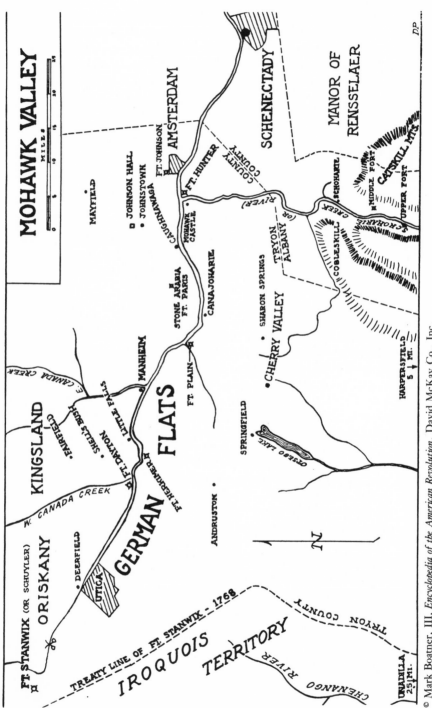

Indians, perhaps a determination "not to make a Ticonderoga of it," but the Tryon county men were full of fight and anxious to get at the enemy. The party set out, divided roughly into three regiments, and accompanied by a number of ox carts carrying their provisions. Despite their lack of discipline the militia made good time and by the evening of August 5 they were encamped about ten miles down the river from Fort Stanwix. Herkimer now sent several messengers to make their way through the Indian lines to the fort. They were to tell Gansevoort to make a diversionary attack from the fort, signalling his sally by firing three cannon shots. Herkimer would then move to his relief.[13]

The messengers got through but not until late in the morning. Herkimer's men were astir before daylight of the sixth and still spoiling for a fight. When the commander insisted on waiting for the signal from the fort their impatience mounted. A stormy council of war ensued, Herkimer advising that they should wait for the signal guns, the regimental commanders urging an immediate advance. There were ugly imputations, first of the general's courage and then of his loyalty. Finally the little German's temper snapped and he ordered the advance. With a screen of Oneidas in the van the militia moved out, 600 of the main body leading the way followed by the provision carts, and then a rear guard of about 200.

St. Leger's "discovering parties" brought him news of Herkimer's approach on August 5. It caught him at a bad time. ". . . I had not two hundred and fifty King's troops in camp, the various and extreme operations . . . having employed the rest, and therefore could not send above eighty . . . rangers and troops included, with the whole corps of Indians." Sir John Johnson was placed in command, accompanied by Joseph Brant and Butler's rangers. They moved down the river about six miles and laid an ambush on either side of a narrow defile.

About ten o'clock on the morning of the sixth Herkimer's van reached a point not far from the Indian village of Oriskany. The militia column was strung out for nearly a mile along the road as the forward companies moved into the narrow ravine and crossed a log bridge spanning a transverse gulley. It was approaching a second bridge, the rear of the column not yet fully into the defile, when the impatient Mohawks opened fire.

Why the Oneidea scouts did not discover the ambush is a puzzle, but the surprise was complete. Probably a hundred Americans were cut down in the first rush of the Indians and rangers. The militiamen scrambled out of the road and up to some high ground on the north. Herkimer's horse was shot from under him and he was badly wounded in both legs. He ordered his men to place him on his saddle against a tree and proceeded to rally his men in a loose circle on the hill above the road.

At this point a violent thunder storm broke, the wind and rain so intense that men on both sides were driven to cover. During the interlude, Herkimer posted his men in pairs so that one could protect the other during reloading.

When the battle resumed the militiamen had recovered from their panic. There were savage exchanges, not only of musket fire, but of hatchets and bayonets and knives and clubbed muskets. The fighting raged for the better part of four hours before the toll taken by the Americans finally discouraged the Indians and they broke off the fight. They had lost about thirty killed and forty wounded, including several of their chieftains. Herkimer's men also had paid a bloody price. Seventy-five of them were killed and as many more were wounded. Perhaps fifty of them were taken prisoner. There was now no question of relieving Fort Stanwix. The wounded, including the courageous commander, were placed on crude litters and the little army made its painful way back to Fort Dayton.

While militiamen and Indians fought at Oriskany Gansevoort made his diversion, though not in time to affect Herkimer's desperate situation. He sent Colonel Willett out of the fort at the head of 250 men to attack the nearly deserted Indian encampment at the Lower Landing. Willett and his men made a swift descent, driving off the few defenders. They then thoroughly looted the camp of its provisions, blankets, clothing, muskets, and camp kettles, altogether several wagon loads of spoil. By the time St. Leger could react Willett was back inside the fort. When Brant and his Indians returned from Oriskany, gloomy over the number of their people lost in the fight, they were outraged to find that St. Leger had allowed their camp to be plundered.

So although Herkimer had failed to relieve Fort Stanwix St. Leger's situation was not a happy one. He found that his 6-pounders made no impression on the walls of the fort and the range was too great for the shells from his mortars and howitzers to reach its interior. The British commander tried to bluff Gansevoort into surrender by threatening to massacre the garrison if it continued its resistance. The defenders were not impressed, and Willett denounced the threat as "a stigma upon the name of Britain." St. Leger's only alternative was to begin the slow work of digging parallels to bring his guns within effective range of the fort.[14]

Gansevoort's problem was ammunition. Though the fort was well supplied with provisions of food constant skirmishing with the Indians had obliged the defenders to burn a good deal of powder. Gansevoort decided to send for help and on the night of August 10 Willett and a companion slipped through the enemy lines and started down river.

At his headquarters at Stillwater Schuyler was aware of the critical situation at Fort Stanwix even before Willett's arrival. Despite the menace of Burgoyne's advance and the fact that there were less than five thousand troops in the American camp Schuyler called a council of war on August 12 to discuss a relief expedition. The meeting was the final bitter episode in the last days of his command of the Northern Department. The officers, with one exception, adamantly opposed the relief of Fort Stanwix and there were mutterings that Ticonderoga was about to be repeated. The exception was Benedict Arnold who had just returned to the army after his promotion to major general. When

Schuyler overruled his dissident officers Arnold volunteered to lead the relief force and within five days he was at Fort Dayton with 700 Continentals. Here he paused, hoping to strengthen his force with militia, but Oriskany had taken the heart out of the Tryon County men.

Finally Arnold tried a desperate stratagem. Among the Tories arrested by the committee of safety was Hon-Yost Schuyler, who had been sentenced to be executed as a spy. Hon-Yost had some kind of mental illness, possibly epilepsy, which made him highly respected by the Indians. (White men attributed mental illness to the baneful influence of the devil and put such people in dungeons. The barbarian viewed them as touched with the Great Spirit and treated them with consideration and respect.)

In return for his life Hon-Yost was induced to go to St. Leger's camp with an alarming story of swarms of Americans approaching under the command of the general whom the Indians called "The Dark Eagle." Friendly Oneidas followed Schuyler and added their elaborations. It is questionable whether such stories convinced Brant's Iroquois, but they were looking for an excuse to abandon St. Leger. The fighting had not been easy and they were still angry over the looting of their camp. The siege had now lasted three weeks and St. Leger's parallels were not yet complete; the warriors had little taste for such tiresome maneuvers. When St. Leger called a council of war on August 21 nearly 200 of his red allies had already drifted away. "In about an hour they insisted that I should retreat, or they would be obliged to abandon me." On the 22nd he lifted the siege and began a retreat to Lake Ontario, his column occasionally harassed by his erstwhile warrior allies. "[They] seized upon officers' liquor and clothes . . . and became more formidable than the enemy we had to expect."[15]

Even before the news of St. Leger's failure reached him Burgoyne had written a gloomy assessment to Germain:

> I am afraid the expectations of Sir J. Johnson greatly fail in the rising of the country. On this side I find daily reason to doubt the sincerity of resolution of the professing loyalists. . . . The great bulk of the country is undoubtedly with Congress, in principle and zeal; and their measures are executed with a secrecy and dispatch that are not to be equalled. . . . The Hampshire Grants in particular, a country unpeopled and almost unknown in the last year, now abounds in the most active and rebellious race on the continent, and hangs like a gathering storm on my left.

On August 20 Nicholas Herkimer lay in his bed at his home in German Flats, cheerfully smoking his pipe, and bled to death.

TEN

———

Saratoga:
The First Battle

———

THE MORE OF HISTORY THAT WE READ THE MORE IT IS APPARENT THAT HEROES
must to a considerable degree be endowed with what the eighteenth century
called presence and what today is called image. Suppose that George Washington had been short, dumpy, and bald and John Adams had been six feet
two and a splendid horseman. Might not the latter rather than the former have
been the Father of His Country?

A case in point is Horatio Gates. Middle-aged, stoop-shouldered, near-
sighted, he was not only consumed with ambition but his egotism and vanity
were so obvious as to be offensive. His supporters in Congress spoke of the
admiration and adulation that he inspired in the troops, especially New
England militia. But there is little evidence from the soldiers themselves that
Gates was any more than a welcome change from Schuyler's arrogance and
pessimism. Yet Gates had a sound military mind and his victory over Burgoyne may have been the most important of the war. History has been nig-
gardly in its praise and this is perhaps simply because Gates cannot pass history's physical exam, cannot project the image that history requires of its
heroes.

THE COMMAND OF THE NORTHERN DEPARTMENT

The Northern Department was created soon after Congress assumed direction of the war in the summer of 1775. Its evolution was the natural outgrowth
of the New England expedition that seized Ticonderoga and the Congressional
decision to launch an invasion of Canada. It was treated almost as a separate
command and even after General Washington was named commander in
chief, "I have never interfered further than merely to advise, and to give such
aid as was in my power. . . ." Philip Schuyler, who was one of Congress' four
original appointments to the rank of major general, was placed in command.
As related above, Schuyler directed the Canadian offensive and he was still in

command fifteen months later when the American forces were shattered and driven back to Ticonderoga in 1776.

By that time Schuyler had experienced a number of difficulties which were to plague him for the rest of his military career. Although he could be a gracious and urbane gentleman Schuyler had a strong streak of arrogance and irrascibility—perhaps in even greater degree than could be expected from one of his standing and background. He was sensitive to any challenge to his authority or criticism of his motives. And his chronic illness undoubtedly contributed to his displays of bad temper.

In June, 1776, General Gates had been appointed to replace John Sullivan after the disaster at Trois Rivieres and the retreat to Lake Champlain. Gates leaped to the assumption that his command was independent of Schuyler's authority. The confusion was a combination of Gates' ambition and Congressional bumbling. Sullivan's appointment in 1776 to "the American army in Canada" had been designed to give him discretionary authority, since it would have been difficult for him to communicate from the St. Lawrence to Schuyler's headquarters in Albany. By the summer of 1776 Sullivan's (now Gates') command was no longer in Canada but Congress had never formally restored it to the jurisdiction of the Northern Department. Schuyler was furious at what he regarded as Gates' effrontery and he vented his spleen in several angry letters to Congress. After some hesitation that body decided that Ticonderoga and its garrison was part of the Northern Department and affirmed Schuyler's authority, but the episode was a forewarning of strained relations between Philadelphia and Albany.

Another source of Schuyler's troubles was the long-standing quarrel over the disputed boundary between New York and New Hampshire. Part of Schuyler's large land holdings lay in this area and he had been prominent among the Hudson land barons in their efforts to evict settlers from New England, who from Schuyler's point of view were squatters and land pirates. The Yankees were slow to volunteer for service in an army commanded by a New York patroon. So, at least, ran the argument of the New England members of Congress, who set out to displace Schuyler after the failure of the Canadian campaign. It might be added that the cantankerous, willful Yankee troops irritated Schuyler as much as his patrician hauteur offended them.[1]

Horatio Gates, champion of the New England Congressmen in Philadelphia, was in his fiftieth year. Somewhat older than most of Washington's generals, he was the son of lower middle class English parents. His mother was a housekeeper and his father held a minor civil service post, but they managed to catch the eye of the Walpole family who saw to it that young Gates secured a commission in the army. He was assigned to Nova Scotia in 1749 and remained in America until the close of the Seven Years' War. He was badly wounded at Braddock's debacle on the Monongahela in 1755, and after his recovery he held a series of staff positions until the war ended.

With little money and no social position Gates was doomed to retirement at half-pay. His tenuous connection with the Walpoles and his wife's family position (she was an army officer's daughter) allowed him a place on the outer fringe of English society, but this was perhaps merely frustrating to a man of Gates' ambition. He came to America in 1772 and bought a small estate in Western Virginia. He counted George Washington his friend and he became an outspoken supporter of the Whig cause. Congress welcomed the services of this regular army veteran and appointed him a brigadier general.

His first assignment was as Washington's adjutant general and he rendered important service to the commander in chief during the first months of the organization of the American army. He was promoted to major general in May, 1776, and was assigned to the Ticonderoga command where he had his first skirmish with Philip Schuyler. Gates had a profound respect for the British army and a thoroughly realistic appreciation of the limits of American military capabilities. Perhaps even more than Washington he advocated a cautious and defensive strategy.

In the latter part of 1776 Congress ordered eight regiments detached from Schuyler's command to meet Washington's critical situation in New Jersey. Fearful that the British would attack from Canada over the winter ice on Lake Champlain, Schuyler castigated Congress for its neglect of the Northern Department, but he complied with the order. Gates seized this opportunity to leave Schuyler's headquarters as commander of the detachment, but he did not remain with Washington after he delivered the troops. Instead he went to Philadelphia where it must be presumed that he made the most of the opportunity to further his own advancement. It was suggested that he resume the position of Washington's adjutant general but Gates protested that he "had last year the honor to command in the second post in America. . . . After this, to be expected to dwindle again to the adjutant general requires more philosophy on my part than could be expected."[2]

By mid-March Gates' backers in Congress had instigated a movement to censure Schuyler for disrespect of Congress, a charge not difficult to substantiate from some of the northern commanders' scathing remarks in his correspondence with that august body. The result was a Congressional vote of reprimand. The Gates faction now pressed its advantage and induced Congress to order Gates back as commander of Ticonderoga with authority to appoint his own subordinate officers. The strategy was clear. By giving Gates the semiautonomous position it had denied him the previous summer the New Englanders hoped to provoke Schuyler into resigning. They mistook their man.

When the rumors that Gates was to supplant him reached Albany Schuyler decided it was high time that Congress heard from him directly. But he did not intend to appear as a supplicant. Before leaving for Philadelphia he arranged for the New York legislature to name him as a delegate to Congress.

He then, in effect, abdicated his command leaving Gates to take over the Northern Department (and to learn that procurement of men and supplies was more easily said than done). Schuyler arrived in Philadelphia in mid-April, 1777, and demanded an investigation of the charge of disrespect of Congress. His prestige was considerably enhanced by an invitation from the governor of Pennsylvania to take charge of that state's military forces. Schuyler accepted the position and worked diligently at it during his brief stay. He also served on a Congressional committee to reorganize the Commissary Department.

All the while he and his New York colleagues, William Duer, James Duane, and Philip Livingston were mounting a counteroffensive. They pressed for action on Schuyler's reprimand and demanded an investigation of the gossip that whispered that Schuyler had embezzled government funds. Late in May they were successful. Congress voted to withdraw its censure and expunge it from the records. The investigation of finances in the Northern Department was a source of considerable chagrin to Schuyler's enemies. It revealed that the government owed Schuyler $3,750—in specie. On May 22 Congress voted a resolution declaring that "Albany, Ticonderoga, Fort Stanwix, and their dependencies, be henceforth considered as forming the Northern Department." Schuyler was ordered to resume his command and Gates was given the option of remaining as Schuyler's subordinate or reporting to Washington for further assignment. The vote was six states to three, with two states divided and two absent.

It turned out to be a hollow victory for Schuyler. He returned to Albany in June to find the Northern Department much as he had left it two months before. Despite the claims of Gates' admirers that his name would attract volunteers and militia the ranks were not filled and there were still shortages of provisions and equipment. Before another two months had passed Ticonderoga had fallen, the forces of the Northern Department had collapsed before Burgoyne's onslaught, and Schuyler had retreated to the mouth of the Mohawk. Although the British had been checked at Bennington and Fort Stanwix little of this redounded to Schuyler's credit. Stark, Gansevoort, Willett, and Arnold were the heroes of the hour. Not much notice was taken of the fact that Schuyler had gotten supplies to Stanwix in the nick of time and that it was his stubborn insistence that had sent Arnold's expedition to disperse St. Leger.

During the intervening weeks Horatio Gates had not been idle. By mid-June he was not only back in Philadelphia but managed to gain the floor of Congress to promote his case. It was not an auspicious occasion. For some time Gates harangued the members, not only about his qualifications for command but his entire life history. His voice querulous, his spectacles resting on the end of his nose, "peering over his scattered notes," his delivery "incoherent and interrupted with frequent chasms," he rambled on until he was finally interrupted by several members who demanded that he leave the floor.

In the ensuing debate "Granny" Gates stood by unembarrassed, "interrupting several times in the debates which arose. . . ." At last he withdrew and Congress voted that he "not again be admitted on the floor."

Congressional sensitivity being what it was the episode should have been the end of Gates' ambitions. Most members, according to Duane, "declared that there was no room for supposing it [the Northern Department] ever had been invested in him." But all this was before the gloom of Ticonderoga and the retreat down the Hudson. It appeared that Burgoyne would sweep down to Albany unopposed. John Stark refused to bring his men in and it was said the New Englanders would never fight as long as Schuyler commanded (some New Yorkers said *they* would not fight if he did not). Congressional critics recovered from their embarrassment at Gates' performance. The attack on Schuyler intensified. "It is indeed droll . . . to see a general not knowing where to find the main body of his army!" said Sam Adams, and even Pierre Van Cortlandt was "disgusted, disappointed and alarmed."[3]

Clearly Schuyler's days were numbered. His reputation declined further when he made an unsuccessful attempt to win the governorship of New York. He was defeated by George Clinton and it was said that his failure was due to a special law passed by the Provincial Congress that allowed the soldiers to vote. His bad temper, his stormy relations with Congress, above all the fact that around him was an aura of defeat and bad luck—all these doomed him. The opposition in Congress demanded an investigation of the loss of Ticonderoga and on August 1 General Schuyler was ordered to report to Philadelphia. General Washington was directed "to order such general officer as he shall think proper, immediately to repair to the northern department, to relieve Major General Schuyler in his command there. . . ." The commander in chief refused to become involved in the squabble. It was clear that Congress intended to get rid of Schuyler and that it wanted Gates to have the command. Washington had no wish to participate in Schuyler's humiliation. "The present situation of that department is delicate and critical, and the choice of an officer to command may involve very interesting and important consequences," was his non-committal answer to Congress. On August 4 Congress named Gates.and two weeks later he relieved Schuyler of the command of the Northern Department.

Young James Wilkinson, who had been appointed deputy adjutant by Gates and had continued to serve under Schuyler may have given the best evaluation. Gates' appointment, he said, came "precisely in season to profit by the reverse of fortune, which radically affected the physical forces of the adverse armies; and to engross all the eclat which attended that conspicuous change. . . . Schuyler . . . was obliged to resign the fruits of his labours. . . ."[4]

THE ARMY OF THE NORTHERN DEPARTMENT

One of the factors that upset British strategy in 1777 was the difficulty of ascertaining the strength of the armies that would oppose Howe and Burgoyne. This is not surprising since neither Congress nor Washington was ever very sure how many men would be recruited, or how many of these could be retained in the ranks. The situation of the Continental Line had improved somewhat after Congress authorized three-year enlistments; at least commanders were now able to reckon the approximate strength of Continental regiments. But there was still no knowing what militia reinforcements would be raised in the states although in many instances the commander in chief was pleasantly surprised at their response to his appeals.

The exaggerated importance that both sides attached to Ticonderoga and the ease with which Burgoyne overwhelmed the American garrison had, as noted, produced elation and perhaps overconfidence on one side and despair on the other. For a time Burgoyne believed that there was virtually no American opposition between Lake Champlain and Albany. Yet between the first week in July and the third week in September a formidable force larger than his own appeared in Burgoyne's path and destroyed his army. Having watched the swarms of militia that had appeared around Boston in 1775 the British commander believed that he was the victim of similar spontaneous rising of American farmers. "Wherever the King's forces point," he wrote Germain, "militia, to the amount of three or four thousand, assemble in twenty-four hours; they bring with them their subsistence, &c., and, the alarm over, they return to their farms."

History has tended to take the general's word at face value. In its pages the Saratoga campaign is the story of Yankee militia rising, as it were, from the ground, stirred to righteous wrath by the presence of an invader accompanied by alien mercenaries and red barbarians. The real story of the army of the Northern Department is not quite so simple.

Of the American army of 10,000 men that was sent north for the spring offensive into Canada in 1776 less than half could be mustered when Governor-General Carleton withdrew that same fall. For most of the winter Schuyler lived in constant fear that the British would resume the offensive when Lake Champlain froze and sleds could be used to transport men and supplies. During the mild winter of 1776–1777 the lake never froze but Schuyler could keep only about 2,500 men at Ticonderoga. Another 1,500 were dispersed in small garrisons from Skenesboro to Fort Stanwix. It was difficult to recruit men to serve at Ticonderoga, for it was widely known that the troops there had suffered severe losses, mostly from sickness, and that the garrison was ill-clothed and badly fed.

By the end of the spring of 1777 the situation had not significantly improved. As noted above, the principal reason that St. Clair abandoned Ticonderoga was that there were simply not enough troops to man the fortifications. On June 28, just a few days before the enemy appeared, the troop return of the deputy adjutant general, Colonel Wilkinson, showed ten undermanned Continental regiments totalling 2,066, two militia regiments of 225 men each,

229 artillerymen, and 183 rangers and engineers (whatever one may think of the subsequent career of this "tarnished warrior" it was Wilkinson's job to keep track of troop strength and there seems to be no reason to question his figures). It might be noted that during the two-month tenure of General Gates (April and May) the situation of the northern army remained virtually unchanged.[5]

As the army retreated to the Hudson after the fall of Ticonderoga Schuyler hurried to Fort Edward to pick up the pieces. St. Clair brought in what was left of the Ticonderoga garrison and Schuyler decided to leave Seth Warner in the Hampshire Grants with his 600 men to threaten Burgoyne's flank. Warner held a Continental commission but most of his men were Green Mountain Boys who were probably as reluctant as Stark's militiamen to serve under "them." Schuyler was in a desperate situation. He warned Washington that "with less than three thousand continental troops and not quite a thousand [New York] militia, I am faced with a powerful enemy from the north." Thanks to Schuyler's industrious axemen and his subsequent withdrawal down the Hudson, his army was granted almost six weeks' respite. But the outlook was grim. "Desertion prevails and disease gains ground; nor is it to be wondered at, for we have neither tents, houses, barns, boards or any other shelter except a little brush. . . . We are in want of every kind of necessities, provisions excepted."

Washington was plagued by the uncertainty of Howe's intentions but he sent General John Nixon with nearly 600 Massachusetts Continentals and by mid-July Schuyler could muster 4,500 men present and fit for duty. Of these, five brigades of Continentals totalling 2,842 men composed the nucleus of his army. New York militia, almost all from Albany County, amounted to 1,625 rank and file. "With this small body we have to encounter a much more numerous body of the enemy, well-appointed, flushed with success, and daily increasing by the acquisition of Tories. . . ." Schuyler's appeals for militia brought little response; New Englanders still professed an unwillingness to serve under him. The western districts of New York, according to Wilkinson, were intimidated because "hostile Indians let loose by the British commander . . . penetrated the frontier settlements, committing murders and spreading terror all over the country."[6]

On July 27 occurred one of the most notorious atrocities of the war. Jane McCrae, reputedly tall, lovely, and fair, had arrived at Fort Edward and taken up residence with a Mrs. McNeill. Jenny was to meet her fiance, Lieutenant David Jones, a Tory serving with Burgoyne. As the British advanced from Skenesboro toward the Hudson the local residents fled, but Jenny and her hostess, who was a cousin of General Fraser, remained at Fort Edward. On the morning of the 27th a party of Indians drove off an American picket, seized the two women, and hurried them off. What happened to Jenny is uncertain, for the captives were separated. According to an American soldier who had also been captured by the Indians, Jenny was murdered, scalped, and her body mutilated. In any event, the Indians appeared in the British camp with a scalp that both Mrs. McNeill and Lieutenant Jones identified as Jenny's. General Burgoyne ordered St. Luc de La Corne to hand over the murderers for punishment, but the hard-bitten old frontiersman pointed out that the Indians were already restive under the restrictions imposed on them. Any reprisals for the murder might result in further desertions by Burgoyne's red allies. The British commander relented and the red fiends went unpunished.

This, in bare outline, is the story of Jenny McCrae. It has been both embroidered and debunked, but as with most such episodes, the legend is more important than the fact. As the historian Christopher Ward has put it, "That the Wyandot Panther killed Jenny McCrae is just as certain as that Hamlet stabbed Polonius." The story was believed and it was said, then and later, that New Englanders were outraged by the atrocious crime and turned out by the thousands to seek revenge on Burgoyne and his savage horde. And it is just here that that legend runs into trouble.

One suspects that Yankee farmers might not be especially enthusiastic about avenging the sweetheart of a Tory, rather inclining to the view that Jenny got what was coming to her. Moreover there is evidence that although the story was widely circulated in New York and New England, it evoked almost no response. It should be remembered that John Stark had drummed in his 1,400 militiamen by July 24, four days before Jenny was killed. Seth Warner's brigade numbered the same 600 men at Bennington (August 16) as when Schuyler detached it to the Grants on July 10. If the militia turned out, they did not march to Schuyler's headquarters for the army he turned over to Gates on August 19 had no additional militia units. Where, then, did the army that faced the British at Bemis Heights in September come from?[7]

Although Schuyler's appeals to state officials fell on deaf ears, those to Washington did not. He was alive to the crisis in the Northern Department, especially after the news of the fall of Ticonderoga. Although Washington was still puzzling over Howe's intentions, his concern for the northern frontier led him to detach several regiments to Peekskill and to direct General Israel Putnam, who was guarding the Hudson Highlands, to release "four of the strongest Massachusetts regiments [who] will proceed immediately to Albany." Putnam sent John Glover's veteran brigade of 750 Continentals and they reported to Schuyler on August 1. On August 22 two New York Continental regiments, Philip Van Cortlandt's 2nd and James Livingston's 4th, came in and were sent to support Arnold's expedition up the Mohawk (thus accounting for the fact that Arnold set out with 800 men and returned with 1200). By this time Washington finally had certain word that Howe's expedition was in the Chesapeake, so he detached Daniel Morgan's riflemen, 331 tough Indian fighters who arrived on August 30. Finally, on September 6, Major Henry Dearborn noted in his journal that a force of Connecticut militia reached the American camps. These must have been the regiments of Colonel Thaddeus Cook and Colonel Jonathan Latimer who were added to Poor's brigade. If they were average militia regiments their total was not more than 300 rank and file (a return of Poor's seven regiments for October 4 lists 831 men present and fit for duty).

In summary, then, Wilkinson's return of July 20, seven days prior to the murder of Jenny McCrae gives Schuyler's force a strength of almost 4,500 men, including Nixon's brigade which had come up from Peekskill on July 10. On August 1 Glover's Massachusetts Continentals arrived, probably about 750 men (the October 4 return shows 918). On August 22 the 2nd and 4th New York regiments, 400 strong came in and were sent up the Mohawk. They returned with Arnold's command on August 31, the day after Morgan's 331 riflemen arrived. This brings the total of the northern army to 6,280 men. On September 8, according to Wilkinson, "the American army, about six thousand strong, began to retrace its steps toward the enemy . . . and reached Stillwater the next day." Of this force, seventy percent were Continentals, and of these forty-five percent had been ordered forward by the commander in chief after Ticonderoga. It was the Continental Line, not the militia that "turned out" to face Burgoyne's invaders.[8]

As the American army moved up the Hudson, General Gates cast his professional eye about for suitable ground on which to make his stand against the British. He had the able assistance of Colonel Thaddeus Kosciuszko, a Polish engineer who had been with the Northern Department since early spring. Kosciuszko was one of the few who had foreseen the disastrous consequences of leaving the Sugar Loaf undefended at Ticonderoga and he had remained as Schuyler's lieutenant during the long summer on the Hudson. Gates halted the army at Stillwater where Schuyler and Kosciuszko had earlier laid out some field works, but the position afforded no protection to the west. On September 13 the army moved north again, this time to Bemis Heights where heavily forested hills pushing to within two miles of the river afforded an anchor to Gates' left flank. He sited his right on the bluff overlooking the river and the road along its bank which led down to Albany. From here Kosciuszko laid out a line that stretched in a convex arc north and west. The center occupied Bemis Heights, a broken elevation rising about 300 feet above the river. Linking the two segments of the works was a barn which was converted into a rude fortress. The line then extended to the west, curving back to the south where it was anchored on a steep knoll. The chord of the arc thus formed was about a mile long.

Kosciuszko and his sappers fell to work with the troops and by September 17 a line of entrenchments and breastworks of logs, trees, and fence rails had been constructed, along with revetments for the guns. Commanding the right wing was General John Glover with his own brigade and those of Nixon and Paterson. The left was commanded by Benedict Arnold and consisted of Ebenezer Learned's brigade and Enoch Poor's oversize brigade of seven regiments. On the extreme left, outside the entrenchments and masking the

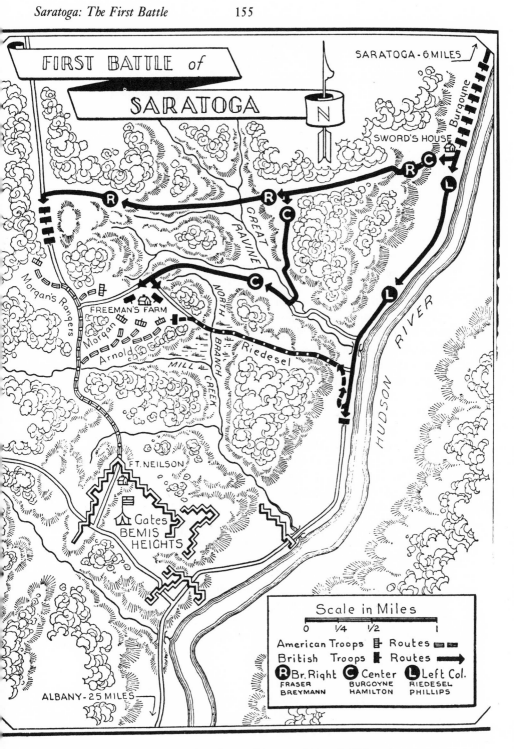

FIRST BATTLE of SARATOGA

SARATOGA - 6 MILES

SWORD'S HOUSE

Burgoyne

N

GREAT RAVINE

Morgan's Rangers

FREEMAN'S FARM

Morgan

Arnold

NORTH BRANCH

MILL CREEK

Riedesel

HUDSON RIVER

FT. NEILSON

Gates
BEMIS HEIGHTS

ALBANY - 25 MILES

Scale in Miles

0   ¼   ½   1

American Troops 🏴 Routes ▭▭
British Troops 🏴 Routes ➡

R Br. Right   **C** Center   **L** Left Col.
FRASER   BURGOYNE   RIEDESEL
BREYMANN   HAMILTON   PHILLIPS

Lynn Montross, *The Story of the Continental Army*, Harper and Row, Publishers, Inc.

western flank, was Morgan's corps of riflemen and a light infantry regiment commanded by Major Henry Dearborn.

On the morning of the 18th Gates was heartened by the arrival of General Stark who had finally been persuaded to join the main army. The addition of his 1,500 men would give the American commander a decided numerical superiority, and the army "was animated by the arrival of [this] band of citizen-soldiers who had conquered the Germans and killed their commander near Bennington." But it was quickly evident that Stark and his men were only passing through. The militia enlistments expired that very day and by noon, despite the vehement urgings of Gates and his officers, it was obvious that the New Hampshire men were determined to go home. Stark seems to have done little to try to dissuade them, and by early afternoon they had departed; "neither officer nor private was left behind."[9]

FREEMAN'S FARM

To the north of the American lines for the next few miles the country was rough and wooded, cut by numerous ravines and creeks meandering from the western hills down to the Hudson. One of these lay immediately in front of the American position. Another, called the Great Ravine, cut a deep gash from west to east about two and a half miles to the north. Where these and lesser water courses led to the river they cut the Albany road. With their usual thoroughness the Americans had destroyed all the bridges, making tedious work for Burgoyne's engineers. The woods between Bemis Heights and the Great Ravine were interspersed with a few clearings around small farms whose owners had long since abandoned them.

On the day that Gates began to dig in on Bemis Heights Burgoyne's army crossed the Hudson from Fort Miller to the west bank at the little village of Saratoga. He had now accumulated his store of provisions for thirty days, most of which moved on bateaux down the river. The troops and the artillery train crossed on a boat bridge and once it was dismantled Burgoyne broke his last link with Lake Champlain and Canada; "from the hour I passed the Hudson's river and proceed towards Albany, all safety of communication ceases." The news from Howe was almost two months old at which time the British commander in chief had told him only that "my intention is for Philadelphia," and assuring him of support if Washington turned north. Clinton in New York could be counted on only to "act as occurrences may direct." Knowing his friend as he did Burgoyne probably did not expect substantial assistance from the lower Hudson.

But he was determined to press forward; ". . . I had dislodged the enemy repeatedly, when in force and more strongly posted; my army was conscious of having the superiority, and eager to advance. . . ." Had he not gone forward he would have fallen under the same stigma of caution and indecision that had threatened the reputation of his fellow generals. Whether he really believed that his orders left him no choice, his flamboyant nature and his driving ambition would scarcely have permitted him to retreat until he had "tried a battle with the enemy." Besides, Gentleman Johnny was a gambler. Unfortunately, there was somewhat more than a drunken young nobleman contending for the stakes.

The army that moved down the Hudson was lean and spare compared to the grand parade that had ascended the Richelieu almost four months before. The English troops were nearly intact except for the regiment left behind to guard Ticonderoga. Three hundred recruits had joined at Fort Edward bringing the redcoat rank and file to 2,900 infantry and 150 artillerymen. Riedesel's Germans had suffered more severely. One regiment was detached at Ticonderoga and nearly 400 of his regulars had been lost at Bennington. With Captain Pausch's gunners the Baron mustered 1,800 rank and file. All but about 100 of Burgoyne's Indians had vanished into the forest and his Canadian and Tory provincials did not exceed 500 men. As the army moved down the right bank of the Hudson its total strength was about 5,500 men.[10]

Ever since Fort Edward Burgoyne's reconnaissance had been deteriorating. On August 4 St. Luc de La Corne had presided over a council at which the Indians had again insisted on a free hand in the conduct of their operations. When this was refused the Indians began to desert in droves thus depriving the British of "scouts and outposts, and all the lesser but necessary services for giving due repose to the Camp." The few Indians who remained, perhaps sensing the changing fortunes of the campaign, became less enterprising and more cautious. From the time he crossed the Hudson Burgoyne was uncertain of both the numbers and the position of his opponent.

The Americans, conversely, became bolder, especially after the arrival of Morgan's men. These forest-wise frontiersmen constantly harassed Burgoyne's pickets and advance parties, restricting the range of his scouts so that they had little opportunity to obtain information. On the east bank of the river parties of American militia were also able to keep track of enemy's movements.

On the 16th the British moved down river and Burgoyne conducted a limited reconnaissance that moved as far as Sword's Farm about four miles from Bemis Heights. He made no contact with the Americans and during the next two days the entire force with its baggage and artillery was brought up. Bridges were repaired and the road improved for the next forward movement. Toward evening of the 18th "regiments of the enemy with banners, could plainly be seen."

These troops were undoubtedly part of a scouting force led by Arnold. They surprised an enemy party digging for potatoes and gathering forage. The Americans opened fire killing and wounding several redcoats but then withdrew to the American lines. This was the first contact between the British and the army of the Northern Department since the retreat from Ticonderoga.

On the morning of September 19 a thick fog delayed the British until the

late forenoon. Burgoyne mustered his troops in three divisions for a reconnaissance in force which he expected would bring on an engagement. Fraser's
advance corps contained the flank companies (grenadiers and light infantry)
of all the British regiments, plus the 24th Regiment, the Brunswick grenadiers
and light infantry, and the few remaining Indians and provincials. Altogether
Fraser had with him nearly 2,000 men. His task was to move to the right as far
as the line of hills west of the river and attempt to flank the American left. The
center under General Hamilton consisting of the English 9th, 20th, 21st, and
62nd Regiments also moved away from the river and then turned south forming on Fraser's left. Burgoyne accompanied this force of about 1,100 men.
Riedesel and the Germans moved on the road which followed the right bank
of the Hudson, making repairs in the bridges and fills, clearing the way for the
rear elements which guarded the baggage. The German wing consisted of
Regiments Rhetz, Specht, and Riedesel, and mustered 1,100 bayonets. From
his artillery train Burgoyne had allocated eight guns to the advance corps and
six to Hamilton's center; eight guns of Captain Pausch's Hesse-Hanau artillery accompanied Riedesel's command. Altogether the strike force had about
five guns per thousand men. By noon the British force was deployed and ready
to move south, but its component parts were separated by the woods and the
rough terrain. This seems not to have disturbed Burgoyne; he merely ordered
Fraser to await the firing of three guns as the signal for a general attack.[11]

Word that the British were on the move reached American headquarters
from scouts sent out early in the morning. Gates' inclination was to sit tight
and let the enemy come to him. But General Arnold strongly objected. Up to
this point there seems to have been little trouble between the two major generals. The argument this morning over tactics seems to have been vehement
but not ill-tempered. Arnold urged that in the forest the Americans would
be able to employ the kind of harassing tactics at which they excelled. He also
argued that it would be folly to allow Burgoyne to bring up his guns unopposed to batter the American fortifications.

Gates' decision was a nice compromise. Morgan's corps was directed to
advance and make contact with the enemy. The rest of Arnold's wing was held
in readiness to support Morgan. The riflemen and the light infantry moved
out and after marching a little more than a mile they reached a clearing about
seven or eight hundred yards long and almost four hundred yards across. This
was Freeman's farm. Burgoyne's center had crossed the Great Ravine and was
drawn up just north of the clearing waiting for Fraser to get in position farther to the west. A British picket had been sent forward to occupy a small shed
on the edge of the woods. One of Morgan's detachments spotted the enemy,
advanced, and opened fire. Since they were well beyond musket range the
British skirmishers probably did not take cover, for the rifle fire hit them with
telling effect. They hastily retreated and Morgan's men pursued them—
squarely into the main British line. A volley of musket fire slammed into the
Americans and they took to their heels. Colonel Wilkinson, riding forward to

ascertain the progress of the advance, found the riflemen scattered, Morgan almost alone and, according to Wilkinson, sobbing in frustration. More likely the "Old Waggoner" was filling the forest air with a special brand of frontier profanity. But he was soon sounding his turkey call and pulling his command back together.

In the meantime Poor's brigade had been sent forward in support. Its leading regiments. Cilley's and Scammell's, drifted off to the left and struck Fraser's corps on the British right. The grenadiers and light infantry counterattacked vigorously and the American advance was brought to a halt. At this point Poor's men tried to drive between Fraser and Hamilton. They were checked and driven back as the 24th Regiment and Breymann's Brunswickers extended into the gap and formed on Hamilton's right. By about three o'clock the battle, which had begun at the break between the right and center wings, had shifted to the clearing opposite the English regiments composed, from right to left, of the 21st, the 62nd, and the 20th, with the 9th in reserve. Some of Learned's men were now fed into the American line although some of the Massachusetts brigade drifted off to the left. The Americans now advanced across the clearing of Freeman's farm and drove the enemy back into the trees north of the open ground. They even overran the British guns but the redcoat artillerymen had prudently carried off their linstocks, so that their guns could not be turned on them. The British reformed and came surging back, counterattacking with the bayonet and driving the Americans back across the open ground.

The seesaw battle of advance and retreat raged for the next three hours. The British, outnumbered on this part of the field by about two to one, fought stubbornly. Their guns played havoc with the American attacking line and drew the concentrated fire of every assault. Captain Jones, commanding the battery, and four other officers were killed, and thirty-six gunners were cut down by the Americans. Lieutenant Hadden, the only officer who had not been hit, called on General Hamilton for men to serve the guns but the hard pressed infantry could not spare them. Before the day was over these four regiments would lose thirty percent of their force, 76 killed, and 250 wounded. With most of its guns silenced, with the 62nd reduced to 60 or 70 men, the British line was on the edge of disaster.

Along the river General Riedesel was making his way unopposed except by broken bridges and washouts. All afternoon he had listened to the sound of firing which rolled down from the heights to the west, but no orders came. Finally Riedesel sent one of his own officers to find out what was happening. About five o'clock the officer returned with orders from Burgoyne to reinforce the line on the left. Riedesel did not hesitate. Snatching up the nearest troops, two companies of Regiment Rhetz and two of Pausch's guns, he hurried up the bluff ordering his own Regiment Riedesel to follow. He rushed through the woods until he came to the flank of the hard-pressed 20th. Without waiting for his own regiment he threw the two Rhetz companies in against the Americans and Pausch's guns opened with grape. In a few moments Regiment Riedesel came up and the Baron sent them scrambling across an intervening ravine and up the far side to attack Poor's men. The Americans were driven back, and in the gathering darkness the British line reformed, now bolstered by Riedesel's fresh troops.

This was the turning point of the battle. Morgan and Poor pulled back their regiments, Learned disengaged on the left, and the battered redcoats retained possession of the field. They had lost 140 killed and 360 wounded. The Americans had suffered substantially less, 65 killed and 254 wounded and missing.

Although the American withdrawal was orderly there was no elation of the sort that usually accompanies a victory. That night anxiety over the possibility of an attack kept most of the army from generals to privates awake and standing to arms. The plain fact was that the Americans believed that they had been beaten and that as soon as the British caught their breath they would storm Bemis Heights. The next morning there was a good deal of confusion; "we were badly fitted to defend [our] works," reported James Wilkinson. The troops of the left wing had expended most of their ammunition and it had not been replenished. Indeed, the whole army was short of powder and shot. Again a morning fog concealed the approaches from the north. A deserter from the 62nd regiment reported that the British were about to renew the attack. Anxiously the men peered into the fog expecting redcoats to loom out of the mist at any moment. Then, about nine o'clock, the sun burned away the mist and there was no enemy in sight. The deserter's report lost some of its credibility, and the Americans finally began to persuade themselves that they had delivered an effective blow against the invaders. Yet for the next four days the soldiers looked anxiously northward from their trenches and breastworks; "we hourly Expect a General Battle," said Major Dearborn on the 22nd.[12]

American fears of an impending action were not unfounded. Burgoyne wrote to General Powell commanding at Ticonderoga, "We have had a smart and very honorable action, and are now encamped in front of the field, which must demonstrate our victory beyond the power of even an American newswriter to explain away." He was prepared to follow up this success and actually deployed his regiments on the morning of September 20. But he had second thoughts undoubtedly induced by the severe casualties suffered by his best regiments. Burgoyne decided to postpone the attack, and on the 21st he received a message from New York. Sir Henry Clinton was bestirring himself and the dispatch asked if a diversion on the lower Hudson might not be welcome. Burgoyne immediately replied, urging "an attack, or the menace of an attack. . . . Do it, my dear friend, directly." Thus heartened, the British dug in to wait for help.[13]

On the whole, the action of September 19 was a curious one. Of the two commanding generals Gates had clearly demonstrated his superiority. Knowing that time was on his side he had prudently pursued his defensive strategy. He permitted the left wing to deliver its attack but despite Arnold's urgent pleas Gates refused to commit any more reinforcements after Poor and Learned went into action. Nixon, Paterson, and Glover remained firmly in place on Bemis Heights against the possibility of a disaster at Freeman's Farm. On the battlefield itself the American command did not distinguish itself (Arnold's precise role is not clear). The attempt to split the gap between Hamilton and Fraser was sound, but thereafter no overall command was exerted over the various brigades. Continuous charges across the clearing unsupported by artillery was playing the British game. After all, Burgoyne was committed to the advance. If the Americans had, for example, held to the woods south of Freeman's Farm and employed the flexible tactics at which they were allegedly expert, they could have received the British attack across a clear field of fire while protected themselves by the cover of the forest. Instead they repeatedly threw themselves against the devastating fire of the British guns and infantry—and painfully learned what history has to teach about "the thin red line."

If American leadership was faulty Burgoyne's was deplorable. In rough and broken country he divided his force so that coordinated action was impossible (one wonders if he would have sent for help from Riedesel if the German had not sent his own messenger to offer it). But the most shocking lapse was Fraser's. Not only did he have the elite regiments, the grenadiers and light infantry, but he had almost as many troops as the other two corps combined. It was his right wing that was to deliver the decisive blow and turn the American flank. Yet after repulsing the initial American attack he stood fast in his position while the center absorbed the full weight of the American assault. For this Burgoyne must share the blame, for when he finally called for help he sent to Riedesel who was a mile and a half away while Fraser could not have been more than a third that distance to his right. Whatever the reason for Fraser's strange immobility, it was buried with the fearless Scot on October 8.

What happened on the field at Freeman's Farm, then, was that Burgoyne, who was committed to an offensive designed to dislodge Gates from his blocking position, stood on the defensive. The Americans, whose task was simply to check Burgoyne's advance, hurled themselves against the British line until they had spent their energy and were driven from the field. Yet as Lieutenant Anbury observed several days later, "Notwithstanding the glory of the day remains on our side, I am fearful the real advantages resulting from this hard-fought battle, will rest on that of the Americans, our army being so much weakened by this engagement, as not to be of sufficient strength to venture forth and improve our victory, which may, in the end, put a stop to our intended expedition. . . ."

On the American side young Henry Dearborn grasped the full significance of the battle more clearly than anyone. The major's journal is terse and to the point, the daily entries often limited to a phrase or two. Although he was in action for seven continuous hours on September 19 his account runs to only 300 spare words, concluding with the laconic comment, "on this Day has Been fought one of the Greatest Battles that ever was fought in America. . . ."[14]

ELEVEN

Philadelphia
Takes Howe

If Sir Henry Clinton was baffled and disbelieving over General Howe's decision to take ship for Pennsylvania, George Washington was completely disconcerted. Even after the British fleet was reported in Delaware Bay Washington professed:

> I am now as much puzzled by their designs, as I was before; being unable to account, upon any plausible Plan, for General Howe's conduct in this instance or why he should go Southward rather than cooperate with Mr. Burgoyne. The latter appeared to me so probable and of such importance and still does, that I shall with difficulty give in to a contrary belief, till I can be obliged by some unequivocal event.[1]

By Sea to Philadelphia

There had never been any doubt in Howe's mind about his destination for the summer campaign of 1777. Yet, as always, the British commander moved as though time meant nothing. He had shifted his headquarters to his brother's flagship, the *Eagle*, on June 24, but it was a full month before the fleet finally weighed anchor. The army, 13,000 strong, was embarked on July 9 but Sir William so far acknowledged his responsibility for Burgoyne as to say he could not leave without some word from the upper Hudson. His concern was somewhat odd in view of the fact that he had made up his mind to sever his connection with the northern army.

On the 15th he received a dispatch from Burgoyne written as the latter was preparing to attack Ticonderoga. The next day Howe sent his own dispatch to Germain, a typical hodgepodge of self-justification and bad logic. Sir William noted that Washington was moving toward the Hudson for the purpose of "preventing a junction between this and the northern army, which will no further affect my proceeding to Pensilvania. . . ." If this movement of the enemy represented a threat to New York city "I shall . . . strengthen Sir Henry Clinton still more by the reserve which is already ordered to remain here. . . ." (Three days later, over Clinton's protests, he detached a full brigade from the New York garrison and added it to his own force.)

Should Washington move against Burgoyne Howe thought the northern commander would have sufficient forces "to leave me no room to dread the event," despite the fact that Washington and Schuyler between them would outnumber Burgoyne more than two to one; "but if Mr. Washington's intention should be to retard the approach of General Burgoyne to Albany he may soon find himself exposed to an attack from this quarter." If by "this quarter" Howe meant Clinton's command, Sir Henry himself noted that his garrison force had been reduced to a point that "would leave no surplus whatsoever for offensive operations." If Howe meant that he himself would go to Burgoyne's assistance it is difficult to see how he would have timely news of Washington's movements if he were at sea en route to Philadelphia.[2]

Having thus, in his own mind, prepared for all possible contingencies Howe took another week to tidy up his affairs, including, no doubt, a fond farewell to his mistress, Mrs. Loring. On July 23 Lord Richard Howe's fleet, 267 sail in all, cleared Sandy Hook and turned south. For a week the great task force plodded down the Atlantic and on July 30 entered Delaware Bay. Here Captain Andrew Snape Hammond, commanding HMS *Roebuck* which patrolled the Bay, reported to the *Eagle*. He recommended to Howe that the troops be disembarked on the western shore at Reedy Island, about twelve miles below Wilmington. Here Howe would have been thirty-five miles from Philadelphia.

To Hammond's astonishment Howe announced his intention to go on to Chesapeake Bay. He was, he said, afraid the rebels would oppose his landing with floating batteries and fire ships; besides, a landing at the head of the Chesapeake would put his army between Washington and American supply depots at York, Reading, and Carlisle.

The reaction of the officers of the expedition to Howe's decision ranged from puzzlement to outrage. Even Admiral Howe entered a mild demurrer, a rare occasion, for his Lordship meticulously refrained from interfering with his brother's military decisions. But keeping men and animals jammed aboard the transports for additional weeks in the August heat was bound to be extremely debilitating. Lord Howe's staff secretary, Ambrose Serle, remarked, "May GOD defend us from the Fatality of the worst Climate in America. . . ."

A glance at a modern map will show that the two sites are at approximately the two ends of the Chesapeake-Delaware Canal, less than twenty miles apart. A landing at the head of Chesapeake Bay would cut the American army off from its supply bases only if Washington wished it so. But Sir William was adamant. Once more the fleet put out into the Atlantic, a move so puzzling to Washington that he halted his movement toward Philadelphia.

The appearance of the fleet off Cape Henlopen had appeared to confirm Philadelphia as Howe's objective. Until this news reached Washington he had prudently kept his army near New York so as to be in position to contest a thrust up the Hudson. Howe's embarkation and southward course had induced Washington to move cautiously toward Philadelphia, but he was figuratively looking over his shoulder, suspecting a feint that would find Howe back on the Hudson to cooperate with Burgoyne. The report of Howe's appearance in Delaware Bay caused him to start the whole army southward, and he himself rode to Philadelphia to inspect its defenses. When the British again put to sea there seemed reason to believe that Howe was indeed playing a foxy game, so on August 10 the commander in chief started the army on a slow march back toward New York. Finally, on August 22 came definite news that the English fleet was in Chesapeake Bay. With a feeling of vast relief Washington again reversed the army's march and started for the capital, now certain that Howe "must mean to reach Philadelphia by that Route, tho' to be sure it is a very strange one." What with all the marching and countermarching, the men in the ranks must have thought their own commander's route equally strange.[3]

Washington's decision to defend the capital was based partly on political considerations, so he decided to put the army on display en route to his meeting with the British by parading it through Philadelphia. In the course of campaigning in the first half of 1777 the haphazard organization of the Continental Line had become more stabilized. Both the regiments and Washington's generals had acquired experience, not only in combat but in troop movement and administration. The army was now organized into divisions, and several major generals were beginning to emerge as competent commanders. Already marked as the ablest tactician and strategist of them all was Nathanael Greene. Not only was his division the best organized but when the army formed for battle Washington always gave him command of that part of the field where the danger seemed greatest.

William Alexander, who refused to abandon his Irish title of Lord Stirling, had emerged as one of the hardest fighters in the army. He had also earned a reputation as one of its hardest drinkers, but no one ever accused him of being drunk in combat. His division contained two outstanding regiments, Smallwood's Marylanders and Haslet's Delaware Continentals. John Sullivan had had the misfortune to command the American left at Long Island, and he had also briefly commanded the disastrous American expedition to Canada in the summer of 1776. But he had performed brilliantly at Trenton and, despite a botched affair at Staten Island in August, he still enjoyed Washington's confidence. When Congress voted to relieve him in order to investigate his conduct, the commander in chief refused to release him in the face of the imminent threat of Howe's invasion.

Adam Stephen, a Virginian, was so given to exaggerated reports of his prowess that Washington finally had to tell him flatly that one of Stephen's reports of "an orderly retreat" was, in fact, "a disorderly rout," and that "the disadvantage was on our side, not the enemy's." Like Stirling, Stephen was fond of liquor but, unlike the Irishman, there was growing evidence that the Virginian was beginning to rely on the bottle to stiffen his resolution in battle.

Washington tolerated him because they had fought together in the Seven Years' War, and because there were simply not enough major generals available. The fifth division was Benjamin Lincoln's and in his absence the command fell to "Mad Anthony" Wayne. The nickname should be taken in its eighteenth century context when it often meant fiery or impulsive. Wayne was thirty-two years old and had fought in the Canadian campaign of 1776. He had preceded Gates as commander of Ticonderoga and had been promoted to brigadier general in February, 1777. He commanded the Pennsylvania Line and had impressed the commander in chief as an able administrator, but he had not had combat experience as a division commander. Wayne was belligerent and pugnacious in battle, but not mad.[4]

The grand parade through the capital was led by General Washington, as always an impressive and heroic figure. There were bands and the clattering hooves of the mounted troops, led by Colonel Theodorick Bland's First Virginia Dragoons; the rumbling wheels of Henry Knox's guns, and the tramp of rank on rank of infantry—14,000 officers and men. "The best clothed men were the Virginians and the smartest looking troops were Smallwood's Marylanders." The regiments passed in files of twelve and the long column took two hours to pass through the center of the city. John Adams, self-styled military expert, watched with a critical eye. "Our soldiers have not yet quite the air of soldiers," he noted. "They don't step exactly in time. They don't hold their heads quite erect, nor turn out their toes exactly as they ought. They don't all of them cock their hats; and such as do, don't all wear them the same way."

One untoward episode marred the scene toward the end of the display, and Washington, at the head of the column, was probably not aware of it. He had ordered that "not a woman belonging to the army is to be seen," so the rather considerable number of camp followers were "spirited off into quaint little alley ways and side streets." As they tramped along parallel to the army's line of march they seethed with resentment. It was *their* army and *their* men. Somewhere in the middle of the city their resentment exploded. They "poured after their soldiers, their hair flying, their brows beaded from the heat, their belongings slung over one shoulder, chattering and yelling in sluttish shrills as they went, and spitting in the gutters." So the women made it their parade, too.

Riding at Washington's side at the head of the column was a young Frenchman whose name was destined to pepper the American landscape with place names. The Marquis de Lafayette had arrived from France a few weeks before, one of the cloud of foreign officers whose ambitious pretensions were usually inversely proportionate to their abilities. But the twenty year old marquis was an altogether different case. Scion of one of the truly old and aristocratic families in France, he offered to serve without salary or expenses. He accepted the rank of major general but did not ask for a command. He had come, he said, only to learn, and he impressed the commanding general, who had come to loathe most of the foreign officers foisted on him by a Congress eager to gain sympathy abroad. Lafayette's modesty, his quick intelligence, and his eagerness to learn earned him, first Washington's regard, and then his respect and affection. Lafayette's modest charm extended to the rest of the officer corps and ultimately to the men in the ranks. And the young Frenchman's admiration for Washington developed into an extreme case of hero worship.

The army moved on from Philadelphia to Wilmington where Washington established his headquarters on August 25.[5]

It took the British fleet two weeks to reach Cape Henry, for the ponderous armada could only proceed as fast as the slowest ship. Ten days were consumed sailing up the great bay to the Head of the Elk. Twenty-five days from Delaware Bay Howe landed his army—ten miles farther from Philadelphia than if he had landed at Reedy Island. Altogether it had taken the British commander thirty-three days to bring his army some twenty miles closer to Philadelphia than it had been at Perth Amboy in June. Moreover, it was an army whose men were exhausted from more than a month at sea in the summer's heat. The army's horses—those that survived—were physical wrecks.

But the most severe blow was the fact that there were virtually no Loyalists to welcome Howe. Many farms and villages were deserted and in some cases the people of the neighborhood had burned their crops to prevent the enemy from using them. No more than a handful of people came forward to greet Sir William and pledge their allegiance to the English cause. So the hope of a Loyalist rising in Pennsylvania and a campaign that would end with the conquest of the middle states secured by an occupation force of provincial troops disappeared in the smoke of the burning fields. Howe abandoned his intention of seizing the supply depots (if indeed he ever had such intention) and ordered his victualling ships back to the Delaware—presumably to brave the fire ships and floating batteries which he had earlier avoided. He would, he told Admiral Howe, allow ten days for them to reach New Castle, by which time he expected to be in position to destroy the rebel army.

On August 30 Howe finally replied to Germain's May 18 dispatch which had approved the movement to Pennsylvania by sea on condition that Burgoyne was properly supported. Howe had received this on August 12 while he was still at sea. Now his belated reply revealed between its lines the ruin of Sir William's strategy. He would, he said, be unable to cooperate with Burgoyne; and "the prevailing disposition of the inhabitants [of Pennsylvania] . . . I am sorry to observe, seem to be, excepting a few individuals, strongly in enmity against us. . . ." He reminded Germain that his previous request for reinforcements had not been met, and that "in the present extended situation of the King's southern army" the American Secretary should not expect the war to be ended by the present campaign. Read out of context Howe's dispatch makes it appear almost as if Germain were responsible for the deplorable state of affairs. Sir William had by now become quite accomplished at laying his faults on others.[6]

The one bright spot in this otherwise gloomy prospect was the news that Washington's army was only a few miles away, and from the disposition of the American troops it was obvious that they were looking for a fight.

As soon as Howe's landing was reported to headquarters at Wilmington Washington began to call in his various detachments: Sullivan, from his "unlucky" attack on Staten Island; Colonel George Baylor, who was recruiting for the dragoons; and most of all, to the militia regiments from Pennsylvania, Maryland and Virginia. "It is to be wished that every Man could bring a good Musket and Bayonet into the field, but in times like the present, we must make the best shift we can, and I would therefore advise you to exhort every Man to bring the best he has." Washington also ordered the formation of a regiment of light infantry made up of 100 men from each of the nine brigades of Continentals to be used for such special duties as reconnaissance, advance guard, and covering force. The command was given to Colonel William Maxwell who had served as a provincial officer with the British army in America for twenty years.

On the 27th Washington and his staff rode southwest to find the British. It was obvious that his fox hunter's blood was up and his eagerness brought him within sight of the enemy, although he could make no satisfactory estimate of its numbers. On that day and the next he rode the countryside trying to familiarize himself with the terrain. By the 29th he was back in Wilmington where he ordered out Maxwell's light infantry "to be watchful and guarded on all the Roads."[7]

By this time Howe's command had sufficiently recovered from its sea voyage and begun to stir itself. The British force consisted of about 13,000 men divided between eight German regiments and seventeen regiments of redcoats. Mounted troops were scarce although raids through the countryside had procured enough horses for the artillery and a few dragoons for reconnaissance. But Howe still lacked a sufficient force of mounted troops that could be used to perform the classic functions of screening and pursuit.

Howe divided his force into two "grand divisions." One of these, composed of four German regiments and nine of redcoats, numbered about 5,500 men commanded by the Hessian general, Baron Wilhelm von Knyphausen. The other division was led by General Cornwallis and consisted of twelve English regiments and three of Hessians. It included a brigade of the Guards and seven regiments of grenadiers and light infantry. Its total strength was 7,500 rank and file.

On September 8 the British army broke camp. The early hours before dawn were lit by the eerie northern lights, the aurora borealis, as the regiments filed off to the northeast. Howe's intelligence had reported the enemy across his path, obviously ready to dispute his passage to Philadelphia. The British moved toward the American right flank causing Washington to shift to the northwest. He took up a position along the left bank of Brandywine Creek at Chadd's Ford. The Brandywine was not a formidable obstacle, but its deep sharp banks compelled the British to use its fords. These were numerous and Washington's decision to defend Chadd's was because it was on the principal road to Philadelphia, and because rough country to the southeast would make it possible to hold his left flank with militia.

By September 10 the British army was encamped at Kennett Square, six miles west of Chadd's Ford and twenty-six miles from Philadelphia.[8]

The Brandywine

William Howe may not have been a military genius, but he was perfectly at home on the battlefield. Although he was fighting in the enemy's country his knowledge of terrain and road networks was invariably superior to Washington's. He used his information to good advantage and his execution was nearly flawless. In the pre-dawn darkness of September 11 Howe's army was in motion along the Nottingham Road which led toward Chadd's Ford. About five miles west of the Ford this road intersected the Great Valley Road which led northward toward West Chester. Howe planned a wide turning movement against Washington's right flank, so when the British reached the intersection Cornwallis' division, accompanied by General Howe, swung left and filed northward, while Knyphausen's division continued directly eastward on the Nottingham Road. About a mile beyond where the two divisions separated, Knyphausen's van, Major Patrick Ferguson's Queen's Rangers, came to Welch's Tavern. There some American videttes were refreshing themselves in Welch's tap room, and they barely escaped by dashing out the back door.

From Washington's post at Chadd's Ford the Brandywine flowed from the north slightly to east of south toward the Delaware, ten miles away. Above Chadd's, at about one mile intervals, were Brinton's Ford, Wistar's Ford, Jones Ford and Buffington Ford, the latter located at the forks of the Brandywine. These names and other local landmarks were not thoroughly familiar to Washington or his generals, and he seems not to have taken the precaution of having at hand someone who knew the countryside. His army was formed into three wings. Downstream the left was guarded by 1,500 militia posted at the one usable ford. Rough terrain and the widening of the river as it approached the Delaware seemed to preclude any danger in this sector. Greene and Wayne, with their divisions, were in the center with Sullivan on the right. Stirling and Stephen were in support, prepared to reinforce either Greene or Sullivan. The American right extended beyond Jones Ford, and Sullivan had been told by the people of the neighborhood that above Jones there was no usable ford for twelve miles. Colonel Moses Hazen, guarding Jones Ford on Sullivan's right, was ordered to scout to the north and west. A perusal of the orders and dispositions issued by Washington and his generals indicates that they were quite vague about the geography of the area. In fact, during the battle the commander in chief needed a guide to take him from one part of the battlefield to the other.[9]

As reports of Knyphausen's advance began to come in Washington ordered Maxwell's regiment across the Brandywine to establish contact with the enemy. It was the videttes of the light troops that Ferguson's Rangers flushed at Welch's Tavern. Supported by the jägers, the Rangers pushed the Americans back until they came within sight of Chadd's Ford. There Maxwell's men stiffened and their stubborn fighting brought the British van to a halt. Three more regiments of redcoats had to be brought up before the 800 light infantrymen could be dislodged. Washington ordered Maxwell back to the east side of the Brandywine as the rest of Knyphausen's division came up and began to deploy. By about 10:30 the British had formed a line opposite the Ford and a desultory artillery duel began; ". . . the [American] balls and grapeshot fell right among us, [but] this cannonade had little effect because the battery was placed too low." Howe and Cornwallis were almost to Trimble's Ford, six miles upstream on the West Branch of the Brandywine. Here the flanking column turned eastward.

Eleven o'clock came and went and there was no movement from Knyphausen. Washington became increasingly uneasy as memories of Long Island began to plague him. He had earlier ordered Colonel James Ross and a small party of Pennsylvanians to reconnoiter west of the Brandywine, and all of the light dragoons were patrolling to the north of Sullivan. He had finally found a man who was familiar with the neighborhood, Major James Spear of the Pennsylvania militia, and had sent him off to scout the British movements.

The first warning came from Colonel Hazen who commanded what was known as the "Canadian Regiment" on Sullivan's right. He reported a strong British column to the west headed toward the forks of the Brandywine. Soon afterward a message from Colonel Ross reported a column of at least 5,000 men on the Great Valley Road at about 11:00 o'clock. Ross was hanging on the rear of the column and some of his men had skirmished with the British rearguard.

Here was the answer to the curious inactivity of the British across Chadd's Ford. Howe was repeating the maneuver of Long Island. This offered a great opportunity, for if Howe had as many as 5,000 men Knyphausen, with only slightly more than half the strength of the American force, was vulnerable. Washington began issuing orders. Colonel Bland and his dragoons were to reconnoiter and confirm the flanking movement. Stirling and Stephen were to move into a blocking position at the Birmingham Meeting House, two miles beyond Jones Ford, and check Howe's flanking column. Greene, Sullivan, and Wayne were to prepare to cross the river and smash Knyphausen. It was now about noon.

At this point a message arrived from Sullivan at Brinton's Ford:

Since I sent you the message by Major Morris I saw some of the Militia who

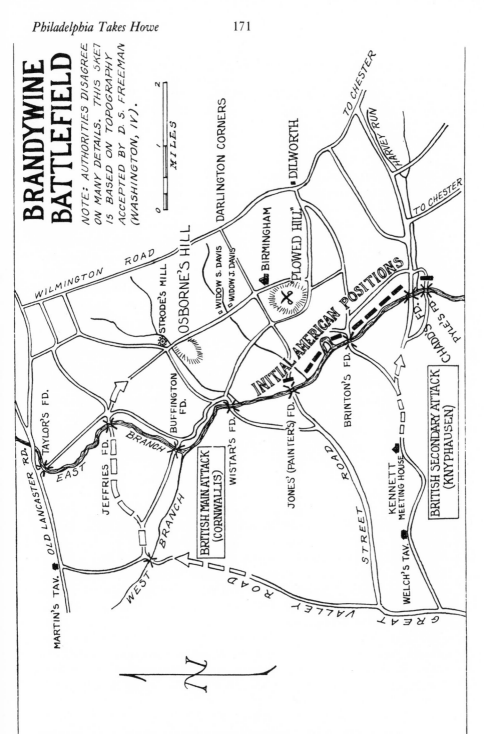

BRANDYWINE BATTLEFIELD

NOTE: AUTHORITIES DISAGREE ON MANY DETAILS. THIS SKETCH IS BASED ON TOPOGRAPHY ACCEPTED BY D. S. FREEMAN (WASHINGTON, IV).

© Mark Boatner, III, *Encyclopedia of the American Revolution*, David McKay Co., Inc.

came in this morning from a tavern called Martins on the forks of the Brandy-wine. The one who told me, said that he had come from thence to Welches Tavern and had heard nothing of the Enemy above the forks of the Brandywine and is confident that [sic] are not in that Quarters. So that Colonel Hazen's Information must be wrong. I have sent to the Quarter to know whether there is any foundation for the Report. . . .

The information came from the Pennsylvania militia officer, Major Spear, and it may be that he himself brought Sullivan's dispatch to Washington. This might explain why Washington believed this report in the face of those of Hazen and Ross. What Spear did not make clear, and what Washington failed to perceive because of his vague knowledge of the neighborhood was that Martin's Tavern was not "on the forks" of the Brandywine, that is, at Buffington's Ford, but three miles up the West Branch and a mile above Trimble's Ford where Howe and Cornwallis had turned east. Howe's column was probably at Trimble's Ford about the time that Spear reported to Sullivan. Spear's information was undoubtedly correct. But neither Washington nor Sullivan asked the crucial question: *When?* When had Spear made his ride, and at what time had he intersected Howe's presumed route? The British column had covered a huge circuit of ten miles, crossing the West Branch at Trimble's Ford and continuing east to Jeffries' Ford which it reached about 2:00 p.m. Spear had evidently ridden from Martin's Tavern past Trimble's Ford early in the morning. He then continued downstream, checking each ford as he went until he arrived at Welch's Tavern. There had been some fog earlier in the day which might have obscured sound as well as sight of the British from Spear as he moved along the river east of the Great Valley Road.

Washington's lapse was understandable, if unfortunate. What was not understandable was why he credited the report of a militia officer (who knew nothing of the tactical situation or the troop dispositions) and refused to believe the reports of two experienced Continental officers, one of whom had actually skirmished with the British column.

But Washington concluded that Howe's entire force faced him across the Brandywine. Previous orders must be countermanded. Greene and Sullivan were to halt their movements and pull back to the high ground above the creek. Stirling and Stephen should halt where they were and be ready once more to support the center and right.

Whether there were other reports seeming to confirm Spear or not, there was one that contradicted him. About 2:00 in the afternoon an excited man named Thomas Cheney arrived at headquarters. The big, black-eyed farmer shouldered Washington's aides aside and insisted on seeing the commander in chief. The army, he told Washington, was nearly surrounded. He himself had seen a huge column on the eastern side of the Brandywine. Washington refused to believe him, but he seems to have been doubtful enough to start off to see for himself. At this moment a dispatch arrived from Bland who had at last discovered the enemy north of the Birmingham Meeting House. A message from Sullivan confirmed the bad news. Washington ordered Stephen and Stirling to resume their march at once. Sullivan was sent in support and given overall command of the right wing.[10]

Sullivan immediately took the road and soon met Hazen coming down from Wistar's Ford. For the first time the division commander learned the full import of the contradictory reports, and the fact that he was faced with an enemy who was in great strength. Hurriedly he pressed on toward the Birmingham Meeting House where Stirling and Stephen were already in position. In his haste Sullivan overshot, for as he deployed his troops into line he found the other two divisions to his right and rear defending a strong position on a plowed hill. Only the fact that Cornwallis insisted on resting his men for a full hour after their seventeen mile march allowed Sullivan to come up. His appearance was the signal for the British to go into action. Cornwallis attacked toward the American right, causing Stephen and Stirling to shift their positions and further disrupting Sullivan's attempt to form on Stirling's left. Despite the confusion the American position on the hill overlooking the Meeting House held for nearly three-quarters of an hour. But Sullivan's men never got their line stabilized and under the pressure of the British assault the division broke and began to retreat in confusion.

Washington now made the decision which may well have saved his army. He ordered Maxwell and Wayne to fend off Knyphausen who was now advancing to the attack across the Brandywine. He sent Greene's division hurrying north to stem the disaster on the right, and followed them himself to be present at the critical point. As Greene's van, George Weedon's 3rd Virginia brigade, neared the Meeting House they met Sullivan's men retreating in disorder. Weedon's men calmly opened ranks to let the fugitives through, then closed and threw a hard check into the British advance. The fighting was violent and chaotic, and the tangle of American formations dictated a withdrawal southward to Chester. But the combined efforts of the American divisions had checked Cornwallis for the better part of two hours. Although he was in the thick of the battle, Washington was untouched. Young Lafayette got a bullet in the leg but continued at Washington's side, helping to rally and steady the troops.

The battle became almost as confusing to the British as to the Americans. Said one officer, "Describe the battle. 'Twas not like those of Covent Gardens or Drury Lane. . . . There was a most infernal fire of cannon and musquetry. Most incessant shouting, 'Incline to the right! Incline to the left! Halt! Charge!' etc. The balls plowing up the ground. The trees cracking over one's head. The branches riven with artillery. The leaves falling as in the autumn by grapeshot. . . . The misters on both sides showed conduct."

At Chadd's Ford Wayne and Maxwell fought a stubborn holding action, but they were hopelessly overmatched. "The enemy's [American] left flank began to fall back, and we took the battery. Our regiments, which pushed across one by one, gained one height after another, from which the enemy withdrew. They withstood one severe attack behind some houses and ditches. . . . Had not darkness favored their retreat we might have come into possession of much artillery, munitions and horses." But Wayne had done his job, holding off Knyphausen until the retreating army could pass to the south.[11]

The aftermath of the battle found many of Washington's formations badly disorganized. The roads along which the soldiers retreated were jammed, men separated from their commands, blundering along in and out of the ranks of regiments who were trying to keep their own troops in order. But there was little panic, none of the blind flight that had followed Long Island and Kip's Bay.

Not until midnight when the army reached Chester did officers bring some sort of order out of the chaos. Morning muster on the 12th seemed to indicate that losses in the battle had been heavy, but as the day passed more and more men straggled into camp. General Greene set the losses at between 1,200 and 1,300 men, killed, wounded and missing, slightly more than ten percent of Washington's force. The British lost 575. But the most significant aspect of the defeated army was its equanimity. Washington reported to Congress, "Notwithstanding the misfortune of the day, I am happy to find the troops in good spirits. . . ." Nor was this wishful thinking. Captain Enoch Anderson of Haslet's Delawares observed that "there was not a dispairing look nor did I hear a discouraging word. . . ." 'Come, boys, we shall do better another time,' sounded throughout the little army." Congress itself took heart—at least to the extent of voting thirty hogsheads of rum to be dispensed to the soldiers.

Perhaps the best proof was the fact that within two days the army had pulled itself together, crossed the Schuylkill to Germantown, and stood once more between Howe and the capital, its commander ready for a fight.[12]

THE CAPITAL FALLS

Philadelphia lies at the tip of a peninsula bounded on the east by the Delaware river and on the west by the Schuylkill. The latter was fordable in several places but the former was not. Washington, encamped at Germantown, five miles north of the city, was faced with a difficult problem. On the one hand he was still determined to defend the capital. On the other, his principal supply depots had been established outside the capital so that the priceless stores would not be lost along with the city. In fact, it is probable that Washington never intended to defend Philadelphia at the risk of a defeat that would leave him pinned against the Delaware with no line of retreat. Nor must he allow Howe to get too far to the north between him and the stores, the nearest of which was at Reading. In short, to move northwest from Germantown to cover his supplies would expose the capital. To take a strong position before Philadelphia was to uncover the route to Reading. Washington therefore concluded that he must once more seek out Howe and attack in order to gain the initiative. On September 14th he led the army back across the Schuylkill at Swede's Ford (modern Norristown) and advanced along the Lancaster Road, throwing out Wayne and Maxwell as an advance guard.[13]

Howe had spent four days tidying up after the battle of September 11 and was now once more on the road. On the 16th the two armies came within sight of each other and occupied adjacent heights. At this moment a northeast gale of unusual violence struck the two armies. The driving, soaking rain "came down so hard that in a few moments we were drenched and sank in mud up to our calves."

So the two armies faced each other unable to fire a shot. If the British generals considered an attack with the bayonet, the gusting northeast wind which drove sheets of rain into the faces of Howe's men discouraged the notion. Washington was forced to withdraw because the inadequate cartridge boxes his troops carried could not protect ammunition against such a deluge. Four hundred thousand rounds of powder were ruined.

The nearest ammunition depot was at Reading Furnace (modern Warwick) twenty-one miles away. The army had left its baggage east of the Schuylkill so, hungry, soaked, and as usual badly shod, the army slogged off in the rain (Colonel Alexander Hamilton was sent to Philadelphia to requisition shoes but the merchants hid them against the day when they could sell them for British gold). After replenishing their cartridge boxes at the Furnace the troops turned back toward Philadelphia, and by the 19th Washington was again between Howe and the capital. The soldiers had marched fifty-two miles in a little more than forty-eight hours. Warned by Washington, the Continental Congress had packed its records and evacuated the city, moving briefly to Lancaster before settling in at York.[14]

Washington detached Mad Anthony Wayne west of the Schuylkill to screen the army's movements. Wayne attempted to conceal his little force near Paoli Tavern, hoping to ambush some unwary British detachment. Whether enemy scouts discovered him or whether his presence was reported by Loyalists, the hunter became the prey. On the night of September 20–21 Wayne's sleeping men were surprised by Major General Charles Grey at the head of five British regiments. Grey ordered a bayonet attack with unloaded muskets. Wayne's sentries got off warning shots but the redcoats were into the American camp before the troops could form. The "massacre" cost Wayne 150 men killed and wounded and was widely reported as the slaughter of defenseless men. But the fact was that Wayne was caught napping. And the "English brutes" were careful to see that forty of the American wounded were left in homes in the neighborhood to be cared for (Mad Anthony was humiliated and his resentment smoldered until he vented it on the British garrison at Stony Point two years later).

But all this maneuvering and fighting was to no purpose. On the day after the fight at Paoli Howe turned north toward Reading Furnace. Washington moved northwest to guard his stores and in the night Howe countermarched, crossing the Schuylkill and made for Philadelphia. By a simple feint Howe had again outmaneuvered his opponent. Four days later Cornwallis' van entered the city, half deserted because not only Congress but most of the Patriot residents had taken a hasty leave. Howe's long delays, both before and after the Brandywine, had allowed the removal of all military stores and other public property. The British and their German allies saw "a lovely city of considerable size . . . laid out with parallel streets. The public squares are beautiful. For the most part, ordinary houses are moderately large and built of brick in the Dutch style. Classical architecture and its embellishments are met with only in the churches and in a few public buildings. . . ."[15]

Ever since the battle of September 11 Washington had been calling for reinforcements. General Putnam, guarding the Hudson Highlands, was ordered to send 2,500 Continentals, and when General Alexander McDougall arrived with only 900 Washington lashed out at "Old Put." He was directed to send 1,600 more men without delay. "That you may not hesitate about complying with this order, you are to consider it as peremptory and not to be dispensed with." General William Smallwood was urged to bring up his Maryland militia and harass Howe's rear as he made for Philadelphia. President Thomas Wharton of Pennsylvania had already called out additional regiments of Pennsylvania militia and General Philemon Dickinson brought 1,200 men to Washington's camp, about thirty miles north of Philadelphia. By the 27th of September with the arrival of 1,000 additional Continentals from Putnam, Washington's army was at full strength, nearly 11,000 rank and file.

The next day came glorious news. Burgoyne's army had been repulsed at Freeman's Farm on September 19. Dispatches from General Gates to Congress—but not to the commander in chief—informed Washington, with some exaggeration, of "the total ruin of Burgoyne." Washington ordered the soldiers paraded, cannon to fire a thirteen-gun salute and an issue of a gill of rum to every man in the ranks.

With the cloud of worry and doubt about the northern invasion removed Washington was now free to set in motion a strategy he had been contemplating for some days. Howe had indeed taken Philadelphia, but could not this be turned to the American advantage? For in all the marching and countermarching one important fact had not escaped Washington's notice. Lord Howe's fleet was still down the Delaware from the city and must penetrate the river defenses and obstructions erected by the Americans to block its passage. Here was a great opportunity. ". . . Genl. Howe can neither support his Army in Philadelphia, if he is cut off from Communication with his ships, neither can he make good a retreat should any accident befall him."[16]

Washington had already ordered Colonel Samuel Smith to take a contingent of the crack 1st Maryland to strengthen Fort Mifflin, a fortification on an island in the middle of the Delaware. On the Jersey shore at Red Banks was Fort

Mercer, occupied by Rhode Island Continentals and New Jersey militia under Colonel Christopher Greene.

In Paris Doctor Benjamin Franklin, head of the American diplomatic mission in Paris, heard the news of the defeat at the Brandywine and the fall of the capital. He did not join in the lamentations of the Americans on his staff. Instead, the venerable philosopher pointed out that "instead of saying Sir William Howe had taken Philadelphia, it would be more proper to say, Philadelphia has taken Sir William Howe." As September drew to a close Washington advanced his headquarters closer to the capital and watched for an opportunity to prove Dr. Franklin's point.[17]

Sir William Howe's southern strategy had turned out to be a debacle. He had expected two results. The fall of their capital city would, he thought, discourage the Americans and sap their will to resist. But the capture of Philadelphia had been dreaded for so long that the actual event made comparatively little impact on American morale. Wrote one observer, ". . . I am satisfied at all times, that the loss of a battle or of a town will detract nothing, finally, from the Americans; and the acquisition of victories and territories will serve only to weaken General Howe's army, and to accelerate the period when America shall establish her freedom and independence. . . ."[18]

The second objective had been to lend support to a Loyalist rising and thus pave the way for the conquest of the middle states. It was this conviction fostered by men like Loyalist Joseph Galloway, who were undoubtedly overenthusiastic in their exaggerated reports of the sentiments of Pennsylvania, that led Howe to abandon Burgoyne. Only when it was too late to assist the northern army did Howe discover the reality of a hostile or indifferent populace.

The campaign had once again demonstrated Howe's singular indolence. For six months he had corresponded with Germain, proposing and modifying a plan of campaign. Yet when the time came to execute he seemed to flinch from plunging into action, making one impromptu maneuver after another, and finally leaving himself no alternative but the hollow conquest of Philadelphia.

Yet this indolence and indecision seemed to vanish once Sir William reached the battlefield. At the Brandywine he acted with a promptness and certitude that brought his army a victory, as on every occasion when he himself was in personal command.

Washington, by contrast, had demonstrated a considerable talent for overall strategy. His movements in the face of the bewildering confusion of Howe's movements were sound and only at the end of the Pennsylvania campaign had he been outmaneuvered. But on the battlefield Washington still showed his lack of experience, his inability to analyze a situation and respond quickly to changing conditions. Above all, he was inclined to ask too much from his commanders and expect too much from his men.

The most notable development of the campaign was in the quality of the American army. The Brandywine has often been compared with Long Island, since Howe had flanked Sullivan on both occasions. But at the Brandywine the reconnaissance had been good—only the analysis of it at headquarters had failed. And even though errors were made Sullivan had come very close to retrieving the situation on the right. The men had fought well and although they finally broke, it was not the kind of blind, disruptive panic that had so often marred the soldiers' performance. The conduct of Wayne and Maxwell at Chadd's Ford at the end of the day received little notice (then or later in the history books). Faced by Knyphausen's attacking force which was twice as large as his own, Wayne fought off the British division for two hours, that is, as Major Baurmeister testifies, until "darkness favored their retreat." And in the aftermath what was remarkable was not the number of desertions (mostly militia), but the number who finally came straggling into camp at Chester, twenty-four and even forty-eight hours later. Three days after the battle Washington was able to write, "Our Troops have not lost their spirits and I am in hopes we shall soon have an Opportunity of Compensating for the disaster we have sustained. . . . We brought the army to this place [German-town] . . . and are just beginning our march to return towards the Enemy." The Continentals had developed a certain toughness of spirit which is the mark of veteran soldiers.[19]

TWELVE

Saratoga:
The Forlorn Hope

ON THE UPPER HUDSON THE AUTUMN AIR WAS BRINGING A CHILL TO BURGOYNE'S army. Parties of Americans hovered just beyond the lines, and "not a night passed without firing, and sometimes concerted attacks on our picquets. . . . By being habituated to fire, our soldiers became indifferent to it, and were capable of eating and sleeping when it was very near them. . . ." It may have been so. But as the men shivered in their blankets surely their sleep was troubled by the howling of wolves, drawn to the battle field by the odor of corpses hastily buried in their shallow graves.[1]

THE HUDSON HIGHLANDS

On September 21 as the British worked at entrenching their positions they were alarmed by the sudden booming of guns from the American lines. Hastily the redcoats stood to arms but there was no movement from the enemy. Not until several days later did Burgoyne learn that the firing was in celebration of the news that troops commanded by Benjamin Lincoln had won victories on Lake Champlain.

By mid-September Lincoln had persuaded between 1,500 and 2,000 militia to come in to his headquarters at Pawlet in the Hampshire Grants (although they refused to go west of the Hudson). He dispatched three regiments to attack Skenesboro and Ticonderoga. Colonel John Brown made a surprise attack on the Lake George portage south of Ticonderoga and drove in the German and British outposts although he could not dislodge General Powell from Ticonderoga itself. But he captured 300 of the enemy, freed 100 American prisoners, and seized 200 batteaux and a sloop. Another American force attacked Mount Independence with indifferent success. Brown then attempted to seize a British post at Diamond Island on Lake Champlain but was driven off. The Americans also occupied Skenesboro after it had been abandoned by the British. In themselves these actions were of little importance but the fact that small detachments could roam at will behind the British made it clear that the road back to Canada was very nearly closed.

So Burgoyne was forced to rely on the slender hope that Clinton might somehow extricate him. While he waited the British commander fortified his camp. On the right farthest from the river at the northwestern edge of Freeman's Farm the German grenadiers under Breymann were posted in a redoubt. They were supported on the left by another redoubt manned by the light infantry under the Earl of Balcarres. Next came the main line of British troops extending toward the river where Burgoyne constructed a strong work called the Great Redoubt, which guarded headquarters and the army's stores.[2]

Sir Henry Clinton, left in command of New York city after General Howe put to sea, had spent two months in virtual idleness, although his inactivity was not accompanied by peace of mind. His garrison force of 7,700 men, half of them Loyalists, was barely sufficient to guard the city surrounded as it was by "an extended coast, of nearly two hundred miles altogether." He beat off a token attack on Staten Island by the Americans in mid-August and Clinton himself sallied into New Jersey in a brief and ineffective show of British force. But mostly Sir Henry waited. He waited for news from Burgoyne who had told him on August 6 that he would be in Albany by the 23rd. News of Bennington worried him and no news from Howe worried him even more.

By the middle of September Clinton became restless. For some time he had had his eye on the Hudson Highlands forty miles to the north. Here two forts, Montgomery and Clinton, guarded the approaches to the upper Hudson. General Israel Putnam commanded an American force of about 1,500 men at Peekskill on the eastern side of the river opposite the forts. Although Clinton had no idea of penetrating to Albany or even of occupying the Highlands he did believe that he might make a swift ascent up the river, drive off Putnam, and destroy the two forts. Two things were necessary, more troops and an excuse to leave New York, since the defense of the city was his primary responsibility.

It was this latter that inspired the letter that Burgoyne received on September 21. If Washington was now preoccupied to the south and Burgoyne asked for help, surely Clinton could not be faulted for responding and furthering the ministry's intention to open communication with the northern army. So the inquiry as to whether General Burgoyne might "be in want of some little diversion" was designed to elicit a request for help, furnishing thereby the excuse Sir Henry needed to attack the Hudson forts.

It took ten days for Clinton's message to reach Burgoyne. The country between Saratoga and New York swarmed with suspicious militiamen, and several British couriers travelling between the two commands were caught and hanged as spies. Each dispatch was sent by two couriers and sometimes three in order to make sure of delivery. If the dispatches were of special importance the messengers were officers. By September 29 Clinton had Burgoyne's answer and its tone of urgency was underscored by the officer messenger who reported that less than thirty days' provisions remained and that the line of retreat to Canada was threatened.[3]

Five days earlier a reinforcement of 1700 men had arrived in New York from England, providing Clinton with the additional troops he needed. For once a British commander wasted no time. By October 3 Sir Henry had embarked 3,000 men and two days later he landed at Verplanck's Point, three miles below Peekskill. Putnam took to the hills frantically seeking a defensive position from which he could defend against the superior British force. Clinton's landing was a feint and its effect was exactly what he had hoped for. The troops were reembarked and, under cover of a fog, landed on the west bank at Stony Point. Marching inland through the rugged hills he split his force and launched simultaneous attacks on the two forts. By October 8 Forts Clinton and Montgomery were overrun and the British were in possession of the Highlands.

Sir Henry had every right to be pleased with himself. He had sustained virtually no losses, his action had been a model of neatness and daring precision, and he had delivered his promised diversion. But it was not enough. Captain Alexander Campbell brought news from Burgoyne that his army was only 5,000 strong, that Gates had cut his line of retreat to Ticonderoga, and that militia pouring into the American camps had almost doubled the numbers of the enemy. (Now that the Americans sensed that Gates' army was a winner, the militia turned out in droves.) Burgoyne still believed that he could force his way to Albany (this may have been inserted for the benefit of the Americans should his dispatch be intercepted), but suggested three alternatives: attack Gates again; remain where he was; or retreat to Lake Champlain. To Clinton's amazement Burgoyne asked for "most explicit orders" as to which course he was to pursue.

It was obvious that the northern commander was desperate and looking for someone on whom he could lay at least a share of the responsibility for his situation. Having previously contended that his orders gave him no latitude but a direct advance to Albany, Burgoyne now asked for modifications from a man whom he knew was not authorized to give them. His suggestion that he should have been supported from New York was justified but he had known for weeks that Howe had gone to Pennsylvania and had never before intimated that he needed help to reach Albany.

Clinton's reply was coldly formal. "Sir Henry Clinton cannot presume to give any orders to General Burgoyne. General Burgoyne could not suppose that Sir Henry Clinton had any idea of penetrating to Albany with the small force he mentioned in his last letter." Yet Clinton, irritated as he was, would not abandon his friend. The dramatic success of his expedition led him to hope that if Burgoyne could reach Albany Clinton might be able to push through a relief expedition. His formal refusal to take responsibility for Burgoyne's action was followed by a series of encouraging personal messages: "I sincerely hope that this little success . . . may facilitate your operations;" on the 10th he noted that Sir James Wallace was taking a squadron up river; "the Commodore and I [will] do our utmost to force a communication . . . and supply . . . provisions." Not a single message reached Burgoyne.[4]

In the American camps recruits were finally beginning to swell the ranks. Most were fed into the existing regiments increasing their strength by about thirty percent. By the first week in October Gates had over 7,000 men present and fit for duty at Bemis Heights. Stark had finally returned with 1,000 New Hampshire men and was sent up the eastern side of the Hudson to threaten the British rear. Lincoln and Seth Warner also brought their men in.

It was inevitable that the uneasy truce between those two towering egos, Gates and Arnold, would eventually erupt. The occasion was Gates' report of the action of September 19 which did not mention either Arnold or the brigades of Poor and Learned which he had commanded. The victory, said Gates, was due "entirely to the valour of the Rifle Regiment and the corps of Light Infantry under the command of Colonel Morgan."

It was, intentional or not, a gratuitous insult to Arnold. Gates, a regular army man, knew that after such a victory a commander was normally either generous in his praise for everyone who had participated or omitted reference to any individuals, thereby implying that the glory was shared by all. Arnold was infuriated. He exploded into Gates' headquarters and vented his wrath in no uncertain terms. Gates replied with equal asperity, and it may be presumed that the volume, if not the words, of the altercation was heard for some distance in the vicinity of the commanding general's quarters. The quarrel brought into the open the resentment that Schuyler's friends had felt towards Gates ever since August 19. Richard Varick and Henry Brockholst Livingston, former aides to Schuyler who had attached themselves to Arnold, added fuel to the fiery controversy, and so did Gates' adjutant, Colonel Wilkinson. Arnold retired to his tent and then erupted in a blast of correspondence to Gates, the tone of which was that his gallant services were not appreciated by the commander of the Northern Department. He called on Gates to explain why he had been treated "with affront and indignity, in a public manner" and demanded "an opportunity of vindicating my conduct." He ended by offering to resign.

To his amazement and considerable discomfiture Gates acquiesced and issued a pass for Arnold and his aides to go through the lines. Arnold, his bluff called, declared his intention "to sacrifice my feelings . . . to the public good and continue in the army at this critical juncture, when my country needs every support." Gates allowed him to remain but he relieved Arnold of the command of the left wing and replaced him with Benjamin Lincoln. Colonel Wilkinson, despite the fact that he was a Gates partisan, may have had the last word. It was, he said, "traced to official presumption on the one side, and an arrogant spirit and impatience of command on the other."

The source of all the trouble, Philip Schuyler, had all the while remained at Albany, using his quartermaster's talents to keep supplies moving up the river to Bemis Heights. By the end of September Gates' command had full cartridge boxes and plenty of provisions.[5]

BURGOYNE CASTS THE DIE

In the British camp the soldiers went on half rations October 3. His outposts constantly harassed, his soldiers threadbare and shivering, his supply line closed, Burgoyne's situation was rapidly becoming intolerable. Anxiously he waited for word from Clinton but no couriers came up from the south. His efforts to reconnoiter Gates' position to get some idea of the size and deployment of the American army was unsuccessful. Although some of his wounded had recovered there was still a sizeable hospital which precluded rapid movement. Without really knowing, he sensed that the enemy was growing stronger every day.

On October 4 Burgoyne called his first council of war. It appeared that Gentleman Johnny was about to take a high-risk gamble for big stakes. To Phillips, Fraser, and Riedesel he proposed another attack. This time he would leave only 800 men to guard the baggage and boats. With 4,000 men he planned to strike again at the American left in an attempt to gain the flank and rear of the fortifications on Bemis Heights. It was a bold and audacious plan but it was also a desperate one. Yet considering the cold courage of his infantry and the cool efficiency of his gunners one wonders what would have been the outcome if Burgoyne had managed to throw the full weight of his force in against the Americans.

His subordinates were appalled. To leave the entire store of provisions under such light guard was to invite its destruction. Even if the attack succeeded it would leave the army separated from its supply base and the river. Its success depended on the ability of the British not only to flank a force nearly twice its size but to drive it into disorder. Burgoyne's generals persuaded him to postpone the decision. The next day Riedesel proposed a more limited action, a reconnaissance in force to test the American left; ". . . if it were impossible to get in the enemy's rear in one day, it would be more adviseable to recross the Hudson and again occupy their old position on the Battenkill [Fort Edward]." Burgoyne at first refused to discuss any plan involving a retrograde movement, but he was finally persuaded to "undertake another great reconnoitering expedition against the enemy's left wing to ascertain . . . whether it would be advisable to attack him. . . ." If the results were negative it was agreed to retreat to Fort Edward. The attacking force would consist of the 24th Regiment, Balcarres' light infantry, Acland's grenadiers, the flank companies of Riedesel's command, and Breymann's jägers. The total numbers of this force would be 1,500 men.[6]

This decision risked both too much and too little. To repeat the maneuver of

September 19 with less than half as many men served no purpose other than as a hollow gesture of defiance. Burgoyne's original plan, even though the odds against it were astronomical, promised dazzling rewards. But by this time "the Gamester," as Gates called him, had lost his gambler's nerve. He settled for the "reconnoitering expedition."

Late in the morning of October 7 Burgoyne, accompanied by all three of his major generals, led his reconnaissance force out of the British lines. Moving south across the western edge of Freeman's Farm the British and Germans moved to within less than a mile of the American position on Bemis Heights. Of the ten guns accompanying the column two were 12-pounders. About one-thirty in the afternoon Burgoyne halted his column and deployed into line with Balcarres and the light infantry on the right, the German flank companies under Lieutenant Colonel Speth in the center, and Acland's grenadiers on the left. For the next hour and a half the command remained in position, strange behavior for a force whose purpose was "to ascertain definitely his [Gates'] position and whether it would be advisable to attack him." Nothing could be seen of the American troops or their fortified line. It was as if Burgoyne had thrust out this slender force and invited the enemy to attack it. If this was indeed his intention the Americans soon obliged.

The British movement was observed almost as soon as it began and reported to Gates' headquarters. Colonel Wilkinson was sent forward to locate the enemy and found them just as they were forming their line. According to Wilkinson, the redcoats then "sat down in double ranks with their arms between their legs and I soon after observed several officers, mounted on the top of a cabin . . . endeavoring to reconnoiter our left." When this was reported to Gates he ordered out Morgan.

The "Old Waggoner" noted the exposed British position and moved to make a wide circle of the enemy right. Enoch Poor directed his brigade against the enemy left and Learned led his men against the center. This would bring a total of 2,100 men against Burgoyne's 1,500. Before the day was over Gates would commit another 3,000 to 4,000 men, but it was the three brigades of the left wing that bore the brunt of the fighting.[7]

About three o'clock the first elements of Learned's brigade, which had the shortest distance to go, collided with the Germans of Burgoyne's center but did not press its attack. Within half an hour Poor's men struck at Acland's grenadiers across a shallow ravine. The grenadiers met the attack with musket and artillery fire. Their volleys, directed downhill may have been high for they failed to check the Americans. The New Hampshire men drove forward up the slope and the grenadiers fell back under the pressure. Acland, galloping furiously among his men trying to reform the line, went down, shot in both legs. The fight raged back and forth but the grenadiers were finally overwhelmed and broken. Wilkinson rode up in time to see Colonel Cilley astride a British gun, shouting with excitement; a surgeon dressing the wounds of a British officer and exclaiming, "Wilkinson, I have dipt my hands in British

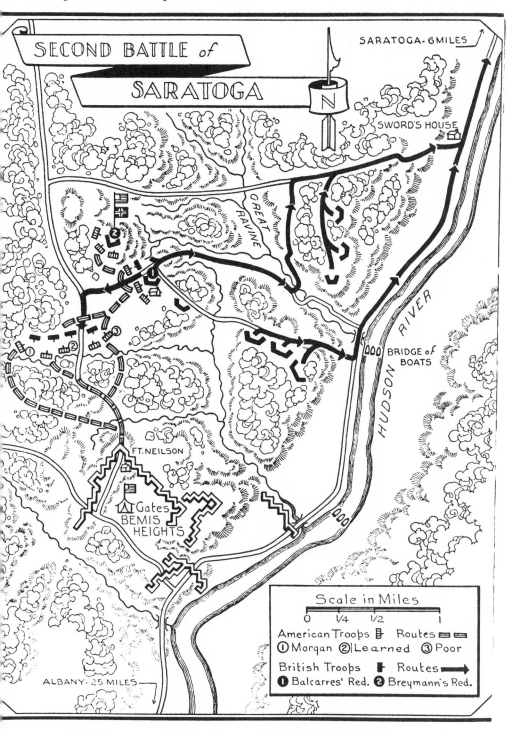

blood;" a fourteen-year old lad aiming his musket at Acland as he lay helpless in the angle of a rail fence. Two of his soldiers had tried to carry the burly major to the rear, but he had finally been left behind and was taken off by the Americans.

Meantime Learned's Massachusetts men had attacked the center. The 300 Brunswickers cooly beat back the five regiments of the American brigade. Captain Pausch's battery, slightly in advance of his line, poured salvo after salvo into the advancing ranks. He emptied three wagon loads of ammunition and his guns became too hot to touch. His crew was reduced to four gunners and a single subaltern but Pausch still fired his 6-pounders. After nearly an hour the Germans began to feel the pressure on their left as the Americans exploited the flank exposed by the retreat of Acland's men.

By this time Morgan had delivered his assault on Balcarres' light infantry and the 24th Regiment. Since Morgan was almost directly west of the British position and threatening to turn it Balcarres was forced to refuse his flank. This in turn put severe pressure on the Brunswickers. Seeing the danger Simon Fraser rode forward to rally the British on the right. He directed part of the 24th to the support of the Germans in an effort to restore the line. At this point Morgan ordered his riflemen to direct their fire at Fraser. Tradition has it that an Irishman named Tim Murphy posted himself in a tree and shot Fraser out of his saddle. The fall of the veteran Scot ended the British resistance on the right. Unsupported on both sides, the Germans in the center collapsed. Pausch, forward of his line, "looked back towards the position still held as I supposed, by our German infantry, under whose protection I, too, intended to retreat—but not a man was to be seen." The tough Hessian captain barely escaped capture, but he brought off one of his guns. In his report to Germain (Oct. 20) Burgoyne did not mention the Germans except to note that they occupied the center. It was perhaps too much to expect that Gentleman Johnny would acknowledge that the Brunswickers held their part of the line until the collapse of the British on both flanks compelled them to retire.[8]

Burgoyne ordered a withdrawal to the right wing of his main position at Freeman's Farm where he hoped to make a stand at the field works called Breymann's and Balcarres' redoubts. The American commanders probably would have broken off the fight at this point since they knew that headquarters was committed to the defensive. But at this moment a short, compact man on a big bay horse came storming onto the field. It was Benedict Arnold.

Arnold had been alternately sulking and raging at headquarters ever since Morgan's troops had marched out to battle. He was without a command but he could not resist the music of the gunfire. Whether, as one account has it, he secured Gates' reluctant permission, or whether he simply mounted and rode to the front with one of Gates' aides in pursuit, he reached Learned's brigade as the British began their retreat.

Arnold rounded up some of Learned's regiments and placed himself at their head as the pursuit reached the British main line. Urging the Massachusetts troops forward Arnold struck at Balcarres' redoubt, but the light infantry did not budge and the attackers were thrown back. Arnold then shifted to the left, picked up some men from Morgan's corps, and drove between Balcarres and Breymann, routing a force of Tories and Canadians who held the gap between the two redoubts. He then turned his attention to the log breast-works of Breymann's redoubt. Furiously Arnold rammed his men against the Germans and swept into the enemy position. Breymann was shot down (some said by his own men) and at almost the same moment Arnold's horse fell and rolled, breaking its rider's leg. In the gathering darkness the attack spent itself. The tired men returned triumphantly to Bemis Heights bearing their disabled general, six captured guns, and 240 prisoners.[9]

Baroness Riedesel, whose breakfast that morning had been disrupted by the sudden departure of her husband and his staff, had nonetheless prepared a dinner party for that evening. But "in place of the guests who were to have dined with me, they brought in to me, upon a litter, poor General Erazer (one of my expected guests), mortally wounded. Our dining table, which was already spread, was taken away, and in its place they fixed a bed for the general." By nightfall when the rest of the army returned "the entry and the other rooms were filled with the sick. . . ." The little baroness spent a fitful night and early in the morning General Fraser died in the adjoining room.

In the battle of October 7 the British lost about 600 killed, wounded, and taken prisoner; the American losses were about 150. The effect on Burgoyne's command was devastating. Altogether, since Ticonderoga (where he had left a garrison of 900 British and German troops) he had lost 730 of his regulars killed or taken prisoner. Riedesel's command had lost 750. On October 8 Burgoyne had over 700 wounded and sick in his hospital. Thus of the 7,250 infantry and artillerymen who had left Canada he now had no more than 4,100 men present and fit for duty. Losses in the officer corps were especially severe. The British had lost 50 officers dead or captured including General Fraser, Major Acland, and Burgoyne's senior aide, Sir Francis Clarke. Riedesel's command had lost 40, including Colonel Baum and Colonel Breymann.

On the night of October 8 a heavy rain began to fall. At nine o'clock Burgoyne's command began to move north toward the Fishkill and the little village of Saratoga.[10]

THE SURRENDER

At the Highlands of the Hudson Sir Henry Clinton refused to abandon Burgoyne. He had still not received any word from Howe as to the situation in Pennsylvania but he felt that he had enough troops to hold the Highlands position as long as it seemed likely that he could assist the northern army. At about this time General Pigot, commanding the British forces in Rhode Island, offered to make 1,000 men available to New York. For Clinton this represented unlooked-for abundance. He hurried to Manhattan and ordered six months provisions for 5,000 men loaded on transports. By October 13 he was back at the Highlands where he detached General Sir John Vaughan and 2,000 men, ordering them to feel their way toward Albany. Clinton was determined to leave no stone unturned in his attempt to open communications with Burgoyne.

His efforts were finally frustrated from two directions. From the north came word from Vaughan that the increasing difficulty of navigation made it impossible to go further up the river. American militia were beginning to join Putnam and there were now 6,000 of the enemy swarming along both banks of the Hudson. Vaughan was still forty-five miles from Albany. Clinton was nonetheless determined "to retain the footing we are now possessed of in the Highlands." But from Pennsylvania the long arm of his commander in chief reached out to frustrate even this hope. Although Howe had defeated Washington and was safely ensconced in Philadelphia he ordered Clinton "without delay" to detach 4,000 men and start them to Pennsylvania. Only if he were "on the eve of accomplishing some very material and essential stroke" was he to delay, and even in that event he was to allow only "a few days" before releasing the troops—"for what purpose, after all the victories we heard of, he best knows," remarked Sir Henry sourly.

Howe's insistence on immediate compliance is interesting as indirect evidence of his attitude toward Burgoyne's expedition. He actually sent two dispatches to Clinton, the first before and the second after he had received news of Burgoyne's precarious situation (i.e., the dispatch of September 21 and the officer who carried it, both of which Clinton had forwarded to Howe). Howe's second dispatch underscored the peremptory tone of the first. In other words, if Clinton were in the midst of an operation which would relieve pressure on Burgoyne he was to conclude it within a few days after which he must detach more than one third of his command. This would have forced Sir Henry to abandon any such operation and return to Manhattan, as it did. It hardly mattered. By October 17, the day Clinton received Howe's orders, Burgoyne was surrendering his army.[11]

The British retreat ground to a halt at Saratoga on October 10 after a number of delays. General Riedesel thought that a swift march to the Battenkill might have given the army time to cross the river and try for Fort George. On the 11th the column was completely bogged down by the rain and mud. The Americans had now not only occupied the east bank but had patrols west of the river between the British and Lake George.

The British came under almost constant fire not only from enemy muskets but from artillery. Baroness Riedesel and her children took shelter in the cellar of a house filled with wounded. As the American bombardment became heavier, cannon shot began to fall on the house and "threw us all into alarm. Many persons . . . threw themselves against the door [of the cellar]. My children were already under the cellar steps, and we should all have been crushed, if God had not given me the strength to place myself before the door, and with extended arms prevent all from coming in. Eleven cannon balls went through the house, and we could plainly hear them rolling over our heads."

Patrols and outposts skirmished constantly and "the army was under constant fire the whole day, both front and rear." Riedesel proposed abandoning the baggage and wounded and retreating up the west side of the Hudson, crossing above Fort Edward, and fighting through to Fort George. "Burgoyne, however, could not make up his mind that evening [the 11th], but allowed the precious moments to pass unimproved. . . . Every hour the position of the army grew more critical, and the prospect of salvation grew less and less."[12]

On October 12 Burgoyne called a council of war to which he invited Brigadiers Hamilton and Gall as well as the major generals. He noted that the American army was now estimated at 14,000 men. British boats and wagons had been almost entirely destroyed or captured, and even by cutting rations again the army could not last more than thirty days. He proposed three alternatives: forcing a passage northward, with or without baggage; attempting to fight southward to Albany; or staying where they were and waiting "for coming fortunate events." Riedesel reiterated his belief that without the encumbrance of baggage they could cut their way through to Fort George, and this was finally agreed to. A delay ensued while six days' rations were distributed among the troops. The task was completed about ten o'clock in the evening, but when Riedesel asked for the order to march he was told that the movement had been postponed. "That evening the retreat was possible. A movement of the enemy made it impossible the following day." Colonel Skene sardonically suggested that Burgoyne scatter his baggage "at proper distances and the militia will be so busy plundering that you and the troops will get clean off."[13]

The next day the Americans finally slammed the door on the escape route to the north. John Stark and his New Hampshire militia were finally persuaded to cross the Hudson and take a blocking position north of the Fishkill. Thousands of militia were now pouring into the American camps, some in organized regiments, some in platoons and companies, roaming the enemy flanks under no orders but their own (Wilkinson would report 18,000 three days later). Burgoyne called another council, this time including all the field officers. They were unanimously of the opinion that the army had no alternative but to surrender. A flag of truce was sent to Gates' headquarters.

There now began the intricate formalities of arranging surrender terms. Gates, a former British regular, went through the ritual, but beneath his air of triumph there were nagging worries. He had intercepted Clinton's messages to Burgoyne and he was aware of the threat to his rear. Moreover, Israel Putnam, panicked by Sir Henry's swift and overwhelming thrust, had sent exaggerated reports telling of defeat and disaster. So when Gates presented his terms to Captain Kingston he was not as confident as his bearing indicated. The American terms, which amounted to unconditional surrender, were rejected by Burgoyne who then made a counterproposal. The British would march out with "the honors of war," surrender their arms, and be returned to England "upon condition of not serving again in North America during the present contest." In other words, Burgoyne was avoiding surrender by asking that the army be paroled back to England where they could relieve other troops which could replace them. It was Burgoyne's last gamble, a magnificent bluff against long odds. And Gentleman Johnny saw his opponent fold. Gates accepted the terms. Although he had more reassuring news from Putnam and Governor George Clinton, he was still worried about the threat from the south. In accepting the terms Gates set a deadline. The acceptance must be complete by three o'clock on the 15th and the army must lay down its arms two hours later.

The alacrity with which Gates accepted the terms and the deadline gave Burgoyne food for thought. If he read the signs correctly Gates was worried about something. The British commander decided to push a little. He asked for a further delay so that the details of the "convention"—rather than surrender—could be worked out by representatives of the two commanders. Again Gates agreed. All day on the fifteenth the officers from both headquarters worked on the provisions and stipulations and by evening the terms were settled. The British would march out under arms; they would not surrender their colors or their equipment, only their shoulder arms and guns; they would be marched to Boston where they would be transported to England on parole.[14]

That night a Tory arrived at Burgoyne's headquarters. He brought news at last of Clinton's movement to the Highlands, and reported erroneously that a British advance corps was in Albany. Burgoyne called a council of war the next morning and announced the news to his officers. He proposed that the American terms be rejected and that they should hold out until help could arrive from the south. By a vote of fourteen to eight the officers decided that the terms of the convention had already been agreed to and that they could not honorably be repudiated. Even if the report was true the army could hold out only a few more days.

Burgoyne refused to accept the decision. He informed Gates' aide, Colonel Wilkinson, that he believed that large numbers of the Americans had left their camps. He demanded that a British representative be allowed to count the American troops in order to be assured that his army was hopelessly outnumbered.

But Gates' patience was at an end. Wilkinson was sent to announce that the negotiations were broken off. He did so and was returning to the American lines when he was called back. Gentleman Johnny had finally had his hand called. The British agreed to capitulate.

On the morning of October 17 the British and German soldiers of Burgoyne's army marched out of the mud and stench of their camp. The drums beat "The Grenadiers' March." The women straggled after their men as they moved past the silent ranks of the Americans to stack their arms. General Gates received General Burgoyne's sword and gallantly returned it.

A German soldier described the army that had defeated him and his comrades:

> . . . nature had formed all the fellows who stood in rank and file so slender, so handsome, so sinewy, that it was a pleasure to look at them, and we were all surprised at the sight of such finely built people. And their size! . . . [The soldiers] had their musket with bayonet affixed in hand, and their cartridge box or powder horn slung on their backs; they had their left hands on their hips and their right foot advanced slightly. . . . I must say in praise of the enemy regiments that there was not a man among them who showed the slightest sign of mockery, malicious delight, hate, or other insult; it seemed rather as if they wished to do us honor.

Philip Schuyler had come up from Albany. While Gates entertained Burgoyne, Phillips, and Riedesel, General Schuyler escorted Baroness Riedesel and her children to his tent where they had dinner. "Never," said the baroness, "have I eaten a better meal. I was content."[15]

On August 20 Burgoyne had complained of the fact that his orders left him no latitude, "being positive 'to force a junction with Sir William Howe.'" This ignored a clause in Germain's original instructions (delivered through Sir Guy Carleton) "that they [Burgoyne and St. Leger] act as exigencies may require and in such manner as they shall judge proper. . . ."

On October 20 Burgoyne, in his report to Germain, was still justifying his actions on the ground that he was bound by his orders, "that . . . a passage to Albany was the principle, the letter, and the spirit of my orders." On the same day he wrote to a friend, "If the State thought it necessary to devote a corps of troops for general purposes, it was no more within the General's duty to decline proceeding, upon motives of prudence . . . than it would be justifiable in a sergeant who heads a forlorn hope at the storm of a breach to recede because his destruction was probable—mine was a forlorn hope with this difference that it was not supported."[16]

THIRTEEN

Stalemate

To those who sought to compare Washington to the Roman general, Fabius, who carefully kept his army out of reach of the enemy, the weeks following the battle at Chadd's Ford posed a serious contradiction. For he continued to seek out the enemy and he called at least one council of war to suggest an attack on Philadelphia. The officers voted him down, ten to five. Yet Washington was convinced that "Gen'l Howe's Situation in Philadelphia will not be the most agreeable; for if his supplies can be stopped by Water, it may easily be done by land. To do both, shall be my utmost endeavor, and I am not yet without hope that the acquisition of Philadelphia may instead of his good fortune, prove his Ruin." It may well be that his pride was stung by the contrast between his own failure and Gates' repulse of Burgoyne on September 19, but he said only, "I am in hopes, it will not be long before we are in a situation to repair the consequences of our late ill-success, and give a more happy complexion to our affairs in this quarter."[1]

GERMANTOWN

By September 28 Washington had moved his command within twenty miles of Germantown. It was obvious that Howe was becoming concerned about his naval support from the fleet commanded by Lord Howe, for he had begun to send detachments to escort supplies that were landed below the river defenses and brought by wagon to the city. This was only a temporary expedient, which could provide neither the volume nor the security of a permanent winter supply line.

Howe's main force was encamped at Germantown, five miles north of Philadelphia. Intelligence reports indicated that the British troops were rather loosely deployed, their outposts just north of the village. Howe had erected no fortifications or entrenchments and most of his guns were in his artillery park rather than distributed with the regiments.[2]

All this convinced Washington that this was the opportunity he had been seeking. For the third time in less than a month he decided to attack. There is no record of a council of war and Washington did not refer to one in his report to Congress, saying only that "I communicated the Accounts to my General Officers, who were unanimously of the Opinion [a rare event in a council of war], that a favourable Opportunity offered to make an Attack upon the Troops, which were at and near Germantown." Washington's fighting blood was up, and it may be that he decided not to risk an adverse vote of a council, choosing to persuade the senior officers individually. On October 1 he moved the army to within fifteen miles of Germantown, close enough to make a night march to the enemy's lines, but not so close as to alarm him.

Since Washington and his officers had been in and out of Germantown several times during the last weeks there appeared to be no problem so far as knowledge of terrain and roads was concerned. No doubt the success of his coordinated attack on Trenton was in his mind as he laid out a plan that called for converging columns moving down on the enemy by different routes. The brunt of the fighting, the attack on the center would be delivered by Sullivan and Greene, with Washington accompanying the unwary Sullivan to insure against "bad luck." Greene would command his own and Stephen's divisions, and on his left flank would be General Smallwood with nearly 2,000 Maryland militia to envelop the British right and rear. Sullivan, with Wayne's division, would be to the right of Greene and on the extreme right would be General John Armstrong with 1,500 Pennsylvania militia to turn the British left. Stirling's division would be the reserve, moving behind Sullivan.

From Washington's camp at Pennypacker's Mill the direct route to Germantown led down the Skippack Road. Two miles to the west, close to the Schuylkill, was Manatawney Road, and about the same distance to the east was the Lime Kiln Road. In the center of Germantown was a cross street called School House Lane to the west, and Church Lane to the east. Sullivan's command, coming down Skippack Road, was to be supported by Greene advancing on the Lime Kiln road to Church Lane and then turning west toward Germantown. Armstrong's militia would close by way of the Manatawney Road and School House Lane. Smallwood was to complete the encirclement by striking Church Lane east of Greene and coming up in support.

It was a complicated plan, one that would have taxed the energy and skill of officers and men far more experienced than Washington's Continentals. The distance across the whole American front from Armstrong on the right to Smallwood on the left was seven miles.[3]

Washington put the army in motion on the night of October 3 hoping to get into position before dawn and rest the men prior to the attack. But it was daylight before Wayne struck the British advance guard—daylight which was shrouded by "a low vapour lying on the land which made it very difficult to distinguish objects at any considerable distance."

Wayne's division drove through the enemy pickets, swarming into the camp of the 40th Regiment and the 2nd Light Infantry. The British quickly discovered that these were Wayne's men, for there were shouts of "Have at the bloodhounds!" and "Paoli! Paoli!" After a hot exchange of fire the redcoats

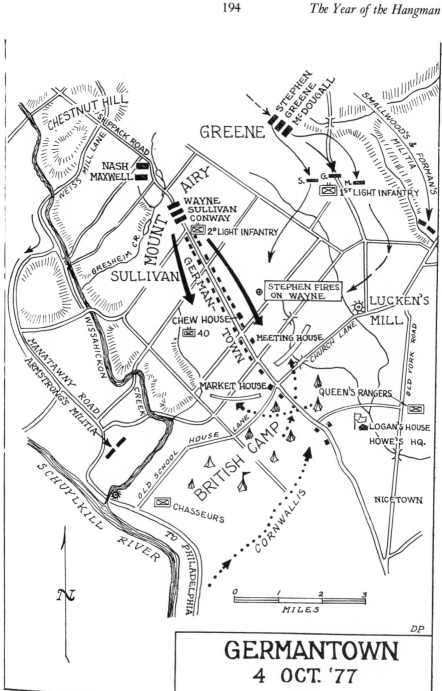

© Mark Boatner, III, *Encyclopedia of the American Revolution*, David McKay Co., Inc.

fell back toward Germantown with the Americans at their heels. Despite the efforts of the officers to stop them, Wayne's men ruthlessly bayonetted the British who tried to surrender and even some of the wounded.

Behind Sullivan, Stirling's division suddenly struck a snag. British Colonel Musgrave's 40th Regiment had put some men into a large stone mansion owned by Judge Benjamin Chew, from which neither musket fire nor cannon could dislodge them. For more than half an hour Washington tried to reduce what Knox called "a castle in our rear" (Knox was doing it by the book). Finally it was decided that the position posed no threat and the attack moved on.

Sullivan and Wayne now made good progress despite the blinding fog. Wayne shifted his division to the left, grouping for contact with Greene. By now the sound of firing aroused the British main camp and General Howe himself rode out to the fight; ". . . seeing the battalion retreating, all broken, he got into a passion and exclaimed, 'For shame, Light Infantry. I never saw you retreat before. Form! Form! It's only a scouting party.'" At that moment Sullivan's column came out of the fog. At its head were three guns which greeted Sir William with a blast of grape. The light infantry "all felt pleased to see the enemy make such an appearance and to hear the grape rattle about the Commander-in-Chief's ears. . . . He rode off immediately full speed." But the rest of the British main body was up, and as the regiments of Grant and Agnew began to put pressure on Sullivan's right, the American attack was checked.

In the meantime Greene's advance was lagging since the left assault column had further to go and had briefly lost its way. However, by the time Sullivan reached the crossroad Greene had reached Church Lane and was coming up on Sullivan's left. Fog still shrouded the field. As Greene's troops groped their way forward Private Joseph Martin remembered,

> The curs [muskets] began to bark first and then the bull dogs [guns]. . . . We saw a body of the enemy drawn up behind a rail fence on our right flank; we immediately formed into line and advanced upon them. Our orders were not to fire until we could see the buttons upon their clothes, but they were so coy that they would not give us an opportunity to be so curious, for they hid their clothes in fire and smoke before we had either the time or leisure to examine their buttons. . . . The enemy were driven quite through their camp. They left their kettles, in which they were cooking their breakfasts, on the fires, and some of their garments were lying on the ground, which their owners had not had time to put on.[4]

The thrust of Greene's attack drove deep into the enemy's lines—so deep that Muhlenburg's Pennsylvanians were momentarily in the British rear and had to counterattack in the opposite direction in order to rejoin Greene. On Greene's right Stephen was extending toward Wayne when he heard firing, so he thought, in his rear. Possibly it was from the Chew house; in any case, Stephen changed his line of advance further toward the north and probably lost his sense of direction in the fog.

At this point the attack suddenly collapsed. Some of the other regiments may have been rattled by bursts of musket fire in the rear. Stephen's division, moving toward the Skippack Road, came up on the left rear of Wayne's flank. In the confusion of the fog the two commands fired on each other. At the same moment, Sullivan's men were not only under heavy pressure from the British but their ammunition began to run short. For one or all of these reasons the troops between Sullivan's left and Greene's right suddenly broke and ran.

Washington was riding exultantly forward to press home a general attack when out of the fog in front of him burst the wild-eyed, panicky fugitives. In vain he and his aides attempted to halt the fleeing men, but there was no stopping the frightened soldiers. The wave of dispair that engulfed the commanding general can only be imagined, for there was no outburst, as at Kip's Bay, and his subsequent report of the battle only emphasized the nearness of victory. Nor was the panic universal. Private Martin, at age seventeen already a veteran of two campaigns, "never wanted to run (if I am forced to run) further than to be beyond the enemy's shot, after which I had no more fear of their overtaking me than an army of lobsters. . . ." Citizen Tom Paine, who observed the withdrawal, found that "the retreat was extraordinary. Nobody hurried themselves. Everybody marched at his own pace."

Instead of pursuing the fugitives the British were forced to turn their attention to Greene's disciplined men. Although he had hit the British hard the Rhode Islander's attack soon lost its momentum. Smallwood had not come up on his left. Stephen's division was lost in the fog, its men in a panic, its commander thoroughly drunk. Cornwallis and Grant now had twelve regiments in action and Greene felt the full force of the British counterattack. He was forced to retreat, pressed hard by the British, but with his regiments preserving their formations. By ten o'clock the fight was over. Tired and hungry, exhausted by almost three hours of fighting, the men managed a twenty-four mile march back to their camp at Pennypacker's Mill.[5]

Here it was evident that the army still retained that remarkable resilience it had somehow acquired in this, the third year of the war. Washington reported to Congress, "Upon the whole it may be said the day was unfortunate rather than injurious. We sustained no material loss of Men and brought off all our artillery except one piece. . . . The Enemy are nothing better by the event; and our Troops, who are not in the least dispirited by it, have gained what all young Troops gain by being in Actions." Whether the loss of 600 killed and wounded, and 400 prisoners could be considered "no material loss," Washington, as usual, was being his most optimistic when the outlook appeared most dismal. He continued to believe that victory had been snatched from him by the accident of the fog and the inexplicable panic of the men.

Intelligence from the enemy camps seemed to confirm this. A report from Philadelphia related that "in my presence several British Officers who had returned from the action of the 4th Instant Confessed that they had never met with so severe a Drubbing since the Battle of Bunker Hill, that the Attack was made with great Judgement and Supported with equal Bravery. . . ." The British loss in the battle was nearly 500 men and 34 officers killed and wounded.

This time Sullivan could not be blamed. He had put his men into action promptly and had fought his division well. The fog and the shortage of ammunition he could not help, and the confusion of the formations was as much Wayne's doing as his. General Stephen was another case altogether. He was found asleep in a fence corner, and it may have been that his collapse was as much from exhaustion as from drink. But he had led his division astray and had been totally confused in the direction of his men. That he had been drinking heavily was later attested to, and when he was cited for a court martial Washington would not defend him. Stephen was convicted of "unofficerlike behavior" and dismissed from the service. Washington gave command of his division to Lafayette.[6]

Of the many factors in the defeat the one least mentioned may have been the most obvious and the most important. It was succinctly expressed by the French engineer, General du Portail, who told Washington, "Your Excellency, in that instance, really conquered General Howe, but his Troops conquered yours." Though they had been surprised and driven, the redcoats did not panic. Their commanders formed them for a counterattack and delivered it with coolness and precision. The American army had developed neither the skill of command nor the steadiness under fire that could bring them to victory in the open field against an opponent nearly equal in strength to their own. The Continentals could be counted on to win only when they had a clear tactical superiority of either numbers or position.

Yet it remained a fact that Washington's confidence in the ability of the soldiers to maintain their spirits seemed to be justified. What was obvious was that, with Howe on the defensive, American numerical superiority became increasingly important. So the commander in chief continued to send out calls for militia. But his principal reliance was on the return of his veteran Continentals from the Northern Department. The battle at Freeman's Farm seemed to demonstrate that Gates now had Burgoyne well in hand. Washington believed that the time had come to press home his strategy of pinning Howe to Philadelphia and the Delaware while denying him the support of Lord Howe's fleet.

Ten days before Germantown, when Washington had asked Gates to return Morgan's corps, Gates replied that since the British still occupied the ground at Freeman's Farm "Your Excellency would not wish me to part with the Corps the Army of General Burgoyne are most afraid of." If Washington recognized an incipient insubordination, he gave no sign.

But the failure of the militia at Germantown underscored the fact that a serious challenge to Howe made necessary the return of the regular regiments from the north, for these amounted to almost 3,000 seasoned troops. Nor was there any question of Washington's authority to order them back to Pennsylvania. On August 23, in answer to a query about his relationship to the Northern Department, Congress had passed a resolution "that Congress never intended . . . by the Establishment of any Department whatever to Supersede or Circumscribe the powers of General Washington as the Commander in Chief of all the Continental Land Forces within the United States."

It was news from the Northern Department that now brought a surge of hope for the American cause. On October 16 Washington received a report (premature, but, as it turned out, accurate) that Burgoyne's army had surrendered. This incredible news sent a shock wave of jubilation throughout the entire country. No single event of the entire war so galvanized American spirits. General orders for October 18 directed that *"Thirteen* pieces of cannon are to be discharged at the park of artillery to be followed by a *feu-de-joy* with blank cartridges. . . ."[7]

The victory also meant that virtually the whole of Gates' army would be available for reinforcements in Pennsylvania. Confirmation of the victory came on the 20th—but not by direct communication from Gates to headquarters. It was beginning to appear as though Gates had drunk deeply of the heady wine of victory. He asked Congress to promote Wilkinson to brigadier general, presumably for nothing more outstanding than bringing Congress the terms of the surrender convention—a feat that took Wilkinson two weeks. Although this rankled the senior colonels, Congressman Nathaniel Folsom pointed out, "I was glad Gates asked no more at this time, for assured I am that if he had it would have been granted. . . ." Congress was indulging in that paradoxical behavior that was to characterize it for the next two hundred years—denouncing standing armies and the influence of the military, while fatuously fawning over hero-generals. Gates' arrogance eventually strained even Washington's monumental patience to the limit.

Adding to his problems were the continuous demands of foreign officers for rank and command. One especially unpleasant affair involved a French artillery officer, Phillippe du Coudray to whom Silas Deane in Paris had promised command of the army's artillery corps with the rank of major general. The problem was happily solved in mid-September when the arrogant Frenchman's horse threw him overboard from a ferry and he was drowned. It was, of course, important that cordial relations be maintained with foreign nations, especially France. Yet the promotion of an officer like Thomas Conway over the heads of brigadiers who had fought and marched through two years of hard campaigning had a devastating effect on the morale of Washington's generals.

Conway was an Irish-born Frenchman who had spent twenty years in the army of Louis XVI. He had been made a brigadier general in the summer of 1777 and commanded a brigade at Germantown. His courage and capabilities were obvious, but Washington questioned his tendency to substitute his own discretion for orders from his superiors. After Germantown Conway pressed for a promotion and proclaimed his superior qualities to all who would listen. Washington characterized him as having "that after kind of sagacity which qualifies a Man better for profound discoveries of errors, that have been committed and advantages that have been lost [rather] than for the exercise of . . . foresight and provident discernment. . . ." He came to despise Conway as he did no other man, but for the moment he was only concerned that Congress might undermine his generals by yielding to Conway's threat to resign unless he was promoted.

All this did not divert Washington's attention from his basic strategy: Hold the Delaware defenses until his regiments could return from the north. With a superior force of Continentals at his back, and Howe cut off from his supplies, the war might be won now, this year.[8]

THE FIGHT FOR THE DELAWARE

When Colonel Samuel Smith and his handful of Maryland Continentals arrived at Fort Mifflin on September 27 they found that post in a sorry plight. It was occupied by 40 militiamen whom Smith immediately detached as unfit for duty, along with 30 of his own men who were either sick or worn down by exhaustion. This left him with less than 200 men. His subordinates were Major Simeon Thayer of Rhode Island and Captain Samuel Treat, an artilleryman. Soon afterward a French engineer, Major the Marquis de Fleury reported for duty. Fleury was one of a number of officers granted leave from the French army to enlist in America, but who were expected to return to the French service when the war ended. Fleury's performance at Fort Mifflin proved him to be, in Colonel Smith's words, "a Treasure that ought not to be lost." Fleury had already fought at the Brandywine and Germantown, and he was to win one of only nine Congressional medals awarded during the entire war. He had supervised the defenses of the Delaware which consisted of three strong points. A fort at Billingsport several miles down river was abandoned by its militia garrison at the first threat of the British advance. On the New Jersey side of the river near Red Bank was Fort Mercer, manned by a Rhode Island regiment commanded by Christopher Greene. Fort Mifflin lay in the middle of the Delaware on an island which was not much more than a mud flat thrown up by the current of the Schuylkill as it flowed into the Delaware.

The two forts were so placed that their guns guarded a two-tiered line of *cheveaux de frise* which blocked the main channel between Fort Mifflin and the Jersey shore. *Cheveaux de frise* were made of heavy spars ballasted on the river bottom at a forty-five degree angle, their sharpened, iron-shod tips pointing downstream about four feet below the surface. They could rip the bottom out of any ship that tried to pass up the channel, and the guns of the two forts guarded against any attempt to raise them. To the west of Fort Mifflin was a low, marshy mud flat, separated from the Delaware shore by a slough. It was dignified by the name of Province Island but it offered only limited sites for enemy guns. Commodore John Hazelwood, commander of the Pennsylvania state naval forces on the river, assured Colonel Smith, "A mosquito could not live there under the fire of my guns." Hazelwood's force consisted of an assortment of row galleys and floating batteries, and two small frigates, one of which had already run aground and been destroyed.[9]

Smith and his men set to work repairing the dilapidated works. In addition to the masonry wall which faced the main channel and masked the principal batteries, blockhouses mounting four guns each were built at the four corners of the fort. An open platform mounting a 32-pounder was erected to bear on Province Island. Walls of pine logs and earth were erected connecting the batteries, and revetments were constructed to protect the men when they were not manning the guns.

All this took a great deal of effort. Living conditions in the fort were miserable and the men were short of every sort of supplies and equipment—shoes, clothing, and blankets. The soldiers became so sickly that Smith was constantly detaching men and asking for replacements. It is doubtful if one third of the troops who garrisoned Fort Mifflin at the beginning of October served until the end of the siege.

Soon after the battle of Germantown the British established a battery on one of the few dry hummocks on Province Island, unhindered by Hazelwood's naval batteries. When Smith asked the commodore to attack the battery Hazelwood refused. In exasperation Smith procured the use of some of the gunboats and led the assault himself, driving off the redcoats and nearly capturing the guns. But by October 14 the British were back. This time they quickly threw up an earthwork behind which they mounted a battery. Smith's force had been reduced to 156 men so he could not risk an attack. Fort Mifflin was soon being bombarded by the guns from Province. The little garrison hung on, although "at least 60 of our small force are without breeches, many of whom have scarce so much as to cover their nakedness."

By the third week in October the British had raised the obstructions at Billingsport and their frigates moved into a position just below the *cheveaux de frise* at Fort Mifflin. Until they could breach these, the fleet ferried a trickle of supplies by night in small boats up the shallow channel between Province Island and Fort Mifflin. Smith called on Hazelwood to use his small vessels to block this line but the cautious commodore explained that a single shell would wreck one of his little ships. The indignant Smith retorted, "Yes, and [a shell] falling on your head or mine will kill, but for what else are we employed or paid? . . ."[10]

Nonetheless, the blockade of the river was a serious matter for the Howes. Supplies brought up Province Channel and what little could be brought overland from New Castle would not suffice for a garrison that intended to winter in Philadelphia.

Fort Mercer was located on the New Jersey side of the Delaware opposite

Fort Mifflin. The distance between them was almost 2,000 yards, too far for mutual fire support, but close enough so that the guns of both could rake the main channel which lay between them. Fort Mercer, like so many of the European designs in America, was too large to be properly defended by the 400 Rhode Islanders under Christopher Greene, but another French engineer, the Chevalier du Plessis, had built an interior wall across one section of the fort thereby reducing the defense perimeter. Greene had fourteen guns of which five were mounted on the walls facing inland.

The Howes seriously underestimated the strength of the American positions. On October 22 the 64-gun *Augusta*, the frigates *Roebuck*, *Vigilant*, and *Fury*, and the sloop *Merlin* moved in to take Fort Mifflin under fire. At the same time Colonel Karl von Donop led a mixed force of 2,000 English and Hessians against Fort Mercer. He divided his force and sent storming columns against opposite sides of the fort. One penetrated the ditch and the abatis without drawing a shot. The other swept over the north wall—and found itself in the dead space formed by du Plessis' interior wall. Only then did the Americans open fire. The soldiers sent their volleys into the British at thirty yards. The guns slammed charges of grape into the close packed ranks. The walled-off interior of the northern redoubt became a slaughter pen. When the British finally withdrew they left 500 killed, wounded, and captured including their Hessian commander who died three days later. The American loss was 38 killed and wounded.

The British had also fared badly in the attack on Fort Mifflin. The five ships were met by furious fire from the fort and from Hazelwood's small craft. Hazelwood claimed much of the credit for repulsing the British but Colonel Smith had noted earlier that "so general a discontent and panic runs through that part of the fleet . . . they conceive the river is lost. . . ." It seems likely that it was the fire of the fixed guns of the fort that threw the British into confusion. As they retired downstream both the 64-gun *Augusta* and the sloop *Merlin* went aground and were eventually destroyed.

The British unwittingly did Sam Smith a favor. The Baron d'Arendt, a tall, imposing Pole, had arrived to take command of Fort Mifflin a few days before. His arrogance and bad judgement had already led Major Fleury to remark, "Par dieu! C'est un poltroon!" When the British guns opened fire the Baron panicked and Smith had to take command. As the *Vigilant* drifted down stream at the end of the engagement she loosed a final broadside. One shot hit a wall near d'Arendt and sent a fragment of brick smashing into his groin. He was promptly evacuated and Fort Mifflin knew him no more.[11]

At headquarters Washington waited anxiously for news of the regiments which should be on their way from the north. It was now clear that Gates considered himself an independent commander since he was making his reports directly to York. "Congress having been requested immediately to transmit copies of all my dispatches . . . I am confident your Excellency has long ago received all the good news from this quarter," he announced grandly in one of only three letters he wrote Washington during November.

By this time Washington's patience had run out. On October 30 he dispatched his aide, Colonel Hamilton, to Saratoga to see to the return of the troops. On his way Hamilton met Morgan's Corps but by the time he reached headquarters it was obvious the Hero of Saratoga had no intention of giving up his army without a struggle. By the first week in November Hamilton had pried loose "near five thousand, rank and file, Continental troops, and twenty-five hundred Massachusetts and New Hampshire militia." These troops, however, struck a snag when they reached Putnam's headquarters at Peekskill. "Old Put," suddenly in command of 9,000 men, conjured up the glorious vision of an attack on New York. Hamilton was wild with exasperation. "Indeed, Sir . . . every part of this gentleman's conduct is marked by blunders and negligence, and gives general disgust." By November 12 Putnam's orders had been overridden and Paterson, Glover, Learned, Poor, and Parsons had started their brigades for Pennsylvania. But "the disposition for marching, in the officers and men in general, of these troops, does not keep pace with . . . the exigency of the occasion."

Three weeks had passed since Burgoyne's surrender.[12]

The victory of October 22 could not disguise the precarious condition of the forts. By the first of November British batteries on Province Island pounded away at Fort Mifflin at a range of 600 yards. Naval vessels just below the *cheveaux de frise* at 1,200 yards added to the cannonade. The fort kept up a steady answering fire and the men settled down into a sort of routine, taking shelter from enemy shells by day and turning to under cover of night to rebuild walls and blinds that had been uprooted and dislodged during the daylight hours.

Like soldiers everywhere they discovered diversions. The 32-pounder facing Province Island had no solid shot. Across the channel the British batteries also mounted a 32-pounder. "The artillery officers offered a gill of rum for each shot fired from that piece. . . . I have often seen from twenty to fifty men standing on the parade waiting with impatience the coming shot, which would be seized before its motion had full ceased, and conveyed off to our gun to be sent back to its former owners. When the lucky fellow who had caught it had swallowed his rum, he would return to wait for another. . . ." (And since the British batteries were equally difficult to supply, is it too much to imagine the same shot passing endlessly back and forth between the rebel and redcoat batteries?)

Early in November an autumn gale lashed the eastern seaboard bringing heavy rains that raised the river level. A good part of Fort Mifflin was submerged under two feet of water. The men, miserable from lack of clothing and bad food, were now denied fires because all the space above water was either built of wood or being used for powder storage. General Varnum, who was acting as senior officer to Greene and Smith, authorized the confiscation of clothing from the nearby towns but, said Colonel Smith, "I fear it will be a very poor Resource—the Garrison must be well cloathed or they will perish."

Boatloads of supplies continued to pass up Province Channel to Philadelphia without interference from Hazelwood. "The Commodore says he cannot prevent the Enemy Boats from passing up and down the River, as they are covered by their Batteries," reported Varnum; ". . . the Commodore appears to be a very good kind of a Man; but his extreme Good Nature gives too great a License to those under his Command."[13]

By November 10 the British began to intensify their bombardment of the battered little fort. Several floating batteries had been built and moved into Province Channel to add to the fire power of the island batteries. Major Fleury wrote almost casually in his journal, "The 24 and 18 pound shot from Batteries No. 16 and 17 broke some of our Palisades this morning, but this does not make us uneasy—they save us the trouble of cutting them to the height of a man. . . ." The storm of shells inflicted surprisingly few casualties and the garrison kept up its spirits. Fleury showed only annoyance as the enemy now "kept up a firing part of the night—their shells greatly disturb our workmen and as the moon rises opposite to us, her light discovers to the Enemy where we are. . . ."

On November 11 a shell crashed into one of the few remaining brick chimneys of the fort. It collapsed on Colonel Smith, temporarily paralyzing him. He had to be evacuated but four days later he was back on his feet. "My Arm will this Night permit me to take the Command at Fort Mifflin. I was there last Night, it is now one Heap of Ruin & must be defended with musketry in Case of Storm. . . . With 600 men I think we could defend it as an Island."

But the fort's hours were numbered. General Varnum reported on the 16th: ". . . last evening we were obliged to evacuate Fort Mifflin. . . . *Vigilant* lay within one Hundred Yards of the Southwest part of the Works [*Vigilant's* shallow draft enabled her to work her way past the *chevaux de frise*], & with her incessant Fire, Hand Grenades, & Musketry from the Round Top, killed every man that appeared on the Platforms.—The Commodore gave positive orders to six Gallies to attack, and take that Ship. . . . I am just told the Gallies . . . did Nothing."

With the fall of Fort Mifflin Fort Mercer lay exposed. It was also evident that General Howe was acutely concerned about the river blockade, for he sent from Philadelphia a column of 3,000 men under Lord Cornwallis. On November 20 General Varnum ordered Mercer evacuated. The Delaware was now a British river.

For seven weeks Christopher Greene and Sam Smith, with a combined force that never counted more than 700 men had effectively scotched the junction of the British army and its supporting fleet. Washington was powerless to capitalize on the situation. Not until additional regiments from Gates gave

him a decided superiority of numbers could he even consider attacking the
trenches and breastworks that Howe had strung across the northern face of the
city from the Schuylkill to the Delaware. He did send Greene after Cornwallis, urging his subordinate to attack and destroy the British detachment.
But Cornwallis, moving by interior lines, outmaneuvered the Rhode Islander.
Despite Washington's urgent desire for a fight, Greene refused to do so without positive orders "under these Disadvantages." Greene then elaborated:

> . . . Your Excellency has the choice of but two things, to fight the Enemy with-
> out the least Prospect of Success, upon the Common Principle of War, or re-
> main inactive, & be subject to the Censure of an ignorant & impatient populace.
> In doing one you may make a bad matter worse, and take a measure, that if it
> proves unfortunate, you may stand condemned for by all military Gentlemen
> of Experience; pursuing the other you have the Approbation of your own mind,
> you give your Country an opportunity to exert itself to supply the present
> deficiency, & also act upon such military Principles as will justify you to the best
> Judges in the Present Day, & to all future Generations.

When Fort Mercer was evacuated on November 20 the brigades of Morgan,
Glover, Paterson, and Poor had not yet reached Trenton.[14]

Valley Forge: End and Beginning

Sir William Howe was at last secure in the rebel capital, his defensive line
drawn from the Schuylkill to the Delaware, his supply line open and guarded
by Admiral Howe's fleet. But General Howe did not regard his achievement
as the conclusion of a successful campaign. If he did, dispatches from Germain
would have disillusioned him. Between August and December the King and
his ministers waited anxiously for word of the outcome of this, their second
campaign of the war. Not since the news of the fall of Ticonderoga had there
been anything to relieve their anxiety. Through July the American Secretary
remained optimistic, although by this time it was known that Major Balfour
and Clinton had failed to deter Sir William from his sea voyage.

By August no news was bad news. Germain's indulgent tone in his dispatches to the Howes was replaced by sarcasm. He complimented Admiral
Howe on his indulgence in allowing American fishermen to ply their trade
(his Lordship had said that if they were allowed to fish they would not join
the American navy), and agreed with General Howe that popular opinion
was no substitute for sound strategy. But, said Germain, despite Admiral
Howe's benign wisdom, there seemed to be enough hands to man the swarm
of American privateers crowding into French ports; and Lord George professed to Sir William, "I shall be happy in seeing you meet with the Applause
and Admiration of the Ignorant, as well as the abler judges of military merit."
The American Secretary was becoming disillusioned with his commanders
even before the news of Burgoyne's disaster and the fruitless Pennsylvania

campaign reached London. Only the fact that Germain's own fortunes were harnessed to those of the Howes prevented him from openly denouncing their leadership.

By the first of December word of Burgoyne's defeat had reached England, and a dispatch from Howe complained as usual of lack of reinforcements. Burgoyne, he said, should not have expected support, since Howe had warned him that the army in New York was going south. Then came Sir William's final effrontery: "From the little attention, my Lord, given to my recommendations since the commencement of my command, I am led to hope that I may be relieved from this very painful service, wherein I have not the good fortune to enjoy the necessary confidence and support of my superiors. . . ."

And on the last day of November, with the surrender of Burgoyne now confirmed, came the denouement: ". . . I candidly declare my opinion, that in the apparent temper of the Americans, a considerable addition to the present force will be requisite for effecting any essential change in their disposition, and reestablish the King's authority; and that this army, acting upon the defensive, will be fully employed to maintain its present position."

Acting upon the defensive! This was the sum of Howe's strategic thinking as the year came to an end. Although Washington did not so consider it, in the lexicon of eighteenth century military thinking, the ultimate victory was achieved by maneuvering the adversary into a situation where he had to yield his ground, because it became impossible to defend it. Howe's avowed objective had been the conquest of the middle colonies, but he had yielded all but the empty shell of the rebel capital, and for its defense "this army . . . will be fully employed."[15]

Howe made one last defiant and empty gesture. On December 4 he marched out of Philadelphia and brought his army north to Chestnut Hill where he faced Washington in a strong, entrenched position. There was sporadic skirmishing, but Howe did not deliver an attack. The British withdrew to Philadelphia and settled in for the winter.

Washington was reluctant to end the year with what was to him an inconclusive campaign. The regiments from Gates' northern command had finally come in, too late to attack Howe while the river was still blocked. Gates' behavior had been very close to insubordination, but Washington was painfully aware that questions of military command were deeply enmeshed in Congressional politics.

The more immediate questions were whether a winter offensive could be undertaken; if not, what were the strategic considerations for locating the army's winter quarters. The former question was posed by the Congress, its members still convinced that a more vigorous policy was needed. To this the opinion of Washington's generals was an emphatic "No!" After reading the statements elicited by a poll which included everyone from Nathanael Greene to Colonel Henry Lutterloh, the deputy quartermaster general, the members of Congress agreed. Despite the increase in the army's strength, there were still the lack of training, the shortage of equipment, "the present temper of the soldiery,"—all these precluded any offensive maneuver. John Sullivan pointed out that "of your Army one third of whom at Least are now confined to their cold Tents & unwholesome Hutts for want of Shoes, Stockings & other Cloathing, a very Large number of them unable Longer to endure the Severity of their Situation have retired (sick) to the Hospitals or to the Country Houses." Many officers were on the point of resigning and another failure would break their spirit.[16]

Some of the officers were aware that Washington was sensitive to the growing criticism but, warned General Weedon, a failure would open the floodgates to those "who want nothing more to blast reputations than a miscarriage, without inquiring into its causes. . . ." How serious this criticism had become was revealed by a letter from Lord Stirling reporting a conversation with James Wilkinson in which the young aide had quoted General Conway as defaming the commander in chief. For the moment Washington contented himself with a brief note to Conway which read:

> A Letter which I received last Night contained the following paragraph.
>
> In a Letter from Genl. Conway to Genl. Gates he says: "Heaven has been determined to save your Country; or a weak General and bad Councellors would have ruind it."

This and nothing more. It brought a spate of protestations from Conway; Gates heard of it and angrily hinted that Colonel Hamilton had snooped in Gates' files when he was at Saratoga. Washington let them stew for the time being, not even bothering to tell Gates that the source of the leak was his own aide, Wilkinson.[17]

Congress began flexing its muscles. It created a new Board of War composed of men outside of Congress, and named Gates as its president. Also named to the Board was General Thomas Mifflin who had become one of the foremost critics of the commander in chief. Congress also made Conway a major general, but as a staff officer in the capacity of inspector general. Some members undoubtedly hoped that these affronts would induce Washington to resign, but it is doubtful if the majority would have voted to accept his resignation. (When Conway arrived at headquarters Washington, with cold formality, asked to see orders specifying his duties. When Conway confessed that he had none Washington informed him that he would have no duties until instructions from Congress were received.)

Meantime the army prepared to go into winter quarters at Valley Forge, a bleak stretch of country on the west side of the Schuylkill near Kelly's Ford (modern Norristown). There had been talk of furloughing the army home but Washington considered that a fatal step. Another consideration was to break it up into cantonments scattered through Pennsylvania, New Jersey, and Delaware. In this way foraging would be easier and the inhabitants would be protected from British marauders. This was also rejected. Howe must be watched and some effort must be made to harass British detachments around Philadelphia. Scattered cantonments brought to mind the fate of the Hessians at Trenton. So it was to be Valley Forge, close enough to keep an eye on the redcoats in Philadelphia, but safe enough from a sudden sally by Howe, since the Schuylkill would guard against a surprise.[18]

The suffering of the army during the winter of 1777–1778 has made Valley Forge a symbol of hardship and privation. A detailed study of the army in that grim winter is not properly part of this study, but a few observations are worth noting. The winter weather was not especially severe, and Pennsylvania and New Jersey had ample food and forage for at least the minimal needs of the army. Washington and his men believed that it was the lack of patriotic spirit among the Pennsylvanians, especially the Quakers, that led them to withhold supplies, preferring to sell them for hard money to the British.

Yet foraging parties sent out from Valley Forge had considerable success. Private Joseph Martin was assigned to this duty. "I do not remember," he says, "that during the time I was employed in this business, which was from Christmas to the latter part of April, ever to have met with the least resistance from the inhabitants, take what we would from their barns, mills, corncribs or stalls. . . . I had to travel far and near, in cold and in storms, by day and by night, and at all times to run the *risk* of abuse, if not injury, from the inhabitants when *plundering* them of their property. . . . But I will give them the credit of never receiving the least abuse or injury during the whole time I was employed in this business."

The real root of the problem was in the army organization. Able men for positions in the quartermaster's department were hard to find. Officers quickly found out that the army offered no financial rewards, which meant that motivation for continuing in the service was confined to patriotism or the rewards of a hero's acclaim. And as General Greene noted, "No body ever heard of a quartermaster, in history."[19]

Even so, early in the war Washington was fortunate enough to find a splendid administrator for the position of quartermaster general. Thomas Mifflin of Pennsylvania proved to be not only an able organizer but a skilful recruiter, and the militia turnout for the Trenton campaign owed much to his silver-tongued oratory. His fine performance earned him rapid promotion and by February, 1777, he was a major general and a close confidant of the commander in chief. His friendship and admiration for Washington began to deteriorate in the summer of 1777 when it was said that he believed Washington was not sufficiently concerned about the defense of Pennsylvania and Philadelphia. By the end of the campaign Mifflin had not only become one of Washington's severest critics but was beginning to neglect his duties as quartermaster general. He finally asked to be relieved for reasons of health (he recovered miraculously when he was appointed to the Board of War), and Congress did not replace him. His duties devolved upon his senior deputy, Colonel Henry Lutterloh, who had neither the rank nor the capacity for the job. The result was that the administrative apparatus for collecting and distributing supplies had collapsed. No preparations had been made for stockpiling supplies for the winter months or for setting up collection depots for foraging parties. Obviously, if Private Martin's experience was typical, the supplies gleaned from "barns, mills, corncribs or stalls" were not reaching the men in the huts at Valley Forge.[20]

Even before the soldiers had built their permanent quarters for the winter they had begun to feel the pinch. Standard fare was "Firecake and water, sir." Firecake was simply unseasoned flour and water mixed into a dough that could be cooked over an open fire, or perhaps flattened on a heated rock and "baked" enough to be edible. In mid-December, after a week without a ration of beef, the hills and valleys around the Forge began to ring with the chant of "No meat! No meat!" The din was interspersed with crow caws and owl hoots until the whole encampment was engulfed in a cacophony of sound. Yet there was no edge of violence in the uproar. "See the poor Soldier . . . —if his food is bad, he eats it notwithstanding with seeming content—blesses God for a Good Stomach and Whistles it into digestion."

The situation was not helped by a Congressional reorganization which had established a maze of red tape for the commissary general's office. Joseph Trumbull, who held that post until the summer of 1777, insisted that his subordinates must be paid by commission rather than by salary. Only on that basis could he induce competent men to serve. When Congress refused to change the system Trumbull resigned. His duties were taken over by William Buchanan who, to put charitably, was not equal to the task.

The army was not only starving but it was freezing. Of all the services that of clothier-general was the most inefficient. This was an army that was seldom fully clothed, much less in uniform. With the approach of winter the situation was desperate. General Sullivan reported that officers who wanted to resign their commissions "assigned as a Reason for not waiting on me that they were so naked they were ashamed to be seen. . . ."[21]

Two days before Christmas Washington sent a dispatch to Congress that must be read in its entirety to understand fully the seething indignation that gripped the commander in chief. Poor Captain Granberry, the aide to whom it was dictated, was the recipient of a veritable flood of words which he never did get into proper sentences. Part of it reads

> . . . since the 4th Instt. our Numbers fit for duty from the hardships and exposures they have undergone, particularly on Acct. of Blankets (numbers being obliged and do set up all Night by fires, instead of comfortable rest in a natural way) have decreased near 2000 Men. We find Gentlemen without knowing whether the Army was really going into Winter Quarters or not (for I am sure no resolution of mine would warrant the remonstrance) reprobating the measure as much as if they thought Men were made of Stocks or Stones and equally insensible of frost and Snow and moreover, as if they conceived it practicable for an inferior Army under the disadvantages I have describ'd our's to be wch. is by

no means exagerated to confine a superior one (in all respects well appointed, and provided for a Winters Campaign) within the City of Phila., and cover from depredation and waste in the States of Pensa., Jersey, &ca. but what makes this matter still more extraordinary in my eye is, that these very Gentn. who were all apprized of the nakedness of the Troops, from occular demonstration thought their own Soldiers worse clad than others, and advised me, near a Month ago, to postpone the execution of a Plan, I was about to adopt (in consequence of a resolve of Congress) for seizing Cloaths, under strong assurances that an ample supply would be collected in ten days agreeably to a decree of the State, not one article of wch., by the bye, is yet come to hand, should think a Winters Campaign and the covering these States from the Invasion of an Enemy so easy a business. I can assure those Gentlemen that it is a much easier and less distressing thing to draw remonstrances in a comfortable room by a good fire side than to occupy a cold bleak hill and sleep under frost and Snow without Cloaths or Blankets; however, although they seem to have little feeling for the naked, and distressed Soldier, I feel superabundantly for them, and from my Soul pity those miseries, wch. it is neither in my power to relieve or prevent.

It was probably during this dreadful time that Washington developed a real affection for what his aide, John Laurens, called "those dear ragged Continentals." And the soldiers recognized that the big, weary general was not entirely responsible for their plight. At the end of a horrible week in February when no rations at all were issued, the men finally protested, but respectfully, "as if they had been humble petitioners for special favors." Later when rumors circulated that Washington might be replaced, the word that came from the soldiers was "Washington or no Army."[22]

So it may be that here at Valley Forge the army won its greatest victory. It survived.

With the men finally in some kind of permanent winter quarters Washington now turned his attention to his American enemies, real or imagined. Shortly after the first of the year he became embroiled in a new dispute with General Conway over the matter of his duties as inspector general. On Washington's part the correspondence was almost prim in its formality; on Conway's there was a lofty pretentiousness that young John Laurens thought was inexcusably insolent. What Colonel Laurens thought might have been inconsequential but his father had just been elected president of Congress. Henry Laurens had at first been inclined to join the critics of Washington, men like Congressman James Lovell of Massachusetts and Thomas Mifflin; but reports from his son and from committees of Congress who had visited Valley Forge led the elder Laurens to an increasing appreciation of Washington's towering stature as the personification of the whole American cause. In this latest controversy with Conway the commander in chief's solution was to lay the whole correspondence before Congress.[23]

At about the same time came Gates' reaction to the "weak General and bad councillors" letter. Gates was disturbed that his private correspondence was being promiscuously circulated, and he notified Washington that he was transmitting a copy of his complaint to Congress. Washington professed to be astonished. Did not Gates know that the source of the letter was Gates' own aide, Colonel Wilkinson? It had been conveyed to him, said Washington, in such a way as to lead him to believe that Gates was warning him against Conway. He had hoped to keep this whole affair "in the family" but since Gates preferred to lay the matter before Congress the commander in chief would do the same with his own correspondence.

As these dispatches reached York the august members of Congress were buffeted from another direction. Nine brigadier generals from seven states wrote to protest the promotion of Conway to major general. A similar blast came from more than forty colonels protesting the promotion of Wilkinson to brigadier. While the members might be sensitive about the authority and dignity of Congress few of them ever forgot that they were also politicians.[24]

With the furor out in the open the air was soon filled with protestations of innocence. Gates brought Conway's offending letter to York and showed a copy of it to President Laurens. The offending phrase quoted by Washington did not appear, but Laurens pronounced the rest of the letter "ten times worse." The letter, it turned out, was a critique of the battle of the Brandywine and probably was filled with much of Conway's "after kind of sagacity." If Gates expected that his arrival at York would promote his cause he was sharply disappointed. On the contrary, it was obvious that Washington's critics were more vocal than numerous, and that Gates would do well to muffle his pretensions. As for Conway, Washington simply gave him the silent treatment, refusing to answer any of his protesting letters. Conway withered on the vine until April, when he once again incautiously threatened to resign. To his dismay Congress accepted with alacrity.

The new Board of War also sank into oblivion. It planned and ordered a winter invasion of Canada. Bypassing Washington's headquarters completely it ordered Lafayette to take command of the expedition with Conway as his second in command (and thus the guiding genius behind the inexperienced young general). But Lafayette scotched this maneuver by refusing to serve with Conway and threatening to return to France. Conway's prestige could scarcely match that of the marquis. The Canadian expedition was, in Washington's words, "the child of folly," and when Lafayette reached Albany at the end of January neither supplies nor troops were at hand, so the invasion was aborted.

The affair ended with professions of loyalty from Gates and a gracious acknowledgement from Washington urging that "those matters which have been the subject of our past correspondence makes me willing to close with the desire . . . of burying them hereafter in silence."[25]

It is idle to say that there was no Conway Cabal. It existed in the minds of men in 1777 and in the histories of the War of Independence ever since. The real question seems to be whether such a term is justified in describing the anti-Washington movement that grew and flourished in the latter part of 1777.

Opposition to Washington came from three principal sources. Congress, imbued with a "new broom" spirit, was determined to assert itself to show its bumbling predecessors how to win the war. As with many of their spiritual descendants they were soon disillusioned and came to appreciate the magnitude of their task (it is notable that not once did Washington visit Congress to plead his cause; instead he invited its committees to the camps—and the effect was invariably devastating). Gates and Conway were simply out to exploit the circumstances to promote their own vaulting ambitions.

To say that these constituted a conspiratorial group of plotters or intriguers is to ignore the bumbling of Gates and Conway, and the ease with which Washington finally disposed of his critics. The conspirators, if such they were, had neither the cohesiveness nor the will to deserve the name.

In the aftermath of recriminations as the participants tried to justify themselves, Wilkinson was appointed secretary to the Board of War. After his complicity in the Conway affair was revealed Gates, the president of the Board, refused to allow him to serve, and Wilkinson was forced to resign his position and his commission (March, 1778). A dual between Gates and Wilkinson was barely averted. Conway could not avoid one with hard-bitten John Cadwalader, the Pennsylvania militia general who had managed to fight in every battle from Trenton to Germantown. They met on July 4, 1778 and Cadwalader, appropriately, shot Conway in the mouth. The Board of War soon sank into that limbo which so often overtakes committees whose members are reluctant to serve and seldom attend.[26]

From the standpoint of personal achievement Washington, who had started the year on a high note of victory, ended it with the bitter taste of defeat in his mouth. His enormous pride was undoubtedly deeply stung, especially as it seemed to him that his very position as commander in chief was being threatened. He had not proven to be the general that the nation—and perhaps he himself—had imagined him to be. His greatest failing was that he could not recognize the limitations of both his men and his officers. He refused to acknowledge that, for the time being, his soldiers, man for man, were not the equal of the redcoats in the field.

Yet in his pessimism he may have failed to give himself sufficiently high marks for achievement. If he bothered to cast his mind back twelve months, he might note that, though this was a tatterdemalion army, it was much more truly a fighting force than in December, 1776. Then he had written, ". . . By the first of next month, then, we shall be left with five [Continental] Regiments of Virginia, one of Maryland, General Hand's and the remains of Miles; reduced by so much sickness, fatigue, &ca. as in the whole not to exceed but fall short of 1200 men;" in December, 1777, "our whole strength in continental troops . . . amount to no more than 8200 In Camp fit for duty."

One accomplishment Washington would not be aware of for some time.

The great victory over Burgoyne has always been cited as a telling point in convincing the French government to conclude its alliance with the young republic. But John Adams, who had gone to Paris to assist Benjamin Franklin in the negotiations (and had joined the chorus of Washington's critics before he left) made an interesting observation:

> General Gates was the ablest negotiator you had in Europe; next to him, General Washington's attack on the enemy at Germantown. I do not know, indeed, whether this last affair had not more influence on the European mind than that of Saratoga. Although the attempt was unsuccessful, the military gentlemen of Europe considered it as the most decisive proof that America would finally succeed.[27]

FOURTEEN

Epilogue:
The French Alliance

TWO YEARS HAS PASSED SINCE GEORGE III HAD DECLARED BEFORE PARLIAMENT his intention to "put a speedy end to these disorders by the most decisive exertions." Since that time the colonies had declared independence and created an army to resist the authority of the Crown. One of the results of the campaign of 1777 was a document whose words had perhaps a greater significance for the history of the war than those of the great Declaration itself:

> . . . and his most Christian Majesty guarantees on his part to the united states, their liberty, Sovereignty, and Independence, absolute and unlimited. . . .[1]

PARIS

As noted above, the upset in the balance of power occasioned by England's great victory in the Seven Years' War had been a serious blow, not only to France's overseas empire, but to her pride. The intervening years had done little to assuage French sensibilities. She had been forced to stand idly by while two of her former allies, Poland and Turkey, had been dismembered by the powers of eastern Europe, Russia, Prussia, and Austria. The Duc de Choiseul, the French foreign minister, saw in a brief span of ten years the loss of much of France's colonial empire and the shift of the power center of continental Europe to the east. His efforts to revive French military and naval power were therefore aimed at two objectives. The more obvious one was to be ready to take advantage of whatever fissures or cracks appeared in Britain's far-flung colonial empire. The other was to restore French prestige on the continent of Europe, to make the court at Versailles once more a power to be reckoned with.

Choiseul labored under two disadvantages. One was the pacific and phlegmatic person of Louis XV who, unlike his great-grandfather, had no desire to impose the Bourbon will on all of Europe. His successor, Louis XVI, was at heart a man of simple piety who disliked disorder and controversy. He believed firmly in the reduction of his government's extravagant spending and in the reordering of the financial chaos into which his kingdom had fallen. In this he was supported by his principal advisor, the Comte de Maurepas, and his comptroller-general, Anne Robert Jacques Turgot. The King opposed an aggressive foreign policy, with its attendant mounting costs for military expenditures and dangerous diplomatic consequences. But Choiseul's successor and protege, the Comte de Vergennes, was no less determined to achieve Choiseul's objectives. The difference was that Vergennes brought to his office tact, patience, and subterfuge which he had developed in a lifetime of diplomatic service.

Both Choiseul and Vergennes believed that the most vulnerable spot in Britain's empire was her North American colonies, and as early as 1764 French agents had been sent to America to take soundings of public unrest and dissatisfaction. The reports were disappointingly accurate. There was ample evidence that the colonists were chafing under some of the restrictions of the British colonial system, but no discernible signs of colonial disloyalty. At this early date Americans were still contending for their rights as Englishmen.[2]

The mounting crisis of 1774–1775 was vastly encouraging to Vergennes. He was soon at work setting up a system through which covert military aid could be channeled across the Atlantic to America. With the help of Caron de Beaumarchais, sometime playwright and man about Paris, Vergennes let it be known that if French merchants would like to engage in arms traffic with the new republic certain arrangements could be made. It was all to be very quiet and unofficial, for France must not give offense to England by meddling in the latter's domestic affairs.

Meantime, even before the Declaration of Independence Congress had created a secret Committee of Correspondence—a committee on foreign affairs— which was soon actively engaged in seeking help from England's enemies. One of the reasons why the radicals pressed for a vote for independence was the fact that they wished to be able to deal with foreign nations as an independent state. By the time Silas Deane, the first American representative to France, arrived in Paris the initial success of his mission was assured. Although the French government carefully avoided official acknowledgement of the presence of an American commissioner, the astonished Deane received a steady parade of French merchants to his door, anxious to press upon him contracts for supplying the Americans with arms and munitions. The arms were available because Vergennes had seen to it that the arsenals of the government were open—strictly to French merchants, of course. And payments for the weapons was assured because Vergennes quietly circulated the word that American credit was good. The subsequent flow of arms and munitions to the United States was crucial to the American war effort in 1776 and 1777. It has been estimated that eighty percent of the powder burned by Washington's army from Bunker Hill to the end of the campaign of 1777 came from France.

The next step in Vergennes' program was to promote an alliance, and here he was confronted with a stubborn Louis XVI. Military supplies to America were not especially costly, and besides French merchants were turning a nice profit. But the King's passion for economy would not brook the possibility of a war with England. Nor was this the fanciful whim of a wilful monarch. One of the ablest of Louis XVI's ministers was Turgot, the comptroller-general of finance, who was not only a capable administrator but a *physiocrat*. He had inveighed against unofficial aid to the Americans in 1775 and 1776; Vergennes, he said, was going back to the old system of overseas empire with the attendant expenses of a fleet and an army to defend it. Not so, replied Vergennes. France claimed no aspirations for territory overseas (American ministers and Congressmen take note). It was England's trade with her colonies that was the key to her wealth, not the possessions themselves. Deprive her of those colonies and divert the trade from the new republic across the Atlantic to France; the profits from this lucrative free trade area would restore prosperity to France and bring disaster and humiliation to England. It was the sort of argument that should have appealed to a *physiocrat*, but Turgot the financier refused to yield to fine-spun theories. The new commercial and industrial imperialism might be the wave of the future but Turgot was concerned with the here and the now. He insisted that Vergennes' policy would lead to another expensive war and that this would be fatal to the financial structure of the kingdom. Fortunately for Vergennes, Turgot was dismissed in 1776 for reasons unconnected with foreign policy. Still the King declared that he was unwilling to make any commitment to the Americans, at least until there was stronger evidence of a favorable outcome of the war.

Only one other concession could Vergennes wring from the King. This was that the government would tacitly allow vessels of the United States to enter French ports. These included privateers, who were not only allowed port facilities but could dispose of their prizes at auction. The British government protested vigorously claiming that a mere declaration of independence did not constitute a fact of international law. The privateers were especially galling to the British. Lightly gunned, swift, and highly maneuverable, they could slip out of French ports, descend like hawks on fat English merchantmen, and be back in Le Havre or St. Nazaire before patrolling British men-of-war could possibly intervene.[3]

The Earl of Sandwich, the First Lord of the Admiralty, was caught in a strategic bind. General Howe's demands on his brother's fleet, especially during the troop lift to Philadelphia in 1777, taxed the navy beyond its capacity. Had the privateers been forced to operate from bases in America or the West Indies they obviously would not have posed a serious problem. As it was, the talk at the coffee tables at Lloyd's was of insurance rates increased by thirty percent, and ship losses in the last eight months of 1777 were set at nearly £5,000,000. Nor had Lord Howe been successful in significantly interfering with the flow of French supplies to America.

Last, but by no means least, Sandwich reminded Germain of the direct threat of the French fleet across the channel. Although diplomats and their agents and spies played their intricate games both London and Paris were pretty well informed about each other's actions, and could make shrewd guesses as to intentions. Thus in making military and especially naval dispositions the Admiralty was not likely to forget that it was an English Admiral

Boscowan who had delivered a sneak attack on Belle Isle prior to a declaration of war in 1756. It was to be assumed that the French had not forgotten it either. This anxiety was reflected in the increasingly sharp warnings of the British ambassador, Lord Stormont, that the flagrant violations of international law were endangering the peace of Europe.

The arrival of Benjamin Franklin in Paris in December, 1776, was not calculated to placate his lordship. Franklin had been a colonial representative in London for some years before the war and his devious ways had earned him the public censure of Parliament. Stormont warned Vergennes that England would regard any dealings with Franklin as an unfriendly act.[4]

Yet the *haute monde* of Paris could no more ignore "Poor Richard" than it could the Deluge. He became the darling of the aristocracy that surrounded the court at Versailles. His simple dress, his unpowdered hair, his lumpy, aged frame moving through the pomp and glitter of Parisian society had a devastating effect. Here was the rustic from the new republic of mankind who was, in fact, no rustic at all, but a renowned scientist and man of letters. The philosophy of the Enlightenment which had pervaded Europe for more than a century had suddenly found the personification of Rousseau's child of nature. Benjamin Franklin became a Paris fashion in the midst of a world that made a tyranny of fashion. Young ladies were "ready to eat him up" and, to borrow John C. Miller's phrase, Franklin was, even at seventy-one, no mean dish.

And it was a triumphant commentary on both his erudition and his charm that the Franklin fashion was not a sometime thing. During the seven years of his stay in Paris his popularity was undiminished until his own declining health forced him into semiretirement.

To say that the alliance with France would not have come about without Franklin's presence in Paris is obviously to overstate the case. His great contribution was that he made the alliance popular with the *aristoi* who by instinct and breeding could scarcely have been expected to welcome republicanism bred in revolution.

The news of the failure of the British campaign of 1777 and the surrender of Burgoyne's army began to filter into Paris early in November. When rumor became fact the wave of enthusiasm that swept through Paris made it appear as though the long sought alliance was now a foregone conclusion. But the King and Maurepas still hesitated. It seemed to Louis XVI that the United States might be capable of winning its independence without the necessity of French intervention. One of the factors in his hesitancy was the tie with Spain in the form of the Family Compact, an agreement between the two Bourbon monarchs to lend mutual support to each other. Only five years before Spain had become involved in a dispute with Great Britain over the Falkland Islands, and had been forced to back down when France had refused its support. Spain, with her far-flung colonial empire in the west, had not the least interest in supporting a colonial war of liberation. Louis was hesitant to give too great offense to his one close ally.

These arguments failed to impress Vergennes. France, he urged, must not lose this opportunity to recover prestige and influence by humiliating Great Britain; if the United States won independence on its own it might still retain its commercial ties with England. Only by positive action on the part of France could the young republic be persuaded to break all ties with the mother country and make France the beneficiary of its trade. There was also the danger that the British, now fully awake to the possibility of losing the war, would make such generous concessions that the Americans would abandon the vicissitudes of war in favor of "a family compact, that is to say, a league against the House of Bourbon."

Franklin was well aware of the objections being raised to the alliance and he shrewdly played on Vergennes' hopes and fears. After the first wave of jubilation over Burgoyne's surrender had subsided Franklin suddenly became less importunate in seeking to open negotiations, and hinted that the United States' position was now radically altered. It must now seek the best terms for a settlement, whether from Paris or London. He carefully nurtured rumors that he and members of his staff were holding secret meetings with English agents.[5]

Two circumstances finally broke the deadlock that seemed to be developing. The first was that Vergennes convinced the King that if an alliance with the United States did lead to war—as it almost surely would—Spain would be forced willy-nilly to honor the Family Compact from the sheer necessity of having to protect her Latin American possessions. The second factor was that it was well-known that the North ministry was ready to present a plan of reconciliation when Parliament reconvened late in January. If Britain came up with a definite and generous proposal while France held aloof, at worst, the Americans would accept; at best, Franco-American relations would be badly damaged.[6]

On December 6 the first formal meeting of American and French representatives took place, although it was a secret session since France was not yet ready to recognize the United States officially. Franklin assured Vergennes that the Americans were not engaged in any conciliatory negotiations with England, but warned that unless France moved quickly, at least concluding a treaty of friendship and commerce (which would be tantamount to recognition), the United States might "be forced by the people into measures with the Power with whom they should most fear any connection."

As rumors and reports ran rife through the diplomatic underground of Paris the advocates of alliance became increasingly strident. Beaumarchais, the playwright whose energetic—and often comic—efforts in behalf of secret aid to America had made him an ardent advocate of intervention, was near despair. "—Promptly enchain the Americans by a treaty," he insisted; "seize the last moment at which they can still say with noble pride; France has been the first to honour our successes by treating with us on an equal footing. . . ." Probably what broke the deadlock was the knowledge that in London Parliament was about to convene and it was certain that the North ministry was ready to present a peace plan for its immediate action.

At a meeting between the American commissioners and Conrad Gerard (who was to become the first French minister to the United States) Franklin applied the final pressure: ". . . The immediate conclusion of a treaty of commerce and alliance will induce the Deputies to close their ears to any proposal which should not have as its basis entire liberty and independence, both politial and commercial." Gerard agreed, and two weeks later, on February 6, 1778, the treaties were concluded.[7]

LONDON

As the autumn of 1777 came to an end an air of deep pessimism pervaded the ministry in London. The word from Stormont in Paris was that France and Spain had no intention of withholding aid from the Americans; on the contrary, there was every indication that their efforts would be redoubled. By the end of October news came from Burgoyne of the reverse at Bennington and the inconclusive battle at Freeman's Farm on September 19. Howe reported from the Head of the Elk that Loyalism was not rampant in the middle colonies as he had supposed and his gloomy prediction that the war could not be ended without another campaign seemed to Germain and the King a masterpiece of understatement. News of the battle on the Brandywine and the occupation of Philadelphia raised no hopes. Washington's army was still very much alive and Lord North was heard to say that "the best we can make of it is to get out of the dispute as soon as possible."

Then, early in December, came a veritable avalanche of disaster: Burgoyne's army surrendered; Howe cut off from the fleet by the Delaware blockade; Washington's army not only intact, but aggressively seeking out his opponent. All this meant that the ministry must completely reshape its policy.

Germain must consider whether Parliament would support the expenditures for another campaign. Certainly such a proposal would be difficult to support unless the Howes were relieved of their commands. This in itself distressed Germain not at all but he foresaw that to accept their resignations (Lord Howe had also offered to resign) could scarcely be done without blaming the Howes for the failure of the ministry's policy. This, in turn, would raise a political storm from their powerful family and friends. Nevertheless, early in February, 1778, Germain informed Sir William that the King "was graciously pleased to signify to you his royal acquiescence to your request to resign your command. . . ." Admiral Howe did not resign until the following summer, but the storm that Germain foresaw continued for the next two years, marked by Parliamentary investigations and bitter recriminations.

Germain also needed to revise the military strategy of the war in America. He suggested to Clinton that the army's role be essentially a passive one, used offensively only in conjunction with the navy in conducting raids along the New England coast and perhaps attacks on French and Spanish possessions. Lord Howe should conduct a tight naval blockade and concentrate his efforts on reducing privateering and cutting off the flow of supplies coming to the United States from France. It was now almost certain that there would be war with France, probably allied with Spain. This meant England must now think in terms of survival, for the rebuilding of the French army and navy during the ministry of Choiseul had not gone unnoticed. What had begun as a rebellion of colonial farmers had now blossomed into a full-scale war as dire in its significance as those conflicts that had been known collectively as the Second Hundred Years' War. Germain and his colleagues agreed that military conquest as a means of solving the American problem was no longer viable. So ended, for the time at least, the policy which ministers, King, and Parliament had so enthusiastically and confidently launched two years before.[8]

Finally, Lord North saw that if anything was to be salvaged from the wreckage of England's American policy a high order of diplomacy was called for—not the kind of deceptive trickery that he had practiced in 1775, but meaningful concessions that would somehow persuade the Americans that empire was preferable to independence. And it was here that North encountered formidable obstacles. He must prepare his proposals in the face of the virtual certainty that France would offer the United States an alliance. To achieve reconciliation England's terms must grant a wide degree of autonomy to the colonies, one that would make them coequal partners in the empire. This was a bitter pill to swallow. Yet both Lord North and the King recognized the gravity of the situation, and both steeled themselves to the task of winning support, not from the opposition, but from the members of their own party in Parliament who had consistently advocated bringing the colonies to a state of submission. In short, any proposition that was acceptable to the Americans was sure to meet with violent and indignant protest from the ministry's own supporters.

Nowhere is the chasm between American and English thinking better illustrated. Americans believed that, while they might still be country bumpkins in many ways, they had developed a political system that was superior to Britain's. Most wars of colonial liberation were waged to win rights and privileges which had their existence only in the hopes and aspirations of the revolutionaries. American goals were not mere fine-spun theories but, in many cases, accomplished fact. They already had representative assemblies, freedom of worship, voting rights. Their struggle for "liberty" in the decade from 1765 to 1775 was against what they considered to be encroachments on these rights by Parliament. The Stamp Act, the tea tax, the Coercive Acts—these the Americans regarded as acts designed to undermine and destroy a system that they had firmly established.

When members of Parliament expressed outrage that Americans should ever consider themselves as the equals of Englishmen, the American answer was, "We already are!" And Englishmen, blinded by national pride, found this beyond belief.

It was this attitude that Lord North encountered when he prepared to present his solution to the House of Commons when it opened its session in January, 1778. His program was embodied in two acts: "An act for removing all doubts and apprehensions concerning taxation by the parliament of Great Britain in any of the colonies; . . ." and an act authorizing the King to appoint a commission to negotiate with the colonists, it being understood that what they were to offer was essentially a return to the conditions prior to 1763. What North was proposing, in effect, was to trade a policy of colonial taxation for a return to the old mercantile system as embodied in the Navigation Acts. Under questioning Lord North expressed his belief that the tax on tea, the Restraining Acts, and the Coercive Acts would all probably have to be repealed. But he did not wish to make concessions prior to negotiations.

The tumult that Lord North had foreseen erupted. There were bitter denunciations and dire predictions of the decline of the empire. But in the end Parliament—even the Lords—choked down the vile thing. By mid-February it was almost certain that a Franco-American alliance had been concluded. No time must be lost. The attitude of most Englishmen was probably akin to that described in the Commons following North's presentation: "A dull melancholy silence for some time succeeded. . . . It had been heard with profound attention, but without a single mark of approbation. . . . Astonishment, dejection, and fear, over clouded the whole assembly."[9]

YORK AND PHILADELPHIA

The Congress of the United States has always been a very deliberate body, seldom allowing the pressure of events to hasten its measured—and sometimes maddening—pace. The Continental Congress was no exception. The nation's first important debate on foreign policy took place late in 1776 when Washington was being pushed out of New Jersey and almost out of the war. The occasion was the nomination of Benjamin Franklin to be an American commissioner to Paris, and the question was over whether or not he and his colleagues were to seek an alliance with France. Congressional pride in its newly declared independence at times almost matched the arrogant nationalism of Parliament. "It is a cowardly Spirit in our Countrymen," said John Adams, "which makes them pant with so much expectation after a French war. I have very often been ashamed to hear so many Whigs . . . Whining out their ears that We must be subdued unless France should step in." It must be remembered that Americans shared the age-old English hatred of all things French, and, as English colonists, they had engaged in the colonial counterparts of the Second Hundred Years' War. Suspicion was rife that France would use an

American alliance to reestablish New France in North America. It was not to be expected that Anglo-American fear of French imperialism, Catholicism, and absolutism would vanish overnight.

Yet such a revolution of opinion did in fact take place in the succeeding months. Despite the persistence of a good deal of Francophobia in Congress the American delegation in Paris became convinced that France was truly aiming at the humiliation of England and an entree to the trade in North America, and that this was the limit of her aspirations. Moreover Franklin and his colleagues succeeded in convincing Congress. This was due in no small part to the steady stream of supplies and munitions that flowed across the Atlantic in 1777. This was accompanied by a somewhat less welcome tide of French officer volunteers. As noted, American privateers found a safe haven in French ports from which they launched their forays against English shipping. Despite all his devious maneuverings and subtle gestures, when Vergennes proclaimed that France's motive was *revanche*, he meant it.[10]

The first packet of dispatches from Paris which was supposed to contain news of negotiations was opened in York and found to contain thick packets of blank paper. Paul Wentworth, a Loyalist agent, and Dr. Edward Bancroft, Franklin's confidential secretary who was also an English spy, were undoubtedly responsible for this admirably clever theft. They hoped that by delaying Franklin's report of the opening discussions of the alliance they would enable the British government to sow the seeds of discord among the Americans. Indeed the essentials of North's proposals to Parliament reached America before the French treaties since North had sent his plan of reconciliation to America even before it had been approved by Parliament. The terms were distributed throughout the states, and the Whigs shrewdly made no effort to suppress them. In fact, they assisted in giving them the widest possible circulation along with their own pamphlets denouncing the proposals as another perfidious offer which Parliament would renounce as soon as the Americans laid down their arms. Lord North's chickens of 1775 had come to roost. It was carefully noted that the bills had not passed Parliament and there was no assurance that they would not be drastically altered in the process.

Loyalists were quick to point out that America was being conceded everything that had been asked for in 1775. In effect, the mother country was renouncing taxation for revenue and going back to a system under which the colonies had flourished before 1763. But Loyalist arguments were to no avail. Too much blood had been spilled, too many dreams for future of the new nation had been born, too many people thought of themselves more as Americans than as Englishmen.

Congress' reply to North's proposals was a demand that either independence be recognized or all British forces be withdrawn from the states as a precondition for opening negotiations. Already news of an alliance with France was filtering across the Atlantic. On May 2 Simeon Deane arrived at York bearing the official treaties, the terms of which exceeded the fondest hopes of the members of Congress. Not only did France specifically renounce any pretensions to territory in North America, but "they mutually engage not to lay down their arms, until Independence of the united states shall have been formally or tacitly assured. . . ."[11]

It was not until June 6 that the Earl of Carlisle and his fellow commissioners arrived in Philadelphia to attempt to implement the settlement with the mother country. Though empowered to grant generous terms Carlisle was supposed to yield these point by point. Yet if pressed to the limit he was authorized to offer what would have been, in a later era, dominion status. But the Carlisle commission was far too long in reaching America. On his arrival his lordship found that General Clinton and Admiral Howe were on the point of evacuating Philadelphia. Orders to this effect had been issued even before the commissioners had left England. Carlisle was outraged. Though he was a novice at diplomacy, even the young earl knew that diplomats can only operate if they have some kind of leverage. How could he possibly convince the Americans when the British army was in retreat? "It appears that we were to be deceived because the cheat could not otherwise be put upon the nation," remarked his lordship bitterly; "by an imposition of this nature the public is wounded thro' us, and those who contrived the cheat, must answer for the consequences."

On March 23 the King was formally notified of the existence of the French alliance with the United States. The same day George III made recommendations to Lord North that clearly expressed the ruin of England's American policy:

> The paper delivered this day by the French ambassador is certainly equivalent to a declaration and therefore must certainly overturn every plan proposed for strengthening the Army under the Command of Lieut. Gen. Clinton with an intent of carrying on an active War in North America . . . it is a joke to think of keeping Pensilvania for we must form from the Army now in America a corps sufficient to attack the French Islands and two or three thousand men ought to be employed with the Fleet to destroy the Ports and Warfs of the Rebels.

And a few days later:

> . . . I think it so desireable to end the War with that country [the United States], to be enabled with redoubled ardour to avenge the faithless and insolent conduct of France that I think it may be proper to keep open the channel of intercourse with that insidious man [Franklin].[12]

FIFTEEN

The Campaign of 1777: Success and Failure

THE STORY OF THE CAMPAIGN OF 1777 IS DOMINATED BY THE PERSONALITIES OF five men: Lord George Germain, Sir William Howe, John Burgoyne, George Washington, and Horatio Gates. Some histories, especially biographies, have been centered on the "great man" theory, that is, that the great events and epochs of history have been caused or decisively shaped by great men. This has at times been amended to say that there are no great men; there are only great challenges which ordinary men are called upon to meet, which suggests that there is greatness in many men if the challenge is strong enough to call forth the best that is in them.

However valid these ideas may be it is surely obvious that history can be drastically altered by men in positions of power who are weak or incompetent when confronted by crises. So it seems proper to try to answer several questions as to why the campaign of 1777 turned out as it did in the context of the failures as well as the successes of the men who had the greatest power to control events.

One should always be aware that these dominant figures are surrounded by a host of lesser individuals who played their roles in the outcome. In England George III loyally backed his subordinates and Parliament was a factor that Germain had constantly to reckon with. In America Washington was acutely and at times painfully aware of his accountability to Congress.

William Howe and John Burgoyne could not win fame and glory without the redcoats and their German allies, and the American "rag, tag, and bobtail" marched and fought through thousands of miles of bitter winter cold and stifling summer heat. And it may well be that the outcome of the campaign of 1777—indeed, of the whole war—was determined by those nameless but deadly little struggles that took place between small parties of Tories and Patriots. As Professor John Shy has pointed out, most Americans in 1776 only dimly perceived the issues of which so much was made in speeches, newspapers, and pamphlets of the time, and in the histories that have been written since. We would do well to heed his admonition that "the war was a political education conducted by military means. . . ."

Yet one is constrained to believe that Americans were inclined to climb aboard the most attractive band wagon, so that military campaigns and battles do assume great importance in determining public opinion. Tom Paine's *Common Sense* may have stimulated the movement for independence in the early months of 1776, but a more important factor may have been that on July 2 there were no British troops on American soil. It is doubtful if Paine's *Crisis* series in the latter part of 1776 would have had much effect without the American victories at Trenton and Princeton. So it becomes important to find out why the leaders and their grand plans failed or succeeded because in the final analysis the War of Independence was won by men who fought each other on the battlefield.

Had the King and his ministers decided to treat the rebellion as a diplomatic and political problem one can go through a whole range of speculation and prediction about the fate of England's American empire. (In fact, both Troyer Anderson and Ira Gruber, in their splendid studies of the Howe brothers, emphasize the efforts of the British commanders, in their roles as peace commissioners, to use just such an approach.) But the fact was that King, ministers, and Parliament never seriously considered anything other than a military solution to the American problem prior to 1778. Imbued by a nationalism that amounted to arrogance, it never occurred to them that a similar sense of national identity had developed in America and that English arrogance would be met by a stiff-necked Yankee pride as stubborn as their own.

So the great campaign was launched that would bring the colonies to heel and end the rebellion. Lord Germain, with the full support of the government, set the ponderous British military machine in motion, a prodigious feat for which he has only recently received recognition.

THE BRITISH HIGH COMMAND

The plan for the campaign of 1777 was essentially a simple one. Using the forces from Canada and the lower Hudson moving toward each other along the axis of the Richelieu river, Lake Champlain, and the Hudson river, British armies would separate the New England colonies from the middle Atlantic area so that the rebel forces would be divided and isolated.

Over the years a great deal has been written about whether such an objective was possible, whether indeed the control of the lake and river line could have effectively crippled the Americans and brought about their defeat. Some modern military strategists have insisted that such a line was far too long to be maintained by the limited forces available to the British command.[1]

It should be noted that this was an offensive plan (much like the Union plan for severing the Confederacy by controlling the Mississippi) that envisioned a chain of posts from which raids could be made especially into western Massachusetts and New Hampshire. American supply and troop movements to and from New England, if they could not be entirely interdicted, would be seriously disrupted. A basic tenet of eighteenth century military doctrine was to conduct a "war of posts" from which the enemy could be harassed— e.g., Ticonderoga, Albany, and the Hudson Highlands.

More to the point, whatever latter day theorists believe is really of little relevance. The fact is that those who planned and fought the campaign believed that it was feasible. There are two extensive memoranda in Germain's papers, one directed to him in 1776 and the other Germain's "Own Account of Plans for the Campaign of 1777," that spell out the objectives and their expected results. And not only the British but the Americans believed that the Hudson river and Lake Champlain were of crucial importance. Even as Washington's army reached its last extremity in December, 1776, he insisted that troops be kept at the Highlands of the Hudson. Forts Clinton and Montgomery and later the fortification at West Point guarding the great chain across the river attest to the fact that Washington shared the British conviction that the river line was an all-important element in the strategy of the war. The historian is primarily concerned with why people did what they did and his judgements are rendered on the basis of discernible results. Only then may he indulge in the "might-have-beens" or the "should-not-have-beens."

Even before the British launched the campaign of 1777 serious flaws were apparent. There were early indications that Germain was not firmly in control of either the planning or execution of the campaign. As Howe's alterations and deviations reached London Germain seemed quite willing to acquiesce, even to the point of accepting Howe's final aberration to virtually abandon Burgoyne and concentrate on Philadelphia and Pennsylvania. It is all very well to say that commanders in the field should be allowed a certain latitude in order to deal with changing circumstances. But overall objectives should have been clear cut and agreed upon by Germain and his generals. Even though communications between England and America were tenuous and time-consuming, the planning for 1777 began late in 1776, and both Burgoyne and Howe's second in command, General Clinton, had opportunities to confer personally with Germain.

Why, then, was not such agreement reached? One explanation is that political leaders from that day to this have proven singularly inept at controlling the military. By this is not meant the acquiescence to military domination that raises *juntas* or military dictatorships, but the kind of accommodation to military wishes and opinions that little by little alters and distorts objectives. This, in turn, stems from the fact that the public—or in this case Parliament— becomes infatuated with generals and the heroic aura that surrounds them, so that political leaders hesitate to bring pressure on these popular demigods for fear of political repercussions (one is reminded of Lincoln and McClellan,

Lloyd George and Sir Douglas Haig, President Truman and General Mac-Arthur). Thus control of overall strategy gradually slips from the grasp of political leaders and military policy becomes an end rather than a means. If someone had raised the question in the spring of 1777 in the cabinet: What terms are to be imposed on the colonies once the war is won, the babel of conflicting views would have revealed that there was little or no agreement as to the answer. The fact that the King immediately relegated the American war to secondary status after France entered the conflict of 1778 suggests that the government's policy of applying a military solution to the American rebellion was simplistic and shortsighted.

If one is to blame Germain as a major architect for the failure of the campaign of 1777 it must be done in the knowledge that he had to work within the framework of British politics. He rose to power because he was a strong advocate of forcible suppression of the American rebellion and the Howes were his chosen instruments for the execution of his policies. In terms of political influence it is rare that even the most influential politician can match the glamor of generals and admirals. This was doubly difficult for Germain who was seldom allowed to forget the cloud that hung over his own military career. Having created the command of the Howe brothers the American Secretary found that he could not get rid of them. There is evidence that as early as midsummer, even before the results of the campaign were known, Lord George had become thoroughly disillusioned with General Howe and only slightly less so with the admiral.

It may have been that Germain realized that Sir William's arbitrary alterations in the basic objectives of the plan for 1777 would make its success doubtful and that the American Secretary's position and prestige were doomed unless he could rid himself of the incubus of his American commanders. Certainly General Howe's gloomy dispatch from the Head of the Elk late in August must have warned Germain that the high hopes for 1777 were at an end. When the Howe brothers finally did resign, the political cost to Germain and the ministry was severe. But Germain had lost his grip on the control of the campaign when he failed to impose his will on General Howe and insist that he adhere to the broad strategic concept which had been laid down as the basis for its success.

William Howe continues to be an enigma and the command of the Howe brothers has provoked at least two brilliant studies which are basic to an understanding of the campaign of 1777. While the reasons cited in these studies are worthy of serious consideration there would appear to be other factors that need emphasis.[2]

Two characteristics of General Howe seem so obvious that they scarcely need to be pointed out. The first was that he was seemingly devoid of any sense of an overall strategy. He never really understood that he was a commander in chief, and therefore responsible for all the King's forces in America. His statement before Parliament in 1779 that Germain had never actually ordered him to cooperate with Burgoyne is ample testimony to his utter lack of comprehension of the scope of his responsibility. His almost casual disregard for the northern army may have been rooted in a subconscious fear that Burgoyne's success would overshadow his own reputation, and the Pennsylvania campaign may have been an effort to outshine the rising star of Gentleman Johnny (although there is little evidence to support this assumption). Only when he received Germain's admonitory dispatch in August did Howe finally seem to realize that he had failed in his obligation to Burgoyne.

The second factor was Howe's incredible indolence. One hardly needs to reiterate the series of interminable delays that characterized the entire two and a half years of his command: the delay in moving his base from Boston to New York in 1775–1776; the seven weeks that elapsed between the time he put his first troops ashore on Staten Island in the summer of 1776 and August 27 when he finally brought Washington to battle at Brooklyn Heights; a delay of eight more weeks until he again caught up with Washington at White Plains. In 1777 Sir William made his decision to go to Philadelphia by sea in early April, but not until the third week in July did he finally sail for Pennsylvania and not until September 11 did he engage Washington on the Brandywine (it might be noted that in the summer of 1778 Clinton took the army back to New York in twelve days).

When the army was not on the march Howe's predilection for rounds of social events, his fondness for the bottle—and for the charms of Mrs. Loring— were the subject of much bitter comment, especially among junior officers and Loyalists. Yet all this may be simply an outward sign of an inner weakness, perhaps an abhorrence of launching a campaign with all its attendant responsibilities and risks. This is not to say that Howe lacked courage. Once on the field of battle he displayed more than adequate tactical skill and his bravery under fire is unquestioned.

Thus in immediate circumstances William Howe performed well. When presented with limited responsibility (such as development of the light infantry tactics) his accomplishments seemed exemplary. It was when broader planning and wider responsibility, with their long-term consequences were involved that his performance became deficient.

Like many others, but unlike truly great military leaders, Howe responded far better to immediate rewards than to delayed gratifications. He gave little evidence throughout his career of a genuine commitment to overriding and far-reaching goals, often deferring to personal pleasures and aggrandizement. His political convictions were conspicuous only by their absence. His adherence to the policies of the Crown were less than steadfast and his strongest efforts seem to have been expended in events of the moment, leaving little for the long term.

While these traits may have been insufficiently pronounced to consider Howe as a disordered personality they certainly precluded the kind of iron-willed persistence displayed by great military leaders. In another profession

Sir William might have been highly successful, but his personality simply did not meet the demands of a commander with his far-reaching responsibilities.

Finally, Howe lacked the killer instinct, the intensity of purpose that leads successful commanders not only to defeat an opponent but to drive him relentlessly until he is destroyed. One may imagine what Napoleon, or Robert E. Lee, or Erwin Rommel would have done in the aftermath of Brooklyn Heights or the Brandywine.

In the annals of 1777 John Burgoyne is usually depicted as the epitome of British futility. After all, he lost an entire army and in the military lexicon glory or disgrace rests squarely on the shoulders of the commanding general. Yet on the whole Burgoyne seems the least culpable of them all. Vainglorious and flamboyant he may have been, and his struttings and bombast make him at times appear almost a character out of comic opera. But of the three principals in the British high command he alone held steadfastly to the task that had been assigned to him. He had been ordered to take his army to Albany and he never swerved from that purpose. Part of his failure was due to bad luck (the appearance of Stark's force at Bennington, the unexpected state of readiness at Fort Stanwix), and part of it was due to his own ineptitude, especially his tactical failures at Saratoga. Yet if Howe and Carleton had given him their unstinted support, if the British commander in chief had even harassed Washington persistently during the summer of 1777, Burgoyne would not have had to fritter away his limited force and Gates would not have had those invaluable Continental veterans from Washington's army around which he built the force that checked and then mated the northern invasion.

THE AMERICAN HIGH COMMAND

The resounding American victory at Saratoga and the subsequent alliance with France have tended to obscure a very important question. Having gone to great lengths to explain why the British failed it would seem logical for history to ask why the Americans did not win the war in 1777. By the spring of 1778 the Carlisle Commission was authorized to grant the colonies virtual autonomy in their domestic affairs and the ministry admitted privately that the American rebellion was secondary to defense against France and other potential enemies who would surely go to war with England. It is not logical to suppose that if Howe's army in Pennsylvania had met with a major setback, this, coupled with the destruction of Burgoyne, would have convinced the government that the suppression of the American rebellion was hopeless, and that by granting the colonies their freedom England would avoid a dangerous and expensive war? In short, would not the government have acknowledged in 1778 what it finally did conclude after Yorktown? Even as events stood, in March, 1778, George III gave serious consideration to granting the Americans their independence in order to assure the safety of British possessions in the West Indies and Canada.[3] It therefore seems pertinent to examine the reasons for the American failure in Pennsylvania where success might have profoundly altered the course toward independence.

By 1777 George Washington had become the personification of the American cause. Among the commanders of both armies he alone seems to have had the clearest grasp of the scope of the war. He alone appears to have thought in terms of truly continental strategy. His generalship on the whole is difficult to evaluate for he was harassed by logistical problems such as few generals have had to cope with. His superiors were the members of Congress and enough has been said of their ineptitude to make it clear that few generals have operated with such a millstone around their necks. One never fails to wonder at his infinite patience with the vagaries of Congressmen, his deference to their opinions and orders, and his insistence on one of the most basic of Whig principles, civilian control of the military. More than any other military leader, Washington recognized the political nature of the war and even when Congress granted him dictatorial powers he seldom used them to the fullest extent. It was a corollary of that intensely developed sense of duty which made him a truly great commander and, by 1777, he was the embodiment of the American struggle for independence.

On the battlefield Washington's abilities were not of a very high order, although in the first thirty months of his command he had obviously developed as a field general. One has only to compare Brooklyn Heights and Kip's Bay with the Brandywine to realize that he had developed the very important ability to keep control of a defeated army and restore it rapidly to a state of readiness.

Far from being a Fabius, during 1777 Washington showed himself to be aggressive and even belligerent in seeking out the enemy. Only the restraining counsel of his officers saved him from disaster on more than one occasion. His principal flaw in battle was that he expected too much of the officers and men under his command.

Although he was not as remiss as Howe, Washington also failed to function as a true commander in chief (unlike Howe, he did feel responsible for, and gave significant help to his commander in the north). He had not been able to weld his subordinate officers and their disparate commands into an organizational team that could execute mutually coordinating strategy. Although his mandate from Congress was clear, that he was the commander of all the land forces of the United States, Washington tended to make almost deferential requests rather than positive orders to senior generals like Charles Lee and Israel Putnam. It should be noted in passing that very few eighteenth century armies had achieved the kind of structured chain of command that was established by Napoleon and became fundamental to the organization of the armies of the nineteenth and twentieth centuries.

Nevertheless, it was this inability to work his will on his subordinates that was a major factor in the failure of Washington's campaign against Howe in the latter part of 1777. When Burgoyne surrendered at Saratoga on October 17

Colonel Wilkinson's returns showed the army of the Northern Department as having a total strength of 18,000 men. This was probably exaggerated to impress Burgoyne but certainly Gates' army numbered close to 13,000 and included in these were 5,000 Continentals of which ten regiments had been detached from Washington's command and sent to Gates' assistance.

Washington's strategy after Howe occupied Philadelphia was obvious. Pen up the British and block the Delaware, denying Howe support from the fleet. The battle of Germantown was more than just a show of belligerence. It was an attempt to deal a severe blow to the British commander and pin him down with his back to the Delaware.

With the surrender of Burgoyne it appeared that at last Washington would have available an abundance of Continentals and militia which would give him the kind of decisive superiority needed to mount a successful siege and, if not defeat Howe, at least lock him up in Philadelphia as tightly as he had confined him in Boston two years before—but without an escape route to the sea. With high hopes, Washington called on Gates for reinforcements, explaining the situation and the opportunity it offered.

Gates, justifiably proud of his victory over Burgoyne, was reluctant to give up all or any part of the superb army under his command. Against whom or what he intended to use it he did not say. That he hoped that his splendid success would result in his displacing Washington is quite likely; that he actively conspired to achieve Washington's removal is doubtful. But it was clear that the Hero of Saratoga had soaring ambitions and his swollen ego led him to snub the commander in chief in a manner that was as offensive as it was insubordinate.[4] Only after Washington had sent a member of his staff to Saratoga was he able to pry loose even those regiments that had originally come from his own command. Had these veteran troops been available while the Delaware blockade held Washington might have punished Howe severely.

The failure must be attributed both to Gates' insubordination and to the commander in chief's refusal to insist on compliance. If Washington held back because he feared the political consequences of a confrontation with Gates, the result was the loss of an opportunity such as would not recur until four more weary years of war had passed.

Notes

The number of notes for each chapter has been kept to a minimum in order to distract the reader as little as possible. Each note cites the source material (including quotations) in the order in which it appears in the text. Occasionally more than one source has been cited for the same material where it was felt that confirmation was needed.

Because some sources have been cited with unusual frequency throughout, the following abbreviations have been used to conserve space.

AA, 4th ser. Peter Force, ed., *American Archives: Fourth Series, Containing a Documentary History of the English Colonies . . . to the Declaration of Independence of the United States.* 6 vols. Washington, 1837–1846.

AA, 5th ser.·———, *American Archives, Fifth Series, . . . from the Declaration of Independence, July 4, 1776, to the Definitive Treaty of Peace with Great Britain, September 3, 1783.* 3 vols. Washington, 1848–1853.

AHR American Historical Review.

CL William L. Clements Library, University of Michigan, Ann Arbor, Michigan.

Geo. III Sir John Fortescue, ed., *The Correspondence of King George the Third, from 1760 to December, 1783.* 6 vols. London, 1927–1928.

HM Historical Magazine.

JCC Gaillard Hunt, ed., *Journals of the Continental Congress.* 34 vols. Washington, 1904–1937.

LCC Edmund C. Burnett, ed., *Letters of Members of the Continental Congress.* 8 vols. Washington, 1921–1936.

LTGW Jared Sparks, ed., *Correspondence of the American Revolution; Being Letters of Eminent Men to George Washington. . . .* 3 vols. Freeport, N.Y., 1853.

MHM Maryland Historical Magazine.

MHS Massachusetts Historical Society.

NJA Documents Relating to the Colonial, Revolutionary, and Post-Revolutionary History of the State of New Jersey. Newark, N.J., 1880–19––. Commonly cited as *New Jersey Archives.*

NJHS New Jersey Historical Society.

NYHS New York Historical Society.

PMHB Pennsylvania Magazine of History and Biography.

SS Report on the Manuscripts of Mrs. Stopford-Sackville. Historical Manuscripts Commission. 2 vols. London, 1910.

State John Burgoyne, *A State of the Expedition from Canada as Laid Before the House of*

Commons, With a Collection of Many Circumstances Which Were Prevented from Appearing Before the House by the Prorogation of Parliament. London, 1780.

WGW George Washington, *Writings*, John C. Fitzpatrick, ed. 39 vols. Washington, 1931–1944.

WMQ *William and Mary Quarterly.*

In citing printed correspondence, addressor, addressee and date have been included only when such data seemed significant.

CHAPTER ONE

1. For Gage see John Richard Alden, *General Gage in America* (Baton Rouge, La., 1948).

2. Gage to Lord Barrington, June 26, Nov. 2, and Dec. 14, 1775, Thomas Gage, *Correspondence*, Clarence E. Carter, ed. (New Haven, Conn., 1931–33), 2, pp. 650, 653–59, 663; John R. Alden, "Why the March to Concord?" *AHR*, 49 (1944), pp. 449–50.

3. Harold L. Murdock, *The Nineteenth of April* (Boston, 1923); Allen French, *The Day of Concord and Lexington* (Boston, 1925).

4. No one, including Ward and the Massachusetts Congress, knew how many men were in the American camps before Washington took command. Allen French, *The First Year of the American Revolution* (New York, 1934), Chaps. V and VI; Hugh Earl Percy to Edmund Harvey, April 20, 1775, *Letters . . . from Boston to New York, 1774–1776*, Charles K. Bolton, ed. (Boston, 1902), p. 48.

5. French, *First Year of the Revolution*, pp. 737–39; Christopher Ward, *The War of the Revolution* (New York, 1952), 1, pp. 59–62; Peter Force, ed., *American Archives: Fourth Series . . . to the Declaration of Independence of the United States* (Washington, 1837–1846), 2, pp. 967–70; Frank Moore, ed., *The Diary of the American Revolution, from Newspapers and other Original Documents* (New York, 1876), 1, p. 94.

6. French, *First Year of the Revolution*, pp. 201–02, 48–49. Security in both armies was extremely lax, although Washington took strict precautions after he took command. Rumors of British plans were out soon after the decision on June 12–14. The Massachusetts Committee of Safety received a warning on June 13. Howe to Germain, June 22, 1775, *Reports on the Manuscripts of Mrs. Stopford-Sackville*, Historical Manuscripts Commission (London, 1910), 2, p. 3; *AA*, 4th ser., 2, pp. 979, 1352, 1040, 1373.

Nomenclature becomes a problem when one talks about the British army. Its forces were almost always a mixture of nationalities, English, Scottish, and Germans, and the latter sometimes contained more than one nationality. I have tried to use the term "British" to denote all troops of whatever nationality who fought under the standard of Great Britain. I have used "redcoats" and "English" to designate troops who came from the British Isles, although I am sure this will offend latter day Scots whose ancestors fought so gallantly in the Highland regiments. The term "Hessian" has been commonly used to describe all German mercenaries, but I have tried to avoid using it unless the units referred to were predominantly soldiers from Hesse-Cassel or Hesse-Hanau.

7. French, *First Year of the Revolution*, Chaps. XV and XVI; Burgoyne to _____, June 25, 1775, *AA*, 4th ser., 2, p. 1094; Rawdon to the Earl of Huntingdon, June 20, 1775, *Report on the Manuscripts of the Late Reginald Hastings*, Historical Manuscripts

Commission (London, 1930, 1947), 3, p. 155; Rev. Peter Thacher, "Narrative," *HM*, 2nd ser., 3, pp. 382–84; "A British Officer to a Friend in England," MHS *Proceedings*, 45 (1910–1911), pp. 101–02; Howe to _____, June 22 and 24, 1775, Sir John Fortescue, ed., *The Correspondence of George III from 1760 to December*, 1783 (London, 1927–1928), MHS 3, pp. 220–24; Rawdon to Huntingdon, June 20, 1775, loc. cit., p. 155.

8. Burgoyne to Lord Stanley, June 25, 1775, *AA*, 4th ser., 2, p. 1095; Rawdon to Huntingdon, June 20, 1775, loc. cit., p. 154; Howe to _____, June 24, 1775, *Geo. III*, 3, p. 224; Sir William Howe, *Narrative . . . in a Committee of the House of Commons . . .* (London, 1780), p. 19; Gage to Barrington, June 26, 1775, *Gage Correspondence*, Carter, ed., 2, pp. 686–87.

9. "Whig-Loyalist" is a term applied by William Allen Benton in *Whig-Loyalism: An Aspect of Political Ideology in the American Revolution* (Rutherford, N.J., 1969), to such people as are here described. Some remained loyal to England, others finally supported the American cause. Radical Whigs, as I have used the term, denote primarily those who earliest and most vigorously supported the movement toward independence. Here and elsewhere I have used the terms "Whig" and "Patriot" interchangeably, as well as "Loyalist" and "Tory." I have also used "American" to denote those who supported the cause of independence unless the context indicates otherwise, although I recognize that Loyalists had just as much right to the claim "American" as the Patriots. See also Merrill Jensen, *The Founding of the Nation* (New York, 1968), Chap. XXIII.

10. Lyman Butterfield, ed., *The Adams Papers: The Diary and Autobiography of John Adams* (Cambridge, Mass., 1961), 2, p. 204.

11. *AA*, 4th ser., 2, p. 620; Edmund C. Burnett, ed., *Letters of Members of the Continental Congress* (Washington, 1921–1936), 1, p. 129.

12. John Adams, *Works*, Charles Francis Adams, ed. (Boston, 1850–1856), 2, pp. 415, 418; Douglas Southall Freeman, *George Washington: A Biography* (New York, 1947–1957), 2, Chaps. XIV and XV for service in the Seven Years' War, Chap. XVII for his selection by Congress; George Washington, *Writings*, John C. Fitzpatrick, ed. (Washington, 1931–1944), 3, pp. 292–93.

13. Washington to John Augustin Washington, July 27, 1775, *WGW*, 3, p. 311; to R. H. Lee, July 11, 1775, ibid., 3, pp. 329–30; *AA*, 4th ser., 2, p. 318; Washington to Lund Washington, August 20, 1775, *WGW*, 3, p. 433; William Emerson to his wife, July 17, 1775, George Washington, *Writings*, Jared Sparks, ed. (Boston, 1834–1837), 3, p. 491.

14. Washington to Congress, Sept. 21, 1775, *WGW*, 3, p. 504; to Joseph Reed, Nov. 28, 1775, ibid., 4, p. 124; Washington to Congress, Dec. 4, 1775, ibid., 4, pp. 142–43; Charles Lee to Benjamin Rush, Dec. 12, 1775, *Lee Papers*, NYHS *Collections*, 5 and 6 (1871–1872).

15. Jonathan Sewall to Thomas Robie, July 5, 1775, MHS *Proceedings*, 2nd ser., 9, p. 414; *Stephen Kemble Papers*, NYHS *Collections*, 16 and 17 (1883 and 1884), 1, pp. 269–70; Washington to Congress, Feb. 18, 1776, *WGW* 4, p. 336.

16. Henry Knox, "Diary," *New England Historical and Geneological Register*, 30, pp. 324–25; North Callahan, *Henry Knox, General Washington's General* (New York, 1958), pp. 33–35.

17. Freeman, *Washington*, 4, Chap. II; James Thacher, *Military Journal of the Revolution . . .* (Hartford, Conn., 1862), pp. 38, 40; Josiah Quincy to James Bowdoin,

March 13, 1776, *The Bowdoin-Temple Papers*, James Bowdoin, ed., MHS *Collections*, 6th ser., 9 (1875–1876), p. 284. The cognomen for the United States for about the first fifty years of its history was "Brother Jonathan" rather than "Uncle Sam."

CHAPTER TWO

1. For Germain see Alan Valentine, *Lord George Germain* (New York and Oxford, 1962). The Minden episode and its political consequences are summarized in Gerald Saxon Brown, *The American Secretary* (Ann Arbor, Mich., 1963), pp. 1–12; relevant documents are in *SS*, 1, pp. 312–22.

2. Brown, *American Secretary*, pp. 14–16, 22, 26; *Parliamentary History of England from the Earliest Period to the Year 1803*, published by T. C. Hansard (London, 1813–1814), 18, p. 192; Germain to the Duke of Suffolk, June [16–17], 1775, *SS*, 2, pp. 2–3; Germain to Gen. Irwin, Sept. 13, 1775, ibid., 1, p. 137.

3. George III to Lord North, Nov. 18, 1774, *Geo. III*, 3, p. 153; Dartmouth to Howe, Sept. 5, 1775, *Parliamentary Register, or History of the Proceedings and Debates of the House of Commons* (London, 1802), 10, pp. 262–64.

4. *SS*, 2, p. 18; Piers Mackesy, *The War for America*, 1775–1783 (Cambridge, Mass., 1964), pp. 50–53; Brown, *American Secretary*, p. 38; George III to Lord North, Aug. 18 and 23, 1775, *Geo. III*, 3, p. 248; *Parliamentary History*, 18, pp. 696, 734–35, 789, 795.

5. George III to Lord North, Sept. 11, 1774, *Geo. III*, 3, p. 131; Mackesy, *War for America*, pp. 55, 22–23, 14–18, passim.

6. Gage to Lord Barrington, Nov. 2, 1774, Carter, ed., *Gage Correspondence*, 2, p. 659; Brown, *American Secretary*, pp. 51, 55–57; Mackesy, *War for America*, p. 60; *Parliamentary History*, 18, p. 1180; the treaties are quoted in ibid., 18, pp. 1157–67; Germain to Howe, March 26, 1777, German Papers, CL; Mackesy, *War for America*, pp. 63–64; Ward, *Revolution*, 2, Chap. 58; Edward E. Curtis, *The Organization of the British Army in the American Revolution* (New Haven, Conn., 1926), Chap. IV, and pp. 97–98, 95; Edward J. Lowell, *The Hessians and Other Auxiliaries of Great Britain in the Revolutionary War* (Williamstown, Mass., 1970 [1st printing, 1884]), p. 56; Mackesy, *War for America*, pp. 62–64.

7. Mackesy, *War for America*, pp. 57–58, 69–70; Howe to Germain, June 8, 1776, *SS*, 2, p. 36.

8. There is no satisfactory biography of William Howe or his more distinguished but less famous brother, Lord Richard. See Maldwyn A. Jones, "William Howe: Conventional Strategist," in George A. Billias, ed., *George Washington's Opponents* (New York, 1969), pp. 39–72, and Ira D. Gruber, *The Howe Brothers and the American Revolution* (New York, 1972). Germain to Suffolk, Aug. [16–17], 1775, *SS*, 2, p. 2.

9. Gruber, *Howe Brothers*, pp. 45–48, 51–54, 61–71, passim, 73; Troyer S, Anderson, *The Command of the Howe Brothers During the American Revolution* (New York, 1936), pp. 52–57.

10. Gruber, *Howe Brothers*, pp. 73–79; Richard Howe to Germain, March 26, 1776, *SS*, 2, pp. 25–26; Germain to William Howe, March 28, 1776, quoted in Mackesy, *War for America*, p. 60. In citing correspondence to and from the Howe brothers, the name "Howe" alone indicates General William Howe; since letters to and from Admiral Lord Richard Howe are infrequent I have used either his first name, title, or naval rank to identify him.

11. Howe to Germain, April 25, 1776, quoted in Anderson, *Command of the Howes,* p. 121.

CHAPTER THREE

1. Howe to Germain, April 26, 1776, *SS*, 2, p. 30.

2. Correspondence of Alexander Wedderburn, Lord Richard Howe, and Germain, March 4 to April 24, 1776, ibid., 2, pp. 24–30.

3. French, *First Year of the Revolution*, Chap. XVI; Allen French, *The Taking of Ticonderoga in 1775: The British Story; A Study of Captors and Captives* (Cambridge, Mass., 1928); *The Narrative of Ethan Allen*, intro. by Brooke Hindle (New York, 1961).

4. *AA*, 4th ser., 2, p. 734; *JCC*, 2, p. 110.

5. *AA*, 4th ser., 2, pp. 1702, 1703; Martin H. Bush, *Revolutionary Enigma: A Reappraisal of General Philip Schuyler of New York* (New York, 1967), pp. 28–39; *AA*, 4th ser., 2, pp. 669, 468; Ward, *Revolution*, 1, pp. 160–62.

6. Ward, *Revolution*, 1, Chaps. XII and XIV; Kenneth Roberts, ed., *The March to Quebec* (New York, 1940), especially the journals of Isaac Senter, pp. 193–241, and Abner Stocking, pp. 543–68; Paul H. Smith, "Sir Guy Carleton," in Billias, ed., *George Washington's Opponents*, pp. 117–21.

7. John Sullivan to Congress, June 1, 1776, *Letters and Papers*, Otis G. Hammond, ed., New Hampshire Historical Society *Collections*, (Concord, N. H., 1930–1939), 1, pp. 212–14; *AA*, 5th ser., 1, pp. 253–54; James Haddon, *A Journal Kept in Canada and Upon Burgoyne's Expedition, 1775 and 1776* (Albany, N.Y., 1884), pp. 16–32; Smith, in *George Washington's Opponents*, pp. 122–27; John Lacey, "Memoirs . . ." *PMHB*, 25 (1901), pp. 510–12.

8. Burgoyne to Clinton, Nov. 7, 1776, Clinton, Mss., CL.

9. Smith, in *George Washington's Opponents*, pp. 137, 138, 23n.

10. Daniel McCurtin, "Journal of the Times of the Siege of Boston," *Papers Relating to the Provincial History of Pennsylvania*, Thomas Balch, ed. (Philadelphia, 1855), p. 40; Gruber, *The Howe Brothers*, pp. 89–92.

11. Morris to Horatio Gates, April 6, 1776, *LCC*, 1, p. 416.

12. *AA*, 4th ser., 6, p. 627; Jensen, *Founding of a Nation*, pp. 696–99, 692–93.

13. Knox to his wife, July 15, 1776, Noah Brooks, *Henry Knox, A Soldier of the Revolution* (New York, 1900), p. 58; Thacher, *Journal*, p. 51; Weldon S. Brown, *Empire or Independence: A Study in the Failure of Reconciliation, 1774–1783* (Baton Rouge, La., 1941), pp. 108–14; Gruber, *Howe Brothers*, pp. 93–100.

14. Mackesy, *War for America*, pp. 57–60; Germain to Carleton and Howe, Feb. 17, 1776, quoted in ibid., p. 60; Howe to Germain, April 26, 1776, *SS*, 2, p. 30; Gruber, *Howe Brothers*, pp. 82–85.

15. Howe to Germain, April 10 and 13, 1776, *SS*, 2, pp. 37–39.

16. For Long Island see Freeman, *Washington*, 4, pp. 153–75; Howe's comments are to Germain, Apr. 3, 1776, quoted in Anderson, *The Command of the Howes*, p. 134; Howe, *Narrative*, p. 215, Louis L. Tucker, ed., "'To My Inexpressible Astonishment:' Sir George Collier's Observations on the Battle of Long Island," *New York Historical Society Quarterly*, 48 (1964), p. 304.

17. Freeman, *Washington*, 4, pp. 181ff; *WGW*, 6, pp. 2–6, passim; Baldwin to his wife, June 17, 1776, quoted in Freeman, *Washington*, 4, p. 85.

18. Gruber, *Howe Brothers*, pp. 117–20; Mercy Otis Warren, *History of the Rise,*

Progress and Termination of the American Revolution (Boston, 1805), 1, p. 323; John Adams to Samuel Adams, Sept. 17, 1776, *LCC*, 2, p. 92.

19. *JCC*, 5, p. 733; Freeman, *Washington*, 4, pp. 191–203; George Weedon to John Page, Sept. 20, 1776, Chicago Historical Society Mss., quoted in George F. Scheer and Hugh F. Rankin, *Rebels and Redcoats* (New York, 1957), p. 182; *WGW*, 4, p. 59; William B. Reed, *Life and Correspondence of Joseph Reed* . . . (Philadelphia, 1847), 1, p. 238.

20. Freeman, *Washington*, 4, pp. 217–31; Washington to Lund Washington, Sept. 30, 1776, *WGW*, 6, p. 138. With respect to the junction with Carleton, Howe seems to have intended to make the effort when he discussed with Germain the problem of command when he joined the northern army (June 7, 1777, *SS*, 2, pp. 34–35). By August 10 Howe's tone was less enthusiastic: "I shall not presume we can flatter ourselves much at the present prospect the season being so far advanced. The extent of my expectations are bounded by the possession of New York and Rhode Island, and a junction with the northern army" (ibid., 2, p. 38). By September 25, "From the present appearance of things I look upon farther progress of this army for the campaign to be rather precarious . . . nor have I any dependence upon General Carleton's approach to act with influence this year . . ." (ibid., 2, p. 41). Yet despite his concern about the "season being so far advanced," it took Howe more than eight weeks after Washington's evacuation from Long Island to bring the Americans to battle at White Plains, thirty-five miles away.

21. Freeman, *Washington*, 4, pp. 241–42, 256–58; James McMichael, "Diary . . ." *PMHB*, 15 (1892), p. 202.

22. Lee to Horatio Gates, Dec. 13, 1776, *Lee Papers*, 1, p. 348; Reed to Lee, Nov. 21, 1776, ibid., 1, pp. 293–94; Freeman, *Washington*, 4, pp. 275–76.

23. Germain to William Knox, Dec. 31, 1776, Knox Papers, CL: Gruber, *Howe Brothers*, p. 163. One is reminded of the confident optimism of Sir Douglas Haig after the ghastly blood bath in Flanders in 1917, and of American leaders in Viet Nam who persistently saw "light at the end of the tunnel" in 1967–1968.

24. Some objectives are mentioned more frequently than others. The seizure of New York and the reference to a "decisive action" are in Howe to Germain, April 25, 1776, quoted in Anderson, *Command of the Howes*, p. 121. The occupation of Rhode Island is frequently mentioned, Howe to Germain, June 7, Aug. 10, and Sept. 25, 1776, and Germain to Howe, Oct. 18, 1776 (*SS*, 2, pp. 34, 38, 41, 42–43). The junction with Carleton is in Lord Howe to German, Sept. 25 and William Howe to Germain, May 12, June 7, and August 10 (ibid., 2, pp. 9, 31, 34–35, 38). For the southern expedition see Henry Clinton, *The American Rebellion: Sir Henry Clinton's Narrative of His Campaigns, 1775–1782*, William Willcox, ed. (New Haven, Conn., 1954), pp. 25–38; William B. Willcox, *Portrait of a General: Sir Henry Clinton and the War of Independence* (New York, 1962), pp. 62–93. Howe mentions the occupation of New Jersey to Germain Aug. 10 and Nov. 30 (*SS*, 2, pp. 38, 49), and Germain suggests the "visit to Philadelphia" October 18, 1776 (ibid., 2, p. 43). Howe's confession that he "has not the smallest prospect of finishing the campaign. . . ." is to Germain, Sept. 25 (ibid., 2, p. 41).

CHAPTER FOUR

1. Washington to John Augustine Washington, Dec. 18, 1776, *WGW*, 6, p. 398;

Thacher, *Journal*, p. 67.

2. Howe to Germain, Nov. 30, 1776, *SS*, 2, p. 49.

3. Leonard Lundin, *Cockpit of the Revolution: The War for Independence in New Jersey* (Princeton, N.J., 1940), pp. 52–59; John Pomfret, "West New Jersey: A Quaker Society, 1675–1775," *WMQ*, 3rd ser., 8 (1951), pp. 493–519; James G. Connelly, "Quit Rents in New Jersey as a Contributing Cause to the American Revolution," New Jersey Historical Society *Proceedings*, new ser., 7 (1922), pp. 13–21.

4. Lundin, *Cockpit of the Revolution*, pp. 60–75; 74–78; NJHS *Proceedings*, 2nd ser., pp. 1236, 1242. I have used "Council" to refer to the Governor's Council rather than to the Council of Proprietors.

5. Lundin, *Cockpit of the Revolution*, pp. 87–92, 96–99, 54–55, 103–05; Richard C. Haskett, "William Paterson, Attorney General: Public Office and Private Profit in the American Revolution," *WMQ*, 3rd ser., 7 (1950), pp. 26–38.

6. Lundin, *Cockpit of the Revolution*, p. 110; Catharine Fennelly, "William Franklin of New Jersey," *WMQ*, 3rd ser., 16 (1959), pp. 74–87.

7. Lundin, *Cockpit of the Revolution*, pp. 119ff; *Documents Relating to the Colonial, Revolutionary and Post-Revolutionary History of the State of New Jersey* (Newark, 1880–1917), 10, pp. 699–700, 720–21; 2nd ser., 1, pp. 152, 162–63, 138. Hereafter cited as *New Jersey Archives (NJA)*. AA, 5th ser., 1, pp. 2, 37, 17, 18, 37; Margaret Morris, *Private Journal Kept During the Revolutionary War for the Amusement of a Sister* (Philadelphia, 1836), pp. 11–13.

8. Freeman, *Washington*, 4, pp. 146–47; *AA*, 5th ser., 1, p. 834; NJHS *Proceedings*, 52, p. 224; *WGW*, 6, p. 333.

9. Lundin, *Cockpit of the Revolution*, pp. 160–65; *AA*, 5th ser., 3, pp. 601, 1169, 1174; *WGW*, 6, p. 397; McDougall's comment in *AA*, 5th ser., 3, p. 1365.

10. Howe, *Narrative*, p. 9; *Examination of Joseph Galloway . . . before the House of Commons, in a Committee on American Papers* (London, 1780), pp. 43–45; Lundin, *Cockpit of the Revolution*, p. 174; *Kemble Papers*, 1, p. 96; Howe's proclamation is in *AA*, 5th ser., 3, p. 927; Congressional report in Moore, *Diary*, 1, pp. 216–17; Captain Fr. Munchausen, *Journal*, quoted in Lundin, *Cockpit of the Revolution*, pp. 185, 178; William Stryker, *The Battles of Trenton and Princeton* (New York, 1898), pp. 329–35. Note that although British and Tory lootings outraged Americans it did not terrorize them. Reprisals were not sanctioned by the British high command and they did not reach the stage that today would be termed atrocities. A reign of terror might have broken American morale, but even if the Howes or Germain had advocated such a policy it is highly unlikely that Parliament would have stood for it. But see Germain to Howe, March 3, 1777 (note 23 below).

11. Reed to Washington, Dec. 23, 1776, Reed, ed., *Joseph Reed*, 1, 275; cf. Freeman, *Washington*, 4, p. 308n.

12. Washington to Gates, Dec. 14, 1776, to Heath, Dec. 16, 1776, *WGW*, 6, pp. 371–72, 385–86; in the exchange of many letters between Washington and Lee I have quoted from Washington to Lee, Dec. 1, 1776, ibid., 6, p. 318, and Lee to Washington, Dec. 8, 1776, *Lee Papers*, 2, p. 326. Washington to John Augustine Washington, Dec. 18, 1776, *WGW*, 6, p. 398; for troop strength about Dec. 16 see ibid., 6, pp. 352, 420–21; quotation is in ibid., 6, p. 432. Cf. Stryker, *Trenton and Princeton*, pp. 59–60.

13. *WGW*, 6, pp. 360, 632, 407; Freeman, *Washington*, 4, pp. 274, 304 and n. It is here suggested that some of the disasters of military history have been the result of key

decisions made by minds exhausted from fatigue and strain. Even military leaders who are considerate of the physical welfare of their men often fail to take similar care of themselves. Attention is invited to Stonewall Jackson in the Seven Days, 1862, American commanders at Savo Island in 1942, and Erwin Rommel in the latter part of the North African campaign (when he was also ill). The strain on Washington from White Plains to the Delaware (Oct. 28 to Dec. 3) had been severe and continuous.

14. Freeman, *Washington*, 4, pp. 303–04 and n.; Stryker, *Trenton and Princeton*, p. 113; Ward, *Revolution*, 1, pp. 292–93 and Stryker, op. cit., say there was a council of war but cf. Freeman, *Washington*, 4, p. 308 and n.

15. Freeman, *Washington*, 4, pp. 311–24 is an excellent account of Trenton and no specific pages have been cited; Marion V. Brewington, "Washington's Boats at the Delaware Crossing," *American Neptune*, 2, (1942), pp. 161–70; Jac Weller, "The Guns of Destiny: Field Artillery in the Trenton-Princeton Campaign," *Military Affairs*, 20 (1955–1956), pp. 1–15. The normal ratio in the British army was two guns per thousand men (but both Howe and Burgoyne exceeded this). Washington's ratio was more than seven per thousand.

16. Von Jungkenn Mss., William L. Clements Library, Ann Arbor, Mich., 1, p. 31; Weller, *Military Affairs*, 20, pp. 8–9; Ward, *Revolution*, 1, pp. 298–301; Stryker, *Trenton and Princeton*, pp. 153–93. Losses as given by Washington, *WGW*, 6, pp. 443–47, passim; cf. Stryker, *Trenton and Princeton*, pp. 188n., 195.

17. *AA*, 5th ser., 3, pp. 1443, 1445–46; Callahan, *Knox*, pp. 89–90; William A. Slaughter, "The Battle of Iron Works Mill," NJHS *Proceedings*, new ser., 4, pp. 22–30; *WGW*, 6, p. 444; Morris, *Journal*, p. 21.

18. Stryker, *Trenton and Princeton*, p. 364; *AA*, 5th ser., 3, p. 1440; Freeman, *Washington*, 4, p. 327, quoting Cadwalader.

19. Washington to Congress, Jan. 1, 1777, *WGW*, 6, p. 464; Sergeant R_____, "The Battle of Princeton," *PMHB*, 20 (1896), pp. 515–16; *Journals of the Continental Congress*, Gaillard Hunt, ed. (Washington, 1904–1937), 6, pp. 1045–46. Congress had finally authorized enlistments for three years or the duration of the war on Sept. 16, 1777. Washington to Congress, Jan. 1, 1777, *WGW*, 6, p. 464.

20. For the second New Jersey campaign see Freeman, *Washington*, 4, pp. 339–59; Alfred Hoyt Bill, *The Campaign of Princeton*, 1776–1777 (Princeton, N.J., 1948); Washington to Congress, Dec. 29, 1776, *WGW*, 6, pp. 451–52; Weller, *Military Affairs*, 20, p. 11. Washington had a gun ratio of eight per thousand, Cornwallis less than four per thousand. Both quotations concerning the retreat are in Freeman, *Washington*, 4, pp. 344–48; James Wilkinson, *Memoirs of My Own Times* (Philadelphia, 1816), 1, p. 141.

21. Weller, *Military Affairs*, 20, p. 13; Sergeant R_____, *PMHB*, 20, p. 518. Moulder's "long" four-pounders were French guns with unusually long barrels, seventy-eight inches as compared with the standard fifty-eight inch barrel.

22. *SS*, 2, pp. 55–56; Lundin, *Cockpit of the Revolution*, pp. 216–26. The quotations are on pp. 224 and 216.

23. See Gruber, *Howe Brothers*, p. 157; Germain to Howe, March 3, 1777, quoted in part in ibid., p. 179.

24. Nicholas Cresswell, *Journal*, . . . 1775–1777 (New York, 1924), pp. 179–80; Moore, *Diary of the Revolution*, 1, p. 193; ibid., 1, p. 198.

CHAPTER FIVE

1. Howard Peckham, *The War for Independence, A Military History* (Chicago, 1958), pp. 199–200; Don R. Higginbotham, *The War for American Independence* (New York, 1971), pp. 389–90.

2. Harold L. Peterson, *The Book of the Continental Soldier: Being a Compleat Account of the Uniforms, Weapons, and Equipment with Which He Lived and Fought* (Harrisburg, Pa., 1968), p. 205.

3. Curtis, *British Army*, pp. 2–5.

4. Ibid., pp. 4–5; Sir John Fortescue, *A History of the British Army* (London and New York, 1899–1930), 3, p. 4.

5. Peterson, *Continental Soldier*, pp. 24, 26–29, 61–62, 64–69, 24–25.

6. Curtis, *British Army*, p. 6; Harold L. Peterson, *Round Shot and Rammer* (Harrisburg, Pa., 1969), pp. 33–48, passim; Captain George Pausch, *Journal . . .* (Albany, N.Y., 1886), p. 126.

7. Curtis, *British Army*, p. 6; Gruber, *Howe Brothers*, p. 31.

8. Curtis, *British Army*, pp. 52, 54, 55, 67, 70–71, 163, 165.

9. Ibid., pp. 22–24, 55–56, 60, 63, 72, 79; Fortescue, *British Army*, 3, p. 41.

10. Curtis, *British Army*, pp. 11n., 28–29, 30–31; Kemble, *Papers*, 1, p. 386; Hannah Winthrop to Mercy Otis Warren, March 10, 1778, Worthington C. Ford, ed., *The Warren-Adams Letters: Being Chiefly a Correspondence Among John Adams, Samuel Adams, and James Warren*, MHS *Collections*, 72 (1917), 2, pp. 451–52; Curtis, *British Army*, p. 30.

11. Curtis, *British Army*, p. 20, 21 and n.

12. Ibid., pp. 25, 159–60.

13. Ibid., pp. 26–28.

14. French, *First Year of the Revolution*, p. 56; *AA*, 4th ser., 2, pp. 620–21; *JCC*, 5, p. 855.

15. *WGW*, 4, pp. 317–18; ibid., 5, p. 112; Elbridge Gerry to John Adams, Dec. 13, 1775, *AA*, 4th ser., 4, pp. 255–56.

16. *JCC*, 5, p. 762; Charles S. Stillé, *Major General Anthony Wayne and the Pennsylvania Line in the Continental Army* (Port Washington, N.Y., 1893), p. 44; *AA*, 4th ser., 2, p. 1630.

17. *WGW*, 6, pp. 6, 11; *JCC*, 5, pp. 854–55; Arthur J. Alexander, "How Maryland Tried to Raise Her Continental Quotas," *MHM*, 42 (1947), pp. 184–96; Higginbotham, *War of Independence*, p. 390; *WGW*, 6, pp. 110–11.

18. *WGW*, 10, p. 366.

19. Ibid., 4, p. 194; Benjamin Quarles, *The Negro in the American Revolution* (Chapel Hill, N.C., 1961), pp. 55–57.

20. Quarles, *Negro in the Revolution*, p. 53; "Some Extracts from the Papers of General Persifor Frazer," *PMHB*, 31 (1907), p. 134; Quarles, *Negro in the Revolution*, pp. ix, 72.

21. Quarles, *Negro in the Revolution*, p. 70; Benjamin Harrison to Thomas Dabney, Oct. 7, 1783, Julian P. Boyd, ed., *Papers of Thomas Jefferson* (Princeton, New Jersey, 1950–00), 6, pp. 430–31 and note; William A. Heming, ed., *Statutes at Large, Being a Collection of All the Laws of Virginia* (Richmond, Va., 1809–1823), 11, pp. 308–09.

22. *WGW*, 3, pp. 309–10, 367, 334, 382.

23. Ibid., 4, p. 202; ibid., 5, pp. 246, 264; ibid., 8, pp. 214, 452; ibid., 7, p. 364; Freeman, *Washington*, 4, pp. 405–06.

24. *WGW*, 3, p. 377; ibid., 6, p. 13; ibid., 6, pp. 107–10.

25. Ibid., 11, p. 237; John S. Pancake, *Samuel Smith and the Politics of Business* (University, Ala., 1972), pp. 24–27.

26. *WGW*, 6, pp. 496–97; ibid., 10, p. 160.

27. *JCC*, 6, 1042–46; Ward, *Revolution*, 1, p. 321; *WGW*, 6, p. 112.

28. Lord Rawdon to the Earl of Huntingdon, Jan. 13, 1776, *Hastings Manuscripts*, 3, p. 167; Christopher Hibbet, *Wolfe at Quebec* (London, 1959), p. 25; *WGW*, 7, p. 33; William Evelyn, *Memoirs and Letters . . . From North America, 1774–1776*, G. D. Schull, ed. (Oxford, 1879), p. 51; *Parliamentary Register*, 14th, 1st sess., 1, p. 135.

29. *AA*, 4th ser., 6, pp. 41–42; *Parliamentary Register*, 14th, 1st sess., 1, p. 421; Hugh Earl Percy to Edward Harvey, April 20, 1775, *The Letters of Hugh, Earl Percy*, Bolton, ed., p. 52; Gage, *Papers*, Carter, ed., 1, pp. 686–87.

30. John Shy, "A New Look at Colonial Militia," *WMQ*, 3rd ser., 20 (1963), pp. 175–85; Wilcomb E. Washburn, *The Governor and the Rebel: A History of Bacon's Rebellion in Virginia* (Chapel Hill, N.C., 1957), p. 31.

31. Shy, *WMQ*, 20, pp. 175–85; French, *First Year of the Revolution*, pp. 38–41, 52–55.

32. Charles J. Hoadly, ed., *The Public Records of the State of Connecticut* (Hartford, Conn., 1894), 1, pp. 94ff.

33. Arthur J. Alexander, "Pennsylvania's Revolutionary Militia," *PMHB*, 49 (1945), pp. 15–25, 18, 53.

34. *WGW*, 6, pp. 110–11.

35. Ibid., 3, p. 490; Peterson, *Continental Soldier*, pp. 42–44.

36. *WGW*, 6, pp. 5–6.

37. For these paragraphs I am indebted to John Shy, "The American Revolution: The Military Conflict Considered as a Revolutionary War," *Essays on the American Revolution*, Stephen G. Kurtz and James Hutson, eds. (Chapel Hill, N.C., 1973), pp. 121–56. Professor Shy and I do not agree on all conclusions, but his is one of the most provocative statements that I have read on the wider significance of the War of Independence.

38. *WGW*, 6, p. 28.

39. Ebenezer Huntington, "Letters," *AHR*, 5 (1900), p. 721; Walter Dorn, *Competition for Empire, 1740–1763* (New York, 1940), pp. 80–94; Alexander Graydon, *Memoirs of His Own Time*, John Littell, ed. (Philadelphia, 1846), p. 135; Adams, *Autobiography*, C. F. Adams, ed., 3, p. 48.

40. Washington to Schuyler, July 28, 1775, *WGW*, 3, p. 374.

CHAPTER SIX

1. Memorandum, "Observations on the War in America," [1776?], Germain Papers, CL, probably not written by Germain; Memorandum, probably 1778, titled "[Germain's?] Own Account of the Campaign of 1777," ibid.

2. Howe to Germain, Nov. 30, 1776, *SS*, 2, pp. 49–51.

3. Same to same, December 20, 1776, ibid., 2, pp. 52–53; same to same, Jan. 20, 1777, *Parliamentary Register*, 10, pp. 377–78.

4. Germain to Howe, January 14 and March 3, 1777, *SS*, 2, pp. 56–59.

5. There is an excellent sketch of Burgoyne by George Athan Billias, "John Burgoyne: Ambitious General," in Billias, ed., *George Washington's Opponents*, pp. 142–92 Francis J. Hudleston, *Gentleman Johnny Burgoyne* (Indianapolis, Ind., 1927) is a popular biography which tends toward the romantic rather than the historical. Edward B. de Fonblanque, *Political and Military Episodes . . . Derived from the Life and Correspondence of the Right Hon. John Burgoyne* (London, 1786), contains many valuable documents. The quotation is on p. 90, quoting an anonymous essayist of the time who wrote under the signature of "Junius." George Coventry, *A Critical Inquiry Regarding the Real Author of the Letters of Junius, Proving Them to Have Been Written by Lord Viscount Sackville* (London, 1825), is not convincing.

6. Howe to Germain, Dec. 31, 1776, *SS*, 2, pp. 53–55; Smith, in *George Washington's Opponents*, pp. 126–28; A. L. Burt, "The Quarrel Between Germain and Carleton: An Inverted Story," *Canadian Historical Review*, 11 (1930), pp. 202–22; Burgoyne's "Thoughts" is conveniently reproduced in Hoffman Nickerson, *Turning Point of the Revolution* (New York, 1928), pp. 83–89.

7. Germain to George III, March 18, 1777, *Geo. III*, 3, nos., 1970, 1971, 1996, 1997, including the King's comments on Burgoyne's plan; Germain to Carleton, March 26, 1777, *SS*, 2, pp. 60–63.

8. Gruber, *Howe Brothers*, pp. 212–13.

9. Freeman, *Washington*, 4, pp. 408–09; Ambrose Serle, *American Journal of Ambrose Serle, Secretary to Lord Howe*, 1775–1778, Edward Tatum, ed. (San Marino, Cal., 1940), p. 226; Nicholas Cresswell, *Journal*, . . . 1774–1777, A. G. Bradley, ed. (New York, 1924), p. 229; Ward, *Revolution*, 1, p. 322; Robert Francis Seybolt, ed., "A Contemporary Account of General Sir William Howe's Military Operations in 1777," American Antiquarian Society *Proceedings*, 40 (1931), p. 4; Charles Francis Adams, "Contemporary Opinion of the Howes," MHS *Proceedings*, 44, pp. 118–20; Freeman, *Washington*, 4, pp. 409–11.

10. Howe to Germain, April 2, 1777, *SS*, II, pp. 63–65; Howe to Carleton, April 5, 1777, ibid., 2, pp. 65–66.

11. Balfour's mission is vague. Gruber, *Howe Brothers*, pp. 210–12; Howe to Germain, June 3, 1777 (two weeks after Balfour arrived), *SS*, 2, p. 68; Germain to Howe, May 18, 1777, ibid., 2, p. 66–67.

12. Freeman, *Washington*, 4, pp. 427–33; Ward, *Revolution*, Chap. 29.

13. Willcox, *Clinton*, p. 160–61; Clinton's notes July 10, 11, 13, and 16, 1777, Clinton Papers, CL; Clinton, *American Rebellion*, pp. 61–65.

After examining the Clinton memoranda I confess that I cannot reconstruct all of the Clinton-Howe conversations. I gratefully accept Professor Willcox's version and confer on him full marks for proficiency in hieroglyphics.

CHAPTER SEVEN

1. [John Spear Smith], "Papers of General [Samuel] Smith," *Historical Magazine*, 17 (1870), pp. 8–10; E. C. Burnett, *The Continental Congress* (New York, 1941), p. 180. This chapter deals primarily with the time and geographical limits of the study as a whole; that is, it is confined to New England, the middle Atlantic states and Virginia, and to the approximate period 1775 to 1778.

2. Alexander Graydon in *The Library of America*, Edmund C. Stedman, ed. (New York, 1891), 3, p. 461.

3. *AA*, 4th ser., 2, pp. 379–80.

4. Robert M. Calhoon, *Loyalists in Revolutionary America, 1763–1783* (New York, 1973), pp. 273–74.

5. Leslie F. S. Upton, ed., *Revolutionary Versus Loyalist* (Waltham, Mass., Toronto, and London, 1968), pp. 8–10.

6. Hamilton to John Jay, Nov. 26, 1775, *Papers of Alexander Hamilton*, Harold C. Syrett and associates, eds. (New York, 1961–   ), 1, p. 176.

7. Calhoon, *Loyalists*, pp. 302–03.

8. Larry Bowman, "Virginia Committees of Safety, 1774–1776," *Virginia Magazine of History and Biography*, 79 (1971), pp. 322–23; Isaac S. Harrel, *Loyalism in Virginia* (Durham, N.C., 1926), pp. 41–42; James Madison to James Madison, Sr., March 29, 1777, *Papers of James Madison*, William T. Hutchinson and William M. E. Rachel, eds. (Chicago, 1962–   ), 1, pp. 190–91, 192n.

9. Richard Bauman, *For a Reputation of Truth: Politics, Religion, and Conflict Among Pennsylvania Quakers* (Baltimore, 1971), p. 148; Mack Thompson, *Moses Brown* (Chapel Hill, N.C., 1962), Chap. 4.

10. Calhoon, *Loyalists*, pp. 292–94.

11. *JCC*, 5, pp. 379–80.

12. Laws dealing with test oaths and treason are conveniently summarized by states in Claude H. Van Tyne, *Loyalists in the American Revolution* (New York, 1902), Appendices B and C; Calhoon, *Loyalists*, p. 301.

13. Higginbotham, *The War of Independence*, p. 270.

14. Van Tyne, *Loyalists*, Appendices B and C.

15. Calhoon, *Loyalists*, Chap. 27, passim. The case of John Davis is on p. 308; that of John Cannon on p. 307.

16. John Cuneo, "The Early Days of the Queen's Rangers, August, 1776–February, 1777," *Military Affairs*, 22 (1958), pp. 65–74; Alexander C. Flick, *Loyalism in New York During the American Revolution* (New York, 1901), pp. 121–30.

17. Richard C. Haskett, "Prosecuting the Revolution," *AHR*, 59 (1954), pp. 578–87.

18. Harold B. Hancock, *Delaware Loyalists* (Wilmington, Del., 1940), pp. 11–32; Hancock, "Thomas Robinson: Delaware's Most Prominent Loyalist," *Delaware History*, 4 (1950), pp. 1–36.

19. Calhoon, *Loyalists*, Chap. 34.

20. *Public Papers of George Clinton*, Hugh Hastings, ed. (Albany, N.Y., 1899–1914), 2, p. 251.

CHAPTER EIGHT

1. Nickerson, *The Turning Point of the Revolution*, has conveniently reproduced Burgoyne's regular and auxiliary troop strength from various sources, and a discussion of their interpretation, as well as the losses sustained. See Appendix II. John Burgoyne, *A State of the Expedition from Canada as Laid Before the House of Commons, by Lieutenant-General Burgoyne, and Verified by Evidence; with a Collection of Authentic Documents* . . . (London, 1780), p. 1; for Gen. Fraser see Henry Manners Chichester,

1106–07; Baroness Fredericke von Riedesel, *Letters and Journals relating to the War of the American Revolution, and the Capture of the German Troops at Saratoga*, William L. *Dictionary of National Biography*, Sir Lesley Stephen and Sidney Lee, eds. (London, 1917), 7, pp. 662–63; for Gen. Phillips, see Robert Hamilton Vetch, ibid., 15, pp. Stone, ed. (Albany, N.Y., 1867), p. 120; *State*, p. 13; Friederich Adolphus Riedesel, *Memoirs, Letters and Journals of Major General Riedesel During His Residence in America*, Max von Eelking, ed. (Albany, N.Y., 1868), 2, pp. 28, 63.

2. Edward J. Lowell, *The Hessians and the Other German Auxiliaries of Great Britain in the Revolutionary War* (Williamstown, Mass., 1884), pp. 30, 16–18, 20, 39–40, 138; Pausch, *Journal*, pp. 108, 116.

3. *State*, pp. 10–12, p. iii, John Albert Scott, *Fort Stanwix and Oriskany* (Rome, N.Y., 1927), pp. 35–43; Bush, *Schuyler*, pp. 52–55; *State*, app., p. xxiii; Thomas Anburey, *Travels Through the Interior Parts of North America; in a Series of Letters. By a British Officer* (London, 1791), 1, pp. 283, 285–86; Fonblanque, *Burgoyne*, p. 243.

4. Burgoyne to Carleton, June 7, 1777, *State*, p. lv; Riedesel, *Memoirs*, p. 104; Anburey, *Travels*, I, 305–06; Pausch, *Journal*, p. 65; E. B. O'Callahan, ed., *The Orderly Book of General John Burgoyne, 1777* (Albany, N.Y., 1870), p. 17.

5. Edward P. Hamilton, *Fort Ticonderoga: Key to a Continent* (Boston, 1964), pp. 40–42, 170; William Henry Smith, *The St. Clair Papers, Life and Public Service of Arthur St. Clair, Soldier of the Revolutionary War* . . . (Cincinnati, O., 1882), 1, pp. 3, 7, 15, 16.

6. James Wilkinson to Horatio Gates, June 25, 1777, Wilkinson, *Memoirs*, 1, p. 178; Smith, *St. Clair Papers*, 1, pp. 407–08; Bush, *Schuyler*, pp. 83–96; Burgoyne to General Harvey, May 19, 1777, *State*, p. lvii; Wilkinson, *Memoirs*, 1, pp. 174–76.

7. Nickerson, *Turning Point of the Revolution*, pp. 140–42; William Digby, *The British Invasion from the North: Digby's Journal of the Campaigns of Generals Carleton and Burgoyne from Canada, 1776–1777*, James Phinney Baxter, ed. (New York, 1887), pp. 202–03; Wilkinson, *Memoirs*, 1, pp. 181–83.

8. Wilkinson, *Memoirs*, 1, p. 184; Digby, *Journal*, pp. 204–09; *State*, pp. xxviii–xxix; Burgoyne to Germain, July 11, 1777, ibid., pp. xxxii–xxxiii; Wilkinson, *Memoirs*, 1, p. 180; Digby, *Journal*, 210–11; Wilkinson, *Memoirs*, 1, pp. 185–88; *State*, pp. xxxiv–xxxvi.

9. Fonblanque, *Burgoyne*, p. 248; John Adams to his wife, Aug. 19, 1777, *LCC* 2, p. 455; Washington to Schuyler, July 11, 1777, *WGW*, 8, pp. 392–93; Schuyler to Washington, July 9, 1777, Schuyler Papers, NYPL; St. Clair to Jay, July 25, 1777, *St. Clair Papers*, 1, p. 433.

10. Bush, *Schuyler*, pp. 125–28; Schuyler to Nixon, Fellows, and St. Clair, July 11, 1777, Schuyler Papers, NYPL; Schuyler to Washington July 9, 1777, ibid.; Wilkinson, *Memoirs*, 1, p. 200.

11. Willard Wallace, *Traitorous Hero: The Life and Fortunes of Benedict Arnold* (New York, 1954), p. 148; *WGW*, 8, p. 459; *State*, p. 15, 54; Digby, *Journal*, pp. 233, 239; *State*, pp. vii, xxxix.

12. Baroness Fredericke von Riedesel, *Baroness von Riedesel and the American Revolution: Journal and Correspondence of a Tour of Duty, 1776–1783*, Marvin L. Brown, ed. (Chapel Hill, N.C., 1964), pp. 55–56; O'Callahan, ed., *Orderly Book*, p. 56; Digby, *Journal*, p. 227.

13. Howe to Burgoyne, July 17, 1777, *State*, p. xlix; *WGW*, 9, p. 77.

CHAPTER NINE

1. *State*, p. 221.

2. Bernard Mason, *The Road to Independence: The Revolutionary Movement in New York*, 1773–1777 (Lexington, Ky., 1966), pp. 26–27, 42. For the evolution and characteristics of parties see ibid., Chap. I, especially pp. 40–41. Cf., Flick, *Loyalism in New York*, pp. 25–36; Mason, *Road to Independence*, pp. 42–43.

3. Flick, *Loyalism in New York*, pp. 40–44; Mason, *Road to Independence*, pp. 8–9, 44–46, 78; Carl Becker, *The History of Political Parties in the Province of New York* (Madison, Wis., 1909), p. 193; William Smith, Jr., *Historical Memoir from 16 March 1763 to 25 July 1778*, William H. W. Sabine, ed. (New York, 1756–1958), 1, pp. 212–13; Dartmouth to Colden, Dec. 10, 1774, E. B. O'Callahan, ed., *Documents Relative to the Colonial History of New York* (Albany, N.Y., 1856), 8, p. 514; Mason, *Road to Independence*, p. 52.

4. Mason, *Road to Independence*, pp. 115–17; Scott, *Fort Stanwix and Oriskany*, pp. 41–43; Mason, *Road to Independence*, pp. 103, 106.

5. Curtis P. Nettles, *George Washington and American Independence* (New York, 1951), Chap. XI; Mason, *Road to Independence*, pp. 131–33, 140, 170–75.

6. Quoted in Mason, *Road to Independence*, pp. 176–77; Livingston to John Rutledge, Sept. 27, 1776, Robert Livingston, *Revolutionary Letters of Importance; The Unpublished Correspondence of Robert R. Livingston* (New York, 1918), no. 95; Flick, *Loyalism in New York*, pp. 95–99; Schuyler to Pierre van Cortlandt, July 27, 1777, Schuyler Papers, NYPL.

7. Digby, *Journal*, p. 248; Baron Frederick von Riedesel, *Letters and Journals, . . .* William L. Stone, ed. (Albany, N.Y., 1868), 1, pp. 101, 126–27; "Instructions for Lieutenant Colonel Baum, . . ." in William L. Stone, *The Campaign of Lieut. Gen. John Burgoyne and the Expedition of Lieut. Col. Barry St. Leger* (Albany, N.Y., 1877), pp. 277–85.

8. John Stark, *Memoir and Correspondence, . . .* Caleb Stark, ed. (Concord, N. H., 1877), pp. 46–47; Riedesel, *Memoirs*, 1, pp. 128–30; Stark, *Memoir*, pp. 55–58; Riedesel, *Memoirs*, 1, p. 131.

9. Ward, *Revolution*, 1, p. 426; *State*, p. xiii; —— Glich, "Account of the Battle of Bennington," Vermont Historical Society *Proceedings*, 1 (1870), pp. 219–23, reprinted in Henry Steele Commager and Richard B. Morris, *The Spirit of 'Seventy-Six: The Story of the American Revolution as Told by the Participants* (New York, 1958), pp. 573–76; Stark's report to Gates, Aug. 23, 1777, Stark, *Memoir*, pp. 129–31; Riedesel, *Memoirs*, 1, p. 255; Breymann to Riedesel, Aug. 20, 1777, ibid., 1, pp. 256–58.

10. Ray W. Pettingill, ed., *Letters from America, 1776–1779, Being Letters by Brunswick, Hessian and Waldeck Officers . . .* (Albany, N.Y., 1924, p. 92; Burgoyne to Germain, Aug. 20, 1777, *State*, pp. lxxv–lxxvi.

11. A contemporary map is in Scott, *Stanwix and Oriskany*, opp. p. 352; John Jay to Gouverneur Morris, July 21, 1777, quoted in Stone, *Burgoyne and St. Leger*, p. 142; Scott, *Stanwix and Oriskany*, pp. 135, 140–41; Stone, *Burgoyne and St. Leger*, pp. 139, 141.

12. Scott, *Stanwix and Oriskany*, pp. 117–29, 157, 164, 166–72; Stone, *Burgoyne and St. Leger*, p. 140; Marinus Willett, *A Narrative of the Military Actions of Colonel Marinus Willett, Taken Chiefly from His Own Manuscripts*, William M. Willett, ed. (New York, 1831), pp. 49–51; St. Leger to Burgoyne, Aug. 27, 1777, *State*, pp. lxxvii–lxxviii.

13. *State*, p. lxxix; Scott, *Stanwix and Oriskany*, p. 139; Stone, *Burgoyne and St. Leger*, pp. 149–51; the quotation is from Thomas Spencer to Herkimer, July 29, 1777, ibid., p. 150.

14. Scott, *Stanwix and Oriskany*, pp. 204–13; *State*, p. lxxviii; Stone, *Burgoyne and St. Leger*, pp. 176–93; Willett, *Narrative*, p. 51; *State*, pp. lxxix–lxxx; Willett, *Narrative*, pp. 53–58, but see Willett's report of August 11, 1777, for a more believable account of the exchange between him and the British emissary, ibid., p. 134.

15. Bush, *Schuyler*, pp. 132–33; Stone, *Burgoyne and St. Leger*, pp. 212–14; Nickerson, *Turning Point*, pp. 273–75; *State*, p. lxxxi; Burgoyne to Germain, August 20, 1777, ibid., pp. xxv–xxvi.

CHAPTER TEN

1. Samuel White Patterson, *Horatio Gates: Defender of American Liberties* (New York, 1941), pp. 50–51; George Athan Billias, "Horatio Gates: Professional Soldier," in Billias, ed., *George Washington's Generals*, p. 80; Busch, *Schuyler*, pp. 26–27; *JCC*, II, pp. 99, 109–10; Washington to Congress, Aug. 3, 1777, *WGW*, 9, pp. 8–9; Bush, *Schuyler*, pp. 60–63, 95; *JCC*, 5, p. 448.

2. Patterson, *Gates*, pp. 4–9; Billias in *George Washington's Generals*, pp. 80–86, 89; Gates to Hancock, Feb. 26, 1777, Gates Papers, NYHS.

3. Schuyler to Congress, March 8, 1777, Schuyler Papers, NYPL; *JCC*, 8, pp. 180–81; Bush, Schuyler, pp. 86–92; *JCC*, 7, pp. 273, 326–27, 375, 364; James Duane to Schuyler, June 19, 1777, *LCC*, 2, p. 383; William Duer to Schuyler, June 19, 1777, ibid., 2, pp. 384–86; Bush, *Schuyler*, p. 129; Samuel Adams to R. H. Lee, July 15, 1777, *LCC*, 2, p. 413.

4. Bush, *Schuyler*, pp. 99–103; Wilkinson, *Memoirs*, 1, p. 217; *JCC*, 8, p. 595; Washington to Congress, Aug. 3, 1777, *WGW*, 9, p. 9; *JCC*, 8, p. 604; Wilkinson, *Memoirs*, 1, p. 222.

5. Burgoyne to Germain, Aug. 20, 1777, *State*, p. xlvi; Wilkinson, *Memoirs*, 1, p. 175; ibid., 1, Appendix A, pp. 155ff.

6. Schuyler to Gens. Nixon, Fellows, and St. Clair, all on July 11, 1777, Schuyler Papers, NYPL; to Washington, July 9, 1777, ibid.; Wilkinson, *Memoirs*, 1, pp. 194–95; Schuyler to Washington, July 14, 1777, *LTGW*, 1, p. 397; Wilkinson, *Memoirs*, 1, Appendix B; Schuyler to the New York Council of Safety, July 24, 1777, ibid., 1, p. 201; ibid., 1, p. 200.

7. Digby, *Journal*, pp. 235–37; Burgoyne to Gates, September 9, 1777, Gates Papers, NYHS; Ward, *Revolution*, 2, pp. 497–98, 898 n. 18; James A. Holden, "The Influence of Jenny McCrae on the Burgoyne Campaign," New York Historical Association *Proceedings*, 12 (1913), pp. 249–310; Seth Warner to John Stark, July 24, 1777, Stark, *Memoirs*, p. 121. Some authorities say Jenny was murdered on July 26.

8. Washington to Schuyler, July 22, 1777, *WGW*, 8, p. 450; Gates to Washington, Aug. 22, 1777, *LTGW*, 2, pp. 427–28; Henry Dearborn, *Revolutionary War Journals*, . . . Howard Peckham, ed. (Chicago, 1939), pp. 103–04; Wilkinson, *Memoirs*, 1, p. 232.

9. Wilkinson, *Memoirs*, 1, p. 232; Benson J. Lossing, *Pictorial Field Book of the American Revolution* (New York, 1850–1852), 1, p. 51; Wilkinson, *Memoirs*, 1, pp. 248–49; Dearborn, *Journal*, p. 105.

10. *State*, p. lxxxiv; Anburey, *Travels*, p. 404; Howe to Burgoyne, July 17, 1777, *State*, pp. xlvi–xlvii; ibid., pp. 22–23.

11. George F. R. Stanley, ed., *For Want of a Horse: Being a Narrative of the British Campaign . . . in 1776 and 1777 by an Officer Who Served Under Lt. Gen. Burgoyne* (Sackville, N.B., 1961), p. 172; *State*, p. li; Anburey, *Travels*, pp. 373–74; *State*, pp. 130–31; Riedesel, *Memoirs*, 1, p. 144; Anburey, *Travels*, pp. 407–10; *State*, p. 83, pp. lxxxv–lxxxvi.

12. Billias in *George Washington's General*, pp. 93–94; Wilkinson, *Memoirs*, 1, pp. 236–38, 243; Digby, *Journal*, pp. 270–73; *State*, pp. lxxxvi–lxxxvii; Wilkinson, *Memoirs*, 1, pp. 238–40; Dearborn, *Journal*, pp. 105–06; Stanley, ed., *For Want of a Horse*, p. 155; *State*, pp. 103–04; Wilkinson, *Memoirs*, 1, p. 241.

The presence of Arnold on the battlefield is examined in Nickerson, *Turning Point*, Appendix XI, and Ward, *Revolution*, 2, Appendix F. The best evidence seems to be from Arnold's own protest to Gates (September 22, Gates Papers, NYHS), in which he does not mention being on the field. See also Wallace, *Traitorous Hero*, p. 148.

Riedesel, *Memoirs*, 1, pp. 147–50; Wilkinson, *Memoirs*, 1, pp. 249–50, 243–44, Appendix D; Dearborn, *Journal*, pp. 106–07.

13. Burgoyne to Gen. Powell, Sept. 20, 1777, Wilkinson, *Memoirs*, 1, p. 242; *State*, p. lxxxvii; Digby, *Journal*, pp. 266–67; Burgoyne to Clinton, Sept. 23, 1777, Wilkinson, *Memoirs*, 1, p. 251.

14. Anburey, *Travels*, pp. 448, 417; Dearborn, *Journal*, p. 107.

CHAPTER ELEVEN

1. Washington to Gen. Ward, Aug. 11, 1777, *WGW*, 9, pp. 57–58.

2. Howe to Germain, July 16, 1777, *SS*, 2, pp. 72–73; Clinton, *American Rebellion*, p. 63.

3. Mrs. Loring came to Philadelphia after Gen. Howe occupied the city.
W. H. Moomaw, "The Denouement of General Howe's Campaign," *English Historical Review*, 79 (1964), pp. 498–512; Serle, *Journal*, p. 241; Washington to Gates, July 30, 1777, *WGW*, 8, p. 499; same to same, [Aug. __?], 1777, ibid., 8, 503–05; to Putnam, Aug. 22, 1777, ibid., 9, p. 115.

4. Whittemore, *Sullivan*, Chap. IV; Kemble, *Papers*, 1, pp. 127–31; Freeman's evaluation of Washington's lieutenants may be found in *Washington*, 4, pp. 367–83 (Greene), 495–96 (Sullivan), 461–62 (Wayne), 241–42 (Stirling), and 417–18 (Stephen); Washington to Stephen, May 12, 1777, *WGW*, 8, p. 53. See also Billias, ed., *George Washington's Generals*, Theodore Thayer, "Nathanael Greene: Revolutionary War Strategist," pp. 109–36; Charles P. Whittemore, "John Sullivan: Luckless Irishman," pp. 137–62; Hugh Rankin, "Anthony Wayne: Military Romanticist," pp. 260–90.

5. *WGW*, 9, pp. 124–27; Sydney George Fisher, *The Struggle for American Independence* (Philadelphia, 1908), 2, p. 20; Charles Francis Adams, *The Familiar Letters of John Adams and His Wife, Abigail Adams, During the Revolution, with a Memoir of Mrs. Adams* (New York, 1876), p. 298; Walter H. Blumenthal, *Women Camp Followers of the American Revolution* (Philadelphia, 1952), p. 66; for Lafayette see Louis Gottschalk, *Lafayette Joins the American Army* (Chicago, 1937).

6. Washington to Congress, Aug. 29, 1777, *WGW*, 9, p. 146; to Gen. Thomas Nelson, Sept. 2, 1777, ibid., 9, p. 164; Montresor, *PMHB*, 5, pp. 404, 407, 409; Carl Bauermeister, *Revolution in America: Confidential Letters and Journals 1776–1784 of Adjutant General Bauermeister of the Hessian Forces*, Bernhard Uhlendorf, ed. (New

Brunswick, N.J., 1957), p. 99; Montresor, *PMHB*, 5, pp. 410–17; Paul H. Smith, *Loyalists and Redcoats* (Chapel Hill, N.C., 1964), pp. 46–47, 51–53; Gruber, *Howe Brothers*, p. 238; Howe to Germain, Aug. 30, 1777, *SS*, 2, p. 75.

7. *WGW*, 9, pp. 131–47, passim; the quotation is to Col. John Thompson, Aug. 28, 1777, p. 141; to Congress, Aug. 27, 1777, ibid., 9, pp. 136–37; to Gen. Maxwell, Aug. 30, 1777, ibid., 9, p. 147.

8. Bauermeister, *Revolution in America*, pp. 106–07; Montresor, *PMHB*, 5, p. 414.

9. Bauermeister, *Revolution in America*, pp. 107–10; Freeman, *Washington*, 4, pp. 471–72; Ward, *Revolution*, 1, p. 342.

10. Washington to Congress, Sept. 11, 1777, *WGW*, 9, p. 206; for accounts of the battle see Freeman, *Washington*, 4, pp. 471–89, and Sullivan to John Hancock, Sept. 27, 1777, *Papers*, 1, pp. 460–65; Bauermeister, *Revolution in America*, p. 108; Freeman, *Washington*, 4, p. 476; Whittemore, *Sullivan*, pp. 56–66, passim; Montresor, *PMHB*, 5, pp. 416–17; Freeman, *Washington*, 4, pp. 478–79. Despite Sullivan's statement that "Colonel Hazen's information must be incorrect," Sullivan wrote to Hancock after the battle, speaking of Hazen's later report on British strength, that "as I know Colo. Hazen to be an old [veteran] officer & a good Judge of Numbers I gave credence to his report."

11. "Papers of General Elias Dayton," NJHS *Proceedings*, 1st ser., 9 (1860–1864), p. 184; Freeman, *Washington*, 4, pp. 480–83; Whittemore, *Sullivan*, pp. 62–64; Bauermeister, *Revolution in America*, pp. 106–12.

12. Ward, *Revolution*, 1, p. 354; Freeman, *Washington*, 4, p. 484; Archibald Robertson, *Archibald Robertson, Lieutenant-General Royal Engineers, His Diaries and Sketches in America, 1762–1780*, Harry M. Lydenberg, ed. (New York, 1930), p. 147; Washington to Congress, Sept. 11, 1777, *WGW*, 9, p. 208; ibid., 9, p. 212; Enoch Anderson is quoted in Ward, *Revolution*, 1, p. 354.

13. Freeman, *Washington*, 4, p. 491–93.

14. Ibid., 9, p. 493; Bauermeister, *Revolution in America*, p. 114; Washington to Congress, Sept. 17, 1777, *WGW*, 9, pp. 230–31; the story of this aborted battle and march can be gleaned from *WGW*, 9, pp. 212–42; Washington to Hamilton, Sept. 15, 1777, *WGW*, 9, pp. 249–50; Hamilton to Washington, Sept. 22, 1777, *Papers*, Syrett et al., eds. 1, pp. 330–34.

15. J. Smith Futhey, "The Massacre at Paoli," *PMHB*, 1 (1877), 291–307.

16. Freeman, *Washington*, 4, p. 498; Bauermeister, *Revolution in America*, p. 117; Washington's call for troops can be found in *WGW*, 9, pp. 216–63, passim; the reprimand to Putnam is Sept. 23, 1777, pp. 253–54; *WGW*, 9, pp. 276, 283–85.

17. Franklin is quoted in John C. Miller, *Triumph of Freedom* (Boston, 1948), p. 220.

18. Moore, *Diary of the Revolution* (abr. ed.), p. 255.

19. Washington to Heath, Sept. 14, 1777, *WGW*, 9, p. 220.

CHAPTER TWELVE

1. Anburey, *Travels*, 1, p. 431.

2. Digby, *Journal*, pp. 276–77; Wilkinson, *Memoirs*, 1, p. 248; *LTGW*, 2, pp. 529–30; Riedesel, *Memoirs*, pp. 151–52.

3. Clinton, *American Rebellion*, p. 63; Willcox, *Clinton*, p. 175; Clinton, *American Rebellion*, pp. 65–72; *State*, p. lxxxviii; Willcox, *Clinton*, pp. 177–79; Wilkinson, *Memoirs*, 1, p. 251.

4. Clinton, *American Rebellion*, pp. 72–77; Clinton to Burgoyne, Oct. 6, 1777, ibid., pp. 379–80; Willcox, *Clinton*, pp. 181–84.

5. Dearborn, *Journal*, p. 107; Wilkinson, *Memoirs*, 1, Appendix E; Arnold to Gates, Sept. 22, 1777, Gates Papers, NYHS; Gates to Arnold, Sept. 23, 1777, ibid.; Wilkinson, *Memoirs*, 1, 253–61.

6. *State*, pp. lxxxviii–lxxxviv; Digby, *Journal*, p. 285; Riedesel, *Memoirs*, 1, pp. 157–62.

7. Anburey, *Travels*, p. 435; *State*, p. 42; Riedesel, *Memoirs*, 1, pp. 162–63; Digby, *Journal*, pp. 286–87; Wilkinson, *Memoirs*, 1, pp. 268–69; *State*, p. lxxxix.

8. Riedesel, *Memoirs*, 1, pp. 163–64; Digby, *Journal*, pp. 287–88; *State*, pp. xc–xci; Pausch, *Journal*, pp. 166–67; Stanley, ed., *For Want of a Horse*, p. 100; Wilkinson, *Memoirs*, 1, pp. 268–72.

9. *State*, p. xci; Riedesel, *Memoirs*, 1, pp. 164–65; Digby, *Journal*, p. 288; Wilkinson, *Memoirs*, 1, pp. 272–73.

There is some disagreement as to the exact time of Morgan's attack and also about the wounding of General Fraser. Since Morgan had the farthest to go to get into position I have concluded that his was the last of the attacks to be made. This agrees with Riedesel and with the unknown author of *For Want of a Horse*. Burgoyne and Digby, who perhaps could not bring themselves to admit that the Germans had given way only after the British left and right exposed their position, barely mention the presence of Riedesel's command. I am also guessing at the time of Arnold's arrival. One account (Samuel Woodruff, in Charles Neilson, *An . . . Account of Burgoyne's Campaign . . .* [Albany, N.Y., 1844], pp. 254–57) credits him with the direction of the shooting of General Fraser. I doubt that Arnold would have bothered with such a detail, i.e., ordering Morgan to direct one of his men to shoot the general. Arnold would have been totally concentrated on gathering troops to deliver a killing attack on the retreating British. My guess is that he arrived after Fraser was down and at the point at which the British were establishing their second line at the redoubts.

10. Baroness Riedesel, *Letters and Journals*, Stone, ed., pp. 119–20; Stanley, ed., *For Want of a Horse*, p. 174; Riedesel, *Memoirs*, 1, p. 166; *State*, p. xci.

11. Clinton, *American Rebellion*, pp. 79–81; Willcox, *Clinton*, pp. 186–89, Howe to Clinton, Oct. 6 and 8, 1777, Clinton Papers, CL; Digby, *Journal*, pp. 300–05; Baroness Riedesel, *Letters and Journals*, Stone, ed., p. 128.

12. Riedesel, *Memoirs*, 1, pp. 170–74; Baroness Riedesel, *Letters and Journals*, Stone, ed., p. 128; Riedesel, *Memoirs*, 1, pp. 170–74.

13. Riedesel, *Memoirs*, 1, pp. 175–78; *State*, app., pp. xcviii–ci; Nickerson, *Turning Point*, p. 386.

14. Stark, *Memoir*, p. 74; Riedesel, *Memoirs*, 1, pp. 179–80; *State*, app., pp. ci–cii; Digby, *Journal*, pp. 306–07; Riedesel, *Memoirs*, 1, pp. 181–86; *State*, app. ciii–civ; Digby, *Journal*, pp. 308–17; Wilkinson, *Memoirs*, 1, pp. 299–320.

15. Riedesel, *Memoirs*, 1, pp. 183–84; Wilkinson, *Memoirs*, 1, pp. 321–22; Pettingill, ed., *Letters from America*, pp. 110–13; passim; Baroness Riedesel, *Letters and Journals*, Stone, ed., p. 135.

16. Germain to Carleton, March 26, 1777, *SS*, 2, p. 62; Burgoyne to Germain, Oct. 20, 1777, *State*, xci; Fonblanque, *Burgoyne*, p. 316.

CHAPTER THIRTEEN

1. *WGW*, 9, p. 279; Washington to Congress, Sept. 23, 1777, ibid., 9, p. 259; to

General William Heath, Sept. 20, 1777, ibid., 9, p. 287.

2. *WGW*, 9, p. 277; Washington to Congress, Oct. 5, 1777, ibid., 9, pp. 308–09; Freeman, *Washington*, 4, p. 501 and n.

3. Washington to Congress, Oct. 5, 1777, *WGW*, 9, 308–09; ibid., 9, pp. 307–08; John Sullivan to Meshech Weare, Oct. 25, 1777, Sullivan, *Papers*, 1, pp. 542–47. The description of the approaches to Germantown are given as actually executed by the various contingents rather than as they are given in the orders.

The orders to Smallwood illustrate the complexity of Washington's plan. Smallwood was to "pass down the road by a mill formerly Danl. Morris and Jacob Edges mill into White Marsh Road at the Sandy run: thence to white marsh Church, where take the left hand road, which leads to Jenkins tavern, on the old york road, below Armitages, beyond the seven mile stone half a mile from which turns off short to the right hand, fenced on both sides, which leads through the enemy encampment to Germantown market houses." *WGW*, 9, p. 307.

4. [Joseph P. Martin], *A Narrative of Some of the Adventures, Dangers and Sufferings of a Revolutionary Soldier* (Hallowel, Me., 1830), p. 75; "Extract from the Diary of General Hunt," *Historical Magazine*, 4 (1830), pp. 346–47; Freeman, *Washington*, 4, p. 509; letter of Timothy Pickering in *North American Review*, 23 (1826), pp. 425–30; Sullivan, *Papers*, 1, p. 545; *HM*, 4, p. 347; Martin, *Narrative*, p. 75.

5. George Weedon to _____, Oct. 8, 1777, Weedon Papers, Chicago Historical Society; Sullivan, *Papers*, 1, p. 546; *WGW*, 9, pp. 309–10; Martin, *Narrative*, p. 76; Thomas Paine to Benjamin Franklin, Oct. 16, 1778, *PMHB*, 2 (1878), p. 298.

6. Washington to Congress, Oct. 5, 1777, *WGW*, 9, p. 310; Peckham, *Toll of Independence*, p. 42; *WGW*, 9, p. 323n.; *WGW*, 10, pp. 89, 138.

7. Worthington Chauncy Ford, ed., *Defences in Philadelphia in 1777* (Brooklyn, N.Y., 1892), p. 292; Washington to Gates, Sept. 27, 1777, *WGW*, 9, pp. 264–65; Gates to Washington, Oct. 5, 1777, *LTGW*, 1, p. 437; *JCC*, 8, p. 668; *WGW*, 9, pp. 387 and n., 391.

8. *WGW*, 9, p. 440; Wilkinson to Washington, Oct. 24, 1777, *LTGW*, 2, p. 13; Freeman, *Washington*, 4, pp. 537, 601, Washington to Col. Lewis Nicola, Sept. 29, 1777, *WGW*, 9, p. 284.

9. Samuel Smith to Washington, Sept. 26, 1777, Smith-Carter Papers, Alderman Library, University of Virginia; same to same, Oct. 14, 1777, Ford, ed., *Defences in Philadelphia*, p. 142; "General Smith," *HM*, 17 (1870), pp. 86–87.

10. *HM*, 17, p. 86; Smith to Washington, Oct. 10, 1777, Smith-Carter Papers, Alderman Library; same to same, Oct. 11, 14, and 15, 1777, ibid.; *HM*, 17, p. 88.

11. Ward, *Revolution*, 2, pp. 375–76; Bauermeister, *Revolution in America*, pp. 125–26; *HM*, 17, p. 88; Martin, *Narrative*, pp. 87–88; Ward, *Revolution*, pp. 373–76; *HM*, 17, p. 89.

12. Gates to Washington, Nov. 2, 1777, *WGW*, 9, p. 466n.; ibid., 9, pp. 466–68; Hamilton to Washington, Nov. ___, 1777, *LTGW*, 2, p. 29; same to same, Nov. 10 and 12, 1777, ibid., pp. 32–40.

13. Extracts of Fleury's journal in Ford, ed., *Defences in Philadelphia*, pp. 98–99; reports to Col. Smith and Gen. Varnum, ibid., pp. 98–126; Martin, *Narrative*, p. 90; Smith to Washington, Nov. 9 and 11, 1777, Samuel Smith Papers, Library of Congress; Ford, ed., *Defences in Philadelphia*, p. 88.

14. Ford, ed., *Defences in Philadelphia*, pp. 107, 123; *HM*, 17, p. 90; Smith to Washington, Nov. 15, 1777, Ford, ed., *Defences in Philadelphia*, pp. 135–36; Varnum to Washington, Nov. 16, 1777, ibid., pp. 140–41; same to same, Nov. 21, 1777, ibid.,

p. 157; Greene to Washington, Nov. 24, 1777, ibid., p. 166–67; same to same, Nov. 20, 1777, ibid., pp. 149–54.

15. Germain to Richard Howe, Aug. 2, 1777, *SS*, 2, p. 73; to William Howe, Aug. 6, 1777, quoted in Gruber, *Howe Brothers*, p. 221; William Howe to Germain, Nov. 30, 1777, *SS*, 2, p. 81.

16. Ward, *Revolution*, 2, pp. 379–80; the opinions of the officers are quoted in full in Ford, ed., *Defences in Philadelphia*, pp. 212–96; Sullivan to Washington, Dec. 4, 1777, Sullivan, *Papers*, 1, p. 598.

17. Weedon to Washington, Dec. 4, 1777, Ford, ed., *Defences in Philadelphia*, pp. 278, 279; Washington to Thomas Conway, Nov. 9, 1777, *WGW*, 10, p. 29.

18. Burnett, *The Continental Congress*, p. 281; Freeman, *Washington*, 4, pp. 588–89; Washington to Congress, Jan. 2, 1778, *WGW*, 10, 249–50; see opinions of officers, Ford, ed., *Defences in Philadelphia*, pp. 212–96, and especially, Greene to Washington, Dec. 1, 1777, pp. 219–34.

19. Washington to Gen. James Potter, Nov. 12, 1777, *WGW*, 10, pp. 295–96; to Gov. Thomas Wharton, Jan. 1, 1778, ibid., 10, pp. 317–18; Martin, *Narrative*, pp. 112–14; Greene to Washington, Aug. 24, 1779, George Washington Greene, *Life of Nathanael Greene* (New York, 1867–1871), 2, p. 466.

20. Hatch, *Administration of the Revolutionary Army*, pp. 96–97; Freeman, *Washington*, 4, pp. 529–30, 529n. See also Erna Risch, *Quartermaster Support of the Army: A History of the Corps* (Washington, 1962), Chap. 1; Martin, *Narrative*, p. 110.

21. Dr. Albigence Waldo, "Valley Forge, 1777–1778, Diary of Albigence Waldo, of the Connecticut Line," *PMHB*, 21 (1897), pp. 307, 309; *WGW*, 10, pp. 212–24; passim; Hatch, *Administration of the Revolutionary Army*, p. 89; Sullivan to Washington, Dec. 4, 1777, Ford, ed., *Defences in Philadelphia*, p. 245.

22. *WGW*, 10, pp. 195–96; William Gilmore Simms, *The Army Correspondence of Col. John Laurens in the Year 1777–78, with a Memoir . . .* (New York, 1861), p. 136; Greene, *Greene*, 3, 563; Mercy Warren to Mrs. Theoderick Bland, March 10, 1778, Ford, ed., *Warren–Adams Letters*, 2, p. 7.

23. Henry Laurens to Lafayette, Jan. 1, 1778, *LCC*, 3, p. 29; Freeman, *Washington*, 4, pp. 590–92.

24. Gates to Washington, Dec. 8, 1777, Gates Papers, NYHS; Washington to Gates, Jan. 4, 1778, *WGW*, 10, pp. 263–64; same to same, Jan. 9, 1778, ibid., pp. 437–41; Freeman, *Washington*, 4, 594, 604n.

25. Henry Laurens to Isaac Motte, Jan. 26, 1778, *LCC*, 3, p. 52; Thomas Flexner, *George Washington in the American Revolution* (Boston, 1967), pp. 268–69; *WGW*, 10, p. 433; Washington to Gates, Feb. 24, 1778, *WGW*, 10, p. 508.

26. Freeman, Washington, 4, pp. 627–29, and 628n.; Flexner, *Washington and the Revolution*, pp. 268–70.

27. *WGW*, 6, p. 420; ibid., p. 195; Francis Wharton, ed., *Diplomatic Correspondence of the American Revolution* (Washington, 1889), 2, p. 664.

CHAPTER FOURTEEN

1. Hunter Miller, ed., *Treaties and Other International Acts of the United States of America* (Washington, 1931), 2, p. 39.

2. For background on French policy in America and Choiseul's part in it see John F. Ramsey, *Anglo-French Relations, 1763–1770* (Berkeley, Cal., 1939).

3. Brown, *Empire or Independence*, pp. 174–78; *Secret Journals of the Acts and Proceedings of Congress* (Boston, 1820), 2, p. 5 (Nov. 29, 1775); Benjamin F. Stevens, ed., *Steven's Facsimiles of Manuscripts in European Archives Relating to America, 1773–1783* (London, 1889–1895), nos. 1310, 1835, 76.

4. Gruber, *Howe Brothers*, p. 264; Samuel Curwen, *Journals and Letters of . . . an American in England from 1775 to 1783*, George A. Ward, ed. (Boston, 1864), p. 188; Gruber, *Howe Brothers*, pp. 260–65; Stevens, ed., *Facsimiles*, n. 1796.

5. Miller, *Triumph of Freedom*, p. 277; Brown, *Empire or Independence*, p. 186; Stevens, *Facsimiles*, nos. 1769, 1835, 1827.

6. Stevens, ed., *Facsimiles*, nos. 1775, 1805.

7. Brown, *Empire or Independence*, p. 190; Stevens, *Facsimiles*, nos. 1774, 1829, 1831.

8. Stevens, *Facsimilies*, nos. 1811, 1823, 1857; Gruber, *Howe Brothers*, pp. 272, 276; Germain to Howe, Feb. 4, 1778, *SS*, 2, p. 92; Germain to Clinton, March 8, 1778, *SS*, II, pp. 94–99.

9. Brown, *Empire or Independence*, pp. 6, 197–99, 216; *Parliamentary Register*, 21, pp. 133–34.

10. *JCC*, 5, p. 827; John Adams to James Warren, May 3, 1777, *LCC*, 2, p. 355; Brown, *Empire or Independence*, p. 176.

Perhaps the most unusual aspect of the whole negotiation between the United States and France was the fact that French motivation was purely and simply to weaken Great Britain. It is hard to believe that France, once a great colonial power in North America, entertained no territorial designs in America (other than the protection of her West Indian possessions). But such, in fact, was the case. The inquisitive reader is invited to examine the following correspondence: the American ministers (Franklin, Deane and Lee) to the Committee on Foreign Affairs, Sept. 8, 1777, Francis Wharton, ed., *The Revolutionary Diplomatic Correspondence of the United States* (Washington, 1889), 2, pp. 388–91; same to same, Oct. 7, 1777, ibid., 2, pp. 404–06; Lee to the Committee on Foreign Affairs, Nov. 27, 1777, ibid., 2, pp. 429–31; the ministers to the Committee on Foreign Affairs, Dec. 18 (ten days after the first conversations between the American ministers and the French representatives), ibid., 2, pp. 452–54; Franklin and Dean to Congress, Feb. 8, 1777 (two days after the signing of the treaties), ibid., 2, pp. 490–91; same to same, Feb. 28, 1777, ibid., 2, pp. 507–09.

11. Carl Van Doren, *Secret History of the American Revolution* (New York, 1941), pp. 61–63; *JCC*, 10, pp. 374–80; Brown, *Empire or Independence*, p. 258; Miller, ed., *Treaties of the United States*, 2, pp. 38–39.

12. Brown, *Empire or Independence*, pp. 260–66; Stevens, ed., *Facsimiles*, nos. 1059, 509; George III to Lord North, March 23, and March 26, 1778, *Geo. III*, 4, pp. 74, 80.

CHAPTER FIFTEEN

1. Higginbotham, *War of Independence*, pp. 177–78, citing Alexander Hamilton, *Papers*, Syrett, et al., eds., 1, pp. 200–21.

2. The reference here is, of course, to the studies of Troyer S. Anderson and Ira Gruber previously cited.

3. Ayling, *George III*, pp. 260–61; cf., George III to Lord North, Jan. 13, 15, 1778, *Geo. III*, 4, pp. 14–15; same to same, March 27, 1778, ibid., 4, pp. 82–83.

4. Wilkinson exaggerated his return in order to convince Burgoyne (who received

a copy) that his situation was hopeless. Charles K. Lesser, *The Sinews of Independence* (Chicago, 1976), p. 50, gives Gates' army 13,216 rank and file, present and fit for duty.

For the effect of the Saratoga victory on Gates' self-esteem, see Gates to his wife, Sept. 19, Oct. 20, and Nov. 17, 1777. Gates Papers, NYHS.

A Bibliographical Essay

In any research project the writer always has at hand a few basic works that provide handy reference and enable him to preserve a properly broad perspective. Yet these volumes are usually cited infrequently or not at all in the notes on sources. Let it therefore be herewith gratefully acknowledged that the following volumes were always within arm's reach while this study was being prepared: Mark W. Boatner, III, *Encyclopedia of the American Revolution* (1966); Douglas Freeman's fourth volume of his magnificent biography of George Washington, *Leader of the Revolution* (1951); Christopher Ward, *The War of the Revolution* (2 vols., 1952); Hoffman Nickerson, *Turning Point of the Revolution* (1926); Henry Steele Commager and Richard Morris, eds., *Spirit of 'Seventy-Six* (1967), with its splendid guide to source materials, and the equally valuable *Rebels and Redcoats* edited by George F. Scheer and Hugh F. Rankin (1948); John C. Miller, *The Triumph of Freedom* (1948), and Don R. Higginbotham, *The War of American Independence* (1971), which will guide the reader to the bibliographical tools of the history of the war.

Few periods in United States history have produced such a deluge of source materials that have found their way into print. John C. Fitzpatrick has edited the *Writings of George Washington* (39 vols, 1931–44), which is, of course, basic to any study of the War of Independence. Peter Force's monumental *Archives of American History . . .* (4th ser., 6 vols, 1837–46 and 5th ser., 3 vols., 1848–53) contains a mass of material on all phases of the war, as does Edmund C. Burnett's *Letters of Members of the Continental Congress* (8 vols, 1921–36).

On the British side the most important printed sources are Sir John Fortescue, *The Correspondence of George the Third . . .* (6 vols., 1927–28), and the Historical Manuscripts Commission *Report on the Manuscripts of Mrs. Stopford-Sackville* (2 vols, 1904), the latter containing much of the correspondence between Lord Germain and the Howes.

But it is in the area of personal journals and memoirs of people from generals to privates to Mrs. Mercy Otis Warren that one encounters a nearly inexhaustible mine of materials (Professors Commager and Morris list more than one hundred and fifty) ranging all the way from single letters in historical journals to James Wilkinson's three-volume *Memoirs*.

The brief listing here will contain only those which the author found especially valuable. On the American side *Private Yankee Doodle*, edited by George F. Scheer (1962), provides an incomparable story of the unflappable Joseph Plumb Martin. James Wilkinson's *Memoirs of My Own Times* (3 vols., 1818) is indispensable although one must proceed with caution when the "Admirable Trumpeter" is recounting his own exploits. Similar care must be used in William Stone's *The Campaign of . . . Burgoyne and . . . St. Leger* (1877) and John Morin Scott, *Fort Stanwix and Oriskany* (1927) since much of the narratives are shot through with "well known" regional or family legends, but both contain important documentary material. There are innumerable other letters, memoirs and diaries which are valuable for specific episodes connected with the campaigns.

On the British side Sir Henry Clinton tells his story in *The American Rebellion*, edited by William Willcox (1954). John Burgoyne, *A State of the Expedition from Canada . . .* (1780) is obviously self-serving in places but contains many indispensable documents as well as testimony of the participants in the hearings before Parliament. William Howe's *Narrative . . . in a Committee of the House of Commons* (1780) is perhaps more revealing of Howe himself than of the events of his campaigns. William Digby's *Journal . . . 1776–1777*, edited by James Phinney Baxter (1887) is a junior officer's view, as is G. B. Stanley, ed., *For Want of a Horse* (1961). The latter is especially valuable for the summary of Burgoyne's troop strengths and losses at various stages of the campaign, obviously compiled from a variety of sources including Digby, Burgoyne, and Wilkinson.

For the German auxiliaries both Baron Riedesel, *Memoirs*, edited by William L. Stone (2 vols., 1868) and *Baroness Riedesel and the American Revolution*, Marvin L. Brown, ed., give valuable and lively accounts of the northern expedition, and that hard-bitten gunner of the Hesse-Hanau artillery, Captain George Pausch, in his *Journal . . .* gives us splendid scenes from the battlefield but also from the bivouac where his German gunners frequently battled their British allies. Edward J. Lowell, *The Hessians* (1884) adds valuable material as does Ray W. Pettingill, ed., *Letters from America* (1924). One of the best sources for Howe's Pennsylvania campaign is Major Carl Bauermeister, *Revolution in America*, Bernard Uhlendorf, ed. (1957).

The principal government documents were Gaillard Hunt, ed., *Journals of the Continental Congress* (34 vols., 1904–1937), John Almon, ed., *The Parliamentary Register . . .* (17 vols., 1775–80), William Cobbett, ed., *The Parliamentary History of England . . . to the Year 1803* (36 vols., 1806–1820), and Frances Wharton, ed., *The Diplomatic Correspondence of the American Revolution* (1889).

The major manuscript collections that were utilized in this study were the Horatio Gates Papers in the library of the New York Historical Society, the Philip Schuyler Papers in the New York Public Library, and the Germain and Clinton Papers in the William L. Clements Library at the University of Michigan.

Almost all of the major figures on both sides have attracted biographers. Handy references are George A. Billias, ed., *George Washington's Generals* (1964) and his *George Washington's Opponents* (1969). Biographies of Horatio Gates by Paul D. Nelson, and John Burgoyne by James Lunt appeared too late to be included in this study.

The following biographies were especially useful not only for their fine character portrayal but for the depth and range of the setting in which their respective subjects lived and moved: William Willcox's, *Portrait of a General: Sir Henry Clinton and the War of Independence* (1962) is especially valuable when used with Clinton's *American Rebellion*; Louis Gottschalk's three volumes on Lafayette, *Lafayette Comes to America* (1935), *Lafayette Joins the American Army* (1937), and *Lafayette and the Close of the American Revolution* (1942); Thomas Flexner, *George Washington and the American Revolution* (2nd of 3 vols., 1967), Martin Bush, *Revolutionary Enigma: A Reappraisal of Phillip*

Schuyler of New York (1967); Don Gerlach, *Philip Schuyler and the American Revolution* (1964), especially good on the political background in New York to 1776.

There is no good biography of either of the Howes, but Ira Gruber, *The Howe Brothers and the American Revolution* (1972) and Troyer S. Anderson, *The Command of the Howe Brothers in the American Revolution* (1935), have thoroughly explored the participation of the Howes in the war. Alan Valentine has written a fine biography of *Lord George Germain* (1962), but this needs to be supplemented by Gerald S. Brown, *The American Secretary* (1963) and Piers Mackesy, *The War for America, 1775–1783* (1964), both of whom have done much to refurbish Germain's tarnished character. Mackesy is especially valuable on the British government's conduct of the war. Of the several biographies of George III I found Stanley Ayling's *George the Third* (1972) to be the most useful.

For the two armies Edward E. Curtis, *The Organization of the British Army in the American Revolution* (1926), Charles K. Bolton, *The Private Soldier Under Washington* (1902), and Louis C. Hatch, *The Administration of the American Revolutionary Army* (1904) are required reading. For weapons and accoutrements of the soldiers see Harold Peterson, *The Book of the Continental Soldier* (1968) and his *Round Shot and Rammer* (1969). The increasing use—and effectiveness—of artillery in both arimes is discussed in Jac Weller, "The Guns of Destiny: Field Artillery in the Trenton-Princeton Campaign," *Military Affairs*, 20 (1955–56). The role of black Americans is ably treated in Benjamin Quarles, *The Negro in the American Revolution* (1961). The full story of the militia has yet to be told, but when it is, the man who will probably do so is John Shy who has already raised some provocative questions in "A New Look at Colonial Militia," *WMQ*, 3rd ser., 20 (1963) and in "The American Revolution: The Military Conflict Considered as a Revolutionary War," in *Essays on the American Revolution*, Stephen B. Kurtz and James Hutson, eds. (1973).

There have been several recent studies on the Loyalists that finally pick up a story first told by Claude H. Van Tyne in *Loyalists in the American Revolution* (1929). An excellent recent work is Robert M. Calhoon, *Loyalists in Revolutionary America, 1760–1781* (1973). Another essential work is Paul H. Smith, *Loyalists and Redcoats* (1964). William Allen Benton, *Whig-Loyalists in the American Revolution* (1969), deals effectively with the puzzling question of divided loyalties. There have been a number of studies of Loyalism in individual states. Among these are Alexander Flick, *The Loyalists in New York in the American Revolution* (1901), Isaac Harrel, *Loyalism in Virginia* (1926), Robert O. DeMond, *The Loyalists in North Caroline During the Revolution* (1940), and William H. Siebert, *Loyalists in Pennsylvania* (1920).

In reviewing my notes I am appalled to find that nowhere do I cite Samuel Flagg Bemis' *Diplomacy of the American Revolution* (1935). It was, of course, essential to my understanding of the French Alliance. A more detailed treatment of the circumstances surrounding the negotiations is Weldon Brown, *Empire or Independence: A Study of the Failure of Reconciliation* (1941).

This essay deals only with those works that were most useful in preparing this particular study. It does not cover many of the sources cited in the notes nor could it conceivably include the many works read over a period of years that conveyed impressions and generated ideas thereby conditioning the attitudes and conclusions herein expressed.

Index